Governing Africa

Governing Africa

3D Analysis of the African Union's Performance

Thomas Kwasi Tieku

ROWMAN & LITTLEFIELD
Lanham • Boulder • New York • London

Published by Rowman & Littlefield
A wholly owned subsidiary of The Rowman & Littlefield Publishing Group, Inc.
4501 Forbes Boulevard, Suite 200, Lanham, Maryland 20706
www.rowman.com

Unit A, Whitacre Mews, 26-34 Stannary Street, London SE11 4AB

British Library Cataloguing in Publication Information Available

Library of Congress Cataloging-in-Publication Data

ISBN 978-1-4422-3530-4 (cloth : alk. paper) -- ISBN 978-1-4422-3531-1 (electronic) -- ISBN 978-1-78661-031-7 (paper : alk. paper)

♾ ™ The paper used in this publication meets the minimum requirements of American National Standard for Information Sciences Permanence of Paper for Printed Library Materials, ANSI/NISO Z39.48-1992.

Printed in the United States of America

To Mr. and Mrs. Boahen Aidoo and Ms. Hilda Mabel Oppong

Contents

Acknowledgments   xi

List of Abbreviations   xiii

I: The Nature of African Union

1   Introduction: A 3-D Guide to the Study of International
Organizations   1
    IOs as Three-Dimensional Organizations   2
    IOs as Intergovernmental Institutions   3
    IOs as Supranational Institutions   6
    IOs as Outisiders   11
    Indicators of IO Performance   16
    Structure of the Book   22
    Notes   25

2   Theorizing African Union as a 3-D International Organization   31
    Intergovernmental AU   33
    Supranational AU   38
    Outisiders AU   46
    Conclusion   51
    Notes   52

3   The African Union in Historical Perspective   57
    Introduction   57
    The Evolution of International Cooperation in Africa   58
    The Major African Political Paradigms   59
    The 1950s and 1960s Grand Debate   61
    The Formation of the OAU   66
    Statism as a Master Frame Idea   68

Africrats and Agenda Setting for the Formation of AU 76
The "Salim Factor" 79
Phase One of Reforms 80
Phase Two of Reforms 85
The 1990s Grand Debate 89
Notes 92

4 The Impact of Entrepreneurship, Institution, and Social Norms
in the Negotiation of the African Union 99
Introduction 99
The Case: Negotiating the Constitutive Elements of the AU 100
The Procedure 100
The State of Play 101
Negotiation Positions 101
Negotiation Process and Outcome 102
Africrats' Role in Solving the Cooperation Problem 104
Africrats' Role in Finding Policy Solutions to the Cooperation
     Problem 104
Building a Coalition for the Africrats' Text 106
Africrats and the Experts Negotiation 107
Providing Directional Leadership for Experts' Negotiations 108
Providing Intellectual Leadership 109
Africrats' Role in the Experts' Search for a Solution to the
     Deadlock 111
Africrats and the Ministerial Conference 116
Conclusion 119
Notes 120

II: Assessment of the Performance of African Union

5 Promotion of Good Political Governance 127
Introduction 127
Worldview 128
Rules 134
Norms 139
Causal Ideas 146
Decision-Making Structures 150
Notes 154

6 Promotion of Peace and Security 159
Introduction 159
Worldview 160
Rules 168
Causal Ideas 173
Norms 181

	Decision-Making Structures	185
	Notes	191
7	Promotion of Human Rights	195
	Introduction	195
	Worldview	196
	Rules	202
	Causal Ideas	207
	Norms	209
	Decision-Making Structures	212
	Notes	218
8	Conclusion: Summary and Theoretical Implications	221
	Future Research Direction	229
Bibliography		231

Acknowledgments

I have accumulated many debts in the process of writing this book, which would not have seen the light of day without the encouragement and support of mentors, colleagues, students, research assistants, friends, and the good people at Rowman & Littlefield as well as family members.

This book is based on intellectual curiosity inspired by professors David Welch, Bob Matthews, Antoinette Handley, and Dickson Eyoh. I thank them for encouraging me to ask probing questions, search deeply into issues, and to contribute constructively to knowledge production.

Great colleagues make all the difference at work, and I owe Erin Norma Hannah and Renee Soulodre-La France enormous gratitude for their comradeship and stimulating conversations.

I would not have been able to complete this book without dedicated cadre of creative, generous, inspiring, and hardworking students who at times seem more invested in this book than I am. Among them are Hilary Birch, Olive Dooley, Tyler Paget, Sean Norman Gareau, Derek Emanuel Orosz, Michael Kunze, and Kristen Myers who literally gave up her fun-filled 2015 summer activities to work on this book.

I am lucky to have superb friends I can call upon in my hour of need. Friends working for the African Union (AU), UN system, and ministries of foreign affairs in various African countries gave me incredible access to relevant information and people. Others turned themselves into book reviewers and critics. The Opoku Boatengs even sacrificed a weekend in order to read the book and provide piercing commentaries on each chapter.

I would also like to thank Christopher Basso for managing the manuscript through the production processes and Marie-Claire Antoine, senior acquisitions editor at Rowman & Littlefield who enthusiastically supported the book project and worked tirelessly to ensure its completion.

Finally, I would like to thank my dearest wife Patricia whose support and patience have no boundaries and the children Jennifer Boateng, Papa-Kwaku Tieku, Kobby Boahen, and Maame-Yaa Aso. I do not know how you people do it but somehow you are able to tolerate the long nights, frequent traveling, and the ubiquitous absent mindedness.

List of Abbreviations

AAEA African Association of Electoral Authorities
ACP African-Caribbean and Pacific Group
ADB African Development Bank
AEC African Economic Community
Africrats Bureaucrats of the African Union
AfriMAP Africa Governance Monitoring and Advocacy Project
AGA African Governance Architecture
AMISOM African Union Mission in Somalia
AMU Arab Maghreb Union
APC All-African Peoples' Conference
APSA African Peace and Security Architecture
ASEAN Association of South East Asia Nations
ASF African Standby Force
ASG OAU Administrative Secretary General
AU African Union
AUC African Union Commission
AUCISS African Union Commission of Inquiry on South Sudan
AUHIP High-Level Implementation Panel on Sudan and South Sudan
BBWA Bank of British West Africa
CEMAC Economic Community of Central African States
CEN-SAD Community of Sahel-Saharan States
COMESA Community for Eastern and Southern African States
CSSDCA Conference on Security, Stability Development, and Cooperation in Africa
CUS Continental Union School
DDR Disarmament, Demobilization, and Reintegration Programs
EAC East African Community

ECA United Nations Economic Commission for Africa
ECOSOC Economic, Social, and Cultural Council
EDECO OAU's Economic Cooperation and Development
EISA The Electoral Institute for Sustainable Democracy in Africa
EU European Union
EWS Early Warning System
GIZ Deutsche Gesellschaft fur Internationale
GNU Government of National Unity
IAEA International Atomic Energy Agency
ICC International Criminal Court
IEC Independent Electoral Commission
IMF International Monetary Fund
IO International Organization
LI Liberal Intergovernmental Theory
LPA Lagos Plan of Action
MCPMR Mechanism for Conflict Prevention, Management, and Resolution
MOU Memorandum of Understanding
NATO North Atlantic Treaty Organization
NEPAD New Partnership for African Development
NGO Nongovernmental Organization
NPFL National Patriotic Front
OAS Organization of American States
OAU Organization for African Unity
P5 Permanent Members of the United Nations Security Council
PF Peace Fund
POWA Pan-African Women's Organization
PRC Permanent Representative Committee
PSC Peace and Security Council of the African Union
PSD Department of Peace and Security
R2P Responsibility to Protect
RUF Revolutionary United Front of Sierra Leone
SADC Southern Africa Development Community
SADCC Southern African Development Coordination Conference
STAG Statist Group
3DIO Three-Dimensional Organizations
TTCs Troop Contributing Countries
UMA Arab Maghreb Union (Union du Maghreb Arabe)
UN United Nations
UNDP United Nations Development Program
WACB West African Currency Board
WAEMU West African Economic and Monetary Union
WANS West African National Secretariat

WHO World Health Organization
WTO World Trade Organization

I

The Nature of African Union

Chapter One

Introduction

A 3-D Guide to the Study of International Organizations

The chapter contributes to both political science scholarship and African studies in at least two major ways. First, it introduces the idea of three-dimensional international organizations (3DIOs) as a conceptual framework for studying the nature of international organizations. The concept of 3DIOs posits that every major international organization has three principal dimensions. These dimensions are intergovernmental, supranational, and *outisiders* (i.e., actors and institution that are not formal members of international organizations (IOs) but shape IOs in many ways, as explained below). The intergovernmental dimension comprises government representatives, and the supranational feature is made up of international bureaucracy and international civil servants. The third dimension is composed of transnational networks such as think tanks, academics, consultants, experts, transnational civil society groups, and independent commissions, whose ideas and views shape the practices, directions, priorities, and policies of these organizations.[1] This last element, referred to in the chapter as *outisiders*, is very controversial and often overlooked in political science scholarship, but as Weiss, Carayannis, and Jolly's short but insightful discussion of "the Third UN" showed, a critical mass of academics, consultants, experts, transnational civil society groups, and independent commissions formed an integral part of the United Nations Organization (UN) system.

The second contribution of the chapter to political science and African studies literature is that it provides a framework for assessing the performance of IOs. This is important especially because measurement of IO performance has been a neglected subject in political science scholarship until recently. Though some interesting work has emerged on the topic in the last few years, political scientists still do not have a good framework to assess an IO's performance. This chapter draws on the limited literature that has been produced in the area to develop comprehensive indicators that can be adopted to assess the performance of IOs in a wide range of areas. The indicators are grouped under a vertical axis and horizontal axis. The vertical axis provides indicators to measure the extent to which IOs help member states acquire their worldview (broader cognitive orientation or paradigm), rules (usually legal instruments), norms (practices), causal ideas (policies), and organizational structures (decision-making bodies) in given issue areas. On the horizontal axis, the scorecard measures the extent to which the worldview, rules, norms, policies, and decision-making structures are novel, relevant, effective, financially viable, and efficient in addressing specific challenges.

These two ideas and contributions to political science scholarship are explored in detail in two sections below. The first section, which immediately follows this introduction, discusses IOs as three-dimensional organizations. The section has three parts. It shows why it is inadequate to treat IOs as intergovernmental bodies, as many political scientists do. The section outlines the supranational character of IOs. An exploration of the idea of IOs as outisiders concludes this section. The second section provides in detail indicators for measuring the performance of IOs and how these indicators can be used to study other IOs. The final section of this chapter summarizes the other chapters contained in the book.

IOS AS THREE-DIMENSIONAL ORGANIZATIONS

This section of the chapter shows that the best way to study IOs is to treat them as three organizations merged into one. The three elements of IOs have symbiotic relationships; the relative influence of each element in the codependent relationship at each point in time determines the direction of the organization. A more assertive intergovernmental component drives the IO to achieve goals that enhance the interests of incumbent governments of member states of a particular IO. The Organization of American States (OAS), the Association of South East Asia Nations (ASEAN), and the defunct Organization of African Unity (OAU) often behaved as if they were nothing but clubs of incumbent ruling elites because of the dominance of intergovernmentalism. They prioritized the achievement of organizational goals that ensured the survival of incumbent regimes, protected core sovereign prerogatives of member states, and limited the influence of transnational actors and institutions in their decision-making processes. These organizations ensured that the objectives of member states were achieved while those of supranationals and outisiders were held in check or not pursued at all. Because of the fear of the unknown and domestic political considerations, intergovernmentals tend to encourage IOs to pursue status quo objectives, politics, and/or policies that enhance their core sovereign prerogative and to ensure regime survival.

Conversely, the more assertive supranationals or international bureaucrats become in an IO, the more the organization tries to pursue goals that seek to change the status quo and in some cases promote goals that may undermine core sovereign prerogatives of member states. The agent-structure literature suggests that given the chance, supranationals will shift more functional powers to IOs, and pursue their interests as well as goals that serve the interest of the transnational community rather than the narrow interests of incumbent governments. In many cases, international bureaucrats take advantage of their position to enhance their own careers, increase their budgets, and increase their influence within the organizations.[2] Outsiders often, but not always, push IOs to promote goals that reflect the interests of vulnerable groups rather than those held by member states, which sometimes impose heavy costs on incumbent regimes and at times undermines the core sovereign prerogatives of states. Because outsiders do not bear the cost of implementing decisions, policies, and programs agreed upon by IOs, they tend to advocate for ambitious, progressive, and far-reaching policies. IOs tend to strive to achieve goals that reflect social purposes and radical thinking when outsiders have assertive influence over the IO. In summary, therefore, most IOs find themselves pushed in three different directions simultaneously. Intergovernmental bodies push them to be more conservative, supranational entities drive them to be independent and assertive, while outsiders encourage IOs to be radical. Thus, even though intergovernmental actors need ideas, technical skills, and policy recommendations from both supranationals and outsiders, it is often in the interest of intergovernmentals to watch carefully the moves of both supranationals and outsiders. The sections below show the sources of the power and limitations of each dimension of IOs.

IOS AS INTERGOVERNMENTAL INSTITUTIONS

There is broad consensus among political scientists of all stripes that IOs are nothing but intergovernmental bodies. In paradigmatic terms, the idea of IOs as intergovernmental organizations finds theoretical purchase in

> virtually all IR theory: for a realist emphasizing self-interested states within an anarchical system; for a liberal institutionalist looking for a stage where states pursue mutual interests and reduce transaction costs; for a proponent of the English School seeking to foster shared norms and values in an international society; for a constructivist looking for a creative agent for ideational change and identity shaping; and for a pragmatist seeking a place to legitimate specific values and actions.[3]

For rational choice theorists, IOs exist to help self-interested or egoistic governments to optimize their material interests, such as the maintenance of territorial independence of their states, security guarantees, military power, international prestige, and economic domination.[4] There is, however, a disagreement in the literature over the exact material interests (i.e., the utility) that governments seek to maximize. While some theorists believe governments create or join IOs to enhance military power, others emphasize economic interests.[5] The disagreement has led to four major lines of theorizing. These are: rational state power theories (the realist family—i.e., neorealism, regime theory, hegemonic stability theory, voice opportunity theory); economic interests theories (the liberal family—i.e., neoliberal institutionalism, transnational theory, and pluralist domestic interests theory); and preference convergence theory, or what some call liberal intergovernmental theory.[6] Sociological political scientists, who disagree with their rational choice counterparts about almost everything, however, concur that IOs are an intergovernmental forum. According to Michael Barnett and Martha Finnemore, two leading sociological political scientists, the UN is at best "a mechanism for interstate cooperation" and at worst a mere forum "of great powers doing their bidding."[7]

Several factors account for the prevailing view that IOs are just intergovernmental organizations. Among them is the crucial fact that IOs come into existence because of treaties signed and ratified by governments on behalf of states. IOs would not exist without intergovernmental agreements. As the opening statements of a major political science textbook indicates, "[all] international organisations exists in the conceptual and legal space between state sovereignty and legal obligation. They are created by the commitments made by sovereign states and their purpose is to bind those states to their commitments."[8] The UN came into being because fifty-one governments on behalf of their states signed a document in June 1945 agreeing to establish this particular institution. Similarly, the African Union (AU) was born on May 26, 2001, thirty days after the deposit of the instrument of ratification of its Constitutive Act by two-thirds of the fifty-three African governments that constituted the Organization of African Unity (OAU), the predecessor to the AU.

For many political scientists, the logics are simple and straightforward. Because governments created them, intergovernmental bodies are the only players in the IO system. And if governments created IOs, the logic goes, IOs cannot be anything more than intergovernmental bodies. Other actors are epiphenomena or mere servants to intergovernmental bodies. According to this logic, governments are in firm control of every aspect of IOs. They provide direction, strategic leadership, and long-term objectives, monopolize decision making, and remote control any other player in the IO system.

The argument seems fine, except that it is based on both a romantic and ancient view of governments. It is based on the assumption that governments are well-organized entities and that government officials have the competence to supervise other actors in the IO system, set priorities, and give policy directions. There is little room in the analysis for states that do not have the necessary capacity to do this. The American, British, and German governments might well have the capacity to be the all-competent supervisors and visionaries, though we know that silly things happen in Washington, London, and Berlin, too. The majority of governments in the world do not have the capacity and competence that political scientists often associate with states. As we will see in subsequent chapters, many African governments rely heavily on Africrats (bureaucrats who work for the African Union and its predecessor, the OAU) and transnational consultants for policy directions at the regional level. Even functional ones such as the government of Botswana, well-developed governmental machinery like the South African government, and democratically organized governments like the one in Seychelles depend heavily on Africrats.

Another reason why many political scientists think IOs are intergovernmental organs is the fact that governments have the final say in the decision making of IOs. Government agents who often negotiate IO agreements take advantage of the opportunity not only to allocate final decision making to themselves but also to put controlling mechanisms on both supranationals and outisiders. Supranationals and outisiders usually need approval from intergovernmental bodies in order to make any major decisions. In the UN system, government representatives, such as state ambassadors to the UN, make final decisions and approve UN resolutions. The Secretary-General cannot act on his or her own on most major issues and needs approval especially from the UN Security Council to act on them. In the AU, the Assembly of the Union is supposed to have the final say over every major decision. The chairperson of the AU commission and, indeed, any other player within the AU system, must seek the assembly's approval before they can act on a whole host of issues.

Moreover, many supranational and outisiders need anonymity to do their best work. For strategic reasons, some supranational and outisiders decide to keep a low profile while doing their work. For instance, and as documented in chapter 3, Africrats strategically decided to stay out of the public eye while putting in place a very ambitious reform agenda that eventually led to the transformation of the OAU to the AU. In certain instances, it is the public relations machines of governments that enable them to crowd out voices of supranationals and outisiders, even when in reality the latter is in the driver's seat. In many cases, the public relations machine allows intergovernmental bodies to oversell their role in IOs to the public.

Finally, the powers given to intergovernmental bodies in founding legal documents of IOs make them appear as if they have absolute powers in the management of IO affairs. Intergovernmental bodies are often described as supreme organs, the highest decision-making bodies, or final arbitrators, among others, in founding treaties of IOs. They are usually mandated to set the mission, vision, and priorities for IOs. For instance, the charter of the Organization of American States (OAS) mandates the assembly to establish priorities and determine the direction for the organization. Similarly, the Association of South East Asian Nations (ASEAN) empowered heads of states to set the priorities and provide guidance to the organization. Even the European Union (EU) founding treaty expects that European leaders will provide the mission, vision, and strategic goals for the EU. For IR scholars who are willing, or prefer to look usually at formal documents and mandates, this requirement in the documents gives them the evidence to claim that intergovernmental organizations are the main and even the only players in the IO system. What they fail to realize is the fact that other actors often perform these roles behind the scenes. Informal channels, asymmetrical distribution of information, and transnational processes have allowed other actors such as international bureaucrats, nongovernmental organizations (NGOs), and consultants to perform functions that are formally given to intergovernmental bodies in the founding documents of IOs. For instance, the AU Constitutive Act mandated the African Union's Assembly of Heads of States and Governments (the Assembly) to set priorities, mission, vision, and strategic plans for the AU, yet informal processes have allowed consultants and Africrats to actually perform these roles on behalf of the leaders. Africrats with little input from the assembly produced all three strategic plans that the AU has followed since its creation.[9] The only contact many of the Assembly members had with these documents was during summits at which they were asked to approve them. A majority of them did not even see the color of the cover page or had the chance to read even the executive summary before rubber-stamping them.

IOS AS SUPRANATIONAL INSTITUTIONS

A small but significant number of political scientists, however, think some IOs have supranationality.[10] Many of these political scientists agree that institutions, such as the EU, are supranational or at least have some supranational elements. According to political scientists who make this claim, the middle ground that international bureaucrats occupy allows them to take advantage of "slacks" in the supervision of their work by intergovernmental actors to increase "their own authority, advance their careers, expand their budgets and mandates."[11] Similarly, the role the international bureaucrats play as interlocutors with national governments, subnational authorities and groups, and a large variety of interest groups gives them unique bargaining power that they can use to shape the direction of IOs.[12] The strategic middle ground they occupy enables bureaucrats to team up with transnational business groups, such as agricultural associations and transnational networks of activists, to put pressure on governments to accept their proposals, advice, and directions.[13] Ideational scholars tend to highlight international bureaucrats' superior in-house knowledge and access to information as the key to their influence.[14] For rationalists, it is the services that international bureaucrats provide that make governments listen to them. Key among them is international bureaucrats' ability to help governments reduce transaction and information costs.[15] In some instances, it is their ability to orchestrate and mediate collective international problem solving that gives them the upper hand.[16] Interdependence, especially complex interdependence, has enhanced the importance, material power, and the role of international bureaucrats in IOs.[17] The services that international bureaucrats provide have enabled them to gain the trust and confidence of the most powerful people within the government of IO member states. Once the head of the government is captured, the rest will often follow.

Eight functions that supranationals perform for IOs will be highlighted to serve as the guidepost for the empirical sections of the book. These include but are not limited to the role of international bureaucracies in: drafting IO treaties; developing strategic visions and plans for IOs; developing IO regulations; implementing and monitoring IO regulations; helping in decision making for IOs; evaluating IO programs; agenda setting for the IO; and other functional activities that show international bureaucrats or IO secretariats perform roles that go beyond the functions of servants of intergovernmental bodies. First, most international bureaucracies get the opportunity to shape treaties that IOs create. The processes of making treaties significantly dilute the supervisory responsibility that intergovernmental bodies are supposed to exercise over international bureaucrats.[18] Secretariat officials usually take advantage of the powers given to them to assist governments in negotiating agreements in order to advance their own interests. In many cases, they embed their own ideas in new agreements, and draft and revise at least some aspects of new agreements. The degree of involvement and influence in negotiation processes depends on a number of factors, including the availability of technical capacity at IO secretariats, the member states, the issues involved, and the nature of the negotiations. It is common knowledge that international civil servants in UN agencies such as the United Nations Environment Program (UNEP) and International Law Commission play central roles in drafting new agreements. While intergovernmental bodies retain the right to sign and ratify these agreements, some international bureaucrats adopt, make, and amend agreements without explicit approval and ratification by every member state of the organization. The AU, the International Atomic Energy Agency (IAEA), and the International Monetary Fund (IMF) require a certain percentage of members to ratify new agreements before they take effect. Both the AU and IAEA require two-thirds of members' approval and/or ratification, meaning a third of members may not get the chance to exercise their supervisory responsibility.

Second, a number of international bureaucrats exercises regulatory powers. The best-known example of international bureaucrats exercising regulatory powers can be found in the EU Commission and Parliament. But as Johnstone aptly pointed out, the "EU is not the only IO that has regulatory powers."[19] Secretariats of many IOs, including the World Health Organization (WHO), the World Metrological Organization (WMO), and the International Maritime Organization (IMO), have powers to make regulations that are similar to those made by governmental agencies at the domestic level. Governments often play minimal roles when secretariats and experts are developing these regulations, yet they are binding on their states.

Third, most international bureaucrats have powers to enforce regulations, promises, and treaties that intergovernmental bodies make. These enforcement powers usually include the right of IO secretariats to review actions of intergovernmental agencies and public officials. The role given to international bureaucrats to ensure compliance of regulations, promises, and treaties is particularly powerful in IOs that have courts attached to them. Karen Alter estimated that no less than twenty IOs have formal courts that ensure that intergovernmental agencies comply with international rules, regulations, and promises.[20] Many international bureaucrats use this power to drive states to implement changes (sometimes very costly ones) that they would not have made without pressure from IO secretariats. As shown in chapter 5, the AU Women, Gender and Development Directorate (WGDD) used the power given to it to ensure that AU member states complied with the AU Solemn Declaration on Gender Equality to influence African countries to create departments and in some cases entire ministries to deal with women's issues.[21]

Fourth, secretariats of most IOs have mandates to make recommendations to intergovernmental bodies. Some political scientists have a dismissive attitude toward recommendations and have done their best to discredit the political significance of recommendations. For many of them, recommendations are epiphenomena and should best be placed in the category of cheap talk. The dismissive approach to recommendations ignores the fact that many recommendations can have consequential political effects. The reputational cost to intergovernmental bodies for ignoring recommendations made by senior international bureaucrats is often enormous. The reputational impact of the recommendations by the General Assembly on Apartheid played a central role in the eventual collapse of the racialized political system. Other actors, such as NGOs, often use recommendations by international bureaucrats of major IOs in their campaigns. The campaign materials of many NGOs on the Israeli-Palestinian crisis are drawn from recommendations made by international bureaucrats. Often, recommendations by international bureaucrats serve as part of packaged information that NGOs use to pressure states to adopt international instruments of great political consequence.[22] Recommendations also have a powerful name and shame effect on intergovernmental actors. Many of these recommendations are based on commissioned studies in areas that intergovernmental bodies may have limited knowledge and expertise. Decisions of the United Nations Security Council are usually based on recommendations contained in reports submitted by the Secretary-General.[23] Most of these reports are written by leading experts in the field. As such, recommendations carry tremendous weight in the decision-making processes of most intergovernmental bodies. In other words, the power embedded in recommendations that international bureaucrats can and do exploit in managing their relations with intergovernmental bodies is enormous.

Indeed, most intergovernmental bodies find it difficult not to adopt recommendations of commissioned studies. Many governments and intergovernmental bodies are acutely aware of the impact of recommendations and often spend a considerable amount of resources to either prevent commissions and committees from making certain recommendations or to quash the publication of reports by commissions and committees that contain costly recommendations. For instance, the government of South Sudan and the Sudan Liberation Movement in opposition spent considerable political and diplomatic capital to quash the release of the final report of the African Union Commission of Inquiry on South Sudan (AUCISS).[24] The former Nigerian president Olusegun Obasanjo, who headed the Commission, was scheduled to present the report to the AU Peace and Security Council (the PSC) during the January 2015 summit, but in an interesting diplomatic move the Ethiopian prime minister, Hailemariam Desalegn, intervened just when Obasanjo was about to speak and moved a motion to defer the consideration and release of the report.[25] South African president Jacob Zuma, who has developed an equally good rapport with the Sudanese warring parties, seconded the motion. It is widely believed in the AU diplomatic circle that the two African leaders moved to delay the release of the report in large part because of its recommendations.[26] The leaders thought the recommendation that those responsible for atrocities, including the incumbent government, should not be allowed to serve in the transitional government proposed by the Commission will influence the leaders of the warring parties not to sign any peace agreement.[27] The bigger point here is that the Commission's report would not have been shelved if the leaders thought that its recommendations were mere cheap talk. Clever international bureaucrats have often used reports of this nature to advance their interest, shape the direction of IOs, and exercise power over governments.

Operational activities of IO secretariats enable international bureaucrats to exercise tremendous influence way beyond those associated with agents of intergovernmental bodies.[28] These operational activities include peacekeeping, peacebuilding, nation building, postconflict reconstruction, security sector reforms, and resource mobilization, among other things. These activities have allowed international bureaucrats to sometimes manage and even reconstruct nation states.[29] Laura Zanotti's work, for example, showed that the nation-building activity of the UN in places such as East Timor allowed UN staffers to influence the direction of the people of East Timor in ways that no single government, however powerful, can or will be able to do. Similarly, the peacebuilding activity of the UN allows UN staffers to write constitutions of countries emerging from conflict in ways that fundamentally reconstruct and shape the politics, society, identity, and culture of these fragile states. Devon Curtis's insightful collections demonstrated how peacebuilding work enabled international bureaucrats such as UN officials to reconstruct identities of people in countries that have gone through civil war.[30] The UN peacebuilding activities in countries such as Liberia and Sierra Leone gave officials of international agencies the opportunity not only to shape the nature of governments and public institutions that emerged but also the very nature of the society developed. It is not a sheer coincidence that most postwar societies are liberal, market-oriented, and have similar public institutions. Finally, the operational activities of the World Bank Group and IMF allows staffers of these organizations to dictate the economic policies of many countries.[31]

Sixth, a number of works have identified agenda setting as an important instrument that international bureaucrats use to direct, influence, and in some cases shape the thinking of IOs. International bureaucrats increasingly set the agendas for most IOs. The leadership of international bureaucrats (whether they go by the name chairpersons, or executive secretaries, or managing directors, or presidents) has formal responsibilities or have allocated to themselves the powers to draw attention of IOs' matters of interest to that organization. Article 99 of the UN Charter gives the Secretary-General the power to "bring to the attention of the Security Council any matter which may threaten the maintenance of international peace and security."[32] This broader agenda-setting mandate allows a creative Secretary-General to take advantage of and to direct the Security Council to do many things that none of the council members is willing to do. Some Secretary-Generals have used these powers to commission studies that have looked at issues that IOs are unwilling or uncomfortable to discuss. Others have used this power to introduce a reform agenda into the UN system. The former Secretary-General Boutros Boutros-Ghali took advantage of these powers to put peacebuilding on the agenda of the Security Council. The agenda-setting power sometimes allows international bureaucrats to limit the issues that intergovernmental bodies can talk about. Put differently, the agenda-setting powers make some international bureaucrats gatekeepers on many issues, including even those that intergovernmental bodies sometimes want to talk about.

Seventh, international bureaucrats are often informal advisers to governments and intergovernmental bodies. Some of them even tell governments what they should or should not do. It is widely documented that IMF and World Bank staffers often dictate microeconomic policies of a number of developing countries that have borrowed money from these two banks.[33] Even those that were not given intrusive methods use savvy ways to influence intergovernmental bodies to take a direction that they would not have done so otherwise. For example, a number of UN staffers working in various UN departments or agencies, including the UN Economic Commission for Africa (UNECA) and United Nations Development Program (UNDP) have used their advising capacity to sometimes shape economic thinking and policies of many African countries. Policies pursued by African countries are often detected, encouraged, or supported by these international bureaucrats. Other international bureaucrats also provide unsolicited but consequential information and advice to intergovernmental bodies.

Finally, most international bureaucrats are by law prevented from taking instructions from any government or any other authority, and thus, in theory, all staffers of IOs are supposed to be independent. For instance, according to Article 100(1) of the UN Charter, "the Secretary-General and the staff shall not seek or receive instructions from any government or from any other authority external to the Organization." This is an important requirement because it allows international bureaucrats to do their work without any interference from governments. This power has been enhanced in many IOs due to the quality and capacity of most IO staffers. In general, IOs tend to attract some of the best experts in a number of areas. Some of them are often technically stronger than their counterparts in government bureaucracies so much so that some state bureaucrats often defer to the authority of IO staffers. This means that IO staffers can in some cases even direct the work of government agencies. Martha Finnemore showed us long ago that international bureaucrats are sometimes and increasingly are teachers of government and government's bureaucracies.[34]

IOS AS OUTISIDERS

The third dimension of IOs is made up of networks of independent actors who are not formal members of IOs, but whose ideas, consultancy services, advocacy, reports, studies, moral suasion, and policy instruments set parameters of choices available to intergovernmental bodies and supranational agencies. Outisiders are neither on the regular payroll of the executive branch of government nor employed as international civil servants, but they often assist intergovernmentals and supranationals to generate ideas and norms, disseminate ideas and programs, debate, implement decisions, influence decision making, and shape the directions of IOs.[35] They include, but are not limited to, experts (academics and consultants), NGOs, eminent persons (usually retired public servants), commissioners, and donors. Their influence is usually exercised through backdoor channels, informal networks, and intermediary bodies. Outisiders are often absent from the table during meetings at which key decisions, priorities, and policies of IOs are made. But they usually set the ideational and policy parameters that intergovernmentals and supranationals operate at these formal meetings.

Information such as reports, studies, and recommendations that form the basis for intergovernmentals' and supranationals' decision making usually come from outisiders such as academics and consultants. Almost all the ideas in the Secretary-General's reports to the Security Council come from outisiders. Many of these reports are written either in whole or in large part by independent consultants and university-based academics. There is a booming ghost-report-writing industry in the international system. The most influential reports submitted by UN Secretaries-General such as Boutros-Ghali's "Agenda for Peace" and Kofi Annan's "In Larger Freedom" were all based on works written outside of the formal UN system.[36] Similarly, the relatively ambitious reports by Ban Ki-Moon, including the forward-thinking reports on relations between the UN and regional organizations, were written in whole or in large part by actors who are not formally part of the UN system.[37] Regular use of shadow writers forms an integral part of the work of other units of the UN system. The bedrock of ideas and most of the contributors to the UN Human Development Report that is copyrighted to the UNDP are provided by outisiders.

Major IOs have routinized shadow thinkers into their work. There is not a single major IO that does not depend on outisiders for ideas and expertise. Even the World Bank Group and IMF, which have enormous technical capacity, rely heavily on outisiders. Many of their reports are written by researchers who are neither formally on the payroll of these institutions nor work for government agencies. The breadth and depth of analysis in major World Bank reports is usually carried out in the quiet and comfortable Ivory Tower environment. Research, ideas, and thinking in the various World Bank's World Development Reports, which have fundamentally shaped global development discourse and policies during the last fifty years, have often come from outisiders. Academics and independent consultants provide the reports' background papers, analyses, and commentaries. In addition, academics and independent consultants serve as peer reviewers for these reports.

Reliance on ghost report writers in the academic community and consultancy industry for policy ideas has been instrumental to the growth and relevance of IOs. As the World Trade Organization's Director-General Roberto Azevêdo pointed out, most outsiders "can identify not only today's challenges and opportunities, but also those of tomorrow. They are not bound by the silos of specific responsibilities" that characterizes IOs.[38] In his view, the freedom that outisiders have from "day-to-day policy-making means they are better placed than many to take the long view." Dependence on ideas generated by outsiders increases even more as IO policymaking becomes more complex. The imperative for outsiders' ideas drives the increasingly cozy relations that the EU has developed with the academic community over the years.

The more technical the issue that IOs have to manage the more dependent intergovernmental bodies and supranational agencies are on outisiders' ideas. This is the case in the area of international environmental governance, in which NGOs with technical expertise have become increasingly indispensable to intergovernmental bodies and supranational bureaucrats.[39] Even rationalists and intergovernmentalists have grudgingly come to the conclusion that NGOs are both active and effective contributors to the IO system. As Koremenos and others showed, NGOs are doing work traditionally reserved for state representatives and international civil servants. They provide leadership particularly in the area of advocacy, research, monitoring, and enforcement of IO policies and rules. Rational Design scholars claim that the decision to delegate these functions to NGOs is "based on the confluence of governmental incentives and NGO comparative advantages and resources."[40] Whatever the motivation, it is generally agreed among IO scholars that the NGOs' participation in IO processes has increased the legitimacy, effectiveness, and performance of IOs.

In general, NGOs enrich IO debates through advocacy, mobilization, embedding in official government delegations, and organizing parallel sessions during key meetings of intergovernmentals and supranationals. The number of NGOs at key IO summits in recent years has often dwarfed government representatives and international civil servants. NGOs generate ideas and policies for intergovernmentals and supranational officials. Research findings showed that the bulk of ideas and policies advanced by developing countries in the WTO were provided by NGOs such as the International Lawyers and Economists Against Poverty (ILEAP) and Oxfam in UK.[41] They influence IO decisions in many ways. Their influence is often uneven and context driven. While the more technically savvy NGOs, such as the International Crisis Group, combine the power of advocacy, expertise, and reports written to shape IOs decision, others (especially smaller NGOs) use the power of naming and shaming to influence IO decisions. IOs have a reputation for making many paper commitments. Without pressure and third-party monitoring, many of these commitments will not be translated into practice. NGOs reporting on the rate of compliance with and implementation of commitments made by governments have enhanced the enforcement of IO work. Many NGOs generate material resources for IOs that go a long way to enhance the credibility of IOs. NGOs' roles are not always positive. Some people who work for NGOs are more self-serving, corrupt, and resistant to progressive change than government officials and international bureaucrats.

Other members of outisiders are eminent persons such as retired senior public servants. Highly respected former heads of state, prime ministers, and retired diplomats contribute to the IO system as part of a panel of wise, independent commissions, committees, and as special envoys. Almost every major IO uses the services of eminent persons. Eminent persons have access to key decision makers, and often they tend to know where key decision makers stand on issues. In addition, they often have good political instincts and can be used to judge ideational and policy preferences of key decision makers. International bureaucrats often use them to gain the attention of government officials. For instance, when Secretary-General Kofi Annan wanted to develop a consensus for a new humanitarian doctrine to enable the UN to intervene in domestic affairs of member states when the government in power is unwilling and/or unable to protect its people, he delegated it to an independent commission of eminent persons coheaded by the former Australian foreign minister Gareth Evans and former Algerian ambassador to the UN Mohamed Sahnoun. The commission, called the International Commission on Intervention and State Sovereignty (ICISS) built on Annan's idea articulated in his acceptance speech of the Noble Peace Prize in 2001 to develop the idea of the Responsibility to Protect (the R2P).[42] The R2P, which the current UN Secretary-General Ban Ki-Moon described as "a solemn commitment by the international community . . . [and] a profound moral imperative in today's world" was adopted as a document of the World Summit Outcome in 2005 and was selectively invoked by UN members to intervene in places such as Libya.[43]

Eminent persons have expertise such as negotiating skills to manage and solve major problems. For example, when the AU intergovernmentals and supranationals found it difficult to resolve outstanding issues after the separation between the Republic of Sudan and South Sudan, the PSC established the High-Level Implementation Panel on Sudan and South Sudan (AUHIP) on October 29, 2009. The AUHIP chaired by the former president of South Africa Thabo Mbeki was mandated to facilitate negotiations relating to South Sudan's independence from Sudan, including issues such as oil, security, citizenship, assets, and the common border. The absence of the full-blown war between the two states is in large part due to the work of the AUHIP.

In a situation in which eminent persons do not have the necessary expertise, they still have the capacity to bring the best experts in the field together.

For instance, when the World Bank needed new ideas in the 1960s on better ways to deliver its aid, the Bank's then president Robert S. McNamara invited the late former Canadian prime minister Lester B. Pearson in August 1968 to form a commission to review the previous twenty years of development assistance, assess the results, and make recommendations for the future. Prime Minister Pearson in turn brought together over thirty people he considered to be the best experts in the field of international development to produce a report whose recommendations fundamentally shaped both the Bank's work specifically and international development in general.[44]

Eminent persons usually have incredible informal access to major decision makers of the world. In other words, although outsiders such as eminent persons may be absent during formal gatherings, their influence often looms large at formal meetings of intergovernmentals and supranationals. They often prefer to work through private and informal meetings. The presence of outsiders in private and informal meetings is important because it is widely recognized that key decisions, priorities, and policies of IOs are often agreed upon at private and informal settings.[45] As the former Australian ambassador to the United Nations, Richard Butler, documented, private deliberations and decision making consumed over 90 percent of his time when he worked on Security Council files. He argued that public meetings took a mere 2 percent of his time. Thus, those who have access to private channels may often assert more influence in IO decision making than even those with access to official channels. The AU is exceptionally good in making use of eminent persons. It does so in multiple ways. At times, the AU at times calls on eminent persons to be part of a high-level panel, as in the case of the High-Level Panel for Egypt established on July 5, 2013, or on a commission of inquiry such as the one for South Sudan discussed earlier or as part of the AU Panel of the Wise.[46]

Outsiders often set the agenda for both intergovernmentals and supranationals. Through research, outsiders such as academics often bring to the attention of intergovernmentals and supranationals a particular issue and/or problem that may not be on their radar. Outsider researchers usually define the issue or problem, and in some cases provide ways to manage or solve the problem. Research shows that the majority of ideas and the main agenda items of the UN come from outsiders, mostly located in North America and Western Europe.[47] Thus, a neglect of outsiders in the study of IO will be a parody of knowledge and analysis. This is why a conscious effort will be made to highlight the role of outsiders in the discussion of the nature and performance of the AU.

INDICATORS OF IO PERFORMANCE

The second part of the book draws on the few literature that has emerged on IO performance to develop comprehensive indicators that can be used to assess the performance of IOs. Academic writings on IO performance coalesce around two schools of thought. One school places emphasis mainly on process factors.[48] The most comprehensive conceptualization of IO performance in process terms is offered by Jorgensen and coauthors, who identified four core elements of organizational performance: effectiveness, relevance, efficiency, and financial viability. They define effectiveness as the extent to which an organization is able to fulfill its goals, while efficiency is the ratio between outputs produced (achievement of goals) and the costs incurred from achieving those objectives. Relevance is the ability of an organization to meet the needs and gain the support of its priority stakeholders in the past, present, and future. The primary stakeholders include member governments of IOs, the political class and transnational opinion leaders, public institutions, the NGO community, and funders of IOs. Finally, financial viability is the capacity of an organization to raise funds required to meet its functional requirements in the short, medium, and long term. The second literature focuses on policy output in terms of decisions, declarations, rulings, recommendations, or guidelines.[49] Scholars who prioritize outcome-based variables in their assessment of IOs look at IO performance primarily in terms of their ability to make policies and decisions. For them, process-level factors are at best complementary to outcome factors, and at worst just cause background noise.

The two schools provide important pointers, but the emphasis they put on one dimension over the other caricatures and skews the outcome of their studies. Both process-level factors and outcome variables are combed below in order to develop a comprehensive measurement tool and scorecard that can be used to study the performance of IOs. In addition, although these measurements are a good starting point, they do not offer a complete framework to understand and theorize performance at the deeper ideational level. As a result, I juxtapose them on indicators that capture deeper organizational performance and institutional change. The two broad measurements allow for the development of comprehensive IO performance indicators on two axes—the vertical axis and horizontal axis. As table 1.1 below shows, the vertical axis provides indicators to measure the extent to which IOs develop a distinctive worldview, rules, norms, and decision-making structures in a given issue area. The scorecard on the horizontal axis measures the extent to which these institutional variables (i.e., worldview, rules, norms, causal ideas, and decision-making structures) are novel (novelty), relevant (relevance) to the world in general and stakeholders in particular, can be implemented (effectiveness), can generate money (financial viability), and also assesses whether they are the most efficient (efficiency) way of dealing with a given challenge.

	Novelty	Relevance	Financial Viability	Effectiveness	Efficiency
	Introduction of distinctive way(s) of looking at an issue or problem	Stakeholders consider the new paradigm important	Donors and state parties provide money for the spread of new thinking	New worldview adopted by target actor(s)	The most appropriate cost-effectiv to look at the issue
	Introduction of unique rules for actors to follow in an issue area	Stakeholders consider rules important	Donors and state parties provide money for integration into national legalization	New rules operational at state and organizational levels	The cost of producing a spreading th rules are reasonable
	Introduction of new policy instruments to solve challenges in an issue area	Stakeholders consider policy instruments important	Donors and member states give money for promotion of policy instruments	New policy operational at state and organizational levels	The cost of producing a spreading th policies are reasonable
	Introduction of new norms to guide actors in an issue area	Stakeholders consider norms important	Donors and state parties provide resources for institutionalization of new norms	New norms operational at state and organizational levels	The adoptic the norm do impose und cost on par
:ing	Introduction of new organizational structure to manage issue area	Stakeholders consider new organizational structure important	Donors and state parties provide money for the implementation of structures	New structures created at state and organizational levels	The most c effective institutional structures available

Worldviews are the taken-for-granted cognitive paradigms that enable actors to interpret events and identify and perceive occurrences. Because worldviews define the universe of possibilities for action, a change of worldview as a result of the work of IOs is a significant achievement. A noticeable change of worldview occurs when key intergovernmentals and/or supranationals start looking at major IO issues, challenges, and policies from a different perspective. For instance, the practice of Pan-Africanism on the African continent never considered gender as a serious lens until the AU emerged on the scene in May 2001. Though the leading Pan-Africanists on the African continent never looked down on women, they did not think continental institution building was women's business. As a consequence, women never featured in their approach to regional integration and continental institution-building exercises. It took a paradigmatic shift in thinking for African leaders to realize that Pan-Africanism concerns African women as much as it animates African men. All the gender-sensitive legal instruments such as the application of the gender-parity principle to the appointment of people to the highest decision making of the AU Commission would not have emerged without a change of African leaders' worldview on gender. Second, the change of worldview is made more meaningful when it is accompanied by a shift in causal ideas (policy). Though worldview does not need policy to exist, well-designed policies provide precision and impose practical obligations on parties.

Causal ideas have the added value of organizing and simplifying experiences for actors. They can also provide a guide to human action. They guide human behavior "by stipulating causal patterns or causal road map," and by "imply[ing] strategies for the attainment of goals." Research findings show that IOs use policy instruments to strengthen and create legitimacy for themselves. For instance, the EU uses its wide selection of policy levers, including the European Initiative for Democracy and Human Rights (EIDHR), to ensure that it is surrounded by allies with similar democratic systems. It is widely believed in EU policy circles and research communities that EU democracy policy enhances welfare and economic exchange in EU member states as well as minimizes spillover effects from instability elsewhere. Moreover, policy instruments are often used by IOs to attach meaning to concepts. IOs often employ policy instruments to introduce new discourse, label a social context, and indeed mark the boundaries of ethical behavior. As Michael Barnett and Martha Finnemore put it, "Naming or labelling the social context establishes the parameters, the very boundaries of acceptable action."[50] The ability to label is an extremely important source of power. The capacity that IOs such as the UN, EU, and World Bank have to label and control discourse gives them the power to define what constitutes development—who is developed, developing, and which actors can legitimately claim the title of development agencies. Finally, policies allow IOs to exercise power even over the most powerful states in the world. IO officials often have the mandate to verify state compliance with their policies, and many IOs take advantage of this delegated responsibility to influence the behaviors of even the most powerful members in the IO. All of these point to the obvious fact that it is essential to integrate into the performance measurement the capacity of IOs to develop policies that stakeholders consider relevant, that generate resources for the IO, and policies that the IO has implemented. The performance of IOs is enhanced even further when IOs are able to develop rules to ensure compliance.

Rules harden polices, provide precision, and impose higher obligation on parties. Rules are so significant to IOs that most IOs spend the majority of their time and energy developing legal instruments. This is why terminologies and jargons used by IO officials are primarily drawn from the legal community—charters, protocols, and treaties, to name just the three prominent languages about rules. Indeed, rules are the lingua franca of IO practices and scholarship. The dominant position of rules in IO works explains why scholarship on IO performance and its appraisals usually focus heavily (and many times exclusively) on the development and implementation of rules. Though any framework that can capture accurately the performance of IO will inevitably include measurements of the creation and implementation of rules, it will be a mistake to privilege rules in the analytical framework. Rules often need a supportive normative setting to thrive. In other words, meaningful measurement of IO's performance on rules will necessarily involve the assessment of norms. Norms are shared standards of appropriate behavior that a community of actors holds.

Norms help actors separate right from wrong, just from unjust, and also provide moral motivations for actions. Results from research indicate that IOs are norm creators, carriers, and diffusers. IOs for the UN Security Council and the AU Peace and Security Council have become fertile grounds for states and transnational actors to create norms. The classic example in the UN context is the creation and internationalization of the norm of territorial integrity of states. Similarly, the AU Peace and Security Council is spearheading the creation and internalization of R2P-like norms on the African continent. IOs also spread existing norms. As Susan Park indicated, IOs spread norms by embedding domestic norms in international regimes, constructing new discourse, turning rules into norms, and provide the glue that bind states together in the international system.[51] Norms are one of the most vital tools available to IOs; many of them use norms to exercise power over other actors in the international system and to shape the direction and focus of policy, and norms in turn shape IOs' identity. The World Bank Group is a good example. Its prominent position in the international development circle has been attributed to its ability to internalize new norms and then use these new norms to exercise power over other actors. For instance, the Bank was the main proponent of Import Substitution Industrialization (ISI) in the 1960s, but it quickly transformed itself into an agent of neoliberalism when its key actors and priority stakeholders internalized free-market norms. It distanced itself from ISI programs, and its officials became poster boys and girls for Structural Adjustment Programs in the developing world in the 1980s and 1990s. The Bank has been so successful in diffusing neoliberal economic orthodoxy in places such as Africa that it will take careful reading of the development literature to realize that ISI was at some point the Bank's main economic prescription for developing countries. Similarly, the Bank became the main supporter and paymaster general of civil society groups in the 1990s when social capita became a development fad. The bigger point here is that norms play key roles in the life of IOs, and it is vital to capture them in the measurement of the performance of IOs. Norms actually work well when they are embedded in organization (decision-making structures). It is difficult for an IO to function without some form of decision-making structure. Kleine's work informed us that every IO "depends on the member's capacity to take collective decisions."[52] The performance of the EU on a whole range of issues is very much a function of its decision-making mechanisms. Thus, the ability of an IO to create effective and efficient collective decision structures, productive organization behaviors, cultures, and habits is a remarkable thing and should appropriately be included in performance measurement indicators.

A number of observations can be made from the juxtaposition of indicators on both axes. An IO should be deemed to have performed well on worldview if it successfully introduces a paradigm that is novel, appeals to key stakeholders to the extent that they use it to look at issues, attracts new resources to the organization, and is adopted by actors at the state and local levels. An IO can be considered to have done well in terms of creating rules if it manages to develop new and most appropriate rules at a reasonable cost to address a specific problem, if the new rules generate money for the IO, and if they are integrated in domestic national and local legislations. The level of money provided by stakeholders and the adoption of the rules by domestic groups will determine the extent to which stakeholders consider the rules to be important. The performance of an IO in a policy arena should be deemed good if it manages to develop a new and appropriate policy instrument to solve a particular challenge and if those policy frameworks are considered important enough by stakeholders that they provide sufficient resources and political support for the implementation of the policy at transnational, national, and local levels. The creation and spread of norms are a crucial aspect of IOs' work, and any IO that is able to develop new and appropriate norms to govern a particular issue will be performing well in normative development. Commitment by donors to provide resources to spread the norms at the level of the organization, the state, and local settings is an indication that the IO is effective in norm creation. The IO will add efficiency to its achievements if it is able to spread the norm at reasonable cost to stakeholders. Finally, decision-making structures are very important in the management of transnational issues. An IO that is able to develop new and appropriate organizational structures that stakeholders consider so significant that they put resources into the organization will be doing well. The IO will be doing even better if the new organizational structures are implemented at target levels.

This framework is used to analyze the performance of the AU in three key issue areas: promotion of good political governance, human rights, as well as peace and security. The result from the analysis shows that the AU has performed well in terms of creating new, relevant, and to some extent financially viable worldviews, rules, policy frameworks, norms, and decision-making structures. But the effectiveness and efficiency of these new ideas are in serious doubt. The AU democracy promotion agenda has led to a pragmatic shift in terms of a new democratic worldview, rules, policy frameworks, norms, and decision-making structures, yet these new ideas have yet to be translated into national legislations and enforced by member states. The elitist approach the AU has taken to promote its democratic ideals is not the most cost-effective way to strengthen democratic practices across the African continent. Similarly, the AU has developed path-breaking human rights norms and rules, policy instruments, and institutional mechanisms to promote human rights, most of which are yet to be internalized by key stakeholders and are often discussed in air-conditioned five-star hotels or the equally inaccessible African Union building at the AU headquarters in Addis Ababa. Most of the key stakeholders leave them on their way out of the rooms where these ideas are discussed in elegant elite and foreign languages. Finally, the AU has made remarkable inroads in pioneering a new peace and security worldview, rules, policy frameworks, norms, and decision-making structures. Some of these ideas have been implemented and have made noticeable change to the lives of some Africans. Yet efficiency and effectiveness in the operationalization of the ideas still need major improvement. The approach the AU has taken so far in promoting these ideas are ad hoc, improvised, and personality driven. The long-term sustainability of the approach is in serious doubt.

STRUCTURE OF THE BOOK

The book is divided into eight chapters. Chapter 2 following this introduction applies the 3DIO logic to the AU. It shows that the AU has indeed intergovernmental, supranational, and outisider features. The most important intergovernmental institutions are the Assembly of Heads of State and Government (the Assembly), the Executive Council (the Council), and the

Permanent Representative Committee (the PRC). The section on the AU as intergovernmental organization focuses more on the Assembly, the Council, and the PRC. The Assembly is the highest decision-making institution of the union. It is supposed to set priorities and give policy directions to the AU, but most of these roles are delegated to the PRC, which is unknown to many people in both the African studies and IR communities. The supranational AU is represented by the AU Commission (the AUC) and the approximately 1,474 (June 2015 figure) international civil servants who work for the Union. The discussion of the AU Commission focuses on the analytical and strategic leadership it provided to the union in the last ten years. The outisiders include networks of consultants, Eminent Persons, Commissions, transnational African Nongovernmental Organizations (TANGOs), African Regional Economic Communities (ARECs), and donors such as the EU. The central message of the chapter is that the AU Commission, assisted by think tanks and independent consultants, acted as the brain house of the AU.

Chapter 3 explores where the AU as an idea came from. It argues that the best way to understand the AU is to see it as part of a second search for an appropriate and effective political system to replace the colonial project. The first resulted in a decisive victory for the statists and the establishment of the Westphalia state model as a master frame idea for the African continent. The OAU was created in 1963 to defend and protect this master idea. This section of the chapter implies that the dominant view in African studies and political science, especially Africa's international relations that the OAU reflects as a compromise between statists and continental unionists, is a myth. The chapter shows that the formation of the AU was the result of an attempt by a new generation of continental unionists to reform the OAU to reflect their preferences and interests. A strong response from the statist group generated the so-called second grand debate. A group of transnational African bureaucrats, referred to in the chapter as Africrats, became the interlocutor. They helped the two ideational groups settle their differences at an extraordinary summit in September 1999 in the Libyan city of Sirte. The compromise reached there was to replace the OAU with the AU. Though African leaders agreed to establish the AU as the new model for interstate cooperation, they could not agree on specific elements of the empty union that they announced at a fanfare press conference at the end of the summit. They established negotiating teams comprising senior state lawyers, ambassadors, and leading figures in African legislatures and foreign ministers to negotiate specific institutions for the AU.

Chapter 4 reconstructs the negotiations, arguing that Africrats took advantage of the mandate they were given to set up the negotiations to engineer specific outcomes. In particular, they used their entrepreneurial skills, the OAU's institutional mechanisms, informal channels, and arguments to persuade representatives of states to select ambitious principles, rules, institutional structures, and decision-making procedures for the AU. Africrats did not persuade all state representatives, but they did convince sufficient numbers of them to generate a broad agreement on the appropriate institutional mechanisms for Africa. As soon as the broad consensus emerged, then the Pan-African solidarity norm, the expectation that an individual African leader will or must toe the line over issues of which a consensus had been reached, set in to compel the unconvinced governments to sign on.[53]

Chapter 5 turns attention to the performance of the AU in the areas of good governance promotion and defense. The central thesis is that the AU has adopted innovative and ambitious home-grown governance promotion and defense benchmarks, and enforcement measures that are designed to address distinct African political challenges. These measures were consolidated in the African Charter on Democracy, Elections, and Governance (the African Governance Charter) that was adopted on January 30, 2007, during the AU summit in Addis Ababa. The African Governance Charter contains unprecedentedly elaborate and, in some cases, innovative instruments for responding to governance challenges, such as military coups and democratic backsliding. The chapter traces the origins of these ideas and assesses their performances, concluding that the overall record of the AU enforcing its innovative governance ideas at the state, community, and individual levels is decidedly poor.

Chapter 6 tells the relatively successful story of the AU's work on the areas of peace and security. It shows that the AU's peace and security ideas and institutions are among the most ambitious and novel continentwide security governance mechanisms to emerge in the world since the end of the Cold War. They are drawn from a collectivist security paradigm, the responsibility to protect (R2P) framework, the human security ideas, and lessons-learned studies from UN postwar reconstruction activities. The AU peace and security work is anchored by the PSC. The PSC's assertiveness on peace and security issues has put the AU in a position in which it increasingly shares with the UN the primary responsibility of maintaining peace and security in Africa. The power- and burden-sharing roles of the PSC go beyond the UN Charter's paternalistic attitude to regional organizations. The AU has been able to attract significant resources and attention for its peace support operations, and has used mediation to prevent the outbreak of full-blown war and/or to reduce tensions in various African states. These success stories were achieved on a weak foundation, and their sustainability is in serious danger.

Chapter 7 explores the AU's remarkable record of adopting far-reaching human rights instruments only to leave many of them to gather dust at the AU headquarters in Addis Ababa. The AU's work on human rights includes mainstreaming into its work program the African Charter on Human and Peoples' Rights (African Human Rights Charter) originally adopted by the

OAU in 1981; explicit adoption of human rights discourse by AU officials; prioritization of gender equality in appointments to professional positions in the AU Commission; and the establishment of the African Court of Justice and Human Rights (African Court of Justice). Except for highly knowledgeable Africans and some human rights activists who have sometimes used AU instruments to fight state officials, AU human rights instruments have had little practical impact. The African economic, social, and political governance situations would be transformed if the AU could make African states translate its elaborate human rights instruments into domestic legalizations. Yet the AU has done little to promote human rights at the state and community levels.

Finally, chapter 8 offers a summary of the book and theoretical significance of each chapter. It offers a number of foods for thought for Africanists and political scientists, especially international relations scholars. It calls into question the widespread view in African studies, particularly in the study of African politics and international relations, that powerful African political leaders drive politics. The book draws attention to other important players such as international bureaucrats and outisiders in African politics. It also raises doubt about the capacity that political scientists have given to the state. The book suggests that the state does not have the capacity that many political scientists think it has to manage at least continental affairs. The state depends, in some cases exceedingly, on nonstate actors in the management of regional and continental challenges. The subtext here is that less romanticization of the state capacity by political scientists will perhaps help us understand politics and society, at least in Africa, a little better.

NOTES

1. For similar conceptualization of these actors as "the Third UN," see Thomas G. Weiss, Tatiana Carayannis, and Richard Jolly, "The 'Third' United Nations," *Global Governance* 15 (2009): 123–42.

2. Joel E. Oestreich, *International Organizations as Independent Actors: A Framework for Analysis* (New York: Routledge, 2012), 6.

3. Weiss, Carayannis, and Jolly, "The 'Third' United Nations," 125–26.

4. F. Snyder, "Institutional Development in the European Union: Some Implications of the Third Pillar," in *The Third Pillar of the European Union: Cooperation in the Fields of Justice and Home Affairs*, ed. J. Monar and R. Morgan (Brussels: European Interuniversity Press, 1994), 85; Robert O. Keohane and Joseph S. Nye Jr., "Globalization: What's New? What's Not? (And So What?)," *Foreign Policy* 118 (Spring 2000), 104–19; Stephen G. Brooks and William C. Wohlforth, "Power, Globalization, and the End of the Cold War: Reevaluating a Landmark Case for Ideas," *International Security* 23, no. 3 (2000–2001), 5–53; Thomas Pedersen, "Cooperative Hegemony: Power, Ideas and Institutions in Regional Integration," *Review of International Studies* 28 (2002): 677–96; Thomas J. Biersteker, "Globalization and the Modes of Operation of Major Institutional Actors," *Oxford Development Studies* 26 (February 1998): 15–31; Pierre de Senarclens, "Governance and the Crisis in the International Mechanisms of Regulation," *International Social Science Journal* 50, no. 155 (March 1998): 91–104; Debi

Barker and Jerry Mander, "The WTO and Invisible Government," *Peace Review* 12, no. 2 (2000): 251–55.

5. William Wallace, "Regionalism in Europe: Model or Exception?" in *Regionalism in World Politics*, ed. L. Fawcett and H. Hurrell, 201–27 (Oxford: Oxford University Press, 1995); John Mearsheimer, "The False Promise of International Institutions," *International Security* 19, no. 3 (1994–1995): 5–49.

6. I omitted functionalism/neofunctionalism and its spill over hypothesis from the review because the theory was not developed to answer questions such as the dissertation seeks to answer. The theory primarily seeks to help us understand increases in supranational authority. Some IR scholars have caricatured and manipulated the theory in order to make their case. I eliminated it from the review to avoid the temptation of falling prey to such an exercise.

7. Michael Barnett and Martha Finnemore, "Political Approaches," in *The Oxford Handbook on the United Nations*, ed. Thomas G. Weiss and Sam Daws (Oxford: Oxford University Press, 2007), 42.

8. Ian Hurd, *International Organizations: Politics, Law and Practice* (Cambridge: Cambridge University Press, 2011), 1.

9. These are: African Union Commission, Strategic Plan 2004–2008; African Union Commission, Strategic Plan 2009–2012; and African Union Commission, Strategic Plan 2014–2017.

10. Donald Puchala, "Institutionalism, Intergovernmentalism and European Integration: A Review Article," *Journal of Common Market Studies* 37, no. 2 (June 1999); Wayne Sandholtz and Alec Stone Sweet, *European Integration and Supranational Governance* (Oxford: Oxford University Press, 1998); K. Armstrong and S. Bulmer, *The Governance of the Single European Market* (Manchester: Manchester University Press, 1998); Ian Johnstone, "Law-Making by International Organizations: Perspectives from International Law/International Relations Theory," in *Interdisciplinary Perspectives on International Law and International Relations: The State of the Art*, ed. Jeff Dunoff and Mark Pollack (Oxford: Cambridge University Press, 2012).

11. John Brehm and Scott Gates, *Working, Shirking, and Sabotage: Bureaucratic Response to a Democratic Public* (Ann Arbor: University of Michigan Press, 1997), 15.

12. Armstrong and Bulmer, *The Governance of the Single European Market*.

13. See Sandholtz and Stone Sweet, *European Integration and Supranational Governance*.

14. Margaret E. Keck and Kathryn Sikkink, *Activists Beyond Borders: Advocacy Networks in International Politics* (Ithaca: Cornell University Press, 1998); Martha Finnemore, *National Interests in International Society* (Ithaca: Cornell University Press, 1996); A. Stone Sweet and Caporaso, "From Free Trade to Supranational Polity: The European Court and Integration," in *European Integration and Supranational Governance*, ed. W. Sandholtz and A. Stone Sweet (Oxford: Oxford University Press, 1998).

15. Keohane and Nye, "Globalization: What's New? What's Not?"; G. Majone, "Ideas, Interests and Policy Change," *EUI Working Papers* SPS 92/21 (Florence: European University Institute, 1992).

16. E. Bomberg and J. Peterson, "Prevention from Above? Preventive Policies and the European Community,'" in *Prevention, Health and British Politics*, ed. M. Mills (Aldershot: Avesbury Press, 1993): 139–59; Paul Pierson, *Dismantling the Welfare State? Reagan, Thatcher and the Politics of Retrenchment* (Cambridge: Cambridge University Press, 1994); Wayne Sandholtz, John Zysman, Michael Borrus, et al. *The Highest Stakes: The Economic Foundations of the Next Security System* (New York: Oxford University Press, 1992); Wayne Sandholtz, "Membership Matters: Limits of the Functional Approach to European Institutions," *Journal of Common Market Studies* 34, no. 3 (1996): 404–29; James Caporaso, "The European Union and Forms of State: Westphalian, Regulatory or Post-Modern?" *Journal of Common Market Studies* 34, no. 1 (March 1996).

17. Robert O. Keohane and Joseph S. Nye Jr., "Transnational Relations and World Politics: A Conclusion," *International Organization* 25, no. 3 (1971): 721–48; Keohane and Nye, "Globalization: What's New? What's Not? (And So What?)"; Robert O. Keohane and Joseph S. Nye Jr., *Power and Interdependence: World Politics in Transition* (Boston: Little, Brown, 1977), 3–19; Robert O. Keohane, After Hegemony: Cooperation and Discord in the World Political Economy (Princeton, NJ: Princeton University Press, 1984).

18. Donald Puchala, "Institutionalism, Intergovernmentalism and European Integration: A Review Article," *Journal of Common Market Studies* (University of South Carolina, June 1999); Sandholtz and Stone Sweet, *European Integration and Supranational Governance*; K. Armstrong and S. Bulmer, *The Governance of the Single European Market* (Manchester: Manchester University Press, 1998).

19. Ian Johnstone, "Law-Making by International Organizations: Perspectives from International Law/International Relations Theory," in *Interdisciplinary Perspectives on International Law and International Relations: The State of the Art* (Cambridge, Cambridge University Press, 2012), 271.

20. Karen J. Alter, "The Multiple Roles of International Courts and Tribunals: Enforcement, Dispute Settlement, Constitutional and Administrative Review," *Buffet Centre Working Paper*, 12, no. 2 (2012): 5.

21. For details, see "The Chairperson of AUC, the Ninth Report of the AUC Chairperson on the Implementation of the AU Solemn Declaration on Gender Equality in Africa (June 2014) to the Twenty-Third Executive Council."

22. Hurd, *International Organizations: Politics, Law, Practice*, 120.

23. Richard Butler AC, "Reform of the United Nations Security Council," *Penn State Journal of Law & International Affairs* 1, no. 1 (April 2012).

24. In December 2013, the AU chairperson announced that the former Nigerian president Olusegun Obasanjo will lead a team of independent experts to "investigate the human rights violations and other abuses committed during the armed conflict in South Sudan, and make recommendations on the best way and means to ensure accountability, reconciliation and healing among all South Sudanese communities. For details, see Human Rights Watch, "South Sudan: AU Putting Justice on Hold," *Human Rights Watch*, February 3, 2015, http://www.hrw.org/news/2015/02/03/south-sudan-au-putting-justice-hold; African Union Commission, "South Sudan Commission of Inquiry Established and Members Appointed," March 7, 2017, http://www.peaceau.org/en/article/south-sudan-commission-of-inquiry-established-and-members-appointed#sthash.WdBv4VEd.dpuf.

25. Institute for Security Studies, Peace and Security Council Report no. 66, 2–3, https://www.issafrica.org/uploads/PSC66Feb2015ENG.pdf.

26. Institute for Security Studies, Peace and Security Council Report no. 66; David K. Deng, "The Silencing of the AU Commission of Inquiry on South Sudan," *Sudan Tribune*, May 13, 2015, http://www.sudantribune.com/spip.php?article53903.

27. *Sudan Tribune*, "AU Inquiry Wants Kiir Excluded from Transitional Leadership," February 16, 2015, http://www.sudantribune.com/spip.php?article54201.

28. Johnstone, "Law-Making by International Organizations," 275.

29. Laura Zanotti, *Governing Disorder: UN Peace Operations, International Security, and Democratization in the Post–Cold War Era* (University Park: Penn State University Press, 2011), 56.

30. Devon Curtis, "The Contested Politics of Peacebuilding in Africa," in *Peacebuilding, Power, and Politics in Africa*, ed. Devon Curtis and Gwinyayi A. Dzinesa, 1–28 (Athens, OH: Ohio University Press, 2012).

31. William Easterly, *The Tyranny of Experts, Economists, Dictators, and the Forgotten Rights of the Poor* (New York: Basic Books, 2013).

32. Edward Luck, *UN Security Council: Practice and Promise* (New York: Routledge, 2006).

33. See Axel Dreher, Jan-Egbert Sturm, and James Raymond Vreeland, "Politics and IMF Conditionality," *Journal of Conflict Resolution* 59, no. 1 (2015): 120–48. For more information, see, Axel Dreher, "IMF Conditionality: Theory and Evidence," *Public Choice* 141.1–2 (October 2009): 233–67; Will H. Moore and James R. Scaritt, "IMF Conditionality and Polity Characteristics in Black Africa: An Exploratory Analysis," *Africa Today* 37, no. 4 (1990).

34. Martha Finnemore, "International Organizations as Teachers of Norms: The United Nations Educational, Scientific and Cultural Organization and Science Policy," *International Organization* 47 (Autumn 1993): 565–97.

35. Weiss et al., "The 'Third' United Nations," 127.

36. "An Agenda for Peace: Preventive Diplomacy, Peacemaking, and Peace-Keeping" (Report of the Secretary-General pursuant to the statement adopted by the Summit Meeting of the Security Council on January 31, 1992), UN Doc. A/47/277-S/24111 (June 17, 1992); "In Larger Freedom: Towards Development, Security, and Human Rights for All," UN Doc. A/59/2005 (March 21, 2005), http://www.un.org/sg/.

37. UN, Cooperation Between the United Nations and Regional and Other Organizations, A/67/280-S/2012/614 (New York: United Nations, 2012).

38. John Brehm and Scott Gates, *Working, Shirking, and Sabotage: Bureaucratic Response to a Democratic Public* (Ann Arbor, MI: University of Michigan Press, 1997).

39. Barbara Koremenos, "When, What, and Why Do States Choose to Delegate?" *Law and Contemporary Problems* 71 (Winter 2008): 151–92, http://scholarship.law.duke.edu/lcp/vol71/iss1/7; Keck and Sikkink, *Activists Beyond Borders*.

40. Kal Raustiala, "States, NGOs, and International Environmental Institutions," *International Studies Quarterly* 41, no. 7 (1997): 720.

41. Thomas Kwasi Tieku and Sylvia Ostry, *Trade Advocacy Groups and Multilateral Trade Policy-Making of African States* (Toronto: Munk Centre for International Studies, 2007).

42. Thomas Kwasi Tieku and Kristiana Powell, "The African Union and the Responsibility to Protect: Towards a Protection Regime for Africa?" *International Insights* 20, no. 1 and 2 (2005); Thomas G. Weiss, *Humanitarian Intervention: Ideas in Action* (Cambridge, UK and Malden, MA: Polity Press, 2007).

43. United Nations Disarmament, Demobilization, and Reintegration Resource Centre (2009),http://unddr.org/; Mohammed Nuruzzaman, "Revisiting 'Responsibility to Protect' after Libya and Syria," *E-International Relations* (March 8, 2014).

44. "World Bank, World Development Report 2003: Sustainable Development in a Dynamic World—Transforming Institutions, Growth, and Quality of Life ," World Bank, 2003, https://openknowledge.worldbank.org/handle/10986/5985; also see "The Pearson Report, A New Strategy for Global Development*" (The UNESCO Courier,* February 1970), http://unesdoc.unesco.org/images/0005/000567/056743eo.pdf.

45. Butler, "Reform of the United Nations Security Council."

46. The Panel's mandate was to interact with the ruling authorities and other Egyptian stakeholders as well as countries from the Gulf region to establish a constructive political dialogue aimed at national reconciliation, as well as contributing to efforts toward a transition that would lead to an early return to constitutional order and to consolidate the democratic process. Alpha Oumar Konaré, former president of the Republic of Mali and former chairperson of the AU Commission, chairs the Panel. The other members are: Festus Gontebanye Mogae, former president of the Republic of Botswana, and Dileita Mohamed Dileita, former prime minister of the Republic of Djibouti. The Panel was appointed on July 8, 2013, and is assisted by a group of experts. PSC/PR/COMM; CCCLXXXIV.

47. Andy Knight, *Adapting the United Nations to a Post-Modern Era: Lessons Learned*, 2nd edition (Houndmills: Palgrave/Macmillan Press/St. Martin's Press, 2005), 312; Leon Gordenker and Christer Jonsson, "Knowledge," *in The Oxford Handbook on the United Nations*, ed. Thomas Weiss and Sam Daws (Oxford: Oxford University Press, 2007), 82–94.

48. Knud Erik Jorgensen, Sebastian Oberthu, and Jamal Shahin, "Introduction: Assessing the EU's Performance in International Institutions—Conceptual Framework and Core Findings. European Integration," *Journal of European Integration* 33, no. 6 (November 2011): 599–620; Tamar Gutner and Alexander Thompson, "The Politics of IO Performance: A Framework," *Review International Organization* 5, no. 3 (2010): 227–48; Lusthaus et al., *Organizational Assessment: A Framework for Improving Performance* (Ottawa: IDRC, 2005); H. Breitmeier, O. R. Young, and M. Zürn, *Analyzing International Environmental Regimes: From Case Study to Database* (Cambridge, MA: MIT Press, 2006); Miles et al., *Environmental Regime Effectiveness: Confronting Theory with Evidence* (Cambridge, MA: MIT Press, 2002); Volker Rittberger and Peter Mayer, *Regime Theory and International Relations* (Oxford: Oxford University Press, 1993); Oran R. Young, *Governance in World Affairs* (Ithaca, NY: Cornell University Press, 1999); and on organizational performance, see Gutner and Thompson, "The Politics of IO Performance: A Framework," 227–48; Lusthaus et al., *Organizational Assessment*.

49. Volker Rittberger, Bernhard Zangl, and Andreas Kruck, *International Organization* (UK: Palgrave Macmillan, 2012); David Easton, *A Systems Analysis of Political Life* (New York: Wiley, 1965); David Easton, *A Framework for Political Analysis* (Englewood Cliffs, NJ: Prentice-Hall, 1965).

50. Michael Barnett and Martha Finnemore, *Rules for the World: International Organizations in Global Politics* (Ithaca: Cornell University Press, 2004).

51. Susan Park, "Theorizing Norm Diffusion within International Organizations," *International Politics* 43, no. 3 (2006): 342–36.

52. Mareike Kleine, "Trading Control: National Fiefdoms in International Organizations," *International Theory* 5, no. 3 (November 2013): 321–46, http://journals.cambridge.org/action/displayFulltext?type=1&fid=9073727&jid=INT&volumeId=5&issueId=03&aid=9073724&bodyId=&membershipNumber=&societyETOCSession=; Also, see Mareike Kleine, *Informal Governance in the European Union: How Governments Make International Organizations Work* (Ithaca, NY: Cornell University Press, 2013a).

53. For detailed discussion, see Thomas Kwasi Tieku, "The Formation of African Union: Analysis of the Role of Ideas and Supranational Entrepreneurs in Interstate Cooperation," (Ann Arbor: ProQuest, 2006). See Christopher Clapham's discussion of the politics of solidarity and Ali Mazrui's analysis of the concept of "we are all Africans." Christopher Clapham, *Africa and the International System: The Politics of State Survival* (Cambridge: Cambridge University Press, 1996); Ali Mazrui, "On the Concept of 'We Are All Africans,'" *American Political Science Review* LVII: 1 (March 1963), 88–97; and Ali Mazrui, *Towards a Pax Africana: A Study of Ideology and Ambition* (Chicago: University of Chicago Press, 1967).

Chapter Two

Theorizing African Union as a 3-D International Organization

Following the 3-D analytical framework, this chapter argues that contrary to popular belief and conventional academic narratives, the AU is not a single organization but rather three international bodies merged into one. It has intergovernmental, supranational, and transnational organizational features. The most important intergovernmental institutions are the Assembly, the Council, and the PRC.[1] The Assembly is composed of African leaders, the Council is comprised of African foreign ministers, and the PRC is composed of African ambassadors or other plenipotentiaries accredited to the AU and Ethiopia. The intergovernmental AU is headed by a chairperson, who must be a sitting African head of state and government. The chairperson's position is held for a maximum of one year by the head of state of the country hosting the midyear annual summit.

The supranational AU is represented by the African Union Commission (AUC). The AUC is composed of a chairperson, deputy chairperson, and eight commissioners. Each commissioner manages a department.[2] The AUC is supported by approximately 1,474 (June 2015 figure) international civil servants. The chairperson of the AUC is elected by the Assembly together with the Deputy Chair. The chairperson acts as the AU's chief executive officer (CEO), legal representative, and its accounting officer. As the CEO, the chairperson is supposed to assume the overall management of the Commission. This means in practice the chairperson is mandated to develop and execute strategic plans of the AUC, take measures to enhance the performance of the AU, promote its activities, act as secretary at meetings of other AU organs, appoints and manages AUC staff, as well as chairs all AUC meetings when present. In addition, the CEO is supposed to consult and coordinate the AU's work with member governments, African regional economic communities (ARECs), and international partners. The CEO is required to enhance the functioning, decision-making, and reporting of all units of the AUC and also ensure that activities of AU organs are in conformity and harmony with the Union's agreed policies, strategies, programs, and projects. As the accounting officer, the chairperson is supposed to manage the entire finances of the Commission, prepare its budget, and account for the financing of the AU to the intergovernmental bodies (i.e., the Assembly through the Council and the PRC). Finally, the chairperson acts as a depository for all AU and OAU treaties and other legal instruments, and also represents the AU at international forums.

The deputy chairperson is not a typical deputy of an IO as he or she is neither appointed nor can be fired by the chairperson. The statutes of the AUC further strengthened the position of the deputy chairperson by making him or her responsible for the administration and finance of the Commission. This means in practice that the deputy chairperson controls both the purse of the AUC and the international civil servants who work in various units of the AUC. In practice, the AUC staffers report to the deputy chairperson rather than the chairperson. Thus, although the chairperson has the power to appoint AUC staff, it will be difficult for him or her to discipline any of the AUC staff without the support of the deputy. In other words, the deputy chairperson is a powerful chord within the AU system, and the chairperson has little choice but to comanage with the deputy. The chairperson cannot turn the deputy chairperson into his or her glorified assistant. To prevent the deputy from undermining the chairperson, the statutes of the AUC made him or her accountable to the chairperson.

The checks and balances embedded in the management of the AUC does not even end there, as each one of the eight AUC departments is headed by a commissioner, who is selected by the Council and appointed by the Assembly. Although commissioners are accountable to the chairperson, they cannot be fired or disciplined by the chairperson or the deputy. Only the Assembly has the power to terminate the appointment of commissioners. The statutes further enhance the powers of commissioners by making each one of them responsible "for the implementation of all decisions, policies and programmes in respect of the portfolio for which he/she has been elected."[3]

In practice, each commissioner has a selfdom, and both the chairperson and deputy cannot micromanage any department without the acquiescence of a commissioner. Commissioners who have strong personalities and are really good have often operated as if their departments are not under the offices of the chairperson or deputy chairperson. The comanagement style works best with good commissioners. A terrible but politically connected commissioner can basically destroy a department, and the chair and the deputy can do little about it.

The limitation of the comanageable model notwithstanding, it diminishes the possibility of the chairperson becoming a dictator. This is not bad for a continent with a long track record of dictators, and big men and women mentality. A good and an innovative commissioner has all the freedom to build a great department, and the work of a slacking commissioner often becomes painfully obvious. The disparities in the size and work of AU departments are reflective of the performances of commissioners who had the chance to run them. The level of competence and commitment of the first generation of commissioners who run the Peace and Security Department (DPS) and the Department of Political Affairs (DPA) largely explain why the former is three times the size of the latter. The DPS was lucky to get a genuinely committed and savvy Pan-Africanist, while the DPA ended up with a tourist who cared more about travel destinations than doing something that generations yet unborn will remember.

The outisiders include networks of carefully selected Pan-African–oriented academics and consultants (knowledge communities), commissions, transnational African nongovernmental Organizations (TANGOs), ARECs, and other international organizations, such as the European Union (EU) and United Nations (UN). Interactions between the intergovernmentals and the outisiders are mediated by the AUC.

The three dimensions of the AU are explored in detail in the three sections below. The section to follow this introduction shows why the AU is often seen as an intergovernmental organization. The next section argues that it is simplistic to think of the AU as a mere intergovernmental body. Its supranationality is equally significant. The section shows that our understanding of the AU is greatly enhanced by taking the supranational dimension of the AU serious. The final section shows the outisider side of the AU, arguing that outisiders are more fundamental to the entire AU enterprise than most people think or are prepared to admit. The chapter ends with preliminary theoretical reflections of the empirical analysis.

INTERGOVERNMENTAL AU

The AU is widely seen by the general public and discussed in popular media and conceptualized by many experts as an intergovernmental body.[4] This is perhaps unsurprising given that the African governments negotiated, signed, and ratified the Constitutive Act that established the AU. The Constitutive Act and the AU would not have come into existence if at least two-thirds of them had not deposited the instrument of ratification. Moreover, there are layers of intergovernmental institutions formally entrusted with, among other things, powers to make final decisions on all AU matters; to set its long-term goal; to hire, fire, and supervise AU employees; and to establish new AU institutions. At the top of the intergovernmental institutions is the Assembly, which, in the wording of Article 6(2) of the AU Constitutive Act, is the "supreme organ" of the AU. It is supposed to make all major AU decisions, but the Assembly is institutionally ill equipped to do so. It normally meets only twice (usually at the end of January and early to mid June) in a year, and each meeting lasts for only two days. For instance, the Twenty-Fifth AU Summit was held between June 14 and 15, 2015, in Johannesburg, South Africa. Each meeting tends to have many agenda items, which make it very difficult for attendees to review the necessary supplementary reports and documents. The Twenty-Fifth AU Summit had over twenty-six big agenda items and approximately twenty major reports, dealing with diverse topics such as a framework for negotiation for continental free trade, alternative sources of funding for the AU, terrorism and violent extremism in Africa, governance and elections in Africa, UN reforms, and international criminal justice. In addition, the Summit reviewed the equally voluminous reports of activities of other AU bodies with a view to approving their programs for the year. To put this in context, the Report of the Peace and Security Council on its Activities and the State of Peace and Security in Africa alone was over fifty pages long. The Assembly had over ten of such voluminous reports to consider within just two days. To expect heads of states or close advisors who are usually middle-aged to read carefully over five hundred pages and have the energy to sit and thoughtfully discuss these reports is to endow them with superhuman quality. In truth, most of them do not read more than two pages of even the most important reports. In fact, you will be lucky to find presidents and close advisers who know the actual titles of these reports. Moreover, the Assembly meetings are too large; on average, approximately forty-five out of fifty-four Assembly members often attend these summits. Such a large gathering of big men and a couple of women within a short space of time is not the most ideal place for an in-depth discussion of issues and effective deliberations of issues that affect the lives of over a billion people. Often ceremonies and speeches take up a majority of the time, and the little time that is left is used to rubber-stamp decisions made by other entities such as the Council or the PRC. The central point here is that although the Assembly is supposed to be the supreme body and manager of the AU, in practice it cannot do that. Others have to do it in the Assembly's name.

The creators of the AU recognized this and therefore established the Council to make the key decisions and send recommendations to the Assembly for the ceremonial rubber stamps. Incidentally, the Council's institutional challenges are similar to, if not worse than, those of the Assembly. Like the Assembly, Council members normally meet twice each year (often a couple of days before the Assembly session), and because Council members look at the administrative side of the AU as well, they often have more reports and agenda items than the Assembly. On average, Council members get between three to four additional reports to consider. The Twenty-Seventh Council meeting held between and June 11 and 12, 2015, and prior to the Twenty-Fifth Summit had close to forty different agenda items. Some of the agenda items take a considerable amount of time to deal with. For instance, it took significant time for the Council to elect the six members of the African Committee of Experts on the Rights and Welfare of the Child (ACERWC) and the three members of the African Commission on Human and Peoples' Rights (ACHPR).

Unlike the Assembly, Council members do not often travel with a huge delegation, and any major technical support is expected to come from the overstretched embassy staff in Ethiopia. Most Council members are often not in a position to read, let alone digest, these reports. They often rely on their ambassadors to Ethiopia to give them verbal briefing of the most extremely important reports. Moreover, each Council meeting requires a minimum of thirty-five members in order to have a quorum—a figure that is usually exceeded and reaches an average of about forty-five attendees. This large gathering of foreign ministers, who are often great at talking for hours without saying anything substantive, is neither conducive to deliberative decision making nor a good space for plying proper supervisory responsibilities.

To address some of the limitations of the Council, the PRC was created as an advisory body to the Council. Unlike the Council, the PRC members are able to meet on a monthly basis to examine in more detail the necessary documents and reports and to prepare agenda items and draft decisions for the Council's consideration. The agenda items and draft decisions recommended by the PRC are usually forwarded to the Assembly without any major changes. The PRC has thus become the defacto institution that sets the agenda for both Council and Assembly summits and establishes parameters of things African leaders can discuss and decide. The agenda-setting and recommendation powers acquired by the PRC have made it the most decisive intergovernmental institution within the entire AU system. It has become the body, as Kane and Mbelle noted, that ensures that the agenda of the AU is consistent with "the day to day reality of government business in capital cities around the [African] continent."[5] In practice both the Assembly and the Council have become mere rubber-stamping institutions of decisions and recommendations made at the PRC level.

The PRC meetings are too large for serious policy debates and proper supervision of either the work of the AUC or the outisiders. Most PRC members are politicians, career diplomats, or generalists and lack the requisite technical skills to engage competently with ideas and reports from the AUC, which are often put together by experts. Few PRC members have the formal public policy background that the job requires, and its discussions tend to be general, personality driven, and anecdotal in nature. The limitation of the PRC is exacerbated by the lack of technical support from their home countries. The modest technical expertise that does exist tends to be siphoned off from the ministries of member states to the various international organizations, the private sector, and the nongovernmental community owning to better salaries. These institutional limitations make it difficult for the PRC to act as the supreme body on behalf of the Assembly and the Council.

Another reason why the AU is generally perceived as a purely intergovernmental organization lies in the powers given to the Assembly to determine the Union's long-term policy, strategic vision, and its overall direction. The Assembly tries to exercise this power through the Council and the PRC. However, the institutional design of both the Council and the PRC make it difficult for the two intergovernmental institutions to help the Assembly initiative policy and provide strategic policy leadership. The tenure of the chair of Council and the chair of PRC, who are normally supposed to lead the policy process, is too short. The position of the chair of Council rotates annually, and that of the PRC is held monthly. The transient nature of the chair's position makes long-term strategic planning and policy initiative almost impossible.

The PRC chair does not have the time to even deal with the many items that are often on the table for the month, let alone the space to consider new policy and long-term strategic policy planning. Many PRC members often spend three years at their post before they are sent elsewhere. The first year is usually devoted to learning, building networks, and gaining access. The third year is usually devoted to planning for the exit of the PRC member, which sometimes have included lobbying for a position within the AUC. The major window of opportunity for a PRC member to do serious work is the second year, and if in the rare case the term is extended, subsequent years. Given that PRC members are also ambassadors of their countries to Ethiopia, they often devote the bulk of their time on matters important to their countries rather than think about the long-term goal of the AU.

As for Council members who are normally foreign ministers of their countries, they simply do not have the space or perhaps the willingness to devote to initiating long-term policy for the AU. Such an exercise will require long and difficult consultations with stakeholders of member states, and most foreign ministers do not have the time and energy to do that. Except preparing for the biannual Council meetings, which many of them do at the very last minute, most Council members do not usually work on AU files. As a direct result, most of the actual strategic planning and setting up of a long-term goal for the AU had been delegated to the AUC.

The current long-term AU document called Agenda 2063 was initiated and developed in the office of the current chairperson of the AUC, Nkosazana Dlamini-Zuma, with assistance from the UN Economic Commission for Africa (UNECA) and the African Development Bank (AfDB).[6] The institutional design of intergovernmental agencies and the limitations that accompanied them have allowed the AUC and outsiders to determine the long-term policy and strategic vision of the AU, and to provide overall direction for the AU. Indeed, the intergovernmental organs of the AU can at best examine and approve strategic plans and visions developed and submitted by the AUC with strong technical support from outsiders. All three AU strategic plans and visions were developed by the AUC and outsiders with little input from any of the intergovernmental bodies. The first strategic plan, which lasted between 2004 and 2008, was develop by the cabinet of the then chairperson of the AUCA, Alpha Oumar Konaré, with technical assistance from the Institute for Security Studies (ISS) based in South Africa. [7]

Finally, the monitoring role given to AU intergovernmental bodies explains in part why some people think the AU is basically an interstate organization. The Assembly through the Council and the PRC is supposed to monitor the work of the AUC and outsiders. The PRC derives its monitoring powers from the mandate it has to advise the Council on the implementation of policies, decisions, and agreements. In practice, the PRC operates within the AU like a technically weak board of directors of a company. They have positioned themselves as go-betweens among AU bureaucrats and member states. They have taken advantage of this interlocutor position not only to become the spokespersons of AU member states but can in theory mobilize African states in support of or against a particular issue and position. They also monitor the implementation of the budget of the AU. PRC members have turned this role into the position of the controller and accountant general of the AU. They scrutinize budgets of the various bodies and organs of the AU, set parameters for salaries for AU bureaucrats, and set spending limits on other organs of the AU. The power over purse together with the fact that PRC members participate in the preparation of programs for the Council and Assembly give the PRC an important voice in the AU system. But as indicated already, the work of the AU is one of several tasks allocated to PRC members. The heavy workload and the superior technical abilities of senior and professional staff of the AUC have restricted PRC members to exercising only the financial oversight function given to intergovernmental institutions within the AU system. Thus, the broader message of this section is that although intergovernmental bodies were given a lot of formal powers, in practice they have given up most of them except the power of the purse and the power to give the customary stamp of approval to the work of AUC and outsiders.

SUPRANATIONAL AU

It is controversial at least in political science and African studies to suggest that the AU has a supranational dimension. Yet the section below attempts to show that the AUC gives the AU its supranational identity.[8] The composition and competencies of the AUC are spelled out in the Statute of the Commission of the African Union (Statutes).[9] The AUC's supranationality comes from the relative independence that the AUC staff enjoys, and the functional roles and activities that Commission staff and supporting actors such as consultants perform on a day-to-day basis. As international civil servants, the AUC staff are granted autonomy and independence in the exercise of their duties. They are not supposed to "seek or receive instructions from any government or from any other authority external to the Union."[10] In addition, AU bureaucrats are required to be responsible only to the commission. Government agencies and representatives are mandated "to respect the exclusive character of the responsibilities of the Members of the Commission and the other staff and shall not influence or seek to influence them in the discharge of their responsibilities."[11]

The above articles were inserted in the statutes of the AUC to prevent African embassies in Ethiopia and donors from dictating to the AUC. This has not provided 100 percent autonomy to the Commission staff, but they have given AU staffers the platform do their work without major interferences from African public officials and representatives of the donor agencies. There are the occasional personal and backroom interventions by embassy officials to protect and/or advocate for AUC staffers from countries they represent, but over there is little evidence to suggest that AU bureaucrats take instructions from the African missions and even the donors who provide most of the program budget.

Besides the institutional and human resource deficits (discussed earlier) that make it difficult for embassy officials to dictate to the AUC staff, two additional factors restrict African embassy officials from dictating to AUC bureaucrats. Embassy staffers are usually junior colleagues of senior administrators of the AUC, and most of the professionals of the AUC were senior administrators in, and sometimes ambassadors of, their countries prior to joining the AUC. For instance, the current commissioner of DPS was the Algerian ambassador to the AU prior to joining the AU. This makes it difficult, though not impossible, for his successor and those below the ambassador tell the commissioner what he should or should not do. In any case, the professionals at the AUC should in theory be technically superior and more competent than embassy officials. Even though African politics sometimes defies logic and basic principles of political life, experiences show that technically inferior people find it difficult to order their superiors around. In addition, AUC commissioners are ranked above ambassadors, and some of the African ambassadors to Ethiopia are often job hunting at the AUC. These factors have combined to give AUC professionals the necessary room to operate relatively independently. They certainly do work within the parameters often established by political scientists for traditional IO bureaucrats.

The actual works of the AUC, not just those provided on paper, have enhanced the supranationality of the AU. The day-to-day works of AUC professionals have become major sources of power for the Commission. These works go far into areas associated with supranational agencies. Seven of these roles are critically examined below to show how intrusive and powerful AUC officials can be if they seize the opportunities within their grasp. If the AUC roles are combined with the autonomy that the statutes grant to AUC staff, a clear supranational image emerges. At the very least they show that the AUC is more than a servant of AU's intergovernmental bodies.

Rule Making: The AUC plays a central role in the drafting of AU treaties, declarations, decisions, and resolutions. The functions that the AUC performs during the drafting of AU legal instruments reflect that of a supranational actor. The AUC staffers often have so much latitude during the drafting of legal instruments that committed and visionary bureaucrats can easily move the African integration process in a direction that no government can resist. The first draft or zero draft of most AU legal instruments are usually crafted by the AUC legal team or consultants hired by the AUC. This gives AUC officials enormous gate-keeping powers. They can and often do use the opportunity to develop documents in ways that reflect their perspective, what they perceive as the views of key member states, and to delimit the kinds of issues and ideas that are put on the table for negotiation by state parties. In theory, member states are supposed to give the AUC comments on these drafts, but as a former legal counselor of the AU pointed out, "You will be lucky to receive acknowledgment of receipt of these documents from member states."[12] African governments have the habit of not commenting or supervising the drafting of these documents. For instance, only two African governments formally sent comments on the zero draft instrument that eventually became the Protocol Relating to the Establishment of the Peace and Security Council of the African Union (the PSC protocol).[13] The PSC protocol created the AU Peace and Security Council, which has been very influential in the peace and security landscape of the African continent.[14] There is little doubt that the PSC protocol has become one of the most instrumental and seminal legal documents in the entire African international system.[15]

Part of the reason why African governments do not provide any substantive comments or contributions in the drafting of AU legal documents has to do with the dearth of technical capacity in the bureaucracies of African states. With the exception of a few states, these bureaucracies do not attract the strongest human capacity within various African states. The most gifted people in most African states pursue their careers elsewhere. In fact, NGOs even attract stronger talent than most bureaucracies in Africa. The pay system of the AUC, however, allows it to attract considerably stronger candidates than most civil service in Africa. The absence of comments is to some extent an implicit assumption that the documents have passed through technically stronger hands, and it would be an unnecessary use of scarce resources for government experts to go over them.

Some African governments do not pay enough attention to draft legal texts sent by the AUC in part because they often think their experts will get the chance to look at them carefully during intergovernmental expert meetings that the AUC often convenes over many of these documents. But these experts meetings are too large, driven by bureaucratic imperatives, and too complex for any meaningful redrafting of these instruments. There is also the issue of per diem and travel allowance, which are paid in the sought-after U.S. dollars, that the cash-strapped government experts have become very dependent upon. For fear of being dropped from the invitation list, many of these experts "behave properly."[16] In any case, AUC officials provide secretarial duties at these meetings and often have the power to interpret and summarize discussions at these meetings in ways that reflect their cognitive orientations more than anything else. In other words, a savvy AUC leadership can use the power to draft legal instruments to embed their own ideas in the drafting of new agreements in ways that serve the broader interests of supranationality rather than the parochial interests of intergovernmental bodies.

Though some of the AU bureaucrats engage in self-censorship, there is ample evidence to show that at least some AUC officials have used these powers to put progressive ideas on the AU agenda. Some have also taken advantage of this power to make intergovernmental AU adopt instruments that they would not have agreed to otherwise. Many of the AU policy and legal instruments such as the African Charter on Democracy, Elections and Governance (African Governance Charter), postconflict reconstruction policy, the Common African Defense Pact, among others, read like literature reviews of best practices in part because they were all written by Africrats usually in collaboration with consultants.[17] African governments provided little substantive input into the development of these legal instruments.[18]

Representational Duties: The AUC exercises a number of representational powers. It plays an ad hoc representational role in the form of speaking and attending public gatherings, such as international fora on behalf of the AU and its member states. In this role, the AUC is required to articulate views, and it behaves in ways that reflect collective preferences of African states. Demands for AUC's representation are so high that the leadership of the AUC spends most of their time traveling and attending meetings. The high rate of traveling in particular has generated enormous debate within the Commission, as it impacts negatively on the productivity of the AUC. The other representational function the AUC exercises entails the creation of permanent missions by the AUC in important capitals around the world. These missions are tasked with the responsibility to promote the interests and values of the African continent, articulate collective views of African states, and act as a delegate of the African society of states outside of the African continent.[19] As of June 2015, the AU had established permanent representational offices to the United Nations in New York, the World Trade Organization (WTO) in Geneva, the European Union (EU), African, Caribbean, and Pacific (ACP) states in Brussels, the League of Arab States in Cairo, and the United States in Washington, D.C. These presentational offices if staffed properly and its resources should give the AUC enormous clout. There is evidence that some of them actually help African states construct their interests in international negotiation. For instance, the AUC office in Geneva brings together usually on Tuesdays African embassy officials in Geneva to construct their interests, agree on common positions, and share negotiation tactics on major global issues such as the Doha Trade Rounds.[20]

Regulatory Powers: The AUC has powers to create regulations that are binding on member states. It is empowered to initiate proposals that would provide regulations in a number of issue areas such as control of epidemics, disaster management, international crime and terrorism, environmental management, negotiations relating to trade and external debt, food security, refugees, populations, migration, and displaced persons.[21] Some of the departments of AUC have taken advantage of this to develop a number of regulations that are enforceable in member states. The DPS took the lead in helping the AU develop extensive regulations on unconstitutional changes of government in Africa.[22] The regulations adopted first as declarations in Harare in 1998, in Algiers in 1999, and Lomé in 2000 have been used to suspend from the AU states such as Guinea-Bissau and São Tomé and Principe in 2003, Togo in 2005, Mauritania in 2005 and 2007, and Guinea in 2008 after military takeover.[23] The success of the anticoup regulation encouraged Africrats in the DPS to hire a consultant to draft a broader governance charter for the African continent.[24] The African Governance Charter, among other things, made elections the only legitimate means of acquiring state power in Africa.[25] Keen observers of African politics credit these regulations for the reduction by almost half of coup making on the African continent since the AU emerged on the scene.[26] The other document that contained detailed regulations that Africrats in the DPS collaborated with consultants to develop is the African Union Non-Aggression and Common Defence Pact (African Defence Pact). This Pact provides some of the most instructive and detailed regulations on regional defense and security in the world. It criminalizes states' acquisition of new territory by force; commits AU members to prohibit and prevent genocide, crimes against humanity, and other forms of mass murder; and in addition it prohibits member states of AU from entering "into any international or regional commitment which is in contradiction to the present Pact."[27]

Similarly, Africrats in the Department of Rural Economy and Agriculture collaborated with consultants to establish a regulatory framework contained in the Comprehensive African Agriculture Development Program, which, among other things, asks member states to spend 10 percent of their national budget on agriculture.[28] Other areas in which AUC departments have been active in developing rules for Africa are counterterrorism, international criminal justice, children, international negotiations, refugees, and internally displaced persons.[29] Among the most elaborate and instructive instruments developed by an IO are the AUC regulations on youth, counterterrorism, and internally displaced persons.[30]

Some of these regulations have received universal praise; others have generated controversy. For instance, the gender-parity regulations that Africrats in close cooperation with gender advocacy groups pushed intergovernmental bodies to adopt have received worldwide praise. These regulations have been hailed not only because they have led to the establishment of gender parity at the very top of the management of the AUC, they have made the AU one of the most gender-sensitive IOs in the world.[31] No IO has more women at senior management positions than the AU. As of June 2015, the AUC had 50 percent women at the top management positions; most IOs have less than 30 percent women at the senior management positions. Women are more represented at the top of the AUC management than even the European Commission. While five out of ten AUC commissioners, including the chairperson, are women, only nine out of nineteen commissioners of the EU are women.[32]

The AUC efforts to create regulations on international crime and law have been widely criticized, especially by the NGO community. For instance, the draft protocol on the proposed African Court on Justice and Human Rights, which was adopted by African leaders at the June 2014 AU Summit in Malabo, was widely denounced by civil society and rights groups. Although "much of it is ground-breaking stuff," the draft protocol was denounced in large part because it reaffirmed immunity granted by customary international law to African heads of state and senior government officials from prosecution while they are in office.[33] Lost in the simplistic analysis of the protocol is the fact that the draft protocol makes it possible for the African Court to prosecute these leaders when they leave office for serious crimes, including genocide, war crimes, and crimes against humanity, as well as transnational crimes such as trafficking in persons or drugs, terrorism, and piracy. Some also criticized the protocol because the drafting processes were controlled largely by the AUC legal affairs with little input from the NGO community. It was rightly argued that the drafting processes would have benefitted from a process of consultation, not least with relevant expert stakeholders and civil society actors.[34] Whatever the merit of the processes for drafting the protocol, there is little doubt the protocol breaks many legal grounds, and it will fundamentally shape the future of the continent and Africa's relations with the rest of the world when the court gets off the ground. It has been argued that the operationalization of the protocol will effectively kill the ICC's influence and work on the African continent.[35]

Power to Enforce Rules: The AUC has at least three implementation powers: the power to "implement decisions taken by other organs of the AU," the mandate to "coordinate and monitor the implementations of the decisions of other organs of the AU," and the power to "assist member states in implementing AU programs and policies."[36] Attached to all these powers is a mandate to review and report regularly to the intergovernmental AU. The AU has used these powers to pursue supranational goals in many ways. Some AUC officials have taken advantage of this power to name and shame governments that have not implemented policies and decisions of the AU. For instance, as part of its mandate to "ensure the mainstreaming of gender in all programmes and activities of the Union,"[37] the office of the chairperson has been reporting annually and publicly about the regulatory and institutional mechanisms developed by AU member states to promote gender equity. These annual reports submitted to the Executive Council during AU summits carry significant naming and shaming impacts. Though correlation is not causation, it is not just a sheer coincidence that there has been progressive development of institutional mechanisms in African governmental machinery, including the presidency, to promote gender issues since the AUC emerged on the political scene in 2003. The changes in African states may have something to do with the AUC's naming and shaming of governments during summits.

The DPS has used these powers to impose AU's code of conduct and rules of engagement on African security personnel on AU peace support operations. The rules have encouraged the majority of African security forces on AU missions to conduct themselves in professional ways. For instance, the AUC is pushing troops contributing countries to its peace missions to enforce the Union's zero tolerance on sexual abuse. Unlike in the past where IOs basically ignored accusations of sexual assaults by their peacekeepers, the AU appointed an independent team of investigators to examine Human Rights Watch's allegations of twenty-one cases of sexual exploitation and abuse by the Ugandan and Burundian Contingents as well as some civilian personnel to the African Union Mission to Somalia (AMISOM).[38] Though the report was inconclusive in large part because the leadership of the military in the affected countries did not fully cooperate, it was interesting that those who were accused of sexual misconduct were quietly withdrawn from the mission and/or banned from participating in future missions, and in at least one case the accused person is generally considered to have been jailed.[39] The allegations would have been an additional footnote to the massive literature that exists on the culture of impunity that peacekeepers accused of sexual exploitation have enjoyed over the years had it not been in the AUC's power to enforce rules on peace support missions. That said, the AUC should and could do more to fight the culture of sexual exploitation in peace missions in Africa.

Strategic Powers: The AUC has the power to provide strategic leadership for the African Union. This strategic leadership mandate is reflected in the statues of the AU in multiple ways. Some of the strategic powers are explicit in nature, while others are implied in the AUC statutes. Article 2(m) of the statutes empowers the AUC to prepare strategic plans and studies for the consideration of the Council. The AUC has used these powers over the last decade to develop three strategic plans. The first was put in place by the Konaré regime from 2004 to 2008. The major thrust of this strategic plan was to shift the AU from a general-purpose organization to focus more directly on political integration. Jean Ping introduced the second strategic plan from 2009 to 2011. The broader goal of the plan was to develop a common value system for the African continent. The final plan was introduced by the Zuma administration for 2012 to 2016 with the fundamental goal to position the AUC to drive Agenda 2063. All of these strategic plans were developed by Africrats with very little input from intergovernmental institutions such as the PRC, the Council, and even the Assembly. Yet they were adapted as a strategic plan of the AU for the period in question. Their impact has not been long lasting, or at least they have not had the desired impact because of the limited time each regime had to implement them. It often took more than a year for new administration to develop these plans, and by the time these policies were implemented the leadership of the administration was preparing for the exit. These strategic plans have actually replaced the strategic role that the Constitutive Act of the AU assigned to the Assembly. In other words, the Assembly is supposed to provide a strategic leadership for the AU, but in practice the AUC is playing that role.

The power provided in the statutes that has enhanced the AUC's strategic leadership position is the authority given to the AUC to "mobilize resources and devise appropriate strategies for self-financing income generating activities and investment for the union."[40] The power of the purse is an important one. It is a power that the AUC can actually use to make the AU financially independent and further reduce the influence of intergovernmental institutions in the AU system. The PRC's influence would be minimized considerably if the AUC can follow the example set by the Economic Community of West African States (ECOWAS) and come up with a creative financial formula that would reduce its dependence on the annual contributions of member states. Smart and savvy AUC departments have actually shown that they can take advantage of these powers to develop programs and direct the AU in ways that none of the member states can. For example, the DPS has developed enormous income-generating capacity to the extent that it has been able to put in place program of activities that none of the member states have control over. The huge growth of the department and the prestige it enjoys comes from the fact that the department is able to generate enormous program resources from donors. The culture of jealousy that exists in some circles of the AUC makes some bureaucrats berate the DPS for encouraging external dependence, but there is little doubt that the department has used the resources to save many lives in Africa. The Damini-Zuma administration has recognized the extreme importance of developing independent funding sources for the AU and has therefore made it a priority to develop an alternative source of funding for the AU.

The other powers embedded in the AUC statutes that have the potential to enhance the AUC's strategic powers is the mandate to "build capacity for scientific research and development" of member states.[41] This power, if used correctly, can and should put the AUC in a position to commission studies that socialize intergovernmental institutions to pursue goals that they would not otherwise do. It should also put the AUC in a position to build strong relationships with research institutions and knowledge centers around the world that should in theory enhance the power of the AUC considerably. Given the dearth of intellectual capacity within governments and bureaucracies in Africa, these research powers should enhance the AUC's reputation in a way that will help it to push through its agenda.

An equally important mandate that should enhance the intellectual capacity of the AUC is the mandate given to the AUC to "undertake research," collect and disseminate information, and maintain a reliable database on the AU and regional integration in general.[42] This mandate can be used by a shrewd chairperson not only to create a think tank and knowledge production unit in the AUC but can also be used to position the AUC as a strategic thinking institution for the African continent. Some departments have taken advantage of this by building partnerships with carefully selected individuals and think tanks in ways that enable them to exercise intellectual power over the PRC. Others have used it to develop institutional mechanisms that, if well managed, should put the AUC at the forefront of thinking on African issues. For instance, the Department of Human Resources, Science and Technology has taken full advantage of this mandate to develop an African-wide university called the Pan African University with five campuses spread across the continent. The focus of the university on graduate programing and research should in theory enhance the AUC's knowledge-building capacity. The Department of Peace and Security has also used this to build a counterterrorism research institute in Algeria to do research and produce fresh ideas on ways to deal with terrorism issues.

Finally, the AUC has been given the strategic power to develop common African positions on major global issues and to coordinate actions of AU members in international negotiations. This is a major strategic mandate as it puts the AUC in a position to basically dictate Africa's position on international subjects. The AUC has taken advantage of this to develop a common African position on subjects ranging from UN reforms, African representation in international organizations, and international trade. In some instances, the relevant AUC unit basically wrote the common African position and presented it to the Assembly for adoption. For instance, the most recent Common African Position on UN Review of Peace Operations (the Peace Operation Policy), which was submitted to the UN in April 2015, was written almost exclusively by a handful of technically gifted individuals in the DPS. As of the time of writing (June 2015), many members of the AU have not actually read it. Those who have read it did so during the Twenty-Fifth AU Summit held in June when the Assembly adopted it. In other words, they read it at least two months after it was sent to the UN.

Agenda Setting and Proposal Initiation: The AUC also has the power to "initiate" proposals for consideration by other organs of the AU. This power effectively gives the AUC the opportunity to set the agenda, to propose new ideas, and to provide direction for the Union. The AUC took advantage of this power to invent the "sectoral expert meetings" where most of the agenda items for summits are generated.[43] Many of the agenda items for summits are developed at sectoral meetings even though the AU rules provided that agenda items for summits must be provided by the Assembly of the Union, the Executive Council, the PRC, the AU Commission, any other organ of the Union, and any other item formally proposed by member states and regional economic communities. The agenda-setting powers of the AUC together with the power to do research can potentially place the AUC in a position to dictate the pace and direction of the AU.

The AUC has a convening power. It arranges and manages most of the meetings of the African Union. It can effectively bring together the sharpest brains on a particular problem to think and develop creative solutions for, and policies on, the issue. If exercised to its fullest, the AUC's convening power holds enormous supranational promise, especially given that the AUC is dealing with countries that have weak and limited institutional and technical capabilities.

OUTISIDERS AU

The outisiders who are central to the effective functioning of the AU are knowledge communities (academics and consultants), the NGOs, eminent persons, ARECs, and donors. To show the specific role these outisiders play, the section below describes the work of knowledge communities, the NGOs, and eminent persons.

Knowledge Communities: Like most IOs, the AU relies heavily on experts who provide their services as consultants or independent academics. Various units of the AUC have since 2001 built close working relationships with a variety of consultants from the academic community, think tanks, the IO system, and the NGO world. None of the AU organs can claim not to have relied on consultants for ideas, reports, and technical skills. Though each unit of the AU has its own way of dealing with the knowledge communities, three models seem very popular. The first model is the one of consultancy services provided by the knowledge communities. A classic example is the services that consultants from the International Labour Organization (ILO) provided to the Council between 2001 and 2003 when the current structure of the AUC was developed. The Council was mandated by the Assembly to come up with the structure of the AUC. Following the normal working procedures, the Council established a Ministerial Team based on regional representations to look into the issue. The Ministerial Team, however, asked the interim chairperson of the AUC, Edem Kodjo, to provide a report on the AUC for consideration by the Ministerial Team. As it is often the case, the interim chairperson subcontracted it to two consultants hired from the ILO system. They were asked to draft the report with recommendations for the appropriate structure of the AU. The report from the consultants were forwarded to the Ministerial Team, which adopted the report and recommendations in whole. Another group of consultants from the accounting firm Ernst and Young were hired to cost the structure, human resource requirements, and condition of services for the staff of the AUC.[44] The current structure and statutes of the AUC that were adopted by the Council in Maputo in 2003 were basically the combined reports submitted by the consultants.[45]

Consultants also played central roles in the selection of the first commissioners of the AUC. Omar Touray described in some detail how independent consultants influenced the selection of the first commissioners of the AUC.[46] The Ministerial Panel appointed by the Council hired the consultants to recommend candidates for elections as commissioners. Because most members of the Ministerial Panel have little human resource background and time to do thorough background research on candidates, they hired independent consultants to preselect and screen candidates who had put their names forward for consideration as commissioners. The consultants developed scorecards for selecting the candidates, ranked them, and made recommendations to the Ministerial Panel. The first batch of AUC commissioners was basically selected from the small pool of candidates ranked by the consultants. The consultants, therefore, influenced in a fundamental way who eventually became the commissioner and head of department of the first AUC.

The second model of engagement of knowledge communities in the AU system is through a short-term contract employment system. This is the model favored by the AUC. Many departments engage experts as short-term contractual employees of the Commission. Often the individuals have taken a leave of absence from their employers, and they engaged by the AUC in their individual capacities. In a few cases, the experts were seconded or sent to the AUC by their regular employers. Some of these experts use the short stay to make a transition from one job to the other. An increasing number of them end up staying beyond the original contract of six months. Some even become permanent staff of the AUC. These experts are supposed to provide independent thinking, research, and critical analysis. Though some of them have adopted the classic bureaucratic outlook and mindset, preferring to keep to the official script, they play a vital role in the AU system. Their reports, analysis, studies, and recommendations drive the work of AU organs. They often assemble the bulk of information contained in the voluminous chairperson's report. The extent of the Commission's dependence on these experts is reflected in the fact that in some key departments these outisiders outnumber permanent staff of the Commission. For instance, in DPS outisiders account for approximately 90 percent of the professional staff.[47]

The third is the ghost-writing model. The AU uses many experts as ghost thinkers and report writers. Every unit of the AU from the Assembly to the Commission seems to have routinized ghost report writers into their work. The behind-the-scenes expertise is provided to the AU, usually by a few think tanks and independent consultants. Three South African–based think tanks—the Institute for Security Studies (ISS), African Centre for the Constructive Resolution of Disputes (ACCORD), and Electoral Institute for Sustainable Democracy in Africa (EISA)—have been streets ahead of everyone in this area. The ISS fundamentally shaped the formative years of the AU peace and security system. The Institute provided the initial ideas, analysis, and reports on the African Peace and Security Architecture. The AU outsourced so much to the Institute that in the first five years of the AU's existence the ISS had more information and AU documents than any other unit of the AU, or even any member state. Though ISS influence has waned a bit in the last five years in large part because of the growth of the short-term expert contractors, it still wields considerable intellectual influence, especially at the PSC level. Interestingly, the decline of ISS's foothold on AUC seems to have coincided with the rise of ACCORD. Though the leadership of ACCORD has been key intellectual figures in both OAU and AU circles and played a central role in the drafting of the OAU Mechanisms for Conflict Prevention, Management and Resolution (MCPMR), it was not until recently that ACCORD came out of the ISS shadows on AU-related matters. ACCORD is at the moment doing more joint activities with the AU than ISS, though ISS still commands more intellectual clout within the AU than AC-

CORD.[48] If ISS used to remote control AU peace and security, then EISA is its equivalent when it comes to the AUC's work on governance and elections monitoring. Those who worked at EISA provided the critical intellectual leadership in the drafting of the African Governance Charter. People on the official payroll of EISA prepare the entirety of the elections observation reports issued in the name of the chairperson of the AU Commission. There are other important reports, such as the chairperson's report on the partnership between the UN and regional organization submitted to the UN as part of the Security Council's open debate on the matter, that were all written by outisiders.[49]

The second outisiders who play a key role in the AU system are NGOs. NGOs are fundamental to the effective functioning of the AU system. There are at least three types of NGOs that are key to the work of the AU. The first type of NGOs is the big international NGOs such as Human Rights Watch, Save the Children, and OXFAM. These big NGOs provide important research support to the AU; sometimes these groups even set the agenda for the AU. For instance, it was the work of these big NGOs together with AUC officials that persuaded the Assembly members to remove gender-insensitive language such as "Founding Fathers" from the texts of the AU.[50] It was also the work of the big NGOs that educated and socialized African leaders to adapt gender-parity policies in the selection of commissioners for the AU. In many cases these big NGOs provide a source of information for the decision making of AU intergovernmental bodies. The research and publications of organizations such as the International Crisis Group have often contributed enormously to the thinking of AU officials on issues that affect the politics of African states. The big NGOs are also very good at advocating for particular positions and pushing the AUC to adapt them. The content of AU rules of engagement for peace support operations, particularly those that concern the protection of civilians, were shaped by the advocacy work of the International Red Cross and Red Crescents. In some cases these NGO officials are embedded in government delegations to key meetings at the international level. For instance, the South Centre, the International Lawyers and Economists Against Poverty, and OXFAM have often provided a draft of the African common position on WTO issues. In other words, these big NGOs provide ideational support to both the AUC and intergovernmental bodies of the AU. The second type of NGOs are transnational African research centers; these centers have become a major resource that the AU can depend on for consultancy reports, for research output, and in some cases for the secondment of technical experts. There is a revolving door between the AUC and these transnational African-based NGOs. Many consultants within the AU system have often worked for these NGOs prior to joining the AU, and in some cases they return to these institutions at the end of their contracts. The last type of NGOs is the local African-based NGOs. These NGOs often receive 60 percent of their funding from Africa and are not dependent on the generosities of the donor community. The leadership of the AU like them in part because they are seen as indigenous bodies and in part because they bring local issues to the attention of the AU. These NGOs have often influenced the decisions of the AU through advocacy, networking, and through the ECOSOC. They interact periodically with the AU institutions, but their influence is not as great as the transnational think tanks and the big international NGOs. Despite this, there is little doubt that they keep the AU relatively grounded. For instance, most of the rules around gender-based violence were shaped by local African feminist organizations that are often able to bring some of these issues to the AU through the funding that they receive and the report they send back to the AU. Putting it differently, they provide the badly needed feedback loop within the AU system.

The final outsiders are the eminent persons who are usually retired African heads of state, prime ministers, and senior diplomats. The AU relies on these individuals as special envoys, as members of an independent panel or as part of the Panel of the Wise. These individuals have direct access to African leaders, and interact with them on a regular basis. Their opinions often carry enormous weight. For instance, the former president of Nigeria, Olusegun Obasanjo; the former president of South Africa, Thabo Mbeki; and the former president of Burundi, Pierre Buyoya, have become important opinion leaders within the AU system. Mbeki'spanel fundamentally shaped the AU's approach to the Sudanese crisis and even that of South Sudan. What he says or does is often taken as a default position of the AU. Similarly, Obasanjo has become a key ideational carrier within the AU. The report of the Panel he chaired informs thinking of the Assembly and the AUC on alternative sources of funding for the AU. Some eminent persons currently serve as the Special Representatives of the Chairperson. Some Special Representatives are appointed as mediators only. For instance, the job of the the former Malian president Alpha Oumar Konaré, who was appointed as the Special Representative of the Chairperson of South Sudan, is to mediate an end to the war between the government of South Sudan and the opposition forces led by Riek Machar. Other Special Representatives of the Chairperson do more, including managing AU Peace Support operations. A classic example is the Special Representative of the Chairperson for Somalia ambassador Maman Sidikou, who manages the 22,126 military, police, and civilian forces of AMISOM. Other eminent persons serve on the Panel of the Wise and are often asked to help resolve conflicts in different trouble spots in Africa. Without them, the AU will struggle to make any meaningful headway in the peace and security landscape. They are so critical that it is unimaginable to think about the APSA without them. In truth, any account of the AU without these outisiders will be incomplete.

CONCLUSION

The chapter has showed that the AU has complex membership and is influenced by a multiplicity of actors. Singling out government representatives and the abstract concept of the state as the important members of the AU is a disservice to knowledge production, dissemination, and the other hard-working people who make invaluable contributions to the Union. The people who work for the AUC are as important, if not the key, as government representatives. They are neither servants of government representatives nor mere paper pushers. Many analysts see the Commission as a mere secretariat of the IO in part because they usually pay attention to the official mandate of the Commission and not the actual day-to-day work that Africrats do, and in part because the imaginative ceiling of most of these analysts is that of the EU. For these analysts, the AUC is not supranational primarily because it is neither a carbon copy of the EU Commission nor even pretending to behave and act like the EU Commission. The argument is not only fraudulent in many ways, it presupposes that supranationals are the same and play a monolithic role in the international system. The logic carries a lot of imperialist and Eurocentric baggage as well. It appears to these observers that supranational functions can only be legitimately performed only with European ascent. They forget that the EU Commission is a product of particular historical developments and that the AUC is an artifact of another specific human and historical processes. It is unrealistic to expect different historical processes to produce the same outcomes. As the chapter showed, the dearth of the capacity of African civil service and the comparatively better remuneration of AU Commission staffs has actually enabled AUC to play a role that even transcends the actual supranational role ascribed the EU Commission.

Equally damaging to knowledge production is the utter neglect of outisiders in the account of the AU. Yet it will be difficult to understand, for instance, the remarkable improvement of AUC reports from the OAU days without a good grasp of outisiders' role as shadow report writers. Some of the AU's reports are similar to that of the UN not because the AU copied the UN reports but because the same people wrote the two reports. It will equally be difficult to account accurately for how a tiny bureaucratic institution is able to produce so much reports and introduce creative security ideas into the peace and security landscape without a good understanding of the ghost-report-writing industry that some outisiders have created. The programs and decision making of the AU cannot be understood without outisiders such as eminent persons and donors. Thus, to say that the AU is all about governments is both simplistic and a total misunderstanding of the AU.

A 3-D analytical framework captures the nuances and complexities of the nature of the AU. The discussion of the AU within the broader analytical framework of a 3-D IO links the AU literature to the broader political science

debates and research on intergovernmental institutions, supranational organizations, and transnational actors. It contributes to connecting the plethora of
African Studies literatures on African regional institutions to the field of
International Relations (IR). Conceptualizing AU as a 3-D IO also provides
much-needed alternative material to the descriptive body of works on international organizations in African Studies.

The subtext of the argument advanced by the chapter is that it may be
helpful for researchers to rethink the way they approach African politics. It
will certainly be helpful to go beyond African political leaders and governments in any attempt to uncover drivers of African politics. The role of
political leaders is overstated while that of transnational actors such as Africa's international bureaucrats are understated, understudied, and poorly
understood. A little balance in researchers' approaches may contribute im-
mensely to the quest of knowledge. Equally important to underline is the fact
that the transnational bureaucracy in Africa is not a unitary actor with a
single institutional preference. The chapter showed that there were different
people and agencies that promoted different objectives and interests. The
recognition of the internal incoherence of the transnational bureaucracy in
Africa is important because it sets the findings in the chapter apart from the
institutional scholarship that often treats supranational institutions as unitary
actors.[51]

NOTES

1. The rest include the Pan-African Parliament (PAP), the Peace and Security Council
(PSC), the Economic, Social and Cultural Council (ECOSOCC), the African Court of Justice
and Human Rights (ACJHR), and the Specialized Technical Committees (STPs). The STPs
include the Committee on Rural Economy and Agricultural Matters; the Committee on Mone-
tary and Financial Affairs; the Committee on Trade, Customs and Immigration Matters; the
Committee on Industry, Science and Technology, Energy, Natural Resources and the Environ-
ment; the Committee on Transport, Communications and Tourism; the Committee on Health,
Labour and Social Affairs; and the Committee on Education, Culture and Human Resources.
The financial institutions are the African Central Bank, the African Monetary Fund, and the
African Investment Bank.

2. The eight departments are: Peace and Security (Conflict Prevention, Management and
Resolution, and Combating Terrorism); Political Affairs (Human Rights, Democracy, Good
Governance, Electoral Institutions, Civil Society Organizations, Humanitarian Affairs, Refugees, Returnees, and Internally Displaced Persons); Infrastructure and Energy (Energy, Trans-
port, Communications, Infrastructure, and Tourism); Social Affairs (Health, Children, Drug
Control, Population, Migration, Labour and Employment, Sports and Culture); Human Re-
sources, Science and Technology (Education, Information Technology Communication, Youth,
Human Resources, Science and Technology); Trade and Industry (Trade, Industry, Customs,
and Immigration Matters); Rural Economy and Agriculture (Rural Economy, Agriculture and
Food Security, Livestock, Environment, Water and Natural Resources, and Desertification);
and Economic Affairs (Economic Integration, Monetary Affairs, Private Sector Development,
Investment, and Resource Mobilization).

3. For detailed function of the Commission, see the Statute of the Commission of the
African Union, http://www.au2002.gov.za/docs/summit_council/statutes.pdf .

4. For elaborate discussion of the AU as a purely intergovernmental organization, see Omar A. Touray, "The African Union: The First Ten Years 2002–2012," (Forthcoming).

5. Ibrahima Kane and Nobuntu Mbelle, *Towards a People-Driven African Union: Current Obstacles & New Opportunities* (Harare: AfriMAP, AFRODAD: Oxfam, 2007), 14.

6. African Union, Agenda 2063, http://agenda2063.au.int/en/about .

7. *Strategic Plan of the Commission of the African Union Volume 3: 2004–2007 Plan of Action*, May 2004, https://repositories.lib.utexas.edu/bitstream/handle/2152/4763/3851.pdf? sequence=1 .

8. The AUC was established in 2003 by the Constitutive Act. See Article 5 and 20 of the Constitutive Act of the AU for the legal authority of the Commission.

9. For detailed function of the Commission, see the *Statute of the Commission of the African Union* (Durban, South Africa: Assembly of the African Union, July 9–10, 2002). http://www.au2002.gov.za/docs/summit_council/statutes.pdf .

10. See Article 4 of *the Statute of the Commission of the African Union*.

11. Article 4, Sec. 2 of the Statutes of the Constitutive Act of the African Union.

12. Kioko interview. For more information about documents, see Ben Kioko, "The Right of Intervention Under the African Union's Constitutive Act," *International Review of the Red Cross* 85, no. 852 (2003): 807–26.

13. Only Kenya and South Africa sent comments. But as pointed out repeatedly during interactions with officials at both the AUC and African missions in Ethiopia, the comments came after many informal promptings from AUC officials. Ben Kioko, who is a Kenyan, in his usual diplomatic way admitted that he had to force the comments out of the Kenyan government.

14. For the assessment of the impact of the Peace and Security Council, see Paul D. Williams, "The Peace and Security Council of the African Union: Evaluating an Embryonic International Institution," *Journal of Modern African Studies* 47, no. 4 (December 2009): 603–26.

15. For a definition of the African international system, see I. William Zartman, "Africa as a Subordinate State System in International Relations," *International Organization* 21, no. 3 (Summer 1967): 545–64.

16. To behave properly in AU circles is to follow the line of the discourse at the meeting and be a yes person. The expectation is that the experts are there to bless these documents.

17. See Thomas Tieku, Omar Touray detailed discussion.

18. A quick review of the process for creating the postconflict policy that intergovernmental bodies have adopted will give a better sense of the centrality of the AUC in the drafting of these documents. A Brainstorming Retreat for members of the Peace and Security Council and the Permanent Representative Council, held on September 4 and 5, 2005, in Durban, South Africa; a Technical Experts Meeting of AU members, held on February 7 and 8, 2006, in Addis Ababa, Ethiopia; an AU and Civil Society Dialogue, held from April 5 to 7, 2006, in Abuja, Nigeria; a Validation Workshop for the AU Commission, held on May 31, 2006, in Addis Ababa; and, finally, a Governmental Experts Meeting held on June 8 and 9, 2006, in Addis Ababa.

19. For importance of the representation in IOs, see Andy Knight's "The Future of the United Nations Security Council: Questions of Legitimacy and Representation in Multilateral Governance," in *Enhancing Global Governance*, ed. Andrew Cooper, 19–37 (Tokyo: United Nations University Press, 2002); David P. Rapkin and Jonathan R. Strand, "Representation in International Organizations: The IMF," August 29, 2010, http://papers.ssrn.com/sol3/papers.cfm?abstract_id=1667934 .

20. S. Ostry and T. K. Tieku, *Trade Advocacy Groups and Multilateral Trade Policy-Making of African States* (Toronto: Munk Centre for International Studies, 2007).

21. African Union Charter Article 3(2n).

22. United Nations Organization, Lomé Declaration on the Unconstitutional Change of Government.

23. Thomas Legler and Thomas Tieku, "What Difference Can a Path Make? Regional Regimes for Democracy Promotion and Defense in the Americas and Africa," *Democratization* 18, no. 3 (2010): 465–91.

24. The lead consultant is now the director of the Department of Political Affairs.

25. Besides elections, the common means of acquiring power in Africa has been military coups, armed rebellions, and popular protests.

26. Issaka K. Souare, "The African Union as a Norm Entrepreneur on Military Coups D'état in Africa (1952–2012): An Empirical Assessment," *Journal of Modern African Studies* 52, no. 1 (March 2014): 69–94, doi: 10.1017/S0022278X13000785; Samuel M. Makinda, F. Wafula Okumu, and David Mickler, *The African Union: Addressing the Challenges of Peace, Security, and Governance*, 2nd Edition (New York: Routledge, 2015).

27. The African Union Non-Aggression and Common Defence Pact, Adopted by the Fourth Ordinary Session of the Assembly (Abuja, Nigeria, January 31, 2005), http://au.int/en/sites/default/files/AFRICAN_UNION_NON_AGGRESSION_AND_COMMON_DEFENCE_PACT.pdf.

28. CAADP, "The Comprehensive African Agriculture Development Program," http://caadp.net/.

29. *African Youth Charter, adopted by the Seventh Ordinary Session of the Assembly* (Banjul, The Gambia, July 2, 2009), http://www.au.int/en/sites/default/files/AFRICAN_YOUTH_CHARTER.pdf ; *African Union Convention for the Protection and Assistance of Internally Displaced Persons in Africa* (Kampala Convention) (Kampala, Uganda: October 23, 2009), http://au.int/en/sites/default/files/AFRICAN_UNION_CONVENTION_FOR_THE_PROTECTION_AND_ASSISTANCE_OF_INTERNALLY_DISPLACED_PERSONS_IN_AFRICA_(KAMPALA_CONVENTION).pdf.

30. See The African Youth Charter, http://www.au.int/en/sites/default/files/AFRICAN_YOUTH_CHARTER.pdf.

31. See Christine Ocran, the Protocol to the African Charter on Human and Peoples' Rights on the Rights of Women in Africa, adopted by the Second Ordinary Session of the Assembly of the Union, Maputo, July 11, 2003, http://www.au.int/en/sites/default/files/Protocol on the Rights of Women.pdf.

32. The EU data is available on the European Commission website, http://ec.europa.eu/justice/gender-equality/gender-decision-making/database/politics/eu-commission/index_en.htm ; for a more critical analysis and details about the AU gender mainstreaming work, see chapter 7.

33. Allison Simon, "Think Again: In Defence of the African Union," *Institute for Security Studies*, September 9, 2014, http://www.issafrica.org/iss-today/think-again-in-defence-of-the-african-union.

34. Alex Obote-Odora, "An AU Absurdity: African Leaders Promote Impunity for Themselves," *The Nordic Africa Institute*, October 18, 2013, http://naiforum.org/2013/10/an-au-absurdity/.

35. Max du Plessis, "Implications of the Decision to Give the African Court Jurisdiction over Mass Atrocity Crimes," *Institute for Security Studies* no. 235 (June 2012), http://www.issafrica.org/uploads/Paper235-AfricaCourt.pdf ; Amin George Forji, "Should Africa Quit the International Criminal Court?" *Nordic Africa Institute*, October 29, 2014, http://naiforum.org/2013/10/should-africa-quit-the-international-criminal-court/ ; Mehari Taddele Maru, "The Future of the ICC and Africa: The Good, the Bad, and the Ugly," *Aljazeera*, October 11, 2013, http://www.aljazeera.com/indepth/opinion/2013/10/future-icc-africa-good-bad-ugly-20131011143130881924.html.

36. See Article 2c, h, and g of the Statutes of the African Union Commission (2002).

37. See Article 2cc of the Statutes of African Union Commission (2002).

38. African Union, "The African Union (AU) Establishes a Team to Investigate Allegations of Sexual Exploitation and Abuse (SEA) by the AU Mission in Somalia (AMISOM)," http://www.peaceau.org/en/article/the-african-union-au-establishes-a-team-to-investigate-allegations-of-sexual-exploitation-and-abuse-sea-by-the-au-mission-in-somalia-amisom#sthash.3q4PGFRq.dpuf ; for human rights report, see Human Rights Watch, "The Power These Men Have Over Us: Sexual Exploitation and Abuse by African Union Forces in Somalia," *Human Rights Watch*, September 8, 2014.

39. "The African Union Releases the Key Findings and Recommendations of the Report of Investigations on Sexual Exploitation and Abuse in Somalia," *African Union Peace & Security*, April 21, 2015, http://peaceau.org/en/article/the-african-union-releases-the-key-findings-and-

recommendations-of-the-report-of-investigations-on-sexual-exploitation-and-abuse-in-somalia .

40. African Union, *Statutes of the Commission of the African Union, First Ordinary Session* (Durban, South Africa: Assembly of the African Union, July 9–10, 2002).

41. African Union Charter, Article 2(z).

42. African Union Charter, Article 2(z).

43. An informal institutional mechanism with no formal basis in the AU legal framework.

44. Maputo, July 4–8, 2003, Executive Council Third Ordinary Session.

45. Report of the third Ordinary Session of the Executive Council on the Proposed Structure, Human Resources Requirements and Condition of Service for the Staff of the Commission of the African Union and Their Financial Implications (Doc. EX/CL/39 (III), July 4–8, 2003, Maputo, Mozambique, http://webmail.africa-union.org/REFERENCE/EX CL 34 (III) _ E.PDF .

46. Touray

47. Several sources, including interview with the president of the AUC Staff Association, Salah Hammad, on June 18, 2014.

48. ACCORD usually cosponsors the AU High Level Retreat for Mediators and Special Envoys.

49. AU. 2012. Report of the Chairperson of the Commission on the Partnership between the African Union and the United Nations on Peace and Security. PSC/PR/2 (CCCVII). Addis Ababa, Ethiopia: African Union.

50. T. K. Tieku, "Explaining the Clash and Accommodation of Interests of Major Actors in the Creation of the African Union," *African Affairs* 103 (2004): 249–67.

51. Wayne Sandholtz and John Zysman, "1992: Recasting the European Bargain," *World Politics* 42, no. 1 (1989): 95–128; and Wayne Sandholtz and Alec Stone Sweet (eds.), *European Integration and Supranational Governance* (Oxford: Oxford University Press, 1998): 217–49.

Chapter Three

The African Union in Historical Perspective

INTRODUCTION

This chapter places the AU within the broader history of international cooperation in Africa, with a view to providing a comprehensive historical context for the overall analysis. It examines the intellectual discourses engaged in, as well as the institutions that were created, in each period. The argument of the chapter is that the best way to understand the AU is to see it as part of a search for an appropriate and effective political system to replace the colonial project. The first so-called grand debate on the issue, in the late 1950s and early 1960s, resulted in the establishment of the Westphalia state model as a master frame idea for the African continent. The OAU was created in 1963 to defend and protect it. Another grand debate in the 1990s led to the emergence of the regionalist project and the formation of the AU to defend this idea. The debate over the appropriate political system for Africa has historically been shaped by three paradigmatic orientations (worldviews); namely, statism, regionalism, and continentalism. Those who hold the statist worldview believe that the Westphalia state model is the most appropriate political framework for managing the affairs of postcolonial Africa. The regionalists favor the creation of the political community and identity based on the regions of Africa; that is, Central Africa, Eastern Africa, Western Africa, Southern Africa, and Northern Africa. The continentalists, however, consider the Westpahlian African state system as problematic, and even illegitimate, and call for the rebuilding of political organizations in Africa. For proponents of this thesis, a continental union government—in the form of a federation, a confederation, or something similar—that brings all African people together will be the most appropriate way to govern the affairs of postcolonial Africa.

The outcome of the discourse and fight between the three groups over the nature of the political system that is best for Africa accounts for the emergence of both the OAU and the formation of the AU.

The chapter's argument is organized into four sections. The first section provides a concise overview of Africa's international relations prior to 1940. The second section details African elites' struggle to establish a master frame idea as a basis for cooperation in Africa. I examine both the discourse and the process used by proponents of the three paradigms, concluding that the statist master frame emerged out of the debate.

The first part of the third section, therefore, shows some of the political measures African leaders adopted to consolidate the state system. The second part documents African leaders' efforts to develop economic tools to reinforce the state system. The last part of the third section demonstrates that the economic measures were unsuccessful. Many factors, including the conflicts between Chad against Libya, Morocco's protest over the admission of Western Sahara into the OAU, and the ideational influence of neoliberalism, hampered the development of the economic tools. Not only did those factors discourage African leaders from developing the economic instruments, they influenced African leaders to lose interest in interstate cooperation in the 1980s. The last section shows that African leaders, however, revived their interests in the continental initiative in the 1990s. It also sets the stage for the analysis in chapter 4.

THE EVOLUTION OF INTERNATIONAL COOPERATION IN AFRICA

Cross-border dealings between various societies in Africa (empires, kingdoms, and city-states) are not new; they predate the creation of the Westphalia state system in Africa. A rich body of literature exists indicating that African societies engaged in international relations as far back as AD 10.[1] Much of the salient forms of the engagements during that period occurred in the economic realm. Long-distance regional trade in gold and salt was the central feature of relations between the various societies that inhabited contemporary Western, Northern, Eastern, and Southern Africa regions.

The strong linkages that existed between African societies partly explain the heights of prosperity attained by political groups such as the Sudanic kingdoms (Ghana, Mali, and Songhai empires) and the Monomatapa kingdom. As Barnett notes:

> The impressive West African empires of Ghana, Mali, and Songhai gained strength from their central positions in the gold-salt trade between tropical West Africa and arid northern Africa. In southeastern Africa, the kingdoms of Zimbabwe rose due to their control of the regional gold trade, and the city-

states of the Swahili Coast flourished because they linked the African interior with the Indian Ocean and Arabian commerce.[2]

Notwithstanding the strong regional trade networks developed by the various precolonial African societies, there is no evidence that they created any supranational institutions to manage their international affairs.

This, however, changed in the colonial era. The European colonizers built and used international institutions to manage their colonies' trade, finance, monetary affairs, transport, and communications. The British established the West African Currency Board (WACB) and the Bank of British West Africa (BBWA) to administer monetary, financial, and general economic activities of the four British West African colonies and the two Protectorate territories.[3] Areas in contemporary East Africa that came under British authority were also managed primarily through supranational institutions.[4] The British created international institutions to manage external tariff, trade, customs, income tax, transport and communications services (railways, harbors, post, telecommunications, and airways), universities, research services, and the currency of modern Tanzania, Kenya, and Uganda.

Like the British, the French established supranational institutions to administer territories that came under their authority. Similarly to British East Africa, the French established quasi-federal structures to govern French West Africa and French Equatorial Africa.[5]

The subject of this chapter is relatively new. It developed as part of the 1950s to 1960s discourse on the kind of political community that should be created for the diverse peoples who inhabit the geographical territory of Africa. It was inspired by the Pan-African normative goal of seeking to create "the consciousness [of the world] of the right of the African peoples to cultural, political, and economic independence."[6] Though the central normative framework of the Pan-African movement was negative—because it was grounded on the logic of racial exclusivity—it was largely responsible for the emergence of the African consciousness and, by extension, of a vague notion of African identity. The attraction of this African identity invented by African elites, particularly political elites and intellectuals, provided the basis for lively debate about the most suitable political institution to be built for the African people after colonial rule.

THE MAJOR AFRICAN POLITICAL PARADIGMS

Africa's major political paradigms are of three kinds: continentalism, statism, and regionalism. Continentalism, which is influenced by the ideas of Pan-Africanism and, in particular, Marcus Garvey's "Back to Africa" movement, holds that the inhabitants of the African region should be organized within a continent-wide political framework. For those who hold this view, a continent-wide union with "a unified economic planning, a unified military and defence strategy, and a unified foreign policy and diplomacy" would be the more appropriate political system.[7] Continent-wide union in the form of federation, confederation, or something similar would be more appropriate, because it would provide the tools for African people to resist foreign domination and oppression and promote unity and economic independence, and it is also the most effective way to develop the African culture.[8]

With such premises, the school inevitably regards the African state system as illegitimate and problematic. They see it as illegitimate in part because they believe the people who inhabit Africa were allowed to make no contribution in the establishment of the boundaries that created the state system, and in part because they think the present system reversed the organic development of political organizations and institutions. They also see it as problematic because of the many challenges the arbitrary division of African societies into statehood created. African elites, who subscribe to the continent-wide political framework, therefore called for the rebuilding of the African political communities. They want a new form of political community with an African flavor to replace the state system that they inherited from European colonial rule.

The other worldview, however, considers the division of the geographic region of Africa into states as a useful organizing principle. Many of those who hold this view are openly critical of colonial rule, and they also, hypocritically, refer to the boundaries created by colonial authorities as fraudulent and artificial. Yet they feel the demarcations are worth preserving. For this paradigmatic group, therefore, the maintenance and protection of the state system in Africa ought to be the guiding principle of interstate cooperation. They think interstate cooperation in Africa should take the form of loose relationships of economic interdependency along the model of the European Union, and/or mere coordination of issues of common interests.

Regionalists are more interested in creating interdependence among individual African states on the basis of regional identity and regional institution building. For the regionalist, any institutional-building process should take as its starting point African regional economic communities. Rather than a continental union that will undermine regional identity, the regionalists want to see a set of strong regional economic communities such as the Economic Community of West African States (ECOWAS) and the Southern Africa Development Community (SADC). For the regionalists, IOs such as AU serve as fora for the regions to manage themselves and coordinate their international activities. In a sense, the statists and the regionalists share a common interest in limiting the role of the AU and setting strict limits on the involvement of Africrats in domestic affairs of African states. The dominance of the statists and regionalists in the intergovernmental AU in large part account for the slow process in the operationalization of key AU's supranational ideas such as the ASF and the poor performance of the AU at the national level. The regionalists are open to the participation by people who do not reside on the African continent in the activities of the AU, but only to a limited extent.

Like every paradigmatic group or worldview, there are some subtle differences within the statist school, regionalist, and the continental union group. Some of the proponents of the statist school are absolute statists, and they loathe attempts to cede any aspect of sovereignty to supranational authority, however insignificant. Liberia's William Tubman and Madagascar's Philibert Tsiranana led the absolute statist group during the first Pan-African debate in the 1960s. In the 1990s, the statist were led by Egypt's Hosni Mubarack and Guinea's Lansana Conté. Some of the regionalists are willing, though not without protest, to cede to supranational authority such parts of sovereignty as do not undermine the core prerogatives of their states. The latter group is usually willing to cede sovereign prerogatives in the economic realm to a supranational organization. Nigeria's Tafawa Balewa, Tanzania's Julius Nyerere, and Cote d'Ivoire's Felix Houphouët-Boigny were the leading advocates of the statist-interdependency group in the 1960s Pan-African debate. Nigeria's Olusegun Obasanjo, South Africa's Thabo Mbeki, and Algeria's Abdelaziz Bouteflika.

In the case of the continental union group, the subtle differences relate to the kind of organization that they want to replace the Westphalia state system. While some prefer a federal government structure, others are inclined toward a confederal system of political organization. During the 1960s, Ghana's Kwame Nkrumah was the leading advocate of the federal system while Uganda's Obote was a prominent proponent of the confederal system of government. In the 1990s, Libya's Muammar Gaddafi favored the federal system, and Mali's Alpha Oumar Konaré was a big fan of the conferation model.

THE 1950S AND 1960S GRAND DEBATE

The genesis of the major political debate can be traced to the first half of the twentieth century. The first visible sign that African leaders hold different worldviews on the kind of political system that ought to replace colonial rule appeared during the first meeting of the Heads of Independent African States, which took place between April 12 and 15, 1958.[9] Even though the conference was not specifically on the issue of international cooperation, the debate on Ghana's draft resolution that requested the Independent States establish a permanent international institution showed the elites' dissension on that subject.[10] Liberia and Egypt strongly opposed Ghana's resolution on the grounds that the idea was "too ambitious."[11]

Due in large measure to opposition by Liberia and Egypt, the resolution was not adopted. Instead, delegates agreed, among other things, to use their representations to the United Nations as informal institutional machinery for:

- the coordination of all matters of common concern to African states
- examining and making recommendations on concrete steps to implement decisions of the conference of independent African states
- making preparatory arrangements for future conferences of independent African states [12]

Egypt's and Liberia's position, and the subsequent resolution that the conference adopted on the subject of cooperation, were interesting. The delegates' decision on cooperation was interesting because it showed that most of them supported the partitioning of Africa into many states. They did not subscribe, obviously, to the continentalist's quest for a single state (homeland) for the inhabitants and descendants of the African region, although prior to the conference almost all the leaders spoke as if they believed in the Pan-African project. African leaders usually refer to the idea of a single homeland for the African people as the "United States of Africa." [13]

The differences in worldview became clearer when Ghana's Kwame Nkrumah began to push leaders of independent African states to establish the "United States of Africa." Nkrumah's attempts to create this were pursued through two major policy tracks—a non-government-led initiative and a state-sponsored strategy. The origin of the civil society initiative dates back to the mid-1940s. The most significant of these initiatives occurred in August 1946 when Nkrumah, through the West African National Secretariat (WANS), brought together in London representatives from dependent states in West Africa to brainstorm on the future of the subregion. Nkrumah succeeded in persuading the conference delegates to agree "to promote the concept of a West African federation as an indispensable level for the ultimate achievement of a *United States of Africa.*" [14] After this conference, however, no progress was made on the civil society front until Nkrumah convened a West African Nationalist Conference in Kumasi, Ghana, in December 1953 to, among other things, discuss the possibility of forming a Union of West African States. [15]

More meaningful progress was made when Nkrumah convened the first "All-African Peoples' Conference" (APC) in Accra from December 8 to 13, 1958. "[M]ore than 300 political and trade union leaders representing about 20 million Africans in 28 countries" attended. [16] Delegates resolved that the international boundaries separating African states are "artificial frontiers . . . [that] operate to the detriment of Africans and should therefore be abolished or adjusted." [17] Delegates argued that "the existence of the separate states in Africa is fraught with the dangers of exposure to imperialist intrigues and of the resurgence of colonialism," and should be done away with.[18] The APC, therefore, adopted as its "ultimate goal the creation of a commonwealth of free African states."[19]

To sow the seed of the commonwealth, delegates agreed to turn the APC into a permanent institution with a professionally staffed secretariat in Accra, Ghana. The APC, in a resolution, provided steps for creating the United States of Africa. As a first step, "independent states of Africa [will] amalgamate themselves into groups on the basis of geographical contiguity, economic interdependence, linguistic and cultural affinity." African "countries which do not appear to fall naturally into any . . . [of the above categories] should after their attainment of independence decide by democratic processes whether to adhere to existing groups or to evolve different groups." The resolution called on those who will form regional groupings to regard them as building blocks for the United States of Africa. As a result, they (i.e., the regional groupings) "should not be prejudicial . . . [to] a Pan-African Commonwealth by hardening as separate entities and . . . by impeding progress towards a continental Commonwealth." For the avoidance of doubt, the resolution provided the following three benchmarks for creating the regional institutions:

- Only independent states and countries governed by Africans should join together.
- The establishment of regional groupings should not be prejudicial to the ultimate objective of a Pan-African commonwealth.
- Adherence to any group should depend on the wishes of the people, ascertained by referendum on the basis of universal adult suffrage.

While the civil society track continued, Nkrumah also laid the foundation for the Ghanaian state to lead the efforts to encourage other African states to integrate. He established "a Department for African Affairs," and appointed a strong advisory team on Africa that was headed by George Padmore, a well-known writer on Pan-Africanism. Nkrumah also consulted with other African leaders with a view to finding the best way to establish the basis for the continental federal union. The APC resolution, therefore, gave him an unofficial mandate to push through the United States of Africa project. It came as no major surprise when Nkrumah and Guinea's president, Sekou Touré, announced on May 1, 1959, that the two countries had agreed to integrate in order to provide a nucleus for the United States of Africa project. In a public statesment, the two leaders contended, "Inspired by the example of the thirteen American colonies, the Accra declaration [i.e., APC] of the Accra conference . . . we have agreed to constitute our two states as a nucleus of a Union of West African States."[20]

The substance of the Union was outlined in a declaration in Conakry. While the leaders deferred to another date discussions about "the portion of sovereignty [that] shall be surrendered to the Union in the full interests of the African community," they agreed that "nationals of the states or federations which are members of the Union will have a Union citizenship."[21] Citizens of member states of the Union required no visa to travel from one state to another, and the Ghanaian resident representative in Guinea was asked to join the cabinet of the Guinea government, and vice versa. Since the Union was a nucleus of the continental Union government, the declaration created room for other independent African states to join.

The formation of the Ghana-Guinea Union, however, displeased the then "spokesman of national sovereignty," Liberia's president William Tubman.[22] His irritation manifested in the angry protest that the Liberian ambassador in Ghana lodged against Nkrumah's suggestion in a speech in India that "it would be in Liberia's interests to join the Ghana-Guinea Union."[23] The ambassador undiplomatically told Nkrumah that "his government had never attributed to Ghana's premier 'either the ability or the capability to determine better than the Liberian Government . . . its best interests.'" The response of Tubman himself to the formation of the Ghana-Guinea Union was interesting.

In response to the Ghana-Guinea Union, Tubman developed a counter plan, which called for the creation of the "Associated States of Africa." Unlike the proposal of the Ghana-Guinea Union, Tubman's plan called for an intergovernmental association of independent states based on a "convention of friendship" and commercial interests. Not only was the plan carefully designed to preserve the sovereignty of member states of the association, it also stressed that the institutions that would be developed to manage the friendship would promote the national sovereignty and identity of individual member states. Based on ideas articulated in Tubman's plan, it was not surprising that there "was a broad agreement . . . between Ghanaian civil servants and politicians that Liberia was the greatest obstacle" to the U.S. project, and a way had to be found "to get him (i.e., Tubman) to bend."[24] Tubman circulated the plan to the African group at the UN for consideration, consulted other like-minded African leaders on the issue, and then, on April 7, 1959, he invited Nkrumah and Touré to a meeting in Sanniquellie, Liberia.

Tubman convened the meeting, as Immanuel Wallernstein noted, to prevent Nkrumah from teaming up with other African leaders to erect "new structures with supranational powers."[25] Ironically, the Ghana delegation accepted the invitation because they thought the meeting would give them the opportunity to persuade Tubman to join the Ghana-Guinea Union. Because of Tubman's firm beliefs in statist ideas and Nkrumah's strong commitment to the U.S. project, many observers expected nothing from the meeting beyond ritualistic rhetoric. Notwithstanding Nkrumah and Tubman's differences, which prompted Sekou Touré to tell the two leaders that "African unity cannot wait on . . . [their] disagreements," the three leaders, "unexpectedly enough," reached a compromise.[26] They agreed to hold:

> a Special Conference in 1960 of all independent States of Africa as well as non-independent States which have fixed dates on which they will achieve independence to discuss and work out a Charter which will achieve their ultimate goal of unity between independent African states.[27]

A joint statement released by the leaders at the end of the meeting laid down "a Declaration of principles" to serve as "the basis for the discussions of the Special Conference."[28] Borrowing ideas from Nkrumah's United States of Africa project, the declaration suggested that the leaders would request that the Conference explore ways of developing a "community of independent African States" with the aim of promoting "Freedom, Unity, the African personality, independence as well as the interests of the African peoples." The declaration also suggested that the Community's institutions could include an Economic Council, a Cultural Council, and a Scientific and Research Council. It added a distinctive Tubman caveat, however, by suggesting that:

> [E]ach member of the Community accepts the principle that it shall not interfere in the internal affairs of any member [and] each member of the Community shall maintain its own national identity and constitutional structure.[29]

The compromised agreement was, however, short-lived. Ghanaian and Liberian officials had different understandings of the content of the Sanniquellie agreement. While the Ghana government felt it provided a basis for a political union, Liberian officials thought it recommended the formation of a loose intergovernmental organization. The misunderstandings became clearer when the foreign ministers of Liberia and Ghana introduced the Sanniquellie agreement at the conference held in Addis Ababa, Ethiopia, from June 14 to 24, 1960.[30] Each foreign minister presented the Sanniquellie agreement to reflect the view of his government.

Thus, while Liberia's foreign minister claimed that the Sanniquellie agreement called for the creation of a loose intergovernmental organization for continental Africa, his Ghanaian counterpart interpreted the same agreement as a political unification project. In the opinion of Ghana's foreign minister Ako Adjei, it was "clear from the declaration of principles that the Union of African States which the three leaders discussed and agreed upon [at the Sanniquellie meeting . . . [was] intended to be a political Union."[31] It was obvious from the contributions of other delegates that "Tubman's idea of the association of states . . . [was] more acceptable"[32] to the majority of countries.[33] Yet the Ghanaian, the Guinean, and, to some extent, the Tunisian delegations insisted that their interpretation of the Sanniquellie agreement was the accurate version, and that a committee of experts be set up to work out the details of the union.

The relentless defence put up by the continental union group created a congenial atmosphere for other statists besides Liberia to voice their opinions more frankly. The head of the Nigeria delegation, Yussuf Maitama Sule, was particularly candid in presenting the opposition of his country to the continental union idea. He emphatically told the meeting that "the idea of forming a Union of African States is premature . . . too radical—perhaps too ambitious—to be of lasting benefit."[34] The split between the alliance of Liberia and Nigeria, on one hand, and the Ghana and Guinea partnership on the other, led to the dissolution of the meeting without any concrete agreement. The disagreement was such that many observers thought another meeting of African states on the issue was unlikely in the near future. More important, it led to the formation of statist and the continental union schools of African politics.

THE FORMATION OF THE OAU

Through sustained diplomatic pressure and negotiation, the Ethiopian government succeeded in persuading representatives of both schools to attend a ten-day Ministerial Session in Addis Ababa in May to develop the agenda for the Conference of Heads of States.[35] To avoid prolonged discussions on the issue of interstate cooperation in Africa, the Ethiopian government decided to contract M. Truco, Chile's representative to the OAS, as a consultant to develop what the Ethiopian government called "a universal African Charter."[36] Truco's draft charter, which recommended the creation of a coordinating organization to constitute the framework for interstate cooperation in Africa, "drew heavily upon the seminal ideas of the Organization of American States (OAS)."[37]

The Ethiopian government's efforts to develop "a universal Charter" nearly came to an abrupt end when Ghana tabled another proposal during the Ministerial Session.[38] Ghana proposed to the leaders the creation of a continental union government with a single African army, a high command with powers to intervene in trouble spots, and centralized economic planning. In response to Ghana's proposal, the Nigeria delegation proposed that the Charter of the Organization of Inter-African and Malagasy Union be accepted as the basis for African unity.

That development led to heated debate over the type of institution that should govern the international relations of African people. One noticeable thing at the conference was that the discussion transcended previous arguments between the statists and continentalists. The debate was more nuanced, and the voices of the eclectic units within the two paradigmatic schools were much more pronounced. Delegations from the Francophone states and those from Kenya and Tanganyika (Tanzania) even felt that regional association was the best way to organize the international politics of Africa. As the prime minister of Tanganyika, Julius Nyerere, pointed out: "[m]any of us in East Africa believe that the best path . . . to unity is through regional association[s]."[39] In his view, "most East Africans" favor "regional integration" because it leads to "immediate strengthening of . . . economies [while] at the same time [it provides] . . . the benefits of unity."[40]

After a lengthy debate, the Ministerial Session decided to give governments of independent African states the chance to study the three proposals thoroughly, and to meet after each state had had the opportunity to examine them, with a view to developing the Universal Charter. The failure by the ministers to reach agreement on the Universal Charter led informed commentators to suggest that African leaders would at best discuss the issue of cooperation "in generalities and postpone indefinitely the creation of an organization."[41] Woronoff described the atmosphere prior to the Heads of State and Government Conference thusly: "As the Kings and Presidents, Princes and politicians arrived [in Addis Ababa for the summit] tension mounted . . . there was talk of failure in the air. All that was expected were pious resolutions and another meeting, and still another."[42]

Contrary to informed expectations, the leaders agreed to use the Ethiopian proposal to form the nucleus of the Universal African Charter. A special commission consisting of fifteen foreign ministers was appointed to tie up any loose ends of the Ethiopian plan and to develop a resolution based on that proposal for the heads of state and government to endorse as the basic legal framework of interstate cooperation in Africa.[43] The delegations that put forward proposals at the Ministerial Session were asked to submit their plans for the consideration of the policy organs of the new institution that would emerge from the Ethiopian proposal.

The draft charter, called "the Charter of the Organization of African and Malagasy States," that was submitted by the Ministerial Commission marked a huge victory for the STAG. The Charter, as Clapham rightly pointed out, contained the "purest statements [that defend and hold together the rings] . . . of elements of juridical sovereignty ever to be embodied in any international organization."[44] The international organization the Charter created was, primarily, a coordinating agency. It was carefully designed to provide governments of independent African states the tools to consolidate the African state system.

With the exception of two notable changes that were introduced into the draft Charter, the Heads of State and Government Conference approved everything the Ministerial Commission recommended. The leaders accepted a proposal by President Philibert Tsiranana of Malagasy (Madagascar) that the best way to ensure total "respect [for] the principle of sovereignty of different states would be for decisions [of policy organs of the new organization] to be taken unanimously."[45] African leaders' acceptance of President Tsiranana's proposal is indicative of their intention to use the new organization to promote statism in Africa. The leaders also accepted a proposal by President Kwame Nkrumah of Ghana to change the name of the organization from the Organization of African and Malagasy States to Organization of African Unity.[46]

Although the leaders agreed to form a continental institution to strengthen, rather than weaken, the Westphalia state system in Africa, they rhetorically communicated the impression to the outside world that they had committed themselves to developing the organization into a political union. The prime minister of Tanganyika, Julius Nyerere, for instance, gave that idea when he claimed in a speech immediately after the Conference that

> there will be some who will say that this charter does not go far enough or is not revolutionary enough. This may be so. But what is going far enough? No good mason would complain that his first brick did not go far enough. He knows that a first brick will go as far as it can go and will go no farther. He will go on laying brick after brick before the edifice is complete.[47]

The outside impression (obviously a wrong one) allowed procontinental union media in countries such as Ghana, Uganda, Guinea, and Mali to suggest that the outcome of the Addis Ababa summit represented a victory for the CUS.[48] This media representation of the outcome of the summit, and the absence of alternative interpretations in major newspapers—because it was "politically incorrect" within the political context of the times to do so—left that wrong impression intact.

STATISM AS A MASTER FRAME IDEA

The wrong impression notwithstanding, the formation of the OAU effectively made statism the master frame idea (i.e., hegemonic paradigm) for any cooperative arrangement among inhabitants of the geographic region of Africa. The OAU's legitimization of the statist project provided the basis for the leaders, who held the statist view, to become more frank in their opposition to the continental union project. For instance, when the Ghana Delegation, on behalf of Mali and Guinea, resubmitted the continental union government proposal to the first summit of the OAU held in Cairo, Egypt, in July 1964, the Nigerian Delegation made it clear that "Nigeria will not be associated with this (i.e., the continental union project) dream."[49] The submission of the Madagascar Delegation was even more intriguing. They contended:

We Malagasy people have just achieved our independence. Well, we are jealous of this independence. If we are replaced tomorrow by a world government or even by a continental government, the Malagasy people will refuse. . . . We fought for our independence . . . and nobody helped us. . . . And now that we have achieved independence—just a few years after we acceded to it, this independence for which we shed our blood—we are told that there will no more be a Malagasy government but a union government. This is difficult for the Malagasy people to grasp. . . . Therefore we will never subscribe to a union government.[50]

When President Nkrumah requested that a committee be set up to examine its feasibility, Tafawa Balewa replied immediately that it would be "a waste of time, a waste of effort to go into it."[51] The Assembly, however, decided to "refer the proposal (i.e., the union government proposal) to the Specialized Commissions of the Organization of African Unity so that they may study the elements of African Unity in their different aspects and report to the Council of Ministers."[52] This decision to refer the proposal to the not-yet-existing Specialized Commissions was a ploy to remove the continental union issue from the agenda of policy organs of the OAU.[53] The overthrow by the military of the governments of Nkrumah in February 1966 and of Modibo Keïta two years later effectively killed the continental union movement as a competing paradigm in the international politics of Africa.

Since the majority of African leaders' main objective for agreeing to the OAU regime was to consolidate the Westphalia state system, only institutions, rules, norms, and administrative mechanisms that strengthened sovereign prerogatives and the territorial integrity of Africa states were developed and/or allowed to operate properly. Institutions such as the Commission for Mediation, Arbitration and Conciliation, which could have chipped away some sovereign prerogatives of African states, remained only on paper.

Many institutional restrictions were imposed on the OAU Secretariat to make it dependent on member states and to prevent it from becoming a supranational entity. The leaders established a Permanent Representative Committee (PRC), composed of African ambassadors accredited to Ethiopia, to supervise scrupulously the day-to-day administration of the OAU General Secretariat (henceforth, Secretariat). The head of the Secretariat, the Administrative Secretary General (ASG), was institutionally prevented from acquiring powers beyond the role of an administrator.

The ASG was supposed to account to the Council of Ministers (henceforth, Council) and the PRC activities of the Secretariat in detail at least two times in a year. For fear that the Secretariat would develop into a supranational entity, the political leaders were not keen on developing the administrative capacity of the organization.[54] It was also not uncommon to find political appointees recruited to manage issue areas that the governments deemed sensitive.

Within the broader framework of trying to consolidate the state system, emphasis was placed on the development of rules and norms, such as the territorial integrity norm and the noninterference of internal affairs norm. The first major decision the Assembly made at its second session in Cairo in 1964 was to legitimize the borders inherited from colonial rule. Along the same lines, the first session of the Council of Ministers developed the pan-African solidarity norm to strengthen African states' sovereignty, particularly in their relations with the outside world.

The desire by African leaders to use the OAU to develop and consolidate the state system in Africa paved the way for decolonization, as one OAU Secretary-General put it, "to monopolize . . . attention and activities" of the continental organization.[55] Thus, by the time the political leaders were celebrating the tenth anniversary, the OAU had become nothing but an institution for the promotion of statehood and decolonization.

Having used the necessary political and institutional tools to entrench the states system in the first decade of the OAU's existence, the political leaders started exploring possible economic and social instruments that could be used to reinforce the sovereignty of their states. As an internal OAU document admitted, African leaders gave continental economic and social initiatives serious thought because of a "general awareness [within the OAU political leadership that] economic independence is a way of guaranteeing political sovereignty."[56] It was within this context that the Assembly, in August 1970, adopted a memorandum in which they recognized that the OAU had a responsibility and a role in the economic and social fields.[57]

In addition to the memorandum, the Assembly adopted a list of priority areas in the social and economic fields that they wanted the OAU to focus on. The list included promotion of regional economic integration, cultural exchanges among African states, and the preservation of African cultural heritage and education. The Assembly also requested the OAU Secretariat, the African Development Bank (ADB), and the Secretariat of the United Nations Economic Commission for Africa (ECA) to establish an interinstitutional agency and a Special Fund to support the socioeconomic agenda.[58]

For a number of reasons, including the ideational influence of structuralism in the global development discourse in the 1970s, which made regional initiatives attractive to African policymakers, regional economic integration dominated the socioeconomic agenda of the OAU.[59] Regional integration joined decolonization and protection of African state sovereignty as core issues areas of the OAU in the 1970s. The former head of the OAU Economic Cooperation and Development department described the 1970s as "the golden era of integration."[60]

A number of policy documents were developed to push the integration agenda forward. The most important of these documents was the "Cooperation, Development and Independence," which the Secretariat developed in early 1973. This document, which articulated the idea of the African Economic Community for the first time, was adopted by the Council as a Declaration in May 1973.[61] Through it the Secretariat proposed that African leaders develop the regional economic communities into the AEC. To this end, the Secretariat urged African governments to divide the African continent into five economic subregions, and to encourage each subregion to develop one international organization into an exclusive economic community. The plan was to merge the five subregional economic communities to generate the African Economic Community (AEC) within twenty-five years. The Council of Ministers agreed in principle to establish the AEC at their meeting in December 1976. They also requested that the Secretariat develop a plan, with timelines, for creating the community within ten to twenty-five years. OAU ministers of Economic Planning and Finance endorsed it at a summit in Kinshasa (Congo) in February 1977.

The desire by a majority of African leaders to establish the AEC influenced them in part to select Togolese economist Edem Kodjo as the Administrative Secretary General. Kodjo, as many interviewers indicated, was a strong supporter of the continental integration initiatives. He prioritized and speeded up the move to establish the AEC, and also broadened its scope by placing it within a more elaborate development strategy called the Monrovia Strategy for the Economic Development of Africa, which the Assembly adopted in July 1979. The Assembly also agreed to his timelines and program of action to pursue the integration agenda.

In order to place the Secretariat in a better position and on a sound legal basis to implement the AEC, Edem Kodjo persuaded the political leaders to make two significant decisions. First, the Assembly agreed to "set up a Fourteen-member Committee to review the Charter of the Organization of African Unity" at its Sixteenth Ordinary Session held in Monrovia in 1979.[62] Second, it agreed to convene an Extraordinary Summit in Lagos in 1980 to finalize and develop a timetable for the establishment of the AEC.

In addition, Kodjo felt the Secretariat required "fresh orientation" and new structures to implement the AEC.[63] As a consequence, he proposed a new institutional structure that was approved by OAU political leaders in 1979. It increased the institutional departments of the Secretariat and, also, changed the name of the Administrative Secretary-General to simply Secretary-General. The number of departments was increased from four to five.[64] A department called Economic Cooperation and Development (EDECO) was established to manage the integration process.[65] The new structure created a cabinet to coordinate the activities of the office of the Secretary-General, which had direct control of Protocol, Information, Security, Legal Affairs, Inspectorate, Budget Control, and Afro-Arab Co-operation. Thus, by the time the Extraordinary Summit in Lagos in 1980 was convened, Kodjo had placed the Secretariat in a good position to implement the AEC.

Meanwhile, the ECA—partly in response to the integration drive, and partly to African leaders' request that it should assist the OAU Secretariat in the operationalization of the idea of the Economic Community—developed a more elaborate regional economic integration plan. The ECA plan and the AEC proposal were merged and adopted as the "Lagos Plan of Action" (LPA) at the Extraordinary Summit.[66]

The drive to establish the AEC in part led to the creation of many subregional integration institutions. The subregional organizations that emerged at the time included the Southern African Development Coordination Conference (SADCC), the Community for Eastern and Southern African States (COMESA), and the Economic Community for Central African States (EC-CAS).[67] In fact, between early 1970 and the early 1980s, over twenty multisectoral integration institutions and over 120 single-issue organizations were formed.[68]

The momentum to establish the African Economic Community, however, came to a sudden end after the adoption of the LPA and the Final Act. Border disputes between some African states, petty squabbles among African governments, ideological differences, and, more important, the influence of neoliberal ideas combined to undermine the entire integration project.

A few months after the adoption of the Final Act, the OAU found itself embroiled in two major disputes: Morocco's claim to the territory of Western Sahara, and the one between Chad and Libya. They sidelined the implementation of the LPA and created so much division that in 1982, the OAU could not get the required delegations to form a quorum for the Summit of Heads of State and Governments. Disagreements over the admission of Western Sahara as a member of the OAU paralyzed the activities of the organization for almost two years.[69]

It became difficult for the OAU to develop the working relationship among African governments necessary for the implementation of the LPA. The poor relationship that prevailed between African states after 1980 was particularly evident at sittings of working committees. Strong disagreement characterized meetings of the Steering Committee, which was set up to draft a framework with timelines for the implementation of the LPA. The Committee produced virtually nothing. Likewise, the Charter Review Committee could not agree on any substantive amendments at its meetings in April 1980, April 1981, and May 1982 before the committee was adjourned indefinitely. Even the Ministerial Drafting Committee was not formed, as none of the Ministers of Foreign Affairs were prepared to discuss regional integration and the AEC at that moment.

None of these factors had more of an enduring impact on the integration efforts than the influence of neoliberal ideas. It was at the ideational level that the LPA project and, indeed, the OAU suffered the greatest damage. As the OAU Secretariat was trying to resolve disputes among African governments in order to implement the LPA, the World Bank released a major economic development report on sub-Saharan Africa. Formally titled "Accelerated Development in Sub-Saharan Africa: An Agenda for Action" but widely known as the Berg Report, it provided an alternative development paradigm for Africa. It challenged many of the ideas that the LPA advocated. In contrast to the LPA's focus on regionalism, the Berg Report emphasized domestic policy reform and internationalization of Africa's economies as the path to sustained economic growth. Thus, while the LPA advocated regionalism and multilateralism at the continental level, the Berg Report called for nationalism and domestic actions.

The effects of the Berg Report on continental development initiatives and, in particular, on the LPA, were enormous. It undermined African leaders' commitment to the LPA project and interstate cooperation in three major ways. It exposed the weaknesses of many of the economic ideas advanced by the LPA. It also undermined the credibility of the epistemic community behind the continental development project. The ideational marketing strengths of the World Bank, together with its willingness to give financial incentives to countries that were prepared to implement its prescriptions, influenced a number of African states to abandon the LPA in favor of the Berg Report's reform package. Drought, famine, and an extraordinary economic crisis in 1983 to 1984 increased the urgency with which African states sought the help of the Bank. Major driving forces of the LPA, such as Nigeria, Ghana, and Uganda, agreed to implement reform packages.

The decision by many governments in Africa to seek the Bank's help turned African multilateralism and "African solutions to African problems" into hollow slogans. Aside from the liberation committee, which was active on the issue of apartheid, and the Conference Committee, which managed to organize the annual summits, the OAU substantively did not exist in the 1980s.

The shift of focus from regional development cooperation to domestic policy actions influenced some OAU member states to reassess the importance they attached to the continental organization. Many of the governments became extremely reluctant to pay their contribution to the organization's regular budget. On average, less than 20 percent of member states contributed to the regular budget of the OAU within a fiscal year between 1980 and 1989.[70] In sharp contrast was the May 1963 to May 1980 period, when over 50 percent of member states made contributions to the regular budget of the OAU within a fiscal year.[71] Because African states were enthusiastic about the OAU prior to 1980, only a few member states did not pay their dues in full. Less than $5.7 million was recorded as arrears for the period between May 1963 and May 1980.[72] The arrears that stood at $5.7 million in 1980 rose to around $36 million in 1986; and, by 1990, over $50 million of the dues were in arrears.[73]

African governments' reluctance to pay their contributions to the regular budget of the OAU had nothing to do with inability. As the OAU Secretary-General, Dr. Peter Onu, observed at the time:

> Member-states which have the most serious economic problems are among those which make the efforts to meet their obligations. The reason for non-payment of contribution by majority of member-states cannot, therefore, be explained away in terms of economic difficulties.[74] The interesting thing is that the countries that failed to make contributions to the regular budget of the OAU showed no "reluctance in the payment of contribution to other International Organizations," and many of them paid their dues in full to the United Nations during the same period.[75]

The low level of contribution to the regular budget of the OAU is indicative of African leaders' lack of appreciation of the work of the OAU in the 1980s. Some African leaders, such as Uganda's Yoweri Museveni, started to openly question the relevance of the OAU.[76] Others, such as Kenya's Daniel arap Moi, went a step further by threatening not to honor Kenya's financial obligation to the OAU.[77] The ideational inroad that the World Bank made in policy circles in Africa was such that as of the end of the 1980s, the OAU was able to do nothing more than issue long and sometimes meaningless resolutions and declarations on Africa's development.

The OAU reasserted itself, however, as the primary framework for interstate cooperation in Africa in the first half of the 1990s. The integration project was put back on track with the adoption of the Treaty of the African Economic Community (AEC) at the Twenty-Seventh Ordinary Session of the OAU held in Abuja, Nigeria, in 1991.[78] As in the 1980s, the adoption of the AEC treaty led to the revival of subregional economic initiatives across Africa. New initiatives were made to revive defunct integration schemes, such as the East African Community (EAC)[79] and the Arab Maghreb Union (AMU).[80] Efforts were also made to establish new integration institutions, such as the West African Economic and Monetary Union (WAEMU),[81] the Southern Africa Development Community (SADC),[82] the Common Market for Eastern and Southern Africa (COMESA),[83] and the Central African Economic and Monetary Community (CEMAC).[84]

In addition, the OAU assumed a prominent role in the management and resolution of intrastate conflicts by developing a framework for African leaders to deal with them. Many of the conflicts in which African leaders had for years prevented the OAU from intervening were put on the agenda. So were new and emerging ones.

The OAU also assumed a leadership role in a number of important development issues, such as African states' campaign for debt relief. African leaders mandated the OAU to provide the institutional framework for African states to negotiate with creditors for favorable terms of payment for the debt

overhang. Further, the OAU was mandated to lead Africa's effort to negotiate with the European Union for a successor agreement to the Lomé Convention, and was also requested to help the African group participate effectively in the development of multilateral trade rules.

Given that the OAU was, to all intents and purposes, moribund in the
1980s, why did it suddenly emerge in the 1990s to play a leadership role in
continental African politics? The answer to the questions lay in the entrepreneurialship of Africrats (international civil servants at the OAU Secretariat,
now African Union Commission).[85] Africrats took advantage of their strategic position and internal knowledge to consciously engineer African leaders'
interests in a new continental security and regional integration agenda. They
persuaded African leaders to reform the OAU to provide the institutional
framework for the promotion of continental peace and regional integration.
African leaders' attempts to reform the institutional structure of the OAU in
order to pursue the new security agenda led to the creation of the AU.
Africrats did not, however, operate in a vacuum. A number of structural
factors, such as the end of the Cold War and the end of apartheid, provided
policy windows for Africrats to set the new security, integration, and reforms
agenda.

The above observations are surprising given the centralization of decision
making in the hands of political leaders in many African states and the weak
institutional structure of the OAU Secretariat. One would have expected
political leaders and appointees to provide entrepreneurial and intellectual
leadership in setting the agenda for any new initiative. Detailed research,
however, revealed that it was OAU bureaucrats who were at the forefront,
and actually pushed the leaders to adopt the changes that led to the formation
of the AU. In addition, given African leaders' protective stand on state sovereignty, one would have expected them to be highly suspicious of the actions
of Africrats. Africrats' ability to sell the ambitious development projects to
the leaders is puzzling.

For three reasons the observations are significant for the study of politics,
international cooperation, and African politics. First, they show that the general view in African studies literature, which suggests that political leaders
drive regional integrationleaders, is overstretched. It appears that bureaucrats
play a much more vital role in regional integration and interstate cooperation
than has been acknowledged. Second, the observations contribute to the
growing literature on supranational leadership in international cooperation
and regional integration. The chapter shows that the OAU Secretariat was not
a unitary actor with a single institutional preference. There were different
people and departments that promoted different objectives and interests. The
recognition of the internal incoherence of the Secretariat is important because
it sets the findings in the chapter apart from the institutional scholarship that
treats supranational institutions as unitary actors.[86] Third, the observations

contradict the central insight of liberal intergovernmental (LI) integration theory, which predicts that state officials determine the creation and growth of regional institutions. In particular, the findings are at odds with a leading IR scholar's prediction that LI provides the most compelling explanation for interstate "arrangements among African leaders today."[87]

AFRICRATS AND AGENDA SETTING FOR THE FORMATION OF AU

Senior OAU staff members in the period between 1980 and 1994 in the political department, in the EDECO department, and in the legal department, along with Salim Ahmed Salim and his cabinet officials, played the critical role in the revival of African leaders' interest in the latest continental development initiatives. They set the agenda for African governments to promote continental economic integration, to use the continental institutional framework to maintain peace and resolve interstates conflict in Africa and, also, to embark on institutional reforms (i.e., reforming the OAU and promoting popular participation in governance and development). Except for Salim, who played the frontline and high-profile role in the process of setting the agenda and reviving continental development initiatives, all the Africrats worked mainly behind close doors.

Senior Africrats at the political and legal departments played the more dominant role in setting the agenda for the institutional reforms and maintenance of peace and conflict resolutions in Africa. The preference of Africrats in those departments for institutional reforms and conflict management goes back to the 1980s. A former director of the political department explains:

> Many of us here have been wishing for a mechanism for conflict management and popular participation in governance since the early 1980s. We engaged consultants to give professional advice on these issues. We prepared a draft Charter on popular participation in development as far back as 1989. The position of some governments on state sovereignty made it impossible to even have a frank discussion about the issues at the political level. Our leaders felt we will use the mechanism to disturb state sovereignty. None of the Secretaries-General before Salim wanted to spend their political capital to ask the leaders to discuss them. Because they were taboo subjects we also had to keep our views and programs to ourselves. [88]

The appointment of Salim as the SG and his desire to give new policy direction to the OAU provided the opportunity for Africrats in the two departments to ask Salim to add institutional reforms and conflict management in Africa to his agenda.

Like their counterparts at the legal and political departments, Africrats at the EDECO department engineered the revival of the integration project and the AEC. The role played by Africrats at the EDECO department in the revival of the integration project was more interesting. They (i.e., Africrats in EDECO department) kept the LPA/AEC process alive after African governments abandoned them in the 1980s. They also had the difficult task of persuading the skeptical Salim to add the integration project to his priority agenda.[89] Through a series of conferences, workshops, and seminars, the leadership of EDECO kept the AEC project in the public domain throughout the difficult period of the 1980s.[90] The department also reminded African leaders, through reports of the SG to the Council of Ministers, about their obligations under the LPA. The department ensured that each report of the SG to Council Sessions contained some information and a reminder of the LPA/AEC project. In addition, through informal networks, the leadership of EDECO developed strategic partnerships with important African personalities, such as Tanzania's Julius Nyerere, and notable local African economists, including the former OAU Secretary-General Edem Kodjo. The idea was to use the influence of these personalities to encourage African leaders to implement the LPA project and to establish the AEC.[91]

The leadership also contracted consultants to examine different aspects of the AEC, though they knew that few African leaders were genuinely interested in the project at the time.[92] The decision by the EDECO department to contract the consultants was strategic, as the chief of Inter-Africa Cooperation at the time, Charles Awitor, explained:

> We went ahead to ask the consultants to work on the AEC project even though we knew that the political climate wasn't right for the implementation of the AEC. We took that decision to ensure that we sustain interest in the AEC project. With a report we could go to OAU leadership and the PRC for discussions. We also knew that the consultants' reports will give us the opportunity to hold more workshops and to attract media and policy-makers' attention.[93]

Two professional staff members at the EDECO department, Faustin Kinuma (head of Cooperation Division) and Charles Awitor (chief of Inter-Africa Cooperation), were instrumental in pushing through the AEC agenda. In the view of a former head of the EDECO department:

> The integration initiative was the pet project of Charles and Faustin. They made it their personal mission. . . . It was as if their very existence in the world depended on it. They were always on the phone talking to the missions about the project. A conversation with these two people in this house will never end unless you talk about the African Economic Community. Their commitment was such that at some point some people accused them of using the African Economic Community to hijack the OAU.[94]

The two EDECO staff members took advantage of the solidarity that had developed among African states, following Morocco's withdrawal from the OAU in protest against the admission of Western Sahara, to influence the states to set up the Ministerial Drafting Committee to develop the AEC Treaty. Recall that the Assembly at its 1980 extraordinary session directed the Council of Foreign Ministers to establish a Ministerial Drafting Committee to develop a treaty for the AEC. The two Africrats initially tried to persuade African Ambassadors in Addis Ababa and members of the PRC to recommend to the ministers implementation of the Assembly's directives. When success was not forthcoming, they decided to put pressure on Heads of Political Departments at the African embassies in Ethiopia to agree to turn the Steering Committee to AEC Drafting Committee. Charles Awitor provides a detailed explanation:

> We gambled a little and succeeded. You know as part of the implementation of the LPA, a Ministerial Drafting Committee was to be set up to draft the AEC Treaty. We tried our best to get the missions to do that but we got nowhere. So when we heard that a Special Summit was going to be convened to examine the 1980 economic crisis, Faustin and I decided to contact the missions to urge them to turn the Steering Committee which was set up in 1980 to implement the LPA plan into AEC Drafting Committee. It was a desperate move which could have backfired. We're afraid some Delegations will tell us to take our utopian AEC project away and let the Summit concentrate on finding ways to find food for the desperate people who have been hit hard by the famine. So we had to find a good way to present the idea. We presented it as part of the solutions to the economic crisis. We argued that the AEC Treaty could be drafted in such a way that it will enhance productive capacity of African states. We wanted them to know that the goal of the AEC project is not just trade promotion, but the AEC project can also be used to boost productive capacity of African states. I think we got the support because of this. This is why the Steering Committee became the AEC Drafting Team. [95]

The two professional staff members also developed and maintained close working relationships with the Committee during the drafting of the AEC treaty. They provided the Committee with the necessary background reports and papers, summaries of all the major workshops, and a draft text of the AEC treaty.

The 106-Article draft treaty that the Committee agreed upon provided a well-thought-out legal framework for pursuing an ambitious integration agenda.[96] The AEC treaty provided a thirty-four-year time frame and six-stage processes to develop subregional economic communities into the AEC.[97] The Draft Treaty was comprehensive, and African governments were required to delegate substantial portions of sovereign prerogatives in the economic realm to supranational institutions by the time that the sixth stage is reached. The challenge for the EDECO department was getting OAU leadership to persuade reluctant and uninterested African states to approve this ambitious legal instrument. The election of Salim Ahmed Salim provided Africrats with the opportunity to convince Salim to sell the AEC project and the integration ideas to African governments.

THE "SALIM FACTOR"

Salim Ahmed Salim's replacement of Ide Oumarou as OAU SG in early 1989 was critical to the revival of the continental development initiative.[98] Salim not only turned out to be the most reformist-minded SG in the history of the OAU, his entrepreneurial leadership drove the process that led to the creation of the AU. He was also responsible for turning the attention of African governments from domestic matters to the continental level and, indeed, for the recent interests of African governments in continental development initiatives. Salim unveiled his reformist intentions during his acceptance speech. He outlined three priority areas: economic development, the environment, and human rights.[99]

After extensive consultations with various OAU departments, he revised his priority areas to include policy preferences of key OAU departments. The new but closely related priority areas he generated from the Inter-Departmental Report were administrative reforms, institutional development, and policy reforms.[100] Salim wanted to build the capacity of the OAU administrative apparatus to ensure efficiency and to "bring the levels of remuneration and staff performance to the highest standards possible."[101] The overall purpose of Salim's policy reforms initiative was to change the OAU from a general-purpose organization to a specialized institution. The policy document argued that the OAU:

> [W]as henceforth expected to focus its energies . . . on economic integration and the establishment of the African Economic Community . . . to promote popular participation . . . in the process of governance and development and to deepen democratization of African societies and . . . institutions; to work towards the peaceful and speedy resolution of all the conflicts raging on [the African] continent.[102]

Selling the reform ideas to disillusioned African governments, whose attention was focused on implementing the World Bank's policy prescriptions, was never without challenges. It required good framing, excellent articulation of the policy, and good marketing of the ideas. The ideas had to be presented so as to appear that they had originated with a neutral actor with no other interests than protecting and serving African states. They had to be presented at the appropriate time, at the right political moment, and in the right environmental context.

The sudden end of the Cold War provided Salim with an excellent policy window to promote his ideas and push through the reform agenda. His first move was to go to the Council of Ministers to draw the attention of Africa's political leaders to what he called "important changes now taking place in the world," and to ask for "guidelines" on ways to prepare Africa's response to the changes.[103] The Secretary-General's actual reasons for going to the Council were, first, to use the end of the Cold War to set the tone for selling the reform ideas; and second, to request political support for using OAU resources to prepare a paper that examined the implications of the end of the Cold War and the policy options that African states could collectively adopt to deal with the situation.[104]

Having secured the political support, Salim set up "an inter-departmental Task Force within the Secretariat" to explore ways to frame the policy reforms within the post–Cold War context.[105] Using the document prepared by the Task Force and the information he got from "an extended tour of Europe" in the early part of June 1990, Salim managed to persuade OAU political leaders to adopt a declaration on "Fundamental Changes Taking Place in the World and Africa's Response" at the Twenty-Sixth Ordinary Session of the Assembly in June 1990.[106]

The document recognized that the end of the Cold War had fundamentally changed the geopolitics of the world, and that African governments needed to adopt specific measures to adapt to the new world order. The report argued that African states would henceforth have to do things on their own; there would be no geostrategic basis for outside powers to help them. It therefore called on the leaders to revive indigenous development initiatives such as the LPA and the AEC. It also urged African leaders to develop a framework for preventing, managing, and resolving conflicts, since there would be no rationale for the international community to keep peace in Africa in the post–Cold War era. The SG got the attention of the leaders because of the uncertainty of African governments and their incomplete information about the new order that was replacing the Cold War era. The leaders were thus cognitively predisposed to accept the argument, ideas, and new initiatives the SG was promoting. Unsurprisingly, the report therefore urged African governments to revive the idea of "African solutions to African problems." It was adopted as a Declaration of the Twenty-Sixth Ordinary Session of the Assembly.

PHASE ONE OF REFORMS

Encouraged by the Declaration, the SG used his biannual Report to Council Sessions in July 1990 to outline the specific measures that African governments can adopt to cope with the new world order.[107] He emphasized the need to revive continental development initiatives such as the LPA and the AEC. Also, the SG urged African governments to provide a continental institutional framework to prevent, manage, and resolve internal conflicts. It was his view that since the end of the Cold War would increase cooperation and integration elsewhere in the world, African governments might have to strengthen their interstates cooperation and integration to avoid total marginalization.

The Declaration opened the space for Salim to submit to the Assembly at the Twenty-Seventh Ordinary Session, held in Abuja, Nigeria, in 1991, the treaty of the AEC and a framework to enable the OAU to prevent, manage, and resolve conflicts in Africa. [108] The Summit adopted the AEC Treaty. The SG was, however, asked to hold more consultations with member states on the proposal to establish conflict-resolution mechanisms within the OAU. Since the OAU would need reform to take on the new responsibilities, Salim submitted the first phase of the institutional reforms to the Council of Ministers in February 1992 and to the Assembly in June 1992. [109] The Assembly also adopted in principle the security framework called the Mechanism for Conflict Prevention, Management and Resolution (MCPMR) to help the OAU deal with conflicts in Africa at the Twenty-Eighth Ordinary Session held in Dakar, Senegal, in 1992. [110] The MCPMR's specific tasks were: to anticipate and prevent situations of potential conflict developing into full-blown wars; to undertake peacemaking and peacebuilding efforts if full-blown conflicts should arise; and to carry out peacemaking and peacebuilding activities in postconflict situations. [111]

The adoption of the AEC treaty led in part to the revival of the regional economic communities (RECs). Efforts were made to revive defunct integration schemes, such as the EAC and the AMU. Efforts were also made to establish new integration institutions, such as the WAEMU, the SADC, the COMESA, and the CEMAC. Treaties of existing subregional organizations, such as ECOWAS, were revised to reflect the new development. In addition, the SG opened up discussions with the subregional organizations to develop a protocol to govern the REC and the OAU. [112]

African leaders' adoption of the MCPMR and the AEC treaty should have moved the OAU to the center stage of Africa's development initiatives. Progress on the reform initiative was slow, however. It took an unusually long time for the MCPMR and the AEC treaty to come into force. While it took three years for the AEC treaty to receive the required instrument of ratification, it took two years for the mechanism to come into operation.

The consultation process for the operationalization of the MCPMR took two years because many governments were not genuinely committed. Some member states insisted that the principle enshrined in the OAU charter of noninterference in their internal affairs gave them the right to prevent the OAU from putting their conflicts on the agenda of the mechanism. Others wanted to confine its work to peace missions rather than allow it to extend to peacekeeping or a more intrusive conflict management. Others were also unprepared to support the idea of the MCPMR because they felt that effective OAU peacemaking and peacekeeping initiatives would encourage the UN to scale down its conflict-management activities on the African continent.[113] As Margaret Vogt indicated:

> [T]he issue of peacekeeping on which the OAU Mechanism was predicated was controversial. It was widely felt within the OAU political leadership that peace and security were the preserve of the United Nations, which is mandated to keep peace globally and which possesses more resources than the OAU.[114]

The same lack of genuine commitment also explains why it took three years for the AEC treaty to receive the required instrument of ratification. While some of the governments were unprepared to abandon the World Bank's prescribed domestic policy reforms in favor of continental development initiatives, others wanted to bide their time until they noticed real progress on the latest attempt to revive continental development initiatives before committing their states to the project. Thus, although many leaders in Africa were beginning to open up cognitively to the new initiatives, they needed real progress and pressure to convince them to get on board.

The coming into operation of the MCPMR in June 1993 and of the AEC treaty in May 1994 were major victories for Salim and his reformist group. They (i.e., the MCPMR and the AEC) entered into force at a good time. It was a period in which a number of events had combined to make continental development initiatives and the OAU relevant to African governments. Three of these events are worth emphasizing.

First, as of 1994 cracks had begun to appear in the neoliberal ideational influence in policy circles in Africa. Critical works and reports that questioned the ideas and the appropriateness of the World Bank's policy prescriptions for African economic challenges were making inroads. The voices of commentators who frequently highlighted the debt overhang and the social impact of the reforms were not only getting louder, the number of works and commentary critical of reforms were also increasing. These critical voices, particularly from indigenous African intellectuals, created doubts in policy circles and encouraged African governments to seek an alternative model to address the social and debt problems of their states. The obvious point of call was the OAU.

Second, the critical reviews of the reform project appeared at the time that African leaders needed the OAU to coordinate their responses to a number of international issues. African leaders needed the coordinating mechanism of the OAU to negotiate with creditors for favorable terms of payment for the

$300 million debt overhang and to develop a common African position for the World Summit on Human Development in March 1995.

In addition, African states that ceded to the WTO regime in 1994 needed the OAU to help them prepare and coordinate the positions of their governments for the first WTO Ministerial Trade Rounds in December 1996.[115] As of 1994, African trade ministers had started to coordinate the positions of their states to the Rounds. In October 1994 they met in Tunis under the aegis of the OAU: to develop a common position for the Rounds and to appeal to the international community to help them participate actively in the trading regime. Also, African states that had a special relationship with the EU under the institutional framework of African Caribbean and Pacific States (the ACP) needed the OAU to provide them with the platform to negotiate with the EU Commission for a successor agreement to the Lomé Convention.[116]

Third, the demand for an OAU coordinating function came at the time that South Africa had joined the OAU. Nelson Mandela's maiden address at the OAU in Tunis in June 1994 contributed a lot to the newfound interests in African development initiatives.[117] The address had at least three major impacts. First, Mandela's romanticization of the African past and his ability to use that "glorious" past to make a strong appeal for African leaders to embark upon "a new African renaissance" to replace the interlude periods of "bitterness," "anger," and "struggle" added weight to Salim's persistent call on African leaders to revive the idea of African solutions to African problems. Second, Mandela's suggestion that South Africa would lead the drive toward the new African renaissance revived African leaders' sentimental attachment to the ideals of Pan-Africanism. Third, Mandela's proreform message created the much-needed reformist constituency and leadership at the political level, which Salim needed to push through his agenda.

Mandela's address generated so much Pan-African feeling that the assembly agreed to convene, in March 1995, an Extraordinary Session of the Council of Ministers to review Africa's economic and social situations and to map out strategies to solve them.[118] Uncharacteristically, the leaders indicated that the Extraordinary Session should not follow the general practice of meetings of the OAU of coming out with general statements and declarations that cannot be implemented. Rather, they challenged the ministers to come out with an "actionable agenda." They also wanted the ministers to reflect on the shortcomings and other things that hampered the implementation of common OAU initiatives such as the LPA.

Consistent with the OAU's administrative procedures, the Secretariat was mandated to develop a proposal to form the basis for deliberations of the Council of Ministers. The SG took advantage of the opportunity to launch the "African economic and social development" agenda, which was a broad policy framework that captured his entire agenda.[119] He followed it up with "[t]he Cairo Agenda for Action," a programmatic proposal designed to persuade African leaders to abandon the reforms of the World Bank in favor of OAU initiatives. Because the proposal was intended to make African leaders believe in OAU initiatives, emphasis was placed on two issues.

First, the report sought to show that the reforms had failed to improve the economies of African countries, and "had been undertaken at great social cost and political risk."[120] It was emphatic that the reforms had impacted negatively on social programs, doubled Africa's debt within eight years— Africa's debt increased from less than $150 billion in 1987 to over $300 billion in 1995—and had also failed to reduce poverty levels.[121] The report also showed that Africa's overall GDP growth rate of 2 percent in 1991, 0.7 percent in 1992, 1.1 percent in 1993, and 2.5 percent in 1994 that were recorded at the height of the reforms were unimpressive and fell far short of what African countries needed.

Second, the report was written purposely to show that OAU initiatives are better alternatives to the reform package. While the proposal was carefully drafted not to antagonize the World Bank, it was emphatic that the time had come for African leaders to "adopt a new vision . . . and take effective measures within specified time frame to ensure the satisfactory implementation and follow-up of decisions" of the OAU.[122]

The report seems to have made a major impression, as a senior Nigerian bureaucrat who attended the Extraordinary Summit and the Thirty-First Summit observed:

> It was perhaps the first time I had read a report from the SG that was clear and comprehensive about the overall economic and social challenges facing Africa and their solutions. Briefing the political bosses, who usually don't listen well, was easy. . . . The data was there for you to tell them the story and, for the first time in a while, you realized the message was sinking in. The message was: the reforms aren't helping. I had no doubt, after conversations with some of our counterparts during the preparation for the 1995 summit, that there had been a change of heart in many capitals.[123]

The SG's report was adopted by the Extraordinary Summit in March 1995 and, also, by the Thirty-First Summit in June 1995. It is striking, however, that the debate at the Assembly during the report's adoption and the speeches that followed were not the usual ritualistic rhetoric. There was a general sense that African leaders' past policy choices had pushed the continent into a deeper developmental crisis, and there was an urgent need for a new paradigm to reverse the trend.

The turnaround of many African states toward African solutions explains why, after nearly six years of inactivity, the Charter Review Committee resumed its work and, in fact, met prior to the 1996 summit. The change in thinking also accounted for the agreement reached at the 1996 summit on a timetable to operationalize relevant institutions of the AEC.[124] For instance, it was agreed that the first meeting of the Economic, Social and Cultural Council (ECOSOCC) should be held in December 1996. [125]

More important, the revival of African states' interest in continental in-itiatives created the opening for the SG to relaunch the OAU development initiative and the second phase of his reform agenda. In a way similar to his use of the Cold War to justify the necessity for the first phase of the reform, Salim took advantage of African leaders' insecurity about the twenty-first century to persuade them to make a declaration on three important things at the Thirty-Second Ordinary Session of the OAU in 1996. [126] First, they ad-mitted that their past policy choices were responsible for the economic diffi-culties, and there was an urgent need for a new paradigm to "rescue the continent from decline." What is interesting is that they also reaffirmed their faith in "the Lagos Plan of Action, the April 1980 Final Act of Lagos and the Abuja Treaty as an appropriate framework for implementing the African strategy of economic growth." Last, they agreed "to reflect on ways and means of smoothly ushering Africa into the 21st century" in subsequent summit sessions.

The declaration opened up the space for the SG to make two critical moves. First, he placed on the agenda of the PRC, the Council of Ministers, and the Assembly an item on how to prepare Africa for the twenty-first century. Second, he introduce the second phase of the reforms initiatives on the theme "Ushering the OAU into the Next Century: A Programme for Reform and Renewal" at the Thirty-Third Ordinary Session in May 1997. [127]

PHASE TWO OF REFORMS

The goal of the second reform package was to structure the institutions of the OAU in order to change it from a general-purpose organization to a more specialized and focused institution. This, according to the proposal, had to be done because the creation of the OAU institutional apparatus was "predicated on the assumption that the organization had to be involved in every field of endeavour." The proposal noted that the general-purpose orientation of the OAU had made the structures of OAU at the headquarters in Addis Ababa and at a regional level "cumbersome to the extent of inhibiting the organiza-tion's effectiveness and efficiency." The essence of the reform was therefore to reduce the bureaucracy drastically and to redirect its "attention and limited resources on priority activities and at tackling those issues and problems which are of the utmost priority" to the continent. The proposal called on the political leadership of the organization to support the Secretary-General's efforts to restructure the OAU in order "to improve its capacity to deliver, especially in those priority areas." The priority areas outlined were regional integration, popular participation in development, and the resolution of intra-state conflicts.

In order to streamline the work of the OAU, the proposal placed emphasis on enhancing the capacity of the OAU administrative apparatus. It specifically asked the leaders to support the SG's efforts to change the OAU's managerial setup, staff work ethics, and the process of recruiting, promoting, and assessing staff at the Secretariat and regional offices. "[Q]uality and not quantity," the report noted, "will henceforth be the guiding principle in retention and recruitment of people."

What was more critical was that the reform package urged African leaders to develop "one single Act to govern the activities of the OAU/AEC." The request for the new single Act was predicated on two main reasons. First, the SG and his core reformist group were of the view that the OAU Charter does not need a review, but a total overhaul, because many of the Charter provisions inhibit the effective operation of the organization. Second, the SG felt that the OAU Charter did not reflect the new focus of the organization. The AEC treaty that captured his integration agenda did not also provide for any institutional structure to administer its provisions. In addition, since the Secretariat was supposed to manage the AEC, the SG thought it was imperative for African leaders to consider a new Act to harmonize and merge the OAU Charter and the AEC treaty.

While the proposal's request for a new single Act was basically a call to replace the OAU, the SG and his reformist-minded "cabinet" wanted the new organization to maintain the name (i.e., the OAU). They were, however, aware that the OAU had an image problem, particularly in the media and some intellectual circles. It was largely perceived by outsiders as talking shop. To address this image problem, the SG recommended two things. First, it asked the leaders to give the Secretariat of the OAU the mandate to develop an effective communication network, including the creation of "Radio Africa" to publicize the works and activities of the OAU, to correct the poor representation of the OAU in the media, and to make OAU documents relatively accessible to researchers. Second, the proposal requested that the leaders mandate the Secretariat of the OAU to develop an institutional framework for the organization to engage African civil society. Jimmi Adisa, the head of the civil society unit, explains:

> Since the movements which culminated in the creation of the OAU were led by civil society, it was felt at the time that there was no need to establish any separate unit for civil society. With time the OAU became a club of leaders and civil society was ignored. From the mid-1990s onward, it became increasingly clear to the Secretariat that the neglect of civil society was a mistake that had to be corrected. [128]

As a first step toward opening up the OAU to civil society, the SG requested that the Assembly of Heads of State mandate the Secretariat to convey a Pan-African Conference as soon as possible to reflect "on Africa's role and position in the next millennium."

The introduction of the second reform proposal marked an important juncture in the move to create the AU. It provided the basis for the Council and the Assembly to deliberate on the "most appropriate means . . . to take up the challenges" that Africa will face in the twenty-first century at the Thirty-Third Ordinary Session in 1997.

The central issue that animated the debate was whether or not the OAU had the institutional capacity to coordinate Africa's response to the challenges of the new century. One clustered group of countries led by Nigeria and Egypt were content with the measure proposed by the Secretary-General. For these countries, the OAU does not require change beyond the institutional reforms contained in the second proposal of the SG and programs already agreed upon in previous summits.[129] What the OAU needs, they contend, is not new initiatives, but, rather, implementation of agreed-upon programs and measures adopted at previous OAU summits. But South Africa and many SADC members disagreed with the position of the status quo group. South Africa in particular found the reforms and the institutional structure of the OAU inadequate, and therefore wanted radical reforms of the continental organization. A minister at the South Africa embassy in Ethiopia summed up his country's position during the debate thusly:

> We had four simple concerns. . . . First of all, we felt the MCMR did not have enough teeth to bite. . . . We did not want to witness another genocide of the 1994 Rwanda kind or worse before we give the OAU the tools to deal with conflicts. Second, the entry into force of the Abuja treaty created confusion. The confusion stems from the fact that Abuja did not create any secretariat and institutions of its own. Its decisions had to be taken by the OAU. This created confusion as decisions of the AEC got mixed up with decisions of the OAU. My president and certainly a great number of other leaders found it difficult to separate decisions made at the AEC summits and that of the OAU and we wanted to tidy up the situation. We also thought that the focus of the AEC should not be integration but on productive capacity. How can you talk about integration when you do not have the capacity to produce? And of course, we thought the OAU institutions did not reflect the democratic wave of the times.[130]

Following the general exchange of views during the Council and Assembly's sessions on the proposal, the political leaders decided to defer a detailed discussion of OAU reforms to the Thirty-Fourth Ordinary Session in June 1998. Although the Thirty-Third Summit session ended without any concrete decision on the reform proposal, it was nevertheless significant. It provided

Africrats with the opportunity to determine how far they could go with the reform initiative.

Based on the absence of any major opposition to the proposal on the floor of both the Council and the Assembly sessions, the SG decided to expand the scope of the reforms for the consideration of the Assembly at the Thirty-Fourth Ordinary Session in June 1998.[131] The expanded policy document covered three themes: political issues, economic and social cooperation, and institutional development.

The major thrust of the political theme was the question of peace, security, and stability. It urged the political leaders, among other things, to "make the search for peace, security and stability [its] primary concern" and to take concrete steps to "work towards the establishment and consolidation of effective democratic systems, ensure respect for human rights and fight impunity."[132]

The economic and social cooperation aspect rehashed earlier decisions on economic integration and social issues. The majority of the economic cooperation issues basically reworded earlier measures aimed at ensuring that the leaders rededicate themselves to the integration project and to strengthening the economic communities. It, however, placed renewed emphasis on providing the OAU with the tools to assist the African continent to speak as a "homogenous political force in international fora such as the United Nations, the World Trade Organization (WTO) and the African-Caribbean and Pacific Group (ACP), and . . . on the debt question."[133]

The social aspect recapped in a clearer and more concise fashion the declaration on social development contained in the 1995 extraordinary summit of the Council. It also included issues agreed upon as constituting Africa's position for the world summit on social development. The theme on institutional development reproduced the reform proposal submitted by the SG to the Thirty-Third Summit. In particular, it urged the leaders to:

> endow . . . [the] Organization with structures capable of meeting the dynamics of changes unfolding in our societies and worldwide through increased coordination of the activities of sub-regional organizations, coordination of the continent's sectorial policies and implementation of the decisions of the Specialized Commissions.[134]

The OAU Secretariat submitted the document to form the basis of the Assembly's debate on how to usher Africa into the twenty-first century at the Thirty-Fourth Ordinary Session.

THE 1990S GRAND DEBATE

The Heads of State and Government debate was started by the South African president Nelson Mandela on the opening day of the Summit. Mandela used his opening address on June 8, 1998, to state his country's position.[135] It was basically a reincarnation of the argument of the statist interdependency school, with a modern twist.[136] In his view, since none of the African states is a "superstar" that has the capacity to succeed on its own, it is imperative that African leaders deepen interdependence, integrate African markets, harmonize national policies, and ensure collective mobilization of human and material resources for the development of the continent. Mandela added a distinctly modern neoliberal caveat to the traditional interdependency position when he indicated strongly that African leaders must "attend to . . . strengthening" the OAU so that it can provide the institutional framework for African states to:

> [P]revent abuse of sovereignty . . . improve Africa's place in the global econo-my . . . attract African intellectuals in the North back to the continent . . . promote good interpersonal relations and entrench the understanding that, as Africans, we are one people who share a common destiny.

Mandela also supported the reform embarked upon by the OAU bureaucrats, but felt the reform was not extensive enough. Accordingly, he urged African leaders to "attend to . . . [the] strengthening and effective functioning [of the OAU] with the necessary seriousness, understanding that without this all-African organization, we would, one and all, be severely limited in our capacity" to deal with Africa's development challenges in the twenty-first century.

The OAU, he continued, must also be reformed so that it can drive the new generation of African leaders to treat issues on security and stability collectively. Mandela also tried to persuade African leaders to take joint decisions on issues dealing with multilateral institutions such as "the World Bank, the IMF, the UN and the WTO and the EU . . . in the next century."

The address, given prior to the discussions on the first day of the two-day summit, had a major impact on the summit discussions and on the positions of some African governments. What was of the greatest consequence was that Mandela's resurrection and attempts to push the statist interdependency ideas, and his attempt to encourage the OAU to promote liberal norms, angered and also energized two important constituencies of the Assembly. First, almost all the military regimes felt that Mandela's call on African leaders to refrain from "abusing the concept of national sovereignty" and to stop using "sovereign boundaries to protect tyranny" was an attack on their governments. A former foreign minister expressed his impression thusly:

For most parts, all of us were at home with the great man's speech. There were
few occasions when you could tell from the facial expressions on some of my
colleagues that they have been attacked by the speech. It did not surprise me
that I heard on several occasions at informal gatherings that some of our
brothers were offended by sections of the message. A colleague from our
neighbouring country was particularly upset at the speech's underlying assumption that non-elective leaders slaughter their people. Bear in mind that the
speech came after South Africa had earlier attacked Nigeria's human rights
records. [137]

Second, the speech also created unease in the ranks of the so-called African
nationalists (the cultural relativists), who felt that the OAU was being driven
to promote Western values.

In response, a small number of states within the nationalists' camp coun-
tered South Africa by proposing a reform package similar to the ideas of the
continental union school of the 1960s. [138] Two versions of the continental
union proposal were outlined. Libya's Muammar Gaddafi, who was attending the OAU summit for the first time after many years of absence, urged
African leaders to establish a continental organization with a strong army, a
single currency, and a powerful leadership. He wondered why Nkrumah's
United States of Africa proposal had still not materialized after four decades
of beating the drum of African unity. Then Malian president (now chairperson of the AU Commission) Alpha Oumar Konaré felt that the OAU "had
fulfilled its mission and its primary objective" honorably, and should be
replaced with a much stronger supranational organization. [139] He proposed
that the organization that would replace the OAU should have the institutional powers to develop a confederal union for the African continent.

No agreement was reached after the lengthy debate, and a decision was
made to continue the discussions at the Thirty-Fifth Ordinary Session of the
OAU. The debate was, however, significant in two ways. First, African leaders' overwhelming preference for new institutional reforms or replacement of
the OAU emboldened Africrats to push through their reform initiatives. They
prepared three important prodemocracy decisions for the adoption of the
Assembly during the Thirty-Fifth Ordinary Session of the OAU. [140] The first
decision sought to make the promotion of "strong and democratic institutions" a key objective of the OAU. [141] The second excluded from the OAU
states "whose Governments came to power through unconstitutional means,"
and the third gave the OAU the mandate to assist military regimes that may
exist on the African continent to move toward a democratic system of
government. Africrats also wanted the summit to agree on the time frame to
integrate the OAU Charter and the AEC treaty, and to develop the Single Act
requested by the SG at the Thirty-Third Ordinary Summit of the OAU.

Second, the debate provided the platform for the leaders who sympa-
thized with the ideas of the continental union to identify themselves and to

assess their support base. The debate provided Libya's Muammar Gaddafi the basis for Libya to write to the SG on September 28, 1998 (three months after the summit), requesting that the Assembly convene an extraordinary summit in September 1999 "to amend the OAU Charter to achieve . . . stronger African unity." After the General Secretariat pointed out to Libya that a committee reviewing the Charter was already in place, Libya modified the basis of the summit to reflect Africrats' request to the Assembly to reform the OAU to meet the challenge of the twenty-first century.

In its reply, dated April 15, 1999, Libya lifted words from Africrats' proposals, and indicated that the summit would "discuss the question of strengthening the OAU to enable it to meet the new challenges facing it on the eve of the new century."[142] Four countries—Liberia, Niger, South Africa, and Sudan—formally responded to Libya's letter, with only South Africa objecting to the request. Although only South Africa formally rejected the request, as officials of the South African embassy in Ethiopia and Africrats pointed out in an interview, the South African view was shared by other African countries and, in particular, by most states within the Southern African region.[143]

Because of the low number of replies the General Secretariat received from member states on Libya's request, the SG decided to conduct diplomatic consultations to gauge support of African governments for the idea of convening an Extraordinary Summit. It was through the consultations that the SG was informed that Nigeria was preparing to table a motion relating to OAU reforms at the Thirty-Fifth Ordinary Session of the Assembly.[144] The motion was going to, first, request that member states convene a ministerial session to set in motion "the process of re-launching the CSSDCA"; second, declare the year 2000 "as the Year of Peace, Security and Solidarity in Africa"; and third, "restructure the OAU to promote this objective (i.e., to promote peace and resolve conflicts in Africa)."[145] The South African government also indicated that it would be prepared to support the OAU reforms, but only on the condition that the reform empowers the organization to focus "on the strategic objectives of the realization of the African Renaissance."[146] The African Renaissance seeks to:

- promote regional economic integration as a route to strengthen the sovereignty of member states
- promote liberal political systems that take into account African specifics
- enhance Africa's place in the global economy
- promote gender equality
- pursue sustainable development
- find a solution to HIV disease
- rediscover Africa's cultures and creative past

The logical questions that arise from the preceding discussion are: Why the variation of African government preferences? Why did Nigeria/South Africa and others want only to refocus the OAU's attention on economic and security integration, while Libya and others wanted to replace it with a continental federal union? How did they develop these preferences? The next chapter examines the preference formation of African governments.

NOTES

1. This is well documented. See, for instance, Cambridge University, *Cambridge History of Africa, no. 2–4* (Cambridge, UK: Cambridge University Press); and volumes V to VIII of the *UNESCO General History of Africa* (California: Heinemann, 1993).

2. William C. Barnett, "The Geography of Africa," in *African History before 1885, Volume One*, ed. Toyin Falola (Durham: Carolina Academic Press, 2000), 43.

3. The colonies were Gambia, Gold Coast (Ghana), Nigeria, and Sierra Leone. The Protectorates were Transvolta-Togoland (now part of Ghana) and English-speaking Cameroon.

4. Arthur Hazlewood, "The End of the East African Community: What Are the Lessons for Regional Integration Schemes?" *Journal of Common Market Studies* XVIII: 1 (1979): 41.

5. A. F. Addona, *The Organization of African Unity* (Cleveland and New York: World Publishing Company, 1969), 73.

6. Domeico Mazzeo, *African Regional Organizations* (London: Cambridge University Press, 1984), 10.

7. Kwame Nkrumah, *African Must Unite* (New York: International Publishers, 1963), 218–20. Also, see Joseph S. Nye, *Pan-Africanism and East African Integration* (Cambridge: Harvard University Press, 1965), 14.

8. Nkrumah, *African Must Unite*.

9. This first conference of independent states was attended by representatives of Ethiopia, Ghana, Liberia, Libya, Morocco, Sudan, Tunisia, and United Arab Republic (Egypt). For more information, see Carol A. Johnson, "Conferences of Independent African States," *International Organization* 16, no. 2 (1962).

10. The conference's specific aims were: to discuss problems of common interests; to develop mechanisms for promoting cooperation and mutual understanding among participating states; to explore means of protecting their independence and sovereignty; to explore ways of speeding up the decolonization processes; and to plan cultural exchanges and mutual assistance schemes.

11. Scott W. Thompson, *Ghana's Foreign Policy 1957–1966: Diplomacy, Ideology, and the New State* (Princeton: Princeton University Press, 1969), 38.

12. Heads of Independent African State, "Resolutions on Cooperation," Conference of Independent African States, Accra, Ghana, December 13, 1958, 2.

13. Nkrumah, *Africa Must Unite*.

14. Colin Legum, *Pan Africanism: A Short Political Guide* (London: Pall Mall Press, 1962), 33. The emphasis is in the original text.

15. Immanuel Wallerstein, *Africa: The Politics of Independence and Unity* (New York: Random house, 1967), 13–14.

16. Johnson, "Conferences of Independent African States," 429. The delegates were drawn from: Ghana, Liberia, Ethiopia, Libya, the Sudan, Tunisia, Morocco, and United Arab Republic (Egypt) and dependent countries—Angola, Basutoland (Lesotho), Belgian Congo, Cameroon, Chad, Dahomey, French Somaliland, Guinea, Ivory Coast, Kenya, Mozambique, Nigeria, Northern Rhodesia, Nyasaland (Malawi), Occidental Afrique, Senegal, Sierra Leone, South Africa, South West Africa (Namibia), Tanganyika (Tanzania), Togoland, Uganda, and Zanzibar.

17. Heads of Independent African State, "Resolutions on Frontiers, Boundaries and Federations," All-African Peoples Conference, Accra, Ghana, December 13, 1958. This resolution is reprinted in Legum, *Pan Africanism: A Short Political Guide,* 228–32.

18. Heads of Independent African State, "Resolutions on Frontiers, Boundaries and Federations."

19. Heads of Independent African State, "Resolutions on Frontiers, Boundaries and Federations."

20. *Daily Graphic*, May 2, 1959.

21. Heads of State of Ghana and Guinea Summit, "The Declaration of the Ghana-Guinea Union," May 1, 1959.

22. Jon Woronoff, *Organizing African Unity* (Metuchen, NJ: Scarecrow Press, 1970), 74.

23. Thompson, *Ghana's Foreign Policy*, 61.

24. Thompson, *Ghana's Foreign Policy*, 91.

25. Wallerstein, *Africa: The Politics of Independence and Unity*, 37.

26. Woronoff, *Organizing African Unity*, 74; and Thompson, *Ghana's Foreign Policy*, 74.

27. The Sanniquellie Declaration, July 19, 1959, 1.

28. The Sanniquellie Summit, Declaration of Principle numbers 1 and 5 (1959).

29. The Sanniquellie Summit, Declaration of Principle numbers 3 and 4 (1959).

30. Delegates for the Conference were drawn from Algerian Provisional Government, Cameroon, Congo Leopoldville, Ethiopia, Ghana, Guinea, Liberia, Libya, Morocco, Nigeria, Somalia, Sudan, Tunisia, Togoland, and United Arab Republic (i.e., Egypt). The invited quests included the nationalist leaders from Southern and Northern Rhodesia, Kenya, Uganda, Tanganyika, South Africa, and South West Africa, who attended the conference.

31. Legum, *Pan Africanism: A Short Political Guide*, 46.

32. Legum, *Pan Africanism: A Short Political Guide*, 93.

33. Besides Ghana, Guinea, Tunisia, and couple of delegations such as Libya and Egypt whose positions on the issues were ambiguous, the rest of the delegates supported the statist project.

34. W. Scott Thompson and I. William Zartman, "The Development of Norms in the African System," in *The Organization of African Unity after Ten Years: Comparative Perspectives*, ed. Yassin el-Ayouty, ed (New York: Praeger, 1975): 3–46.

35. Woronoff, *Organizing African Unity*.

36. Norman J. Padelford, "The Organization of African Unity," *International Organization* 18, no. 3 (1964): 526.

37. Padelford, "The Organization of African Unity," 527.

38. Thompson and Zartman, "The Development of Norms in the African System."

39. Julius Nyerere, "A United States of Africa," *Journal of Modern African Studies* 1, no. 1 (1963): 6.

40. Nyerere, "A United States of Africa," 6.

41. Padelford, "The Organization of African Unity," 529.

42. Woronoff, *Organizing African Unity*, 128–29.

43. Proceedings of the First Conference of Independent African States in Addis Ababa, Ethiopia (1963).

44. Christopher Clapham, *African and the International System: The Politics of State Survival* (Cambridge: Cambridge University Press, 1996), 111.

45. Proceedings of the First Conference of Independent African States (1963).

46. Proceedings of the First Conference of Independent African States (1963).

47. Proceedings of the First Conference of Independent African States (1963).

48. See, for instance, *Daily Graphic*, May 25–26, 1963.

49. Thompson and Zartman, *The Development of Norms in the African System*, 18.

50. See the submission in Thompson and Zartman, *The Development of Norms in the African System*, 18–19.

51. Organization of African Unity, "Proceedings of the First Summit of Heads of State and Government" (Cairo, Egypt, 1964).

52. AHG/Res.10 (I).

53. Because President Nkrumah and his group were aware that the decision to refer the proposal to the nonexisting commission was designed to kill the project, they also changed their strategy. They tried—though without much success—to persuade the leaders to revise the OAU Charter in order to provide the organization with meaningful supranational powers. This is why Ghana submitted a proposal at the Second Ordinary Summit in Accra in October 1965 asking the leaders to revise the Charter in order to create an executive arm for the OAU.

54. Few professionals were employed at the Secretariat in the first decade of the organization's existence. Vacancies at the Secretariat were largely filled with local Ethiopian citizens and civil servants with some knowledge in ceremonial duties and Foreign Service. Notwithstanding professional advice from two different administrative consultants that the work at the Secretariat should be performed by professionals, African leaders continue to encourage the Administrative Secretary=General to recruit local Ethiopians. Not a single recommendation contained in two cconsultancy reports—the first consultancy report was submitted by a Ghanaian in 1966 and the second one by an Egyptian in 1970—which would have made the OAU Secretariat efficient, was implemented. The debates on the reports by the Council of Ministers show that African governments did not implement the recommendations in the reports because they feared that doing so would turn the OAU into a supranational organization.

55. Dailo Telli, "Introduction to the Report of the Administrative Secretary General covering the period February 1969 to August 1969," (Addis Abbadi: Organization of African Unity, 1969), 22.

56. EDECO/EC/26/1969.85.

57. Charles Awitor, former OAU Chief of Inter-Africa Cooperation, Interview, July 29, 2005.

58. Dailo Telli, "Introduction to the Report of the Administrative Secretary General covering the period September 1970 to February 1971," (Addis Abbadi: Organization of African Unity, 1971), 15.

59. For quotation, see EDECO/EC/26/1969.85, 1.

60. Abdelrahim Dirar (Former Director of EDECO), Interview, July 27, 2005.

61. CM/St.12 (XXI).

62. AHG/DEC. 111 (XVI) and CM/CTTEE.A/RPT (L).

63. Edem Kodjo, "Report of the Administrative Secretary General covering the period September 1970 to February 1971," (Addis Abbadi: Organization of African Unity, 1971), 351.

64. Administration and Finance was split into two departments.

65. Other noticeable changes were that Social Affairs was added to the Scientific, Education and Culture Department and more division were also created. The new EDECO department had six divisions, and this made it the largest OAU Department. It also had the largest number of professional staffs within the Secretariat of the OAU. A number of people with economic background and who share the Pan-African economic vision such as Faustin Kinumaa and Charles Awitor were recruited at this period to work at the EDECO Department. Eden Kodjo increased the Secretariat's staff strengths from about 250 to 366, out of which 99 were professionals.

66. Organization of African Unity, *Lagos Plan of Action for the Economic Development of Africa 1980–2000* (Addis Ababa: 1981). For intellectual analysis of the Lagos Plan, see Claude Ake, *Democracy and Development in Africa* (Washington: The Brookings Institution, 1996).

67. SADCC was established in 1980, COMESA in 1981, and ECCAS in 1983.

68. Adebayo Adedeji, "History and Prospects for Regional Integration in Africa," (1989).

69. Organization of African Unity, "What Type of Economic Community for Africa?" (Addis Ababa: 1985), 2.

70. CM/1233 (XL). Also, see Kodjo, "Report of the Secretary General covering the period June 1980 to February 1981."

71. CM/1120 (XXXVII), 7.

72. CM/1233(XL), 2.

73. CM/1442(L), 3; CM/1681(LV), 2.

74. Peter Onu, "Report of the Secretary General covering the period June 1983 to February 1984," (Addis Abbadi: Organization of African Unity, 1984), 2.

75. CM/1233 (XL), 2

76. Museveni's criticism of the OAU during the Twenty-Second Ordinary Session of OAU in Addis Ababa, Ethiopia, in July 1986 was unique and extraordinary. It was the first time an African leader had publicly criticized the OAU on the floor of the Assembly.

77. Ide Oumarou, "Report of the Secretary General covering the period June 1988 to February 1989," (Addis Abbadi: Organization of African Unity, 1989), 4.

78. For a discussion of the economic treaty, see Kwaku Danso, "The African Economic Community: Problems and Prospects," *Africa Today* 42, no. 4 (1995): 31–55; Muna Ndulo, "Harmonisation of Trade Laws in the African Economic Community," *International and Comparative Law Quarterly* 42 (1993): 101–18. And for security mechanism, Richard Jackson, "The Dangers of Regionalising International Conflict Management: The African Experience," Political Science 52, no. 1(2000): 41–60; Eric Berman, "African Regional Organisations' Peace Operations: Developments and Challenges," *African Security Review* 11, no. 4 (2002): 33–44.

79. The EAC, which collapsed in 1977, was revived and reinaugurated with fanfare on January 15, 2001.

80. The UMA is made up of five countries (Algeria, Morocco, Mauritania, Libya, and Tunisia).

81. The WAEMU, which was established in 1994, is comprised of eight countries (Benin, Burkina Faso, Côte d'Ivoire, Guinea Bissau, Mali, Niger, Senegal, and Togo). It was formed by a merger of the West African Monetary Union and the West African Economic Community.

82. The SADC was created in 1994. It is comprised of fourteen countries (Angola, Botswana, Democratic Republic of Congo, Lesotho, Malawi, Mauritius, Mozambique, Namibia, Seychelles, South Africa, Swaziland, Tanzania, Zambia, and Zimbabwe).

83. The COMESA was created in 1994. It is composed of twenty countries (Angola, Burundi, Comoros, Democratic Republic of Congo, Djibouti, Egypt, Eritrea, Ethiopia, Kenya, Madagascar, Malawi, Mauritius, Namibia, Rwanda, Seychelles, Sudan, Swaziland, Zambia, Zimbabwe, and Uganda).

84. The CEMAC came into existence in 1998. It is composed of six countries (Cameroon, Central African Republic, Congo, Equatorial Guinea, Gabon, and Chad).

85. By entrepreneurialship, I mean committed and well-placed individuals within the OAU Secretariat who invested their time, reputation, and resources to convince African leaders to adopt certain specific ideas and policies.

86. Wayne Sandholtz and John Zysman, "1992: Recasting the European Bargain," *World Politics* 42, no. 1 (1989): 95–128; and Wayne Sandholtz and Alec Stone Sweet (eds.), *European Integration and Supranational Governance* (Oxford: Oxford University Press, 1998), 217–49.

87. Andrew Moravcsik, "Taking Preferences Seriously: Liberalism and International Relations Theory," *International Organization* 51, no. 4 (1997): 532.

88. Interview with Jean Mfasoni, Acting Director of Political Affairs, African Union. Interview took place on February 22, 2005. (Henceforth, interview with Mfasoni.)

89. Salim was primarily interested in political issues such as conflict management and was initially uninterested in the integration project. Some key interviewees pointed out that he repeatedly told senior staffs at the EDECO Department at closed-door meetings to "forget about the integration project."

90. The widely known of these conferences was the Arusha Colloquium in 1986. The Colloquium brought together more than two dozen local African economists, the ECA, and OAU staff to brainstorm on the AEC.

91. Interview with Soanirinela Tsilimbiaza, Director of Trade and Industry, African Union. Interview took place on July 22, 2005. (Henceforth, interview with Tsilimbiaza.)

92. I obtained a copy each of three of the works of the consultants. One of the reports examined the legal implication of the AEC, another looked at the economic implication establishing economic community, and the other assessed the political effects of the proposed AEC.

93. Interview with Charles Awitor, former OAU chief of Inter-Africa Cooperation. Interview took place on July 29, 2005. (Henceforth, interview with Awitor.)

94. Interview with Abdelrahim Dirar, former director of EDECO. Interview took place on July 27, 2005. (Henceforth, interview with Dirar.)

95. Interview with Awitor.

96. Organization of African Unity, "The Draft Treaty Establishing African Economic Community," (Addis Ababa, 1989).

97. The first stage focuses on strengthening the existing regional economic communities (RECs), and creating new ones where they do not exist, to serve as building blocks for the AEC within five years from the date of entry into force of the treaty. The second phase focuses on the stabilization of tariff and nontariff barriers, customs duties, and taxes of member states of each REC within a period not exceeding eight years. The third phase involves the removal of intra-RECs tariff and nontariff barriers and the creation of a Free Trade Area within a period not exceeding ten years. The fourth phase entails harmonization of intraregional tariff and nontariff barriers, the adoption of common African external tariff barriers, and the creation of a Continental Custom Union within two years. Phase five is devoted to the preparation of African countries for sectoral integration and the establishment of an African Common Market within a period of four years. The last stage is committed to the consolidation of the African Common Market and the establishment of institutions such as the African Central Bank, the African Monetary Bank, a single African currency, and a Pan-African Parliament within five years.

98. African leaders appointed Salim (Tanzanian and East African) in part because they wanted to defuse the perception that the OAU was a West African organization and in part because of his foreign affairs experience and academic background. The domination of OAU bureaucratic hierarchy by citizens of West Africa prior to the appointment of Salim had created the impression in parts of Africa that the organization is a West African institution. The appointment was meant to create a regional balance and to diffuse the perception.

99. "OAU: Twenty-Fifth Summit Meeting," *Keesing's Record of World Events*, 1989, 36807.

100. CM/1591(LI) and Salim Ahmed Salim, "Report of the SG to the Fifty-Second Ordinary Session of Council of Ministers" (Addis Abadi: Organization of African Unity, 1990).

101. CM/1691(LV); Salim Ahmed Salim, "Report of the SG to the Fifty-Fifth Ordinary Session of Council of Ministers," (Addis Abbadi: Organization of African Unity, 1992), 4–5. Specifically, Salim wanted to change the managerial setup of the OAU Secretariat; improve conditions of service and the efficiency of staff; change recruitment and promotion policies; change work ethics at the Secretariat; end the practice where unqualified people end up at the top management level of the OAU; end promotion on an exceptional basis; and end the policy that makes it possible for staff to stagnate at one grade for as long as twenty years or, even, throughout their career.

102. CM/1691(LV); Salim Ahmed Salim, "Introductory Note to the Report of the Secretary General," (Addis Abbadi: Organization of African Unity, 1997), 10.

103. Salim Ahmed Salim, "Report of the Secretary General to the Fifty-First Ordinary Session of Council of Ministers," (Addis Abbadi: Organization of African Unity, 1990), 8; Salim, "Report of the SG to the Fifty Second Ordinary Session of Council of Ministers," 10.

104. Interview with Mfasoni; interview with Dirar.

105. Salim, "Report of the SG to the Fifty-First Ordinary Session of Council of Ministers," 8; Salim Ahmed Salim, "Report of the Secretary General to the Fifty-Second Ordinary Session of Council of Ministers," (Addis Abbadi: Organization of African Unity, 1990), 10.

106. AHG/Decl.1 (XXVI). For the document prepared by the Task Force, see Organization of African Unity, "The Political and Socio-Economic Situation in Africa and the Fundamental Changes Taking Place in the World" (Addis Ababa, 1990). Salim held talks with top-ranking officials within the UN agencies and government officials in France, United Kingdom, Belgium, and Switzerland during the trip.

107. CM/1591(LII).

108. For a discussion of the economic treaty, see Kwaku Danso, "The African Economic Community: Problems and Prospects," *Africa Today* 42, no. 2 (1995): 31–55; Muna Ndulo, "Harmonisation of Trade Laws in the African Economic Community," *International and Comparative Law Quarterly* 42 (1993): 101–18. And for the security dimension, see Richard Jackson, "The Dangers of Regionalising International Conflict Management," *Political Science* (2000): 41–60; Eric Berman, "African Regional Organisations' Peace Operations," *African Security Review* 11, no. 4 (2002): 33–44.

109. CM/1681(LV).

110. AHG/Decl. 1 (XXVIII).

111. Sam Ibok, "The OAU Mechanism for Conflict Prevention, Management and Resolution and Conflict Situation in Africa," (Original Document: Addis Ababa, 1999), 1.

112. The Protocol was finally signed between the OAU and four RECs (i.e., ECOWAS, SADC, COMESA, and ECASS) in 1998.

113. Funmi Olonisakin, "African 'Homemade' Peacekeeping Initiatives," *Armed Forces and Society* 23, no. 3 (Spring 1997).

114. Margaret Vogt, "The African Union and Subregional Security Mechanisms in Africa," *Africa: Problems and Prospects* (2002).

115. The African countries that acceded to the World Trade Organization regime at the Uruguay rounds in 1994 and those preparing to sign the WTO agreement needed the OAU to assist them to coordinate their positions and strategies to participate effectively in the Round. They were acutely aware that they stood no chance of having their voices heard at the Round unless they teamed up and spoke with one united voice.

116. The ACP states needed a united voice and stand to ensure that the post-Lomé agreement maintained the benefits, such as the preferential access to the EU market, that they enjoyed under the Lomé regime. It was therefore normal that they will look up to the OAU to coordinate their united response to the two international issues.

117. Nelson Mandela, "Statement of the President of the Republic of South Africa at the OAU Heads of State and Government Summit," Tunisia (June 1994).

118. AHG/Decl.5 (XXX).

119. Salim Ahmed Salim, "The Report of the Secretary-General to the Special Session of the Council of Ministers on Economic and Social Issues in African Development."

120. CM/1789; Salim Ahmed Salim, "Introductory Note to the Report of the SG to the Fifty-Ninth Ordinary Session of Council of Ministers," (Addis Abbadi: Organization of African Unity, 1994), 7.

121. Salim, "The Report to the Special Session of the Council of Ministers on Economic and Social Issues," 132–35.

122. Salim, "The Report of the Secretary-General to the Special Session of the Council of Ministers on Economic and Social Issues in African Development," (1995), 130–31.

123. Interview with Layi-Kayode Iyanda, Head of Mission at the Nigerian Mission in Addis Ababa. Interview took place on September 27, 2005. (Henceforth, interview with Iyanda.)

124. CM/1880(LXII).

125. CM/1880(LXII); Salim Ahmed Salim, "Introductory Note to the Report of the SG to the Sixty-Forth Ordinary Session of Council of Ministers," (Addis Abbadi: Organization of African Unity, 1996), 45.

126. AHG/Decl.3 (XXXII).

127. Salim Ahmed Salim, "Ushering the OAU into the Next Century: A Programme for Reform and Renewal" in the Introductory note to the Report of the SG to the Thirty-Third Ordinary Session, (Addis Abbadi: Organization of African Unity, 1997). I draw the analysis more from the introductory note because the ideas are much more refined and clearly articulated than the document submitted to the Thirty-Second summit. Note that a declaration on preparing Africa for the next century was adopted at the Thirty-Second summit in June 1996.

128. Interview with Jimmi Adisa, Senior Coordinator and Head of CSSDCA, February 20, 2004. (Henceforth, interview with Adisa.)

129. WTO members who had pushed for the measure were frantically pushing for the inauguration of the intergovernmental committee on trade, customs, and immigration of the Abuja so that it could coordinate and develop a common African position and strategies for the second WTO ministerial meeting in May 1998, and they were not interested in the debate.

130. Interview with Henry William Short, minster in charge of African Union, South African Embassy in Addis Ababa, February 22, 2004. (Henceforth, interview with Short.)

131. The document was adopted as the "Ouagadougou Declaration" at the Thirty-Fourth Ordinary Session of the Assembly. See AHG/DECL.1(XXXIV).

132. AHG/DECL.1 (XXXIV).

133. Assembly of Heads of State and Government, "Ouagadougou Declaration," *Organization of African Unity* (1998), 1.

134. AHG/DECL.1 (XXXIV).

135. The speech is available online athttp://www.anc.org.za/ancdocs/history/mandela/1998/sp980608.html.

136. The modern caveat was Mandela's emphasis on Liberal norms building as part of the integration exercise.

137. Interview with Victor Gbeho, former foreign minister of Ghana, June 27, 2005. (Henceforth, interview with Gbeho.)

138. The ideas of the continental unionists underlined the contribution to the debate of Liberia, Libya, Mali, Senegal, and Niger.

139. Interviews with Kioko.

140. AU officials, especially the director for political affairs, claim in an interview that they prepared the document and the decisions as far back as 1996 but were just waiting for the right moment to submit them. In their opinion, the death of Sani Abacha in 1998 and an encouraging political signal on the subject by some member states during and after the Thirty-Fourth Summit opened the gate for them to unveil it finally.

141. AHG/Decl. XXXV. Available online at: http://www.iss.co.za/AF/RegOrg/unity_to_union/
pdfs/oau/hog/9HoGAssembly1999.pdf.

142. The letter was also sent to member states of the OAU. Four countries, namely, Liberia, Niger, South Africa and Sudan, formally responded to the letter, with only South Africa objecting to the request. Although only South Africa formally rejected the request, as William Short, official of the South Africa embassy in Ethiopia, and Jean Afasoni at the O/AU Commission, pointed out in an interview, the South African view was shared by other African countries, and in particular, by most states within the Southern African region.

143. Interviews with Afasoni and Short.

144. Interview with Kioko.

145. AHG/Decl. XXXV. The last quotation comes from a summary of the CSSDCA process from the Department of Foreign Affairs of the Republic of South Africa. About three senior officials I interviewed at the Nigeria embassy in Addis Ababa confirm that the view is accurate. The material is available online athttp://www.dfa.gov.za/for-relations/multilateral/cssdca.htm - sgrep. Senior officials I interviewed at the Nigeria embassy in Addis Ababa confirmed that the view is accurate.

146. Thabo Mbeki, "Speech Delivered on 11 October 1999 at the Launch of the African Renaissance Institute" (Pretoria, 1999), available at: http://www.polity.org.za/html/govdocs/
speeches/1999/.

Chapter Four

The Impact of Entrepreneurship, Institution, and Social Norms in the Negotiation of the African Union

INTRODUCTION

The previous chapter showed that competition between those African national governments that preferred to reform the OAU and those that wanted to replace the OAU with a continental federal union led to the declaration to establish the African Union (AU) at the Sirte Extraordinary Summit. The Sirte Declaration was only a statement of intent, inasmuch as it did not define the nature, powers, functions, or institutions of the proposed union. The thirty-five heads of state who met at Sirte mandated the OAU Council of Ministers to negotiate the specific elements of the AU. The purpose of this chapter is to account for the decision by representatives of African countries to select the principles, rules, institutional structures, and decision-making procedures that constitutes the AU.

I argue that Africrats used their entrepreneurial skills, the OAU's institutional mechanisms, and argument to persuade representatives of states to select ambitious principles, rules, institutional structures, and decision-making procedures. Africrats did not persuade all state representatives, but they did convince sufficient numbers of them to generate a broad agreement on the appropriate institutional mechanisms for Africa. As soon as the broad consensus emerged on the appropriateness of the AU institutional mechanism, Pan-African solidarity then set in to compel the unconvinced governments to sign on. The representatives that Africrats persuaded were mostly foreign ministers, state lawyers, diplomats, and selected members of legislative branches of governments of African countries. I use the phrase *OAU's*

institutional mechanisms to mean rules and norms, decision-making procedures, delegated powers, and resources of the defunct Organization of
African Unity. I use the term *argument* to mean that Africrats used information, reasoning, and ideas intentionally to shape the revealed preferences,
interests, positions, and views of representatives of African states, and/or
persuaded delegates to accept their revealed preferences, interests, positions,
and views.

The chapter is organized into four sections. The first section provides a
concise description and overview of the case. It outlines the negotiation
procedures, the state of play (i.e., the purpose of the negotiations), the respective negotiating positions of the delegations, and efforts by Africrats to provide a solution to solve a cooperation problem. The second section examines
the role Africrats played in helping delegations reach agreement on some
major areas under negotiation during the first meeting of experts. The third
section outlines the issues on which the experts failed to reach agreement. It
also documents the efforts made by Africrats to help the experts break the
deadlock on the outstanding issues. It details reasons for Africrats' failure to
help the experts break the deadlock during the second meeting of experts.
The fourth section provides a discussion of the assistance Africrats gave to
the ministers to reach agreement on the outstanding issues and the inputs
Africrats provided during the development of the final draft of the legal
instrument that was signed by African states in Lomé in July 2000. The
chapter concludes by placing the empirical data within a broader IR theoretical context.

THE CASE: NEGOTIATING THE CONSTITUTIVE ELEMENTS OF THE AU

To demonstrate that it was Africrats who persuaded representatives of
African states to select ambitious principles, rules, and institutional structures
as elements of the AU, a concise overview of the case is needed. When did
the negotiation take place? What kind of procedure was used? Who were the
negotiators? What was the negotiation about? And what was the final outcome?

THE PROCEDURE

The key elements of the AU were negotiated during three separate meetings
of representatives of member states of the OAU (henceforth, delegations).
Experts attended two of the three meetings. The experts were state lawyers,
diplomats (i.e., ambassadors, counselors, political attachés), and selected
members of the legislative branches of governments of African countries

who were employed by those governments to represent them. The first meeting of experts was held in Addis Ababa from April 17 to 20, 2000. It was attended by delegations from forty-three African states.[1] The second experts' session was convened in Tripoli from May 27 to 29, 2000. Delegations from forty-nine African countries attended the meeting.[2] Foreign ministers of OAU member states met between May 31 and June 2, 2000, to examine the work of the experts and to resolve the outstanding issues on which the experts failed to reach agreement. Delegations from fifty-one African states attended the Ministerial Conference.[3] Heads of African states met in Lomé in July 2000 to approve the outcome of the negotiation.

THE STATE OF PLAY

Delegates were supposed to negotiate a legal instrument of the AU based on parameters set by the Sirte Declaration. The negotiators were to arrive at a legal framework that took into "account the Charter of the OAU and the Treaty establishing the African Economic Community."[4] The instrument that the negotiators were to agree on was intended to reflect "the ultimate objectives of the Charter of . . . [the OAU] and the provisions of the Treaty establishing the African Economic Community."[5] They were also supposed to provide institutional structure to "accelerate the process of implementing the Treaty establishing the African Economic Community."[6] In addition, negotiators were mandated to reach an agreement on ways to "strengthen . . . and consolidate . . . the Regional Economic Communities."[7] The Sirte Declaration set a deadline for completing the negotiation. The negotiators were asked to submit the draft legal instrument to the Thirty-Sixth Ordinary Session of OAU/Fourth Ordinary Session of the AEC meeting of the Assembly "for appropriate action."[8]

NEGOTIATION POSITIONS

With the exception of the Libyan Delegation, none of the representatives provided written submission articulating its positions. Instead, delegations verbally presented their states' positions on the critical issues. This is, perhaps, unsurprising because African states seldom use the written approach in dealing with issues and negotiating agreement at the OAU level. It appeared, however, from rapporteurs' reports that the positions of delegations were identical with the stands their heads of state had taken during the last two OAU Summit discussions on African unity.[9] Delegates' positions reflected either the statist/sovereigntist ideas or the continental federal union paradigm. Some delegations were of the view that the AU should be a political union. Nine delegations supported Libya's claim that the AU should be a continental federal union.[10] Senegal and Mali wanted the structure of the federal union to reflect the American model, while Libya felt it should be a hybrid of the American and Soviet models.

The majority of the delegations were, however, of the view that the AU should be an intergovernmental forum and must continue the coordinating work of the OAU.[11] Some of the delegations that felt the proposed union should be an intergovernmental agency suggested that the AU should be designed to help African states coordinate their international activities on economic and security issues.[12] These delegations wanted the AU structures to differ only slightly from those of the OAU. Some suggested it should be modeled along the lines of regional organizations, such as SADC and ECOWAS. But a surprisingly large number of delegations felt there was no need to develop any new rules, institutional structures, and decision-making procedures.[13] Ten delegations out of the status quo wanted the AU to have institutional structures and functional powers identical to those of the OAU and the AEC.[14] They also wanted the AU to pursue its work using the legal framework of the OAU Charter and the AEC treaty. In their view, the OAU Charter and the AEC treaty provided sufficient legal instrument for coordinating African states' activities in the areas of economics and security. The delegations were of the view that the negotiation should concentrate on finding ways to integrate the AEC treaty and the OAU Charter into a single legal framework.

Another sticking point during the negotiation had to do with the authority that would be delegated to the AU. Six delegations were of the view that the AU should have powers over member states on important issue areas such as security and defence, economic and foreign policy, and governance.[15] However, ten delegations felt member states of the AU should retain all core sovereign prerogatives except that of humanitarian intervention.[16] They felt state sovereignty should not be used as a shield to abuse human rights and, therefore, suggested that the AU should be empowered to interfere with state sovereignty in order to deal with humanitarian crises. About a dozen delegations disagreed.[17] They did not want to entertain the idea of humanitarian intervention, and wanted the proposed union to promote the principle of noninterference in the internal affairs of member states. They were of the view that the provision for humanitarian intervention would be used by outside forces as an excuse to disturb African governments.

NEGOTIATION PROCESS AND OUTCOME

The first meeting of experts was relatively successful. Delegates reached agreement on a thirty-four-article preliminary draft text (henceforth, the Experts Text). The delegates reached consensus on all articles in the Experts

Text except two. The outstanding articles dealt with the ultimate objective of the AU and its relationship with other African international institutions. A second meeting of experts was convened to resolve the outstanding issues but failed to break the deadlock. Some delegates even questioned the legality of the text developed at the first meeting of experts, and the authority of the experts to make decisions on behalf of member states. A decision was therefore made to discontinue the discussions at the level of experts, and to refer the outstanding issues, together with the text, to foreign ministers of OAU member states for appropriate action.

The ministers adopted the Experts Text, and upheld decisions made at the meetings of experts. They agreed that the ultimate goal of the AU was to integrate African states into a confederal union. The ministers also agreed that the legal instrument of the AU should supersede the OAU Charter and the AEC treaty. The Ministerial Conference decided to create a working group, under the chairmanship of Mali, to use the Experts Text to develop a draft treaty of the AU that reflected the agreement reached. The thirty-two-articles draft CA (henceforth, the Mali Text) that the fifteen-member Mali Committee submitted was closer to sovereigntist ideas than to a confederation. The Mali Text contained many sovereigntist principles, including a clause that would have prevented the proposed union from interfering in the internal affairs of its members. Aside from some minor and semantic differences, the Mali Text and the OAU Charter were identical. The Mali Text also had many structural and stylistic problems. Moreover, some articles of the Mali Text were ambiguous. The ministers therefore referred the Mali Text to the OAU Drafting Team to revise it to reflect the agreement the Ministerial Conference had reached on the ultimate objective of the AU. [18]

The revised draft CA developed by the Drafting Team and submitted to the Ministerial Conference was completely different from the Mali Text. It contained many new articles that were consequential. [19] It proposed to commit the AU to interfering and intervening in the internal affairs of its members under certain conditions. [20] It also proposed to make the AU a collective security organization. The Drafting Team's treaty included a provision that prohibited member states from using military force or threatening to use military force against each other. Some of the new articles were also development oriented. The draft treaty proposed to make the AU promote equitable and balanced economic development and to reject undemocratic changes of governments in Africa. The document was unanimously approved, and signed as a binding agreement by twenty-five African heads of state and government and two foreign ministers on behalf of their countries at the Thirty-Sixth Ordinary Session of the OAU and Fourth Ordinary Session of the AEC of the Assembly of Heads of State and Government held in Lomé on July 11, 2000. What accounted for the negotiation outcome? The sections below provide a detailed explanation. They show that Africrats were largely responsible for the success of the negotiation and the selection of the ambitious mechanisms.

AFRICRATS' ROLE IN SOLVING THE COOPERATION PROBLEM

Africrats were instrumental in the definition of the negotiation problem. Senior Africrats developed a draft legal instrument that they felt reflected the parameters provided in the Sirte Declaration. They submitted the draft text to the meeting of experts, and succeeded in persuading the delegations to conduct their meeting on the basis of ideas in the text. In other words, Africrats provided policy options for the delegations to resolve the cooperation problem. Africrats also provided directional leadership during the meeting of experts. They were also instrumental in finding solutions to break the negotiation deadlock at the Ministerial Conference. More important, Africrats extensively revised the draft text that Mali submitted. They deleted some of the key conservative principles, such as the one on noninterference in the internal affairs of African states. They also added many new, consequential, institutional mechanisms to the ministerial text.

AFRICRATS' ROLE IN FINDING POLICY SOLUTIONS TO THE COOPERATION PROBLEM

African leaders and the Sirte Declaration originally assigned gave Africrats a peripheral role in the negotiation of the elements of the AU. They were to provide administrative support only to African foreign ministers during the negotiation processes. Following the OAU's administrative procedure, however, the foreign ministers mandated the OAU Secretariat to convene a meeting of experts of OAU member states to translate the Sirte Declaration into a draft AU legal instrument for their consideration. Africrats took advantage of this delegated authority to translate the broadly agreed parameters in the Sirte Declaration into a fully fledged founding treaty of the AU. The text obviously reflected the institutional preferences of senior Africrats. The official reason Africrats used to justify their decision to develop the founding treaty—a task that no one had explicitly asked them to undertake—was that they wanted to speed up the negotiation processes and the development of the legal instrument.[21] They argued that the treaty would, at a minimum, reduce the time the experts would have to subsequently spend debating the meaning of phrases in the Sirte Declaration. It appears, however, that some of the senior Africrats had other motives. They turned the Declaration into a founding treaty at least in part because some senior Africrats wanted to use the draft treaty to shape the discussion and the outcome of the negotiation.

As part of the process of turning the Declaration into a preliminary draft treaty, the Secretary-General asked a team of consultants to develop a legal instrument based on the Sirte document for the consideration of senior Africrats. The consultants recommended that the AU should be created as part of "a pyramidal structure of continental organizations in which the OAU provides the framework and the AEC and the AU becomes it [*sic*] pillars."[22] The AU and the AEC, in the view of the consultant, should be made to perform specialized tasks. They recommended that the AEC should concentrate solely on economic issues and that the AU should be made to "coordinate and harmonize" African states' policies in the areas of foreign policy and diplomacy, defence and security, management of internal conflicts, and science and medicine.[23] The consultants also proposed that the AU should operate within the boundaries of the principle of noninterference in the internal affairs of member states.[24]

Some senior Africrats were not impressed with the consultants' recommendations. Senior Africrats at the political department, legal affairs, and the EDECO were particularly unreceptive to the suggestion that the AU should coexist with the AEC and the OAU. They felt the financial burden involved in operating three separate institutions would discourage African states from ever agreeing to establish the AU.[25] They (i.e., senior Africrats) were also concerned that member states would not provide adequate resources to manage the institutions, even if they agreed to establish them.

Many senior Africrats were particularly unhappy with the consultants' suggestion that the AU should be made to defend the principle of noninterference in the internal affairs of member states. A top-ranking Africrat at the political department felt the suggestion "was a step backwards," and would have undermined efforts they had made to strengthen the OAU's capacity to deal with conflicts.[26] A former acting director of the peace and security department claimed that the recommendation came as a shock, as many of the consultants were aware of senior OAU officials' stands (positions) on the principle of noninterference. They knew, he argued, that "we wanted the principle of non-interference revoked, amended or removed from OAU Charter. We have long held the view that the principle had constrained our ability to craft comprehensive security architecture to drive the peace and security agenda of the continent."[27] Senior Africrats at legal affairs felt the consultants paid insufficient attention to human rights issues, and that they also failed to draw insights from the African Charter on Human and Peoples' Rights.[28]

Key Africrats' dissatisfaction with the work of the consultants influenced the Secretary-General to put together a team, headed by the legal counselor, to examine the draft treaty and to develop a new preliminary draft text. The thirty-two-article draft founding treaty (henceforth, the Africrats' Text) was a synthesis of the OAU Charter, the AEC treaty, the African Charter on Human and Peoples' Rights and the MCPMR.[29] The team also tried to consolidate important decisions taken within the framework of the OAU, such as the "Resolution on Unconstitutional Changes of Governments." It appeared that the team's goal was to provide institutional mechanisms for the AU to perform the responsibilities of the OAU and the AEC. The team also tried to shorten the implementation period of the AEC treaty. Unlike the OAU Charter and the AEC, the Africrats' Text placed much emphasis on both high and low politics. There were articles that sought to make the proposed union a collective security- and development-oriented organization. The team, however, tried not to introduce radical measures. While it provided a basis for the AU's Assembly to authorize intervention for humanitarian purposes, it also prohibited outside powers (i.e., states outside of continental Africa) from interfering in the internal affairs of African states. The Secretary-General accepted the Text, and decided to forward it for the consideration of the experts.

BUILDING A COALITION FOR THE AFRICRATS' TEXT

Africrats set out to persuade African governments to adopt the document as the solution to the cooperation problem. The first move Africrats made to market ideas in the text to African governments was to consult selected African mission staffs (i.e., ambassadors and senior bureaucrats) in Addis Ababa. Africrats were aware that the text had a better chance of being adopted if African diplomats in Addis Ababa supported it. The Secretary-General's cabinet and the office of the Assistant Secretary-General for Political Affairs, together with the OAU legal counselor, held a series of consultative meetings with selected diplomats—ambassadors, heads of missions, and directors of political affairs—in African embassies in Addis Ababa prior to the meeting of experts.[30] Senior Africrats held two consultative meetings each with Algeria, Botswana, Egypt, Lesotho, Libya, Mali, Nigeria, Senegal, and South Africa embassy officials.[31] Senior Africrats consulted these particular mission staffs because they felt their delegations would play the leadership role during the meetings of experts and ministers. The political affairs and the legal departments also informally discussed the draft treaty with Ghana, Côte d'Ivore, Malawi, Lesotho, Tanzania, and Zambia embassy officials. These informal discussions were meant to gauge the reaction to the draft of states whose leaders could be classified as neither strong sovereigntists nor federalists. Africrats thought those countries would be more receptive to the ideas in the text. Senior Africrats felt they would be able to take advantage of the six states' unrevealed preference for either the continental model or the statist form to persuade their delegations to support the draft treaty. The Secretary-General also tried to use informal channels to build a loose coalition involving mission staffs from Ghana, Lesotho, Malawi, and Tanzania to promote the draft treaty at the meetings of experts.[32]

Senior Africrats also felt that civil society support was needed to sell the draft treaty to member states. It was thought that the draft treaty stood a good chance of winning the support of member states if indigenous African civil society organizations and research institutions with continental orientation supported it. Africrats also thought they could use the consultation with civil society to show member states that nonstate actors and ordinary Africans had contributed to the development of the draft treaty. The cabinet of the Secretary-General and the Political and Legal Affairs departments discussed the draft treaty with about half a dozen carefully selected civil society organizations.[33] Africrats emphasized the participation of research-oriented civil society organizations, such as the South African Institute for Security Studies, the African Research Consortium, and the African Capacity Building Foundation, in the consultative processes in part because they wanted to use the research institutions to corroborate the authenticity of the ideas in the draft treaty in the presentation of the document to experts and ministers.

AFRICRATS AND THE EXPERTS NEGOTIATION

Africrats influenced the direction and outcome of experts' negotiations. They presented their draft treaty to the experts as the negotiation Text. Rather than giving the experts the chance to discuss and interpret the Sirte Declaration in their own way, the Secretary-General persuaded them to conduct the meeting on the basis of the draft treaty submitted by Africrats. Notwithstanding the Libyan Delegation's protest that the document could not form the basis of the meeting of experts because it was "not commensurate with the expectation embodied in the Sirte Declaration," the experts "agreed to proceed to examine the [Africrats'] Text."[34] The decision by the experts to conduct the meeting on the basis of the Africrats' Text was significant, not least because it limited the range of issues that the experts could consider, but it also gave Africrats the opportunity to shape the kind of institutional mechanisms that delegations could select to constitute the AU. It at least reduced the possibility of selecting, for instance, another OAU. It also set the parameters of the debate the experts could engage in. Indeed, the decision to use the Africrats' Text meant that the experts were negotiating on the basis of preferences of Africrats rather than of African states.

PROVIDING DIRECTIONAL LEADERSHIP FOR EXPERTS' NEGOTIATIONS

Aside from using the Text to limit the choices of the experts, the Secretary-General intentionally set out to use his opening address to the first meeting of experts to narrow further the range of issues that the experts could discuss. He succeeded in doing so by making two significant moves. First, the Secretary-General tried to condition the experts to think that "the spirit of the Sirte Declaration" was to develop a new institution, superior to the OAU and the AEC. Second, he used the idea of Pan-Africanism to try to make the experts feel that history might not be kind to them if they failed to agree on a strong and a powerful union that could advance the integration of the African continent. Experts, he argued, had "a unique and significant opportunity in the history of the continent and the support of ordinary men and women from different parts of the continent" to help the African continent "transcend linguistic, ideological, ethnic and national differences."[35] They would, on the other hand, be seen by generations to come as major contributors to Africa's problem if they failed to recommend to the leaders an institutional framework of "superior format" to that of the OAU. [36] He then laid out three issues he felt the experts' meeting should explore. It was his view that the meeting should look at ways to develop institutional structures that would bring African states closer together. He also felt the experts needed to agree on a legal instrument that would overcome the limitations of the OAU. It was essential, he suggested, for the experts to provide the required tools that the AU needed to deal with Africa's economic and security challenges. Though the extent to which the Secretary-General's address shaped the thinking of delegates is unclear, he at least succeeded in making the delegations aware that "generations would hold them responsible for Africa's disunity should they fail to give the AU the tools to promote integration of African states."[37] This was significant in the sense that it made the experts take a cautious approach and a less radical stand, as "none of the Delegates wanted his or her state to be the scapegoat."[38]

The Secretary General address also provided a basis for the OAU Legal Counsellor Ben Kioko to use the presentation of the Text to delineate in a more concrete way agenda items for the experts meeting. He called on the experts to examine the articles in the Text, and to pay particular attention to articles on the legal nature of the proposed union and its relationship with the OAU and the AEC, and on the institutional powers of the AU vis-à-vis national sovereignty and the ultimate objective of the union. The meeting of experts proceeded exactly the way the legal counselor outlined. After the lengthy opening addresses, which prompted the chairperson of the session ambassador Smaïl Chergui to urge "delegates to make precise comments and put forward concrete proposals," the experts "agreed to proceed to examine the Text Article by Article."[39]

PROVIDING INTELLECTUAL LEADERSHIP

In addition, Africrats used entrepreneurial skills to influence the experts to adopt ideas in their Text. Africrats used their intellectual skills to shape revealed institutional preferences of delegates, and to influence the perceptions of the experts on the institutional mechanism that would be good for Africa. Africrats also tried to condition the experts to think that adopting ideas from the draft treaty to form the basis of the AU was a good thing. They sought to persuade the experts to reject proposals drawn from sovereigntists and the continental schools. The Secretary-General and his cabinet officials, the legal department, and the political affairs department were the key players in the process of shaping the thinking of the experts. Africrats used arguments to discredit the two traditional ideational frameworks—statism and continental unionism—that shaped the way African elites think about interstate cooperation and also to demonstrate the superiority of ideas in their Text.

An important objective of the Secretary-General's decision to address the experts at the first meeting of experts was to show that the positions of the sovereigntists and the continental federalists were extreme, and that those who continued to think in those terms are not helping the course of Africa.[40] Focusing on the demands articulated in the proposal submitted by the Libya Delegation, although no reference to the document was made, the Secretary-General argued that it was unhelpful to demand that the AU be a continental government. The demand was unhelpful in part because the conditions necessary for creating a continental federal union did not exist, and in part because the time frame that the leaders provided for developing the legal instrument for the AU was insufficient for exploring the political unity question in any meaningful way.

The Secretary-General also sought to portray the statists' position as another extreme view. Using Africa's economic and security challenges, the Secretary-General argued that the past forty years has shown that none of the African states could develop on its own. Moreover, none of the African states possessed the institutional structures to compete favorably in the international system. It was, therefore, imperative for African governments to develop a strong continental institutional framework to assist their states to compete in the international political economy. Creating another OAU, he felt, would not be in the interest of any African state. He therefore urged the experts to provide the AU "with sufficient powers and authority" so that it can "act with vigour and dynamism" in the collective interests of African people.[41]

Having challenged the two dominant ideas and created uncertainty in the minds of the experts, the Secretary-General then went on to show that the draft treaty contained appropriate and substantive ideas and institutional mechanisms that African states needed. As part of the process to demonstrate the quality of the ideas in the Africrats' Text, Salim went to great lengths to underscore the fact that the treaty was developed after the OAU Secretariat had examined and reviewed consultancy studies and held extensive consultations with member states and civil society. The Secretary-General therefore urged the experts to accept the draft treaty because the ideas in it had the broad support of the political elites and had also "captured the popular imagination of ordinary Africans in the various parts of the continent."[42] Thus, the Secretary-General used the consultation with the civil society groups to further verify the appropriateness of the ideas in the Text.

The reward Africrats got for their entrepreneurial efforts was that at least 40 percent of the articles in the Text were adopted without any amendment. Nearly 60 percent (i.e., nineteen out of the thirty-two articles) were amended. But, as one of the experts pointed out, the "majority of the amendments were minor. They were procedural in nature."[43] In fact, with the exception of a clause and two articles that were controversial, the experts seemed to agree with almost everything in the draft Text. Though the majority of the delegates were comfortable with the clause that gave the Assembly the right to authorize intervention for humanitarian purposes, they insisted that there should be another clause to prevent individual states from interfering in the internal affairs of other African states. In other words, delegates were of the view that states could interfere in the internal affairs of African states only through the multilateral framework of the AU. The clause on intervention in the Africrats' Text was amended accordingly. The two articles that turned out to be controversial were Articles 23 and 2. Article 23 sought to provide a framework for civil society to interact with the policy organs of the AU. Article 2 dealt with "the legal nature and the structure of the proposed African Union and its relationship with the OAU and the AEC." The debate on Article 23 was sparked by Libya's suggestion that Article 23 was "not necessary since there would be a parliament, which would represent the views of all ordinary Africans." But Ghana, Tanzania, and Lesotho defended the inclusion of the Article, arguing that the meeting "should take a futuristic view of the Union and allow African civil society a consultative voice in the activities of the Union." At the end of the lengthy debate, Article 23 was maintained.

Delegations from six countries—Burkina Faso, Libya, Mali, Niger, Senegal, and Sudan—ignited the controversy over Article 2. They felt its formulation did not reflect "expectations embodied in the Sirte Declaration" or provide the legal basis for the formation "of a strong institution" that would "transcend the existing institutional framework."[44] They therefore proposed that a new article that would give strong powers to the proposed union be developed. The Libyan Delegation proposed a formulation that would have effectively committed African leadership to a continental union government structure. Others, however, including the Kenyan, Ugandan, and South African delegations, found the Libyan Delegation's reformulation unacceptable. While the Botswanian, Ghanaian, and Tanzanian delegations defended the formulation proposed by the Africrats' Text, others provided alternatives.[45] Following nearly two hours of debate, the experts decided to "adopt a formulation based on the wording in the Sirte Declaration, and to refer the matter to higher authorities for a political decision."[46]

The relative ease with which Africrats influenced the experts to adopt ideas in their Text made senior officials at the legal department and the office of the Assistant Secretary-General for Political Affairs think there was room to push through ideas that were even more consequential. The Assistant Secretary-General for Political Affairs and the legal counselor felt they should have developed a number of articles that limited sovereign prerogatives of African states on human rights, conflict resolution, and humanitarian intervention.[47] The Secretary-General for Political Affairs, Said Djinnit, in particular, was disappointed that the Text did not contain articles that give the AU strong powers in the area of conflict resolution. The two senior Africrats therefore felt that the OAU Secretariat should convene a second meeting of experts so that they could push through some of the more controversial ideas excluded from the Text. In addition, some senior Africrats were also worried that the deadlock over Article 2 and the decision to refer the matter to the political leaders might derail the gains they had made. Some of the senior Africrats did not see the wisdom of asking political leaders to determine the nature of the AU. One of them provided more insights:

> The idea of referring the issue to the political leaders was not the solution, since the lack of clear specification of the exact nature of the AU was deliberate. They did not know the exact form the union should take and, therefore, left it for the experts to fill in the details. The experts' decision to send the same issue back for a political decision was, in our opinion, a non-starter.[48]

AFRICRATS' ROLE IN THE EXPERTS' SEARCH FOR A SOLUTION TO THE DEADLOCK

Senior Africrats who attended the meeting decided, after consultations, to hold another session of experts to find ways to resolve the outstanding issues. Though senior Africrats agreed to use the deadlock to justify the need for a second meeting of experts, as indicated earlier, they wanted to use the session to encourage the experts to provide strong powers for the AU to promote human rights and maintain continental peace. They decided to convene the meeting of experts three days prior to the Ministerial Conference. Africrats' decision to call the second meeting of experts so close to the Ministerial Conference was influenced by two factors. The consensus among Africrats was that the hard work was over. In addition, senior Africrats were of the view that it would not be difficult to find a solution to the deadlock.

As soon as Said Djinnit indicated to delegates that the General Secretariat "intended to convene a second meeting of experts," the Libyan Delegation offered to host the session.[49] The eleven Libyan delegates felt that hosting the meeting would allow them to use the privileges usually given to the host state to influence the experts to revise the Experts Text to reflect "what Libya thought was best for Africa."[50] Unlike the first meeting, in which the Secretary-General and the legal counselor played the key entrepreneurial roles, Said Djinnit provided the directional leadership for the second experts meeting. Thus, for instance, Said Djinnit gave the Secretary-General opening address, which he used to outline the outstanding issues. Because arguing was the currency of the first meeting of experts, the chair of the meeting, in consultation with the Bureau and Said Djinnit, agreed to "hold a general exchange of views relating to the outstanding issues."[51] The open debate was meant to help delegates reach common understanding on issues that were yet to be resolved, and to give each delegation the chance to present its views.

In the course of the debate, the Libyan leader, Muammar Gaddafi, invited the heads of the delegations to a separate meeting to inform them that they should not conduct the meeting on the basis of the Text developed at the first meeting of experts, and should restart the negotiation.[52] Gaddafi provided two reasons. He claimed that the first meeting of experts "deviated from its original mandate as a technical organ" charged with the task of translating the Sirte Declaration into a legal instrument.[53] The experts had no mandate to discuss any other Text except the Sirte Declaration. The experts' decision to work on the basis of the Africrats' Text rather than the Sirte Declaration, he submitted, meant that the first meeting "did not carry out its work in conformity with the Sirte" mandate.[54] He therefore asked the heads of delegations to set aside the Text agreed upon during the first meeting. The Experts Text should be discarded, he also argued, because its content did not reflect the spirit and letter of the Sirte Declaration. The ideas in the Experts Text did not aim at "establishing a strong and effective Union as recommended by the Sirte Declaration, but rather at revitalizing the OAU."[55] Gaddafi therefore urged the heads of delegations to restart the negotiation. It is interesting that he requested that the working document for the new negotiation should consist of the Sirte Declaration and the proposal for the establishment of a United States of Africa.

Though some of the heads of delegations felt Gaddafi had a point, many delegates were unwilling to restart the negotiation. Two factors accounted for the reluctance of many of the experts to do so. The way Gaddafi presented the case made some of them feel they did not "know what they were doing."[56] More important, however, the majority of the experts were of the view that restarting the process would undermine the working procedure of OAU meetings; it would set a new precedent for delegates to challenge an issue they did not agree with but which commanded a broad consensus. As a way out, the Burkina Faso, Malawi, Mali, and Sudan delegations, who felt that Libya had a case, proposed to the experts not that they restart the negotiation, but that they "enrich the Text developed at the first meeting" with insights from Libya's document.[57] But some delegations, including Nigerian, South African, Ugandan, Algerian, and Guinean, were unprepared to discuss Libya's proposal. Their contention was that the meeting was called to discuss outstanding issues, and there was no need to consider any other proposal. They also submitted that every delegation, including Libya, had had the opportunity at the first meeting to present its case, and it would be unfair to other delegations to give Libya another chance. To find a way out of the deadlock, Said Djinnit proposed to the chair of the meeting that they suspend proceedings to allow delegates to hold consultations with their governments on the working document of the meeting.[58]

Many delegations returned after the consultations to inform the chair that they had received the mandate to discuss only the Text prepared during the first meeting and, "as experts, they could not do otherwise."[59] Libya, however, replied that the meeting could not work on the basis of the Experts Text, because it "had watered-down the Union" proposed in the Sirte Declaration.[60] The Libyan Delegation's shift from the original argument Gaddafi had used to justify his call for a restart of the negotiation, together with the inability of their experts to demonstrate in a persuasive fashion that the Experts Text did not reflect the Sirte Declaration, influenced some delegations that had supported Libya's position to now distance themselves from Libya's request. The Senegalese and Malian delegations, two of the key ideational partners, submitted that putting aside the documents prepared in Addis Ababa would mean that many delegations had serious reservations about the Text, which was not currently the case.[61] The delegation suggested that the meeting should be dissolved, and the matter "referred to the Ministerial Conference to take appropriate decision" in the absence of a consensus.[62] Just before the vote for adjournment was held, "the Assistant Secretary General in Charge of Political Affairs (i.e., Said Djinnit) proposed that the deliberations should be suspended for the second time to allow for new consultations to be held at the level of the Bureau" of the session.[63] He also proposed to the experts that they "include Chairmen of the Regional Economic Communities" in the consultative process.[64] The experts accepted the proposal, and appointed Libya, Algeria, Gabon, Lesotho, Ethiopia, Mali, Djibouti, Equatorial Guinea, Mozambique, and Kenya to carry out the consultations.

Said Djinnit requested consultations at the level of the Bureau because senior Africrats wanted to give the leadership of the meeting the chance to examine an idea they had discussed, and thought it might provide a way to break the deadlock.[65] Senior Africrats who attended the meeting felt the majority of the delegations would accept a proposal that would commit the AU to promote a confederal union in Africa within a fifty-year period. They thought the Bureau Session was the best place to hold initial discussions on the proposal. The view was that agreement on the proposal during the consultation would go a long way to break the deadlock. Africrats' optimistic assessment of the decision of the Bureaus was based on the fact that delegates usually do not oppose issues that command a broad consensus at the Bureau level. The Bureau accepted the confederation proposal. [66]

Except for the Libyan and Kenyan representatives, who were not entirely convinced that the proposal from Africrats was good, the rest of the delegates who attended the Bureau meeting felt "it was a brilliant proposal."[67] Even so, the Libyan and Kenyan representatives found it difficult to oppose it at the Bureau. Because Mali leaders had on many occasions called on African leaders to establish a confederation, the Libyan representatives felt they would be setting themselves on a collision course with the Mali Delegation should they oppose it. They also thought that opposing it might create the impression that Libya was trying to be "a spoiler."[68] Such an impression, as Salem Natng of the Libyan embassy in Addis Ababa pointed out, would have "given a legitimate reason for many Delegations to be hostile towards our cause."[69] The fifty-year time frame provided as the period for the AU to evolve into a confederal structure put the Kenyan representative in a rhetorical trap because Kenya's political leaders had repeatedly claimed that Kenyans would want to be part of a United Africa in the future. The fifty-year benchmark meant that the representative could not argue that the time was not ripe for the proposal. The obvious option was for him to indicate that Kenyan officials did not subscribe to the Pan-African vision of a United Africa. The representative was, however, unprepared to take that route. The absence of formal opposition to the confederation proposal during the consultative process encouraged the chair of the Bureau to recommend it to the meeting of experts. Acting on the Bureau's recommendation, the experts decided to revise the Experts Text accordingly. The experts also agreed to draw insights from the Libya document to enrich the Text.[70]

The Libyan Delegation was dissatisfied with the experts' decision. The delegation felt the confederation proposal was not ambitious enough. The head of the delegation also thought the fifty-year period was too long. The reservation, notwithstanding, the Libyan Delegation did not oppose the proposal formally during the experts' discussion. The delegation knew that to do so would break one of the cardinal decision-making norms of the OAU—the expectation that no delegation would formally oppose an issue that has commanded broad support at the Bureau level during its consideration at the Committee of the Whole—if it had formally opposed the proposal. Fearing it might be ostracized, the Libyan Delegation decided not to oppose the proposal. To give Libyan officials the opportunity to express their opposition to the confederation proposal without breaking OAU's decision-making norm, and more significant, to give the Libyan Delegation the space to persuade African leaders to create a United States of Africa instead of a confederation, the delegation requested that the experts refer the issue to the Ministerial Conference to determine the ultimate goal of the AU. Libya's request seemed to be a rushed move, as a delegate who is now the head of mission at the Nigerian embassy in Addis Ababa explained:

> The consensus at the Bureau was a massive victory for Libya and friends. All that Libya needed to do was to allow the meeting to revise the draft Text to reflect the confederal proposal. None of the Delegations was prepared formally to raise objection. After securing this deal, the Libyan Delegation could then have advised their government to persuade the political leaders at the Ministerial and Assembly levels to enhance the powers given to the AU in the draft Text. It was that straightforward, but I guess they wanted everything at one go. [71]

Libya's request for the ministers to take over the negotiation played into the hands of about fifteen delegations, which also had their own reservations about the entire confederation idea. [72] The fifteen delegations felt the confederation proposal was overly ambitious, and might have given "too much power to AU Bureaucrats who may not use it responsibly." [73] Botswana, South Africa, and Madagascar felt the idea could be unpopular at home, and could, potentially, harm the image of their governments. The Nigerian Delegation also had serious "concerns" about the confederation proposal. [74] The delegation felt Nigeria and some few other states might be compelled to provide the bulk of the resources to implement the project. The delegation also feared that external actors might use the confederation to exercise undue influence over Nigeria. The delegations from the fifteen states therefore joined Libya to request that the experts meeting be dissolved, and the matter referred to the Ministerial Conference for a political decision. The South African Delegation formally requested that the issue, together with the Experts Text and rapporteurs' reports, be referred to the Ministerial Conference for its consideration. [75] South Africa also proposed that another Extraordinary Summit of the Assembly should be held in Sirte to decide on the nature and the ultimate goal of the AU should the Ministerial Conference fail to reach agreement. The request was accepted, and the reports of the meetings were forwarded for the consideration of the foreign ministers.

AFRICRATS AND THE MINISTERIAL CONFERENCE

Similar to the central role they played at the meeting of experts, senior Africrats were instrumental in finding solutions to the cooperation problem. They started a rigorous campaign, immediately following the dissolution of the session of experts, to persuade the ministers to adopt the Experts Text and the consensual agreement reached at the Bureau during the second meeting of experts. Salim, Djinnit, and Kioko held a series of consultative meetings with a number of delegates to the Ministerial Conference on May 30, 2000, with a view to persuading them to accept the Experts Text and the consensual agreement. The Africrats' campaign received a huge boost prior to the opening ceremony on May 31, 2000. After consultations between the Secretary-General and heads of state that Libya had invited to help Gaddafi sell the United States of Africa idea to the Ministerial Conference, the foreign ministers agreed to "work on the basis of the consensus agreed upon at the Bureau of the meeting of experts."[76] The stand of the leaders was reflected in the addresses they gave to the opening session of the Conference. Unlike Gaddafi, none of the leaders who addressed the opening session of the Ministerial Conference tried to persuade delegates to adopt the United States of Africa proposal.[77] Rather, they joined the Secretary-General in order to sell the consensual agreement reached at the meeting of experts and to draw the attention of the ministers to the negative impact their failure to reach an agreement would have on Africa's image and place in the world.

Due in large measure to the Africrats' campaign and the seven leaders' intervention, many delegations felt the proper thing to do was to work on the basis of the consensual agreement reached at the Bureau of experts. Some of the delegation also thought it was important to give the Libyan Delegation sufficient opportunities to present its case.[78] The first decision the Ministerial Conference took, after the addresses by the heads of state and the Secretary-General, was to hold a general debate and, in particular, to give the Libyan Delegation the chance to show that the Experts Text did not capture the spirit and letter of the Sirte Declaration. Following the rather repetitive submission of the Libyan case by Dr. Triki—the Secretary of the General Peoples' Committee for African Unity—and rebuttals of the argument by twenty-five other delegations, the ministers agreed to work on the basis of the agreement reached at the Bureau.[79] In response to a suggestion by the South African Delegation that another summit be organized to clarify the Sirte Declaration, the ministers agreed that the "Sirte Declaration is clear."[80] The Declaration, they agreed, proposed an organization whose creation requires a "radical rearrangement of the existing institutional structures" for cooperation in Africa.[81] In addition, the ministers affirmed Africrats' position that the Sirte Declaration provided that the AU should "evolve from the OAU Charter and the AEC Treaty into one strong institution."[82] They also affirmed the consensual agreement reached at the Bureau that the "ultimate objective of the Union should be a Union of African States or Confederation."[83] In the view of the ministers, the mandate of the negotiations was to agree on the nature and structures that would help African states establish the confederation. They therefore "decided to create a working group under the Chairmanship of Mali" to revise the Experts Text in order to plant the seed of the confederation.[84] The vice chairperson of the Ministerial Conference explained why Mali was selected to chair the working group:

> Normally, you will expect the host to chair such a meeting, but there were too many things that did not favour Libya. On one hand, many of the Foreign Ministers saw the Libyan Delegation as trying to push through a proposal of which they did not really have sufficient grasp. On the other hand, President Konaré and his Foreign Minister were seen in OAU political circles as leading intellectuals and technocrats, and many of us had enormous respect for them. Besides, Mali's contribution to the meeting of experts and the Ministerial Conference was such that it would have been a great injustice if the Malian Delegation had been overlooked in the selection of the chair. [85]

The thirty-two-article draft treaty (the Mali Text) that the Mali Committee submitted was a little conservative in outlook. It reflected the position of the sovereigntist more than the confederation idea that the experts and the ministers proposed. It did not give the slightest hint that the ultimate objective of the AU was confederation. The underlying principles and the functions of institutions provided for the AU in the Text were almost identical to those in the OAU Charter. Members of the Mali Committee also lifted the principle of "non-interference in the internal affairs of Member States" enshrined in the OAU Charter, and inserted it as one of the thirteen principles in the Mali Text. The dominant representation of the working group by delegations from the sovereigntist school accounted for the less ambitious nature of the Mali Text. Over 70 percent of the members of the committee had, at some point in the negotiation process, maintained a conservative position on the question of African unity. The bulk of the representatives on the Committee came from the fifteen delegations that were skeptical about the confederation proposal, and were instrumental in the abrupt dissolution of the second meeting of experts. Out of the fifteen members of the working group, only the Ghanaian, Lesotho, and Malian delegations had accepted the idea. Though the three delegations made the effort to recommend articles that were very ambitious, the other committee members used their numerical advantage to modify or reject them. The selection of Mali as the chair also limited the effectiveness of its representative on the Committee. The impartial role that the position of the chair required meant that Mali's representative on the Committee could not debate the statists in any meaningful manner.

Djinnit, Kioko, and a few middle-level Africrats who attended the sitting of the Committee for OAU Secretariat felt that the work of Mali Committee had reversed many of the gains they had made. Senior Africrats, together with other discontented members of the working group, mounted "a short but robust campaign" to persuade the ministers to revise the Mali Text.[86] To dissuade the ministers from adopting the Mali Text, Africrats made sure that delegates who were not part of the committee were made aware of the disconnection between the Mali Text and the consensus reached at the Ministerial Conference and the Bureau of experts. Africrats also discredited the ideational value of the Mali Text by exposing its numerous limitations. Senior Africrats at the legal department devoted much of their efforts to drawing the attention of the ministers to the inconsistencies in the Text and the vague wording of some of the articles. The legal counselor sought to show that the Mali Text was legally illiterate, though for diplomatic reasons he presented the case in a more nuanced way. Said Djinnit and his senior staff also tried hard to make the ministers aware that the Text failed to provide robust mechanisms for the AU to deal with important developmental challenges, such as conflict resolution and the maintenance of peace.

The reluctance of supporters of the Mali Text to respond to Africrats' criticisms of the document made it look worse than it was. It was, perhaps, unsurprising that little debate took place during the ministers' consideration of the Text before a decision was made to rewrite it. The Ministerial Conference, apparently convinced that the work of the Mali Committee was shoddy, decided to mandate the OAU Drafting Team to revise the Mali Text to reflect the consensual recommendations of the Ministerial Conference.[87] Members of the Drafting Team, whose work was closely supervised by the Secretary-General and other senior Africrats, made extensive revisions. Six of the changes proposed in the twenty-nine-article draft Constitutive Act (the draft CA) the Drafting Team submitted were consequential. The draft CA had no place for the principle of noninterference in internal affairs of AU members. However, it proposed to commit "Member States" to intervening in another state's internal affairs "in grave circumstances . . . and where the Assembly of the Union so decides."[88] The draft CA proposed to make AU member states "defend the African continent and its Member States in case of external aggression."[89] In other words, the draft CA proposed to make the AU a collective security organization. Provision was also made to prohibit "the use of force or threat to use force among Member States of the Union."[90] There was also a provision in the draft CA for AU member states to "request intervention from the Union in order to restore peace and security."[91] The draft CA also proposed to compel AU member states to "promote social justice . . . [and] balanced economic development."[92] Last, the CA proposed to make it obligatory for AU member states to "condemn and to reject unconstitutional changes of governments" in Africa.[93]

Though as many as a dozen delegations were not entirely convinced that the Drafting Team treaty was good for their states, the Ministerial Conference adopted it without major revision.[94] The ministers made only one noticeable change. They agreed to commit AU member states "to the establishment of a common defense policy for the African continent."[95] The OAU Legal Affairs Department was asked to develop an article to capture the decision, to "re-organize in logical and related clusters" the Articles, to improve "on the formulation" of specific Articles of the draft CA, and to submit the revised document to the OAU summit in Lomé in July 2000 for the consideration of African leaders.[96] The revised draft CA was unanimously approved and signed as a binding agreement in Lomé in July 2000 without any changes. The instrumental role Africrats played in the negotiation process explained why Jakkie Cilliers suggested the AU would have been less "progressive and ambitious had it not been for the fact that it was drafted in large measure by OAU bureaucrats."[97]

CONCLUSION

Much of the widely known scholarship on African politics and international relations does not acknowledge the independent political impact of Africa's supranational bureaucrats. Though the autonomous impact of supranational entities in Europe has been the subject of debate since the pioneering works of Ernst Haas, there is virtually no major inquiry into the role played by bureaucrats based at the regional or subregional levels in Africa. This chapter suggests that supranational bureaucrats in Africa do not perform merely functional roles for states, as the functionalists seem to think, nor are they mere servants of politicians, as the liberal intergovernmentalists maintain. They are autonomous political players.

The chapter showed that Africrats compelled African governments to commit their states within institutional mechanisms that many of them would otherwise have opted out of. Africrats provided the bulk, and certainly the more ambitious aspects, of the AU's constituents. The empirical data indicates that Africrats defined the negotiation problem, and constructed the legal meaning of the broad guidelines contained in the Sirte Declaration. They then used the reconstructed document to structure and direct the debates and negotiations of African experts. It was also used to set a limit on the menu of institutional options from which the experts could choose to create the AU. Africrats also used carefully chosen words to delegitimize the causal power of the policy solution that was derived mainly from any one of the paradigmatic frameworks that informed thinking on interstate cooperation in Africa, and to enhance the authority of their ideas. They also exploited OAU decision-making procedures and norms wherever possible to drive the state officials to accept their interpretation of and solutions to the cooperation problem. Africrats' entrepreneurial leadership compelled the states to adopt many of the ideas they provided. The CA that now contains rules, norms, decision-making procedures, and structures that will shape Africa's international politics for years to come was developed, in large measure, by Africrats. Africrats were successful in persuading African state leaders in part because the driving mechanism of the selection of AU institutional mechanisms was argument. This observation is at odds with the conventional IR account of international negotiations. Well-known IR works on international cooperation inform us that negotiation is a bargaining act. They tell us actors bargain to reach a compromise, which usually reflects the common denominator of interests of big governments involved in the negotiation process. The selection of the elements of the AU was certainly contrary to this received wisdom.

NOTES

1. The countries that sent delegations were: Algeria, Angola, Benin, Botswana, Burkina Faso, Burundi, Cameroon, Cape Verde, Central African Republic, Chad, Congo, DR Congo, Côte d'Ivoire, Djibouti, Egypt, Eritrea, Ethiopia, Gabon, Ghana, Guinea, Guinea Bissau, Kenya, Lesotho, Libya, Madagascar, Malawi, Mali, Mauritania, Mauritius, Mozambique, Namibia, Niger, Nigeria, Rwanda, Sahrawi Democratic Arab Republic, Senegal, Sierra Leone, South Africa, Sudan, Tanzania, Tunisia, Uganda, Zambia, and Zimbabwe. Absent were Comoros, Equatorial Guinea, Gambia, Liberia, São Tomé and Principe, Seychelles, Somalia, Swaziland and Togo. The Algerian Delegation chaired the Conference. Gabon, The Kingdom of Lesotho, Ethiopia, and Mali were first, second, and third Vice Chairs and Rapporteur, respectively. Together the five countries constituted the Bureau of the Session.

2. The countries that sent delegations were: Algeria, Angola, Benin, Botswana, Burkina Faso, Burundi, Cameroon, Cape Verde, Central African Republic, Chad, Comoros, Congo, DR Congo, Côte d'Ivoire, Djibouti, Egypt, Eritrea, Ethiopia, Equatorial Guinea, Gabon, Ghana, Gambia, Guinea, Guinea Bissau, Kenya, Lesotho, Liberia, Libya, Madagascar, Malawi, Mali, Mauritania, Mauritius, Mozambique, Namibia, Niger, Nigeria, Rwanda, Saharawi Democratic Arab Republic, Senegal, Sierra Leone, South Africa, Sudan, Tanzania, Togo, Tunisia, Uganda, Zambia and Zimbabwe. There was no delegation from São Tomé and Principe, Seychelles, Somalia, and Swaziland. The Bureau elected for the session was chaired by the Libyan delegation, and Mali was elected as the Rapporteur. Delegations from Algeria, Gabon, The Kingdom of Lesotho, and Ethiopia were elected as first, second, third, and fourth Vice Chairs, respectively.

3. The Kingdom of Lesotho chaired the Bureau. Ghana, Uganda, and Congo were the first, second, and third Vice Chairs, and Saharawi Arab Democratic Republic was the Rapporteur. These countries constituted the Bureau of the Session. Libya was elected to chair the working Session.

4. EAHG/Draft/Decl. (IV) Rev.1
5. EAHG/Draft/Decl. (IV) Rev.1
6. Ibid.
7. Ibid.
8. Ibid.
9. Organization of African Unity, "Report of the Meeting of Legal Experts and Parliamentarians on the Establishment of the African Union and the Pan-African Parliament" (Addis Ababa, April 2000); Organization of African Unity, "Report of the Second Meeting of Legal

Experts and Parliamentarians on the Establishment of the African Union and the Pan-African Parliament," (Addis Ababa, May 2000); Organization of African Unity, "Report of the Ministerial Conference on the Establishment of the African Union and the Pan-African Parliament" (Tripoli, May/June 2000). I did face-to-face interviews to clarify ambiguities in the reports and to supplement insights I gained from them.

10. Burkina Faso, Central African Republic, Liberia, Libya, Mali, Niger, Senegal, Sudan, and Togo delegations supported Libya's proposal.

11. Algeria, Angola, Botswana, Cameroon, Congo, Eritrea, Ethiopia, Gabon Ghana, Guinea Bissau, Guinea, Kenya, Lesotho, Malawi, Madagascar, Mauritius, Mozambique, Namibia, Nigeria, Rwanda, Tanzania, South Africa, and Uganda delegations held this view at the meeting.

12. Strong proponents of this idea were: Botswana, Eritrea, Ethiopia, Gabon, Ghana, Lesotho, Malawi, Mozambique, Namibia, Nigeria, Rwanda, Tanzania, Zambia, and South Africa.

13. Algeria, Angola, Benin, Burundi, Cameroon, Congo, DR Congo, Eritrea, Gabon, Guinea Bissau, Guinea, Kenya, Madagascar, Mauritania, Mauritius, Tunisia, and Uganda delegations preferred the status quo.

14. They were Benin, Burundi, Cameroon, DR Congo, Guinea, Kenya, Mauritania, Mauritius, Tunisia, and Uganda.

15. Burkina Faso, Central Africa Republic, Libya, Mali, Niger, and Senegal delegations held this view.

16. Botswana, Ghana, Lesotho, Mozambique, Nigeria, Rwanda, South Africa, Sierra Leone, Tanzania, and Zambia delegations made this point.

17. Algeria, Angola, Cameroon, Congo, Côte d' Ivoire, Eritrea, Gabon, Guinea Bissau, Guinea, Kenya, Madagascar, Mauritius, and Uganda vehemently opposed the idea of intervention.

18. Middle- and upper-level professional staffs at the OAU Secretariat constituted the Drafting Team.

19. Organization of African Unity, "The Draft Constitutive Act of the African Union" (Tripoli, June 2000).

20. Ibid., 6.

21. Kioko interview.

22. OAU Consultants on the Sirte Declaration, "The Draft Treaty Establishing the African Union" (Addis Ababa, February 2000); Organization of African Unity, "Report of the Meeting of Legal Experts and Parliamentarians," 5.

23. OAU Consultants on Sirte Declaration, "The Draft Treaty Establishing the African Union," 5. Six institutional organs, namely, Assembly of Heads of State and Government, Council of Foreign Ministers, Pan African Parliament, African Court of Justice, Ten-Member Commission, and Consultative Forum for civil society and nongovernmental organizations, were tasked with the responsibility of managing the AU's work.

24. Ibid., 5

25. Interview with Couaovi A. L. Johnson, Addis Ababa, July 29, 2005.

26. Mfasoni interview.

27. Interview with Sam Ibok, Addis Ababa, February 20, 2003.

28. Kioko interview.

29. Organization of African Unity, "The Draft Treaty Establishing the African Union" (Addis Ababa, April 2000); Organization of African Unity, "Report of the Meeting of Legal Experts and Parliamentarians," 4–8.

30. Johnson interview.

31. I should also point out that the Ethiopian government was also consulted.

32. The Secretary-General targeted senior mission staffs in the Ghana, Mali, and Tanzanian embassies in Addis Ababa and Ethiopian government officials. The Ghana, Mali, and Tanzania missions have been reliable partners of the Secretary-General for many years.

33. Adisa and Johnson interviews.

34. Organization of African Unity, "Report of the Meeting of Legal Experts and Parliamentarians," 5.

35. Salim Ahmed Salim, "Opening Address to the Meeting of Legal Experts and Parliamentarians on the Establishment of the African Union" (Addis Ababa, April 17, 2000), 2; Organization of African Unity, "Report of the Meeting of Legal Experts and Parliamentarians," 3.

36. Organization of African Unity, "Report of the Meeting of Legal Experts and Parliamentarians," 2.

37. Iyanda interview.

38. Interview with Doe Adjaho, Accra, June 8, 2005.

39. Organization of African Unity, "Report of the Meeting of Legal Experts and Parliamentarians," 5.

40. Johnson, Kioko, and Dirar interviews.

41. Salim, "Opening Address to the Meeting of Legal Experts and Parliamentarians," 2; Organization of African Unity, "Report of the Meeting of L

42. egal Experts and Parliamentarians," 33.

43. ; Adjaho interview.

44. Organization of African Unity, "Report of the Meeting of Legal Experts and Parliamentarians," 5.

45. Two alternative formulations seem to have attracted the attention of many delegates. The first proposal was that the experts should expand the formulation of Article 2 with a view to creating new functional institutions. The other formulation was that Article 2 should be amended to reflect the pyramid idea that the consultants recommended.

46. Organization of African Unity, "Report of the Meeting of Legal Experts and Parliamentarians," 6.

47. Fado interview.

48. Kioko interview.

49. Organization of African Unity, "Report of the Meeting of Legal Experts and Parliamentarians," 13.

50. Interview with Salem Natng, Addis Ababa, July 28, 2005.

51. Organization of African Unity, "Report of the Second Meeting of Legal Experts and Parliamentarians," 8.

52. Adjaho, Kioko, and Gbeho interviews.

53. Organization of African Unity, "Report of the Second Meeting of Legal Experts and Parliamentarians," 12.

54. Ibid.

55. Ibid., 15.

56. Iyanda interview.

57. Adjaho interview.

58. Adjaho, Kioko, and Iyanda interviews.

59. Organization of African Unity, "Report of the Second Meeting of Legal Experts and Parliamentarians," 13.

60. Ibid., 14.

61. Ibid., 15.

62. Ibid., 15.

63. Ibid., 16.

64. Ibid., 16.

65. Nfasoni, Johnson, and Kioko interviews.

66. Fado, Nfasoni, Johnson, and Kioko interviews.

67. Adjaho interview.

68. Natng interview.

69. Ibid.

70. Organization of African Unity, "Report of the Meeting of Legal Experts and Parliamentarians," 16.

71. Iyanda interview.

72. They were Algeria, Angola, Botswana, Cameroon, Egypt, Eritrea, Gabon, Guinea, Kenya, Madagascar, Malawi, Mauritius, Nigeria, South Africa, and Uganda.

73. Interview with Bisi Dara, Addis Ababa, September 28, 2005.

74. Iyanda interview.

75. Organization of African Unity, "Report of the Meeting of Legal Experts and Parliamentarians," 18.

76. Gbeho interview. The heads of state were Chad's Idriss Déby, Ghana's Jerry Rawlings, Liberia's Charles Taylor, Malawi's Bakili Muluzi, Mali's Alpha Konaré, Senegal's Abdoulaye Wade, and Sudan's Omar al-Bashir.

77. There is no record for Déby and Muluzi's addresses, and none of the delegates I interviewed remembered anything they said. I have therefore assumed that they did not address the Session.

78. Johnson, Gbeho, and Fado interviews.

79. While the general consensus is that the AU would have been different had Libya provided good diplomats, Libyan officials blamed Dr. Triki and the Peoples' Committee for African Unity for Libya's failure to persuade the ministers to create a strong AU.

80. CM/2162(LXXII); Organization of African Unity, "Report of the Ministerial Conference," 16.

81. Ibid.

82. Organization of African Unity, "Report of the Ministerial Conference," 17.

83. Ibid.

84. CM/2162(LXXII), 18. The working group was made up of fifteen delegations. Three delegations were selected to represent each of the five subregions. Ethiopia, Kenya, and Uganda delegations represented countries in East Africa; South Africa, Botswana, and Lesotho represented countries in the southern Africa region; East African countries were represented by Gabon, Cameroon, and Central African Republic; and Ghana, Mali, and Nigeria represented West African States.

85. Gbeho interview.

86. Johnson interview.

87. CM/2162(LXXII), 18. Members of the DT were OAU professional staffs working in such departments as Administrative and Human Resource Development, Conference and Events, and Legal Affairs of the OAU Secretariat.

88. CM/2162(LXXII), Annex I, 6; Organization of African Unity, "The Draft Constitutive Act of the African Union" (Tripoli, June 2000).

89. Ibid.

90. Ibid.

91. Ibid.

92. Ibid.

93. Ibid.

94. Algeria, Angola, Cameroon, Egypt, Eritrea, Gabon, Guinea, Kenya, Libya, Madagascar, Mauritius, and Uganda. Even the South African government and Nigeria were not pleased with the outcome. The Libyan government wrote to the legal department with a series of amendments. The legal department felt it did not have the mandate to carry out the request and, therefore, referred it to the Ministerial Conference in Lomé in 2001. See the General Secretariat, "Explanatory Note on the Draft Constitutive Act of the African Union" (Addis Ababa, June 2000). Governments of other disgruntled states, such as Kenya and Uganda, made no effort to change anything. Though some threatened not to sign the CA until a number of changes were made, they all signed the document.

95. African Union Non-Aggression and Common Defence Pact, adopted by the Fourth Ordinary Session of the Assembly, held in Abuja, Nigeria, on Monday, January 31, 2005, http://www.au.int/en/sites/default/files/AFRICAN_UNION_NON_AGGRESSION_AND_COMMON_DEFENCE_PACT.pdf .

96. CM/2162(LXXII). For instance, the Secretary-General asked for the mandate to redraft Article 13, which deals with the powers of the Council of Ministers, to make them legally sound. It also asked for a mandate redraft Article 14 to indicate the sectoral areas of competence of the Specialized Technical Committees.

97. Interview with Jakkie Cilliers, Ottawa, May 10, 2005.

II

Assessment of the Performance of African Union

Chapter Five

Promotion of Good Political Governance

INTRODUCTION

This chapter turns attention to the AU's attempts to promote and defend good political governance across the African continent. These efforts, intensified in the last ten years, have led to the AU creating and adopting innovative and homegrown democracy promotion and defence norms, benchmarks, and institutional structures that focus on African governance challenges. These measures were consolidated in the African Governance Charter that came into force on February 15, 2013. The chapter assesses the performance of the AU in enhancing good political governance on the African continent, arguing that although the AU has introduced innovative, game changing, relevant, and paradigmatic governance ideas, the union has been less successful in making African government integrate them into national policies and legislations. In addition, the AU has been unable to attract funding from the donor community for the governance ideas and has also not been able to make these ideas and institutions work effectively and efficiently. Overall, the record of the AU in promoting good political governance in Africa has been average at best and decidedly poor at times.

The above-outlined insights are demonstrated in five sections. The first section explores the broader orientation that guides the AU governance work and the extent to which the broader idea is novel, relevant to priority stakeholders like African governments, generates money for the AU, and is effective and efficient in addressing the peculiar African governance problems. The second section critically examines the rules the AU has developed in the area of governance and the extent to which the rules are novel, relevant to critical stakeholders, financially viable, and effective in dealing with African governance challenges. In addition, the section documents the level of efficiency of AU governance rules. The third section analyzes the AU's policies on political governance along the novelty-efficiency continuum. The fourth section shows the level of the AU's success in translating its governance ideas into norms and whether these norms are new, effective, and efficient in addressing African governance problems. The final section explores the performance of the decision-making structures that the AU has developed to promote political governance across the African continent.

WORLDVIEW

Nature: The AU has introduced at least two paradigmatic political governance ideas into the African international system. These are standardization of democratic principles and understanding across the African continent and the adoption of a charter that seeks to monitor governance performance of AU member states. The push by the AU to provide a common frame of reference for democracy has gradually and steadily led to the emergence of a region-wide consensus around the meaning and content of democracy. A broad agreement seems to have emerged within the political class that democracy in the African context should reflect a representative form of government similar to those found in European settler societies. The emergence of this conception of democracy is remarkable because since independence African governments have maintained that democracy is both culturally and context driven, and that every state in Africa reserves the right to develop its own brand of democracy. This belief was strong and internalized to the extent that the Assembly of the OAU, in the midst of the third wave of democracy, specifically made a declaration affirming that every state in Africa has "the right [. . .] to determine [. . .], the system of democracy on the basis of their socio-cultural values."[1] In the bureaucratic corridors of the OAU, it was considered taboo to use the phrases *representative government* or *liberal democracy* because they were considered Western and imperial ideas. And as an anticolonial and anti-imperialist organization, the OAU could not be used as a vehicle to promote imperial discourse and agenda. Practices and procedures such as elections, political parties, and free press, which are used in Western democracies to encourage participation in political processes, were seen as divisive and alien to African cultures.[2]

Member states of the OAU were encouraged to use other means to encourage good political governance. The preferred phrase used in the practice of Pan-Africanism to talk about the promotion of good political governance was *popular participation in government*. Thus, for instance, when the then Secretary-General of the OAU, Salim Ahmed Salim, felt it was necessary for the OAU to adopt a charter to promote and defend good political governance, he had to use the codename *popular participation* rather than *democracy* as the title for the document. The OAU Charter adopted by African leaders during the OAU summit in Addis Ababa in Ethiopia in July 1990 would not have seen the light of the day if it had *liberal democracy* in the title. He even made a calculated effort to avoid the "d" word in talking about the document. He had to sell it as a document that would "ensure the involvement of all including in particular women and youth in the development efforts" of African states.[3] Similarly, when the UN brought together African governments and key African nongovernmental organizations at a major conference held in Tanzania from February 12 to 16, 1990, to discuss good political governance as part of the recovery processes of the African continent from the 1980s economic crisis, the African states who attended the conference argued that the most important thing for them is popular participation in governments. For them, it was essential to ensure that the recovery policies reflected aspirations and values of African citizens rather than insisting on participation in the development of these policies. The conference did not only end up adopting the popular participation fad; the Charter that African ministers adopted at the end of the conference was instructive. The Charter only encouraged African governments to "adopt development strategies, approaches and programmes, the content and parameters of which are in line with the interest and aspirations of the people and which incorporate, rather than alienate, African values and realities."

In a fundamental paradigmatic shift from the OAU cultural relativist approach to political governance, the AU seeks to encourage its member states to develop a political culture "based on the holding of regular, free, fair and transparent elections conducted by competent, independent and impartial national electoral bodies." These liberal democratic ideals are described in various AU documents as having universal value. As indicated in the African Democracy Charter, state parties would adhere to "universal values and principles of democracy," including, among other things, respect for human rights, representative government, the rule of law, supremacy of constitutions and constitutional orders, separation of powers, free and fair elections, the independence of the judiciary, gender balance, and the involvement of African civil society in the political process. The AU seeks to internalize and domesticate this definition of democracy in member states by making it the explicit purpose of the Union and by empowering its organs to protect, defend, and promote good political governance.

The second paradigmatic shift in thinking that the AU has pioneered is African governments' acceptance of democratic charter and third-party monitoring of their governance performance. The African Governance Charter spells out in some depth key rules relating to the acquisition of power, management of power, and governance of public institutions. On the acquisition of power, the African Governance Charter outlaws all other means of acquiring political power in Africa except through constitutional means. The constitutional means is intersubjectively understood in the AU system to mean that power can only be acquired legitimately in Africa through the ballot box. This is a significant paradigmatic shift since power in Africa has often been acquired in many ways, including coups, as in the case of Omar Bashir's ascension to power in Sudan in June of 1989, military rebellion as in the case of Yoweri Museveni's acquisition of power in Uganda in 1986, mass street protests, secession, and inheritance, among others.

The African Governance Charter has game-changing rules on management of power in Africa. For instance, it forbids ruling elites from changing national constitutions and other legal instruments in ways that infringe on "the principles of democratic change of government." This is paradigmatic change inasmuch as manipulation of legal instruments to promote authoritarian practices has become a staple of the African governance tapestry or practices, especially in the last twenty years. Finally, the Charter introduces rules designed to strengthen and consolidate transparent, accountable, and responsible public institutions. The adoption of these rules on public institutions reflects a fundamental change in orientation since they were designed to create a Weberian type of public institution for a continent widely known in political science for its neopatrimonial tendencies.

Novelty: The two main paradigmatic ideas are not necessarily novel to the rest of the world, but they are new to the African continent. For example, the definition of *democracy* has always been a hotly contested issue. Until 1990 most African governments and certainly the predecessor organization to the AU maintained that democracy is either alien to African culture or every country should be allowed to practice democracy according to its own sociocultural practices. In other words, there was no consensus that democracy had a specific universal content, and Africans have a right and duty to adapt their own version of what democracy is. This understanding paved the way for populist regimes, such as the late Muammar Gaddafi's government, to claim that their governments are democratic. The insistence by the AU that democracy has a particular universal meaning makes it difficult for regimes similar to Gaddafi's to make a legitimate claim that their system of government is democratic.

The idea of binding states to a democracy charter across a continent is also not novel within the international system. The Organization of American States (OAS) developed a democratic charter that governed the Americas prior to the emergence of the African Governance Charter.[4] What is unique is the breadth and depth of the legal obligations that the African Governance Charter imposes on state parties. Its legal obligation goes far deeper and wider than the Inter-American Democratic Charter.[5] Unlike the OAS system, the African Charter calls for the prosecution of coup makers in the African Court of Justice and Human Rights.[6] The obligation it imposes on parties to respect democratic institutions is also much stronger than those provided in the Inter-American Democratic Charter. The Charter is written in such a way that the AU Commission does not necessarily need the invitation of state parties to monitor elections, although in practice it is difficult to see how the Commission can monitor elections effectively without an invitation from the state holding the elections. Yet the decision to mandate the AUC to monitor elections without the explicit invitation by member states is significant because clever governments in the Americas have often used the "by invitation only" clause in the OAS Charter to negotiate the terms of the observation mission, such as when to issue the invitation (how soon before the election date), who to invite to observe, access to electoral institutions, and shaping the election observation mission to their liking.[7] The African Governance Charter provides for a stronger monitoring and third-party oversight than the Inter-American Democratic Charter.[8] The AU, unlike the OAS, whose compliance tools are mainly political in nature, has a PSC that has many enforcement powers, including a mandate to ensure that state parties comply with the African Charter. In addition, the AU Commission is empowered to monitor the implementation of the Charter. In particular, the AU chairperson is empowered to demand a speedy return to constitutional order.

Relevant: The relevance of the AU's good governance paradigm to stakeholders is not in doubt. Governance is a major issue across the African continent, and most analysts, observers, governments, and civil societies have all praised the adoption of the prodemocracy approach to continental unity. The relatively good image that the AU has so far enjoyed within the international system compared to its predecessor, which was largely considered as a club of dictators, has much to do with the Union's prodemocracy orientation.

The provision of a shared frame of reference for democracy has undercut attempts by the African political class to adopt context-specific interpretations of democracy in AU member states. This has great potential to minimize conflicts over the meaning of democracy in the African context. African political class, civil society, and other stakeholders have a clear benchmark to measure the performance of democracy everywhere on the African continent, except Morocco, which is not a member of the AU.

Financial Viability: Donors are yet to pump money into the spread of the AU's approach to good political governance. The Department of Political Affairs (DPA), which is charged with the responsibility to promote the AU's political governance agenda, received just U.S. $6.6 million ($6,625,547 to be exact) in 2014 compared with the over U.S. $35 million ($35,322,866) that donors gave to its sister department, the DPS, during the same period. The bulk of the money that went to DPA was provided for election observation and EISA rather than the DPA, which played the key role in securing the money from the British Department for International Development. Perhaps it is too early to suggest that the AU's way of promoting good governance is not financially viable, yet so far the financial commitment by donor countries for AU to promote good political governance has not been encouraging. Compared with the amount of money that donors have spent on AU military intervention or even the resources that donors have traditionally put into democracy promotion at the state level, the AU's approach has not received ringing endorsement from the donor community.

It has not received any significant financial support from African governments besides the allocation from assessed contributions. The fact that AU member states have not put money into the promotion of their own idea is perhaps not surprising given the African governments' penchant to free-ride when it comes to continental institution building. Many African governments have been reticent in giving money to the AU beyond their annual contributions. Even the allocation from the annual contributions to the DPA is relatively small compared to the allocation given to the DPS. In 2014, the DPA was allocated just $458,258 from the assessed contributions, while the DPS was given $1,880,225.

One of the major lessons learned since the formation of the AU is that administrators who are determined to build and promote programs within the AU system cannot depend on the annual contribution. African governments are not known for providing resources from the annual contribution for programs. In any case, payment of the annual dues is not even impressive. The AU has not received more than 70 percent of the annual dues at any given year since it was formed. Even in a good year, such as in 2014 in which the AU was able to collect 61 percent (i.e., $84.6 million of $138.5 million), it still had to contend with over 38 percent (53.9 million) in arrears. The arrears carried forward from previous years for 2014 was reported to be approximately $39.5 million.[9] The outlook for the future will not be any different from previous years in which the AU has depended on a few countries (Algeria, Egypt, Libya, Nigeria, South Africa, and now Angola) for over around 65 percent of its operating budget. As Allison noted, "While countries such as South Africa and Nigeria pay more than their fair share, many struggle to meet their financial commitments."[10]

The low rate of dues payment is in spite of the fact that the AU is one of the lowest in the IO community. The AU also has one of the smallest budgets. The entire budget of the AU for the 2014 period was around $281,576,722 million.[11] This is a drop in the bucket when compared with the EU budget of around $162 billion or even the UN operating budget of $5.4 billion for the same period.[12] In fact, carefully crafted, professionally staffed, competently run, properly equipped, and well-grounded programs aimed at promoting good political governance in AU member states will cost in excess of the entire AU operating budget.

Effectiveness: The two worldviews have so far not been adapted across the continent, although over thirty-four African states have constitutional and institutional frameworks that are largely in line with AU good-governance paradigms.[13] Some of these alignments were adopted before the African Governance Charter emerged. The countries whose legal frameworks are out of line with the AU definition of democracy have not embarked on the legal reforms needed to ensure compliance with the new AU worldviews. Some have rhetorically positioned themselves as prodemocracy regimes and to some extent doing some of the things that the AU Charter instructs them to do, such as organizing elections, but the outcome of these elections are foregone conclusions. For instance, Rwanda, Cameroon, and Uganda have political systems that broadly reflect the letter of the AU governance agenda, but the actual governance practices do not reflect the spirit of the AU's approach to good political governance. Most observers generally agree that these countries are not democratic, in the proper sense of the word, but the savvy way that the political class in these countries practice their politics makes it incredibly difficult to invoke the African Governance Charter.

Efficiency: The definition of democracy as well as the content of the African Governance Charter is, broadly speaking, appropriate and tailored to deal with specific African governance challenges, yet there are gaps in the AU's new governance paradigm. Most keen observers of African politics will agree that the AU needs a paradigmatic shift in its approach to term limits.[14] The longevity of governing regimes in some African states is a major problem across the African continent. Attempts by ruling governments to prolong their stay has already created political crises in many African states, including Burkina Faso in 2014 and Burundi in 2015. It will continue to be a major source of conflict unless the AU takes a firm stand on it. The African Governance Charter does not specifically impose limits on African regimes. There was an attempt at the initial stage of the drafting of the African Governance Charter to introduce term limits, and in fact the first two drafts of the Charter had those specific elements, but after protest from political elites and pressure from diplomats the AU rephrased it.[15] Instead of specifically imposing term limits, the African Governance Charter forbids elected state officials from manipulating the national constitution to legitimize authoritarian actions. It mandates that the revision of national constitutions and other domestic laws reflect the spirit and letter of liberal democracy and specifically outlaw changes to national constitutions and other legal instruments that infringe on "the principles of democratic change of government."[16] The spike in the rate of manipulation of national constitutions by incumbents to extend their term or remove term limits in national laws in the last ten years informed the development of this idea. The most spectacular failure to manipulate national constitutions occurred in Zambia in 2001, Malawi in 2004, and Nigeria in 2005. President Yuweri Museveni of Uganda,

President Paul Biya of Cameroon, and Sam Nujoma of Namibia successfully amended the term limit in their national constitutions. There is a strong likelihood that presidents Joseph Kabila of the Democratic Republic of the Congo, Denis Sassou N'Guesso of Congo-Brazzaville, and Thomas Boni Yayi of Benin will create political crises in their countries by trying to amend their national constitutions in order to run for elections in 2016. The change of the term limits by these presidents may likely occur through legal means and pseudo-democratic processes, and the AU may probably have no impactful tools to manage the political crises that will come out these processes. Though the prohibition of undemocratic ways of changing national legal instruments is a good first step to ensuring that incumbents respect existing laws, it does not also address the problem of dictatorship by the majority.

RULES

Nature: The AU has introduced a number of rules that seek to regulate political governance across the African continent. The foundational rules are in Articles 3(g) and 4(m) of the Constitutive Act of the African Union. The former Article encourages the creation and development of democratic principles and institutions, popular participation, and good governance, while the latter Article promotes respect for democratic principles, rule of law, and good governance. The supporting rules can be found in the PSC protocol, protocol of the Pan-African Parliament, and of course, the African Governance Charter. In addition, the AU Assembly has adapted many declarations that strengthen the Union's legal position on good political governance in Africa. The most seminal of these declarations are the Harare Declaration (1997), Algiers Declaration (1999), and Lomé Declarations (2000). The African Governance Charter brings together all the key rules on good political governance.

Novelty: The AU governance rules provide innovative ways to address key and peculiar African political problems, including unconstitutional changes of government. Unconstitutional change of government has been at the root of African governance problems since the 1950s. The rules spell out five grounds for unconstitutional change of government in Africa. These are: a military coup d'état against a democratically elected government; an intervention by mercenaries to replace a democratically elected government; the replacement of a democratically elected government by armed dissident groups and rebel movements; the refusal by an incumbent government to relinquish power to the winning party after free, fair, and regular elections; and finally, amendment or revision of the constitution or legal instruments that infringe on principles of a democratic change of government.[17] The African governance charter made the definition of unconstitutional change of government open-ended by stipulating that the five scenarios indicated above are just examples. The open-ended nature of the definition gives the AU rules the necessary adaptive capacity and flexibility to stand the test of time. It should, however, be noted that the history of abuses by powerful African actors of open-ended clauses in international treaties should serve as a cautionary note.

Although the Constitutive Act and the PSC protocol advanced the precision and enforcement of key principles in these declarations, many of the democracy promotion ideas in the declaration remained aspiration and unforeseeable. Senior Africrats, especially the AU legal team, knew that the Constitutive Act and the PSC protocol did not provide enough legal cover for the Commission to promote good political governance in Africa. Senior Africrats started looking for additional legal tools, which made them team up with the Independent Electoral Commission (IEC) of South Africa and the African Association of Electoral Authorities (AAEA) to cohost a conference on strengthening African initiatives on democracy and governance in South Africa between April 7 and 10, 2003.[18]

The conference, which brought together representatives from AUC, the electoral management bodies, academic community, and civil society organizations in Africa, made a number of recommendations, including the creation of democracy charter. Africrats put the conference recommendations together with a request to African leaders to mandate the Commission to draft a charter on democracy. The request was adopted as a declaration at the 2003 summit held in Maputo, Mozambique.

Though most of the novel ideas in the African Governance Charter came out of this conference, the idea of creating a governance charter for the entire African continent dates back to the mid-1990s. It follows a measure that Africrats and OAU political leaders put in place to restore democratic rule in Burundi in 1996 and Sierra Leone in 1997.[19] These measures led to the adoption of a series of anticoup declarations in Harare in 1997, Algiers in 1999, and Lomé in 2000. The Constitutive Act legalized the key principles contained in the anticoup declarations. The incorporation into the Constitutive Act of all the prodemocracy principles in the declarations proved to be a delicate and difficult exercise. Remnants of the cultural relativist school, including delegates from Guinea, Uganda, and governments that came to power through coups, opposed the wholesale integrations of democratic principles into the Constitutive Act.

The compromise that emerged from the negotiation committed the AU to promote good governance and the rule of law, consolidate democratic institutions and culture, and to ensure that there is respect for human rights in member states. The Constitutive Act tries to make the common values in the declarations legally binding by making respect for democratic principles one of the AU's guiding principles.

The PSC protocol adopted the democracy promotion language in the Constitutive Act and strengthened further their precision and enforcement mechanisms. It empowered the PSC to follow up on progress made in the promotion of democratic practices, good governance, the rule of law, human rights, and respect for freedom of speech.[20] The PSC protocol added new enforcement tools when it made respect for constitutional governance a qualification for the election of PSC members. In addition, the PSC protocol recognized democracy promotion as key to conflict prevention and peacebuilding. As a result, it mandated the PSC, the Early Warning System, and the Panel of the Wise to pay attention to governance as part of their conflict prevention work. And because PSC decisions are binding on all AU member states, the integration of the prodemocracy principles into the PSC protocol moved them from the domain of soft law into the realm of hard law.[21]

The adoption of the PSC protocol and the widespread support it received emboldened Africrats to bring together between May 15 and 17, 2004, lawyers of AU member states to discuss the implication of the Maputo, which, among other things, requested the creation of an African Governance Charter. The AUC recruited a consultant, Khabele Matlosa, who was a major intellectual force at the April 2003 democracy promotion conference in South Africa discussed earlier, to develop the charter.[22]

Relevance: The NGO community, donors, and even African governments consider these rules relevant. They address many of the governance challenges that the African continent has faced since decolonization. The NGO community in particular has taken to these rules. More than a dozen of them working in ten countries came together in 2009 to form the State of the Union (STU) to advocate for the implementation of the AU's prodemocracy "standards and commitments at the national level."[23] Led by FAHAMU (a group of NGOs committed to social justice), the NGOs have been campaigning for full implementation and compliance of the AU's political governance rules in member states of the AU. The campaign and support from the NGO community is reflected in the fact that they published the State of the Union report, a biannual publication designed to measure African governments' compliance with AU governance rules and indicators.

Financial Viability: Similar to the promotion of the worldview, the AU rules on governance have not attracted the resources that one would have expected given the extent to which they can change the governance landscape of Africa for the better. The limited support may be due to the fact that most of these rules emerged during the financial crisis or the period where there was a general feeling of donor fatigue. There is also the perception that these rules were developed not necessarily for the purposes of ensuring that African countries are well governed but were developed primarily to raise resources. Also, the AU has a peculiar problem when it comes to the promotion of governance rules. Its predecessor was very good at developing rules but not great at implementing them, an image that has been projected onto the AU. The AU is an international bureaucracy dominated by unelected officials and those who are not directly accountable to the electorate. The democratic deficit of the Pan-African organization makes it difficult for the AU to make the case to donors that it is well positioned or the most suitable organization to promote democracy across the African continent.

The inability of the AU to attract donor support for its governance rules may also be the result of the fact that some people see it as an elitist institution whose rules do not affect ordinary Africans. In particular, there is a perception in donor circles that the AU is incapable of bringing about fundamental political change in African countries, and the state level is still the best place to invest resources for purposes of bringing about political change. The logic is obviously flawed and old-fashioned, but it seems many donors still hold on to that view. They seem to think their money on democracy promotion would be better spent at the domestic level rather than at the continental level.

Effectiveness: The AU governance rules have so far not been adopted across the continent. Some states may have legal frameworks that largely reflect the spirit and letter of the African Governance Charter, but these alignments were often introduced not necessarily because of the adoption of these governance rules. Some of political systems were established before the AU rules emerged. Countries such Eritrea and Sudan, whose legal regimes do not dovetail neatly with the intent and purposes of the AU governance rules, are not rushing to introduce the measure that will ensure that they are in compliance with the new AU rules. Others have rhetorically positioned themselves as prodemocracy regimes and to some extent doing some of the things that the AU Charter instructs them to do. For instance, almost all African states do organize regular elections in conformity with the requirement of the African Governance Charter.

In some instances, African governments have made changes on paper to reflect broadly the less burdensome obligations in the Charter, but the changes are not reflected in the actual practices and attitudes of governing elites and regimes. African governments such as the regimes in Burundi, Gabon, Egypt, Sierra Leone, and Zimbabwe have developed national legislations and tweaked existing laws and policies to reflect the broad tenants of the AU governance rules, but the actual behaviors of these regimes are anything but democratic. Most observers generally agree that these countries are not democratic in the proper sense of the word, but the AU will find it incredibly difficult within the ambit of the rules to invoke the punishment attached to breaking the African Governance Charter.

The strong sanction regime attached to the African Democratic Charter provides a glimmer of hope for the future. In addition to sanctions that may be imposed on perpetrators of unconstitutional regime change, the Charter provides for the imposition of sanctions on state parties that instigate or support unconstitutional change of government in another state. In 2010, the AU Assembly added more obligations by explicitly debarring AU members from recognizing any unconstitutional regimes and asking other international organizations to do the same.[24] The Assembly specifically asked African regional organizations to refrain from admitting into their organizations states in which a constitutional change of government has taken place. It urges state parties not to give sanctuary to perpetrators of an unconstitutional change of government. Rather, the Charter obligates them to put them on trial or extradite them to states that are willing to prosecute them.

The powers the African Governance Charter given to the PSC is another source of hope for the future. The PSC is empowered by the Charter to take initiatives to restore constitutional rule. Some people in the international legal community have equated the "take initiatives" clause in the Charter to the principle of "all necessary means" in international law.[25] They think the provision endowed the PSC to use all means necessary, including military force, to restore constitutional order. As Omorogbe put it, "Although the coverage of this article is somewhat uncertain, it appears to enable AU military intervention to protect democratic political institutions or legitimate governments."[26] Whether the "take initiative clause" obligates the AU to use military means to defend and protect democracies in Africa or not, it still carries a significant deterrent effect.

Another potential source for optimism is the disincentive embedded in the rules for participants of unconstitutional change of government. The African Governance Charter forbids those who participate in an unconstitutional change of government from gaining political dividends from the democratic order that will emerge. They cannot participate in elections that are held to restore constitutional order or hold any position of responsibility in the government that will come from the processes of restoring constitutional rule.[27] The Charter also empowers AU's judicial bodies to try perpetrators of an unconstitutional change of government, although the institutional mechanism to do so is underdeveloped.

Efficiency: The rules are, broadly speaking, appropriate and tailored to suit specific African democratic challenges, yet gaps still remain in the AU's approach to good governance promotion. For instance, term limits are generally seen to be a major problem across the African continent. It is estimated that of the thirty-four African states that introduced two-term limits into their national legislations, only 20 percent of those governments have actually respected this provision.[28] The total disregard for the two-term limits and regular manipulation of national laws to prolong regimes' hold of power have created street demonstrations in Burkina Faso and political crises in Burundi, among others. Yet AU rules do not specifically impose limits on African regimes. As indicated already, there was an attempt during the drafting stage of the African Governance Charter to introduce term limits in the Charter, but it was rephrased in broad terms. The new language only talks about changes to national laws that infringe on "the principles of democratic change of government." Everyone within the AU system knows the principles were introduced in response to the attempted manipulation of national constitutions in Zambia (2001), Malawi (2004), Nigeria, and Namibia in 2006. Though the definition of the "infringement of the principles of democratic change of government" is unspecified, the prohibition of undemocratic ways of changing national legal instruments is a good first step to ensuring that incumbents respect existing laws. It is only a good first step because the Charter does not address fully the problem of dictatorship by the majority.

NORMS

Nature: The first norm that has emerged within the institutional setting of the AU is obviously the strong anticoup attitude. Coup makers are no longer welcome into the coveted and exclusive political class of the AU, and states in which coups occur are immediately ostracized from the African international system. The anticoup sentiment is both at the political as well as bureaucratic levels. This is a remarkable shift from the practices of twenty years ago when coup makers were welcomed with open arms by the OAU and given red carpet treatment. The origin of the norm dates back to the Lomé Declaration on the Framework for an OAU Response to Unconstitutional Changes of Government, adopted by African leaders during their summit on July 11, 2000, in Togo.[29] The Lomé Declaration broadened the definition of an unconstitutional change of government and provided standard operating procedures for dealing with any unconstitutional change of governments. It asked the chairperson of the AU Commission to "immediately and publicly condemn such a change and urge for the speedy return to constitutional order." The Lomé Declaration mandated that the chairperson and the Central Organ, now the PSC, "convey a clear and unequivocal warning to the perpetrators of the unconstitutional change that, under no circumstances, will their illegal action be tolerated or recognized."

The chairperson and the Central Organ were also supposed to encourage bilateral partners of the affected state and international organizations that the country in question belongs to to align their policy, position, and action with that of the AU. The Central Organ was required to meet to discuss the change of government and proposed further measures aimed at restoring constitutional order. These measures should include automatic suspension from participating in the activities of policy organs of the OAU, and the coup makers should be given six months within which to restore constitutional rule.[30] The chairperson of the AU is required within the six-month period to explore ways, including moral suasion, diplomatic pressure, isolation, and coordination with other regional organizations, to make sure the coup makers restore constitutional rule. Limited and targeted sanctions such as the denial of visas to coup leaders and trade restrictions may be instituted after six months if the regime does not do enough to restore constitutional order. The anticoup idea was legalized by the Constitutive Act of the AU, the PSC protocol, and the African Governance Charter.

The second norm that seems to have emerged from the AU's promotion of good governance is the expectation that every African election has to be monitored and certified by the AU. African political elites' expectation at the moment is that every national election they organize must have AU monitors. In other words, election observation is the new game in town. The AU election monitoring is a culmination of processes that started in the days of the OAU. The OAU started monitoring elections in the early 1990s when it sent diplomatic missions to observe elections in African countries. Namibia was the first country to receive such a diplomatic election-monitoring mission from the OAU. The ad hoc diplomatic type of election monitoring continued until 2002 when the AU started the processes of professionalizing election observations and making it a regular feature of its work.

The paradigmatic shift from the ad hoc and politically driven approach to election observation to a more professional method of monitoring occurred when the AU adopted in July 2002 the Declaration on the Principles Governing Democratic Elections in Africa and Guidelines for Election Observation and Monitoring Missions.[31] Professionalization of election monitoring meant that the AU had to make five important changes. First, it discontinued the practice of sending only diplomats. It broadened the delegation to include technical and professional electoral officers from electoral management bodies in individual African states, members of the Pan-African Parliament (PAP), civil society groups, and the PRC. At the moment, the composition of the AU election observation team is approximately 40 percent PAP members, 10 percent civil society groups, 10 percent PRC, and 40 percent electoral management bodes. Second, the AU moved away from direct involvement in observations. The AU Commission became a sort of coordinating and facilitating agency. The Commission outsourced its election monitoring activities to independent electoral bodies outside of the AU system. It left the actual work such as the training of monitors, deployment of observers, and report writing to the independent agency. The EISA is at the moment doing this work on behalf of the AU. Third, the AUC created a database of experts and trained observers it could send to observe elections in various African countries. The creation of the database gave the AUC both institutional memory and a more reliable approach to selecting observers. Fourth, the AUC developed a code of conduct for the observers that outlined the duties and responsibilities of an observer. Finally, the AU developed policy instruments for its elections observations.

Novelty: The anticoup norm is a recent addition to the African norm system. Since independence, coup making has been a customary way to acquire power and to join the African ruling class. Successful coup makers were welcomed into the OAU until the late 1990s, when the anticoup sentiment began to emerge, and by the mid-2000s it has cascaded, to use Finnemore and Sikkink's terminology.[32] The coup d'état against the Sylvestre Ntibantuganya civilian government on July 25, 1996, by Major Pierre Buyoya and the overthrow of Ahmed Tejan Kabbah's civilian government in Sierra Leone on May 25, 1997, by the Armed Forces Revolutionary Council set the ball rolling. The Burundi coup took place precisely at the time that the Arusha conflict Mediation Team thought it had found the right political formulae to end Burundi's tragic civil war.[33] Ntibantuganya was not only a key player in the Arusha negotiation processes, but his interim government had been given the mandate by both the OAU and East African regional leaders to establish the necessary condition for full constitutional rule in Burundi. Similarly, the Sierra Leone coup occurred not only three days to the 1997 OAU heads of state government summit, and perhaps more important, it took place at the time that West African leaders through the Economic Community of West African States (ECOWAS) and its Monitoring Force (ECOMOG) had established the political system that they thought would end the Sierra Leone catastrophic civil war.

The two coups had at least three impacts on the emergence of the norm. The coups' disruptive impact on the African-led peace processes made OAU political leaders acutely aware of the negative consequences that coups have on African security and the need to address coups as part of their collective effort to resolve conflicts. Second, the coup annoyed a significant number of African leaders to the extent that the OAU for the first time gave political backing to regional leaders to use force to dislodge the military regimes. While the OAU backing encouraged West African leaders to use military force to remove the coup makers and restore Kabbah's government in Sierra Leone, it emboldened East African leaders to impose a total economic blockade on Buyoya's government. The anger that the coups generated created a key anticoup constituency within the OAU leadership. As the then OAU chairperson President Robert Mugabe of Zimbabwe put it, "The OAU merely used to admit coups had occurred, but now we want to address them. There is now a definite attitude to coups and illegitimate governments."[34] The then OAU Secretary-General Salim Ahmed Salim took advantage of the anticoup sentiment within the leadership of the OAU to introduce to the OAU summit held in Harare in Zimbabwe between May 28 and June 2, 1997, specific measures designed to restore constitutional order in Sierra Leone.[35] They were adopted as the Harare Declaration.[36]

In a fundamental departure from the OAU practice, the Harare Declaration called on "all African countries, and the International Community at large, to refrain from recognizing the new regime and lending support in any form whatsoever to the perpetrators of the coup d'état in Sierra Leone." It asked West African leaders through "ECOWAS to assist the people of Sierra Leone to restore constitutional order to the country." The phrase *to assist the people of Sierra Leone*, which was inserted in the declaration with the full support of ECOWAS leadership, was understood to include a mandate to ECOWAS to use all necessary means, including military force, to overthrow the military regime. Finally, the Assembly asked non-ECOWAS countries and the larger international community, especially Western leaders, to assist ECOWAS to restore constitutional rule in Sierra Leone. The Harare Declaration emboldened ECOWAS leaders to mandate a military operation that forced the military junta in Sierra.

The Harare Declaration (1997) and the general antipathy to coups by a significant number of OAU leaders paved the way for Africrats to develop a policy proposal to address the menace of usurpers. OAU leadership discussed the proposal during the Thirty-Fourth OAU Summit held in Ouagadougou in Burkina Faso in June 1998 and adopted during the Thirty-Fifth Summit held in Algiers in Algeria in July 1999.[37] The Algiers Declaration excluded from participating in OAU activities "[s]tates whose Governments came to power through unconstitutional means.[38] The Declaration mandated that states "whose Governments came to power through unconstitutional means after the Harare Summit [i.e., May 1997] restore constitutional legality before the next Summit."[39] Finally, the Algiers Declaration mandated the OAU Secretary-General to "assist in programmes intended to return such countries to constitutional and democratic governments." The Constitutive Act of the AU legalized the anticoup declaration and outlawed it in Article 4(p) in 2001.[40] The anticoup rule developed from this period through repeated practices of condemning, rejecting, and suspending, and it became a full-fledged norm by 2007 when it was incorporated into the African Governance Charter.

Relevance: AU member states and civil society organizations seem to find the AU's electoral observation processes and mission useful. This is reflected in at least three ways. Many civil society organizations in Africa lobby hard to be included in the observation team. AU member states willingly invite and encourage AU observation missions to their countries. Though the AU does not need an invitation to observe elections, the AU Commission prefers to receive invitation from its member states. This is because invitation by incumbent governments often means that it is willing to cooperate and allow the monitors to do their work. There has been no shortage of invitation as almost all the countries that have held elections since 2006 have invited the Commission to monitor the elections. In some instances, such as the May 2015 Ethiopian elections, AU is the only external body invited to observe the elections.

On average, the AU Commission monitors fifteen elections in a calendar year. The invitation has even come when the country in question has significant disagreement with the AU. For instance, the AU Commission controversially accepted invitation to deploy over two hundred election monitors to basically observe and certify the coronation of the former Egyptian army commander, el-Sissi, in the May 26–28, 2014, presidential elections, even though Egypt had been suspended from the AU. Egypt was suspended because of el-Sissi's coup against the first democratically elected president of Egypt. Most analysts and even the AU itself knew that the elections were designed to provide a political cover for the coup, and yet the AU accepted the invitation from Egypt. It should, however, be pointed out that the AU declined to deploy observers to monitor the controversial third-term presidential election of Pierre Nkurunziza. The questionable nature of the invitation from Egypt notwithstanding, the fact that a suspended member of the Union will invite the AU monitors to observe elections it is organizing shows the importance they attach to the work of the AU Electoral Assistance Unit (EAU).

Financial Viability: The donor community also seems to attach some importance to the electoral observation work of the AU Commission. This is reflected in the fact that major donors are providing resources not only to the Electoral Assistance Unit but also to the EISA. The United Kingdom's Department for International Development will finance the funding for the work of the EISA in the next five years. In addition, African states have showed good interest in supporting the work of the Electoral Assistance Unit. They have shown a willingness to provide funding outside of the annual contributions to the Electoral Assistance Unit. A number of them have voluntarily contributed to the Electoral Assistance Fund even if the assistance is often conditioned on the AU agreeing to deploy election missions to observe elections in the country donating the money. The government of Algeria donated around U.S. $2 million in 2014 to the Electoral Assistance Fund. The donation was made close to the April 17 presidential elections, suggesting the resources were meant for the AU Commission to deploy a mission to observe the Algerian elections. It seems to be partly a gift and partly a tactical political move designed to force the AU's hands to observe Algerian elections. Some countries also seem to use the donation to buy legitimacy from the AU. Egypt controversially donated approximately U.S. $2 million worth of monitory resources to the Electoral Assistant Union in 2014 even though Egypt had been suspended from the activities of the AU. The AU Commission used the money to deploy over two hundred elections that ended up given el-Sissi the badly needed legitimacy his government needed. These contributions suggest that the AU election-monitoring norm is financially viable if one sets aside the questionable grounds for the donation and AU's acceptance of the money.

Effectiveness: The AU seems to have implemented its electoral mission reasonably well. It has created an arm's-length technical unit, and outsourced the observation and report writing to a competent outisider. The electoral observation reports that the AU has issued so far are reasonably balanced and professionally written. They are consistent with international standards, and there is often little difference between the AU reports and those issued by international observers such as the Carter Centre and the Commonwealth Secretariat.

There are, however, a number of limitations to the AU process. The AU missions are often deployed two weeks prior to elections. This does not give enough time for the observers to make a fair assessment of the most critical element of preelection processes such as the compilation, revision, and update of voter registration. This is a major drawback as many opposition leaders often accuse incumbent governments of bloating the electoral register with ghost names and under-aged people. The two-week period, meanwhile, does not provide enough space for the AU monitors to assess overall media coverage of political parties. Incumbent governments often do most of their media blitz at least a month prior to the election because they are aware that the eyes of the observers and the media will be on them during the month when elections are held. Thus, the AU mission tends to miss the period that incumbents usually abuse their positions. Studies also show that electoral malpractices start long before the crucial month prior to election, and only less savvy or desperate incumbents will actually cheat during the crucial month prior to the election. To the credit of the AU, they have identified the problem and are putting measures in place to deploy electoral observers three months before elections.

Politicians who usually have favorable predispositions toward incumbent regimes and are sometimes more interested in the material incentives that the process offers than the actual observation itself still heavily dominate the composition of AU missions. Although the AU mission is independently run, incumbent governments often use diplomatic niceties to prevent observers from seeing what they do not want them to see. For instance, in Libya the government provided cars and drivers to the AU monitors and used the excuse of insecurity to discourage observers from visiting certain areas of the country. In some cases, the age, health, energy levels, and interest of observers prevent them from going to rural and remote areas where malpractices can easily happen. The AU observation, just like most international observer missions, are urban centric. Finally, the missions are often too small and are only able to observe a few polling stations. Most of the areas they visit are in urban and affluent neighborhoods where educated people who are less vulnerable to incumbent manipulation live.

Efficiency: It is debatable if the AU election observation missions are the most cost-effective way to ensure respect for good governance principles. The AU spends on average $250,000 dollars on each one of the fifteen elections it observes in a year. This amounts to approximately U.S. $3.7 million on average every year. As indicated earlier, findings and conclusions of most of the election observation missions are similar in nature and in tune with that of other international election-monitoring groups such as the Commonwealth Secretariat and the Carter Centre. In actual fact, there is so much duplication in the current election monitoring system. The major reason why this waste and duplication are allowed and encouraged is that democracy is now the new religion in town, and elections are its main rituals. The question that must be asked is whether it offers value for money for the AU to spend $3.7 million, which in the grand scheme of things is not much but in the context of AU is a significant amount of money, on a process whose results can be obtained elsewhere. The answer to this question is not straightforward. On one hand, Africa cannot afford to continue to rely on the generosity and good will of others for affirmation of its governance process. Societies and even individuals do not innovate and grow in the midst of high dependence. Rather, it is independence mixed with some reasonable level of interdependence that fosters creativity and development. And having an African institution to police its governance and democratic practices is an important step in the continent's maturity processes.

On the other hand, spending $3.7 million by a resource-challenged organization on a process that may turn out to be nothing more than duplication may not be the most efficient use of resources. In addition, the AU election monitoring further encourages Africa's dependence on the outside world. The Election Monitory Unit does not have the $3.7 million the AU spends on elections every year. The total contribution by AU member states to election monitoring is around $2 million a year. The AU Commission has to find the shortfall of around $1.7 million every year. In practice, this has meant that the head of the Electoral Assistant Unit spends most of his time looking for money. To turn a skilled and competent governance expert to a fund-raising agent is certainly not the most efficient way to use skilled manpower. It is even unclear if election monitoring is the most efficient way to promote democratic values in Africa. African political elites have turned elections into another instrument they can use to perpetuate and cover up their autocratic tendencies, and it is doubtful if election monitoring is the best approach to change it. Is election observation the answer, for instance, when the army cuts short the term of a democratically elected government, as occurred in Egypt in 2014? The answer to this question and other related ones will be important as the AU tries to deepen good political governance in African states.

CAUSAL IDEAS

Nature: The policy instrument that drives the AU's democracy and governance agenda is the African Governance Architecture. A cursory look at the AGA reveals many familiar democratic principles and rules, but a closer examination shows it depends on five main ideational pillars. The five include emerging norms and rules designed to standardize the practice of democracy in AU member states, determining the most legitimate means to acquire political power in Africa, regulating the appropriate and inappropriate use of political power by elected officials, encouraging the creation of strong and efficient public institutions, and enhancing minority rights and interests within the context of majority rule.

Novelty: The AGA is not necessarily a new policy instrument, and certainly the terminology is borrowed from the peace and security architecture. The content of AGA is a synthesis of some of the best practices of good governance that the OAU and AU have been advocating for the last ten years. The history of AGA can be traced to the Lomé Declaration, which outlined AGA's key pillars. It suggested that OAU member states adhere to "a common concept of democracy [. . .] and common values and principles for democratic governance."[41] Africrats who developed the common values and principles identified nine principles as key to promoting democratic culture in Africa. They are respect for democratic constitutions, separation of powers, political pluralism, independence of the judiciary, gender balance in the political process, democratic change of government, respect for human rights, existence of vibrant opposition and civil society groups, and the holding of free, fair, and regular elections. The adoption of these democracy promotion principles during the Lomé Summit provided a concrete continentwide conception of democracy. It also signaled the beginning of the end of the dominant influence of cultural relativists in the continental African discussion of democracy.

While the common values and principles of democracy that the Lomé Declaration introduced in continental African politics significantly advanced the emergence of AGA, they were aspirational in nature. The principles needed to be rewritten and embedded in a treaty or treaties in such a way that they are enforceable. Africrats, primarily then OAU Under Secretary-General for Political Affairs Said Djinnit and the Acting OAU Legal Counselor Ben Kioko, recommended to delegates negotiating the Constitutive Act of the AU these principles for integration into the Constitutive Act of the AU. Besides minor changes, the Constitutive Act affirmed the entire Lomé Declaration.[42] The PSC protocol and the African Governance Charter solidified these ideas.

Relevance: The AGA is relevant to African policymakers, donors, transnational civil society groups, nonelite Africans, and AU bureaucrats. AGA has given African governments the policy instruments that they can use to put pressure on each other to ensure that the performance of their states on good governance reflect the policy standards articulated by the AU. Drafters of African state public policy instruments do not need to reinvent the wheel as they have a clear benchmark and in some cases a policy framework they can adapt and modify to suit their local context. They can also help the AU to know how useful this policy framework is by applying it and providing feedback to the AU. For the AU bureaucrats, AGA has given them the rhetorical tools, the language and discourse to talk about governance, and the push for political openness and deepening of democratic processes across the African continent. It also offers a platform that allows AU bureaucrats to engage with external partners.

Donors have a document that articulates an idea of what African elites consider as good governance. Many of the ideas articulated by AGA as well as the policy framework that led to the adoption of the Lomé Declaration are consistent with democratic ideas that donor countries promoted within African states in the 1990s. AGA principles in particular seem to draw extensively from the governance and democracy ideas that donors used as conditions for providing aid to individual African countries. To put it differently, AGA ideas fit with the broader democracy promotion agenda of most donor countries. The AGA should easily provide a common language for donors to work with the AU in the promotion of good political governance across the continent. For nonelite Africans, AGA provides the benchmark that they can use to hold their leaders and political elites accountable. AGA should and has provided the necessary template for transnational civil society groups to demand higher governance standards from every African country. Already a number of groups of civil society associations are using AGA's ideas to put pressure on and to shame certain African countries to deepen good governance.

Financial Viability: Compared with other policy frameworks, such as the policy instrument relating to the African Standby Force, AGA has not captured the imagination of the donor community in any significant way. The anticipated economic windfall is yet to materialize. Perhaps the jury is still out regarding whether AGA can provide the policy framework for the AU to attract the necessary funding for the promotion of governance ideas. It should in theory be attractive to mainstream donors since it seems to fit with the public commitment to democracy promotion by the donor community. Almost all of AGA's ideas are consistent with the conditions that donor countries set for providing political aid. The ideas that AGA seeks to promote reflect the governance ideas that the United States International Development Agency, the British Department for International Development, the Canadian Department for Foreign Affairs, Trade and Development, and the Swedish International Development Agency have publicly stated as things they want to see practiced more in individual African states. Perhaps donors are not queuing to provide support in part because they may be waiting to see if AGA was developed for extraversion purposes. They might be waiting to see clear the AU's commitment to AGA before supporting it.

Effectiveness: AGA as a policy instrument has made very little inroads into policies, decisions, and programs of various African countries. To be fair, AGA is relatively new, and it will take some time for countries to appreciate and change national legislations and policies to coincide with those promoted by AGA. African countries in general tend to be very slow in adopting international policy instruments. They are often relatively quick to sign them, but they take time to turn them into policy instruments. It takes on average about five years for international instruments to make their way into domestic policies, and AGA is just about three years old. That said, the way that AGA has been promoted might not be the most effective way to translate it into public policies.

The administrators of AGA seem to be more interested in what social media has to say about AGA than what African policymakers have to say. The few activities that have been organized in the last two years have focused more on social media publicity than bringing together a critical mass of public policymakers, academics, and opinion leaders who may be able to shape the integration of AGA into national legislation and policies. Like most AU events, the two major retreats put together by the AGA Secretariat have been very elitist and only targeted at people within the upper class of African societies. Few community members who are capable of promoting the ideas at the local level were invited to these events. Even the title of the event—High-Level Retreat—is super exclusive. Current and former African leaders, very senior diplomats, and selective academics and civil society friends, journalists, and bloggers who will write something flattering about the AGA Secretariat are those invited to these events. Middle-level bureaucrats who actually write national policies or those who can actually promote these ideas at the local level or those who will provide contrarian views were all ignored. The doors of the events were completely shut for members of the African civil service who are key to translating AGA into policy instruments.

AGA Secretariat also employs elitist language and discourse. Almost all of AGA's events are organized in English and to a limited extent French. Very little effort is made in translating most of the events or communicating AGA's ideas in the commonly spoken languages in individual African states. Statistically speaking, it is unlikely that the events will reach anywhere near 20 percent of the population of Africans. A majority of those who will be reached are the privileged few who have access to the Internet and social media platforms. The most effective means of communicating with the common person, such as the ubiquitous radio, were ignored in favor of trendy but less effective means of commutating with the majority of Africans. Little effort has been put into translating them into school curriculum at the primary, secondary, or tertiary levels. In all likelihood, more people based outside of Africa may know more about AGA than Africans who are supposed to be the main target.

Finally, AGA as it is currently conceptualized is too broad, overly ambitious, and it seems to include almost everything. According to a policy brief released by the AGA Secretariat, AGA "takes at least 24 different norms (actually rules) and standards into account."[43] It goes on to list almost all the legal instruments that the AU and OAU have developed since 1963. Without a good understanding of the AU system, one would be tempted to think all the departments and units of the AU Commission are under AGA after reading the policy paper. This is problematic on so many levels, and it is a perfect recipe for bureaucratic conflicts. It needs a clearly demarcated ideational boundary, especially given the dearth of human and institutional capacity of the AGA Secretariat. Without a carefully outlined focus for AGA, experienced and savvy civil servants who know all about the pitfalls and dangers of bureaucratic turf wars and conflict-averse experts would stay far away from AGA.

Efficiency: It is difficult to make a cost-benefit analysis of AGA. It is very new and yet to take root. Because it is yet to be integrated into national policies and legislation, it is difficult to know how much cost it will impose on African countries. However, judging from the integration of other AU documents into national legislation, it may not be unreasonably expensive to adopt it and diffuse it at the state level. It appears that it may not impose costs higher than the cost of promoting similar ideas within African states. Most African states already have similar democracy-related policy instruments in place, and it should not be too difficult to mainstream AGA ideas into existing national policy instruments.

The cost for creating and promoting AGA at the AU level has not been exorbitant, and so far a single donor, the Deutsche Gesellschaft fur Internationale (GIZ), has been able to support it in the last two years. The few events that the AGA Secretariat organized did not break the bank. The two High-Level Retreats were relatively well attended, and their publicity blitz reached a considerable number of social media users. The retreat also attracted some funding, especially from the Germans, who have been generous enough to support the AGA Secretariat. The efficiency of running these high-level retreats is yet to be demonstrated, though. As noted already, the audience tends to be self-selected, and it remains to be seen if these high-level meetings are the most efficient ways to promote ideas at the state, community, and local levels. It is unclear if this is the best route to secure buy-in from even African opinion leaders. Though the retreats are able to generate the interest of political, social, and economic elites, it appears those invited may not necessarily need to be convinced about the importance and value of democracy and good governance. The elites in places such as Equatorial Guinea, Angola, and Eritrea, just to mention these three, who do not believe in these ideas do not often attend these events. In other words, these events tend to attract the already converted. Some of the people at the local and bureaucratic levels who may need to be convinced about the importance of democracy are often the individuals that the AU does not deem elite enough to invite to these high-level retreats. The location of these events may not also offer value for money. They are often held in five-star hotels and expensive venues that are not the most accessible places in Africa for the common person. These observations should not in any way obscure the fact that if properly managed, AGA can be a very cost-effective way of pushing African countries to deepen good political governance. Its continental location makes it difficult for political elites to manipulate it in the way they are able to manipulate similar policy instruments at the national level.

DECISION-MAKING STRUCTURES

The AU democracy promotion agenda is managed by the Political Affairs Department through the Democracy, Governance, Human Rights & Elections Division (DGHRE) and the Democracy and Electoral Assistance Unit (DEAU). The DGHRE focuses on governance, human protection and promotion, transitional justice, decentralization and local governance, public service, and administration. The AGA Secretariat was established as a subunit of the DGHRE division to promote the political governance agenda. The mandate of the DEAU revolves around the promotion of good political governance through elections observation, strengthening Election Management Bodies, and enhancing national electoral processes. The Electoral Monitoring Unit was established as DEAU's coordinating and monitoring unit of electoral processes.

Novelty: Both the AGA Secretariat and the Electoral Monitoring Unit look like relatively novel ideas, though in some significant way they are classic examples of an administrative division of understaffed African regional organizations. The AGA Secretariat is in the worst situation. It is technically speaking a one-person management unit with a shared office. Compared to similar governance units in other IOs, the AGA Secretariat looks like a cupboard. Indeed, the entire DGHRE shows all the characteristics of an underfunded, overburdened, and underresourced bureaucratic institutional structure. The underfunding of both the AGA Secretariat and the Electoral Monitoring Unit has compelled them to develop creative ways of doing their work. For instance, the Election Monitoring Unit has developed an innovative partnership with EISA based in South Africa. The unit has basically outsourced the technical and administrative work to this think tank.

These included training of election monitors, the development of a roster for election observers, as well as the writing of observation reports. In other words, they have creatively brought the outsiders into the work of the AU.

Similarly, the AGA Secretariat uses informal and ad hoc relationships with African think tank organizations and selective pubic institutions in promoting and organizing events. The AGA Secretariat has forged a good relationship with African bloggers and those with a strong presence on social media platforms such as Twitter, Facebook, and Instagram. The AGA Secretariat collaborated with them to popularize the high-level retreats. The absence of human and institutional capacity means that the AU institutions promoting democracy have to constantly innovate and find new creative ways to advance the AU's governance agenda.

Relevance: So far the Electoral Assistance Unit seems to have provided services valued most by its priority stakeholders such as African governments, Election Management Bodies in Africa, and donors. It certainly appears from the frequent invitations for the Unit to observe elections that at least African governments consider the work of the Unit important. The Unit receives approximately fifteen invitations annually, and African governments seem to make a conscious effort to ensure that the Unit is available to observe their elections. As indicated earlier, the invitation is sent to the Unit even when the government in question has major disagreements and disputes with the AU. African election management bodies also seem to value the work of the Unit. They have worked with the Unit on a wide range of issues, including participating in various AU observer missions and cohosting events such as training workshops, seminars, and other educational programs. The Electoral Assistance Unit has revived the annual gathering of the Association of African Election Authorities (AAEA). Between July 22 and 24, 2015, the Electoral Assistance Unit held the 3rd Continental Election Management Bodies Forum in Accra, Ghana.

Judging by the financial support they have given to the Unit to observe elections, it appears donors value its work as well. The United Kingdom's Department for International Development signed in 2014 another MOU with the DPA committing to another five-year funding program for the Electoral Assistance Unit through EISA. Civil society groups, in particular those that are interested in elections monitoring, appear to see the Unit as very important to their work. They have made tremendous efforts to work with the Electoral Assistance Unit, and they compete vigorously for the few slots allocated to civil groups in the election observer teams that the Unit deploys. It is, however, unclear whether the Unit's work has had tangible impact on the common African. The inbuilt conflict-prevention mechanism in election monitoring should be relevant to the so-called ordinary Africans, but whether the work of the Electoral Assistance Unit has prevented the outbreak of a conflict or has had an impact on the lives of the commoner in Africa are open questions.

Financial Viability: The Electoral Assistance Unit has received relatively good support from the donor community and African states, but the overall financial flows to the AU to promote good political governance have been poor. The limited financial support to the AU's good-governance work may perhaps be a result of the relatively weak institutional structure and human resource deficit of the divisions tasked with the responsibility to promote the idea. As indicated already, both the DGHRE and DEAU are institutionally weak, understaffed, and underfunded. They have little web or physical presence within the AU system. They have neither regional nor country desk officers. The ratio of governance experts to the population they are supposed to promote good governance is approximately one to over one million people. The extreme human resource capacity deficits in the DPA has forced it to focus primarily on election monitoring at the expense of promoting the broader AU good-governance agenda.

The Germans sought to ameliorate the situation by helping the Department establish the AGA Secretary in 2011, but the unit is also understaffed, overburdened, and managed by a temporary employee of the Commission. Like other units of the AU, there are people working there who would probably be better off elsewhere not because they are incompetent but because they could not be bothered about the whole integration and Pan-African project. Some of them are African nativists and statists who are best suited to working for government agencies or organizations that align with their core beliefs rather than working for an African unity that they do not believe in in the first place. It is a classic challenge for some professionals who settle for jobs because of the money rather than working for organizations they philosophically agree with.

Though it is early for any meaningful assessment of the AGA Secretariat, the early indications are not promising. It seems to lack a clear focus, and the early activities of the unit have focused more on events that generate social media interest and publicity rather than on substantive issues that will advance the governance landscape of the continent. The Secretariat seems to be crying out for bold, continental Pan-Africanists who genuinely believe that it is the AU's business to shape domestic politics of African states.

The human resources deficit notwithstanding, the absence of donor support for the AU's approach to governance is very curious in the sense that democracy promotion is generally considered to be the new religion of the world and the darling of the donor community. Perhaps donors do not think the Secretariat is serious enough about good governance, or maybe they think the Secretariat is institutionally incapable of absorbing more donor resources. Be it as it may, it is clear that the creation of the AGA Secretariat is yet to show financial viability.

Effectiveness: Of the two main units dealing with the AU's governances promotion agenda, the Electoral Assistance Unit seems to be the most effective. It is able to observe elections, write decent reports, and build relationships with stakeholders such as election management bodies and civil society groups dedicated to the promotion of democracy across the continent. It has been able to do this not only because of the human resource capacity and the dedication of the few overworked temporary professional staffers of the Commission, but because it has been able to creatively outsource the work to outisiders. The question then becomes how much impact the AU actually has on the implementation of election observations.

AU officials do not often contribute to the writing of these observation reports. In some cases the senior management of the AU often does not know the content of these reports. This is a dual-edged issue. On one hand, the absence of the AU contribution allows think tanks to write an impartial report and provide independent assessment of each particular election. On the other hand, the absence of AU contribution limits the depth as well as the legitimacy of the reports that are in general seen as AU's reports. In other words, it appears African countries are relying on foreign-funded NGOs rather than the AU to affirm and certify their elections. The EISA itself is made up of unelected people and elite Africans whose lives are far removed from the daily struggles of commoners in countries they are observing the elections for. They are unlikely to be affected by any trouble that their reports will create. The question of input legitimacy becomes an issue particularly given that the opinions and conclusions of these reports carry some weight in political circles of African states. Political parties, the contestants, and especially incumbent governments in Africa often consider the so-called AU's reports perhaps the most important. Increasingly they are becoming the benchmark for other election bodies. A number of these election bodies would often wait patiently to hear the AU's conclusions and verdict. The legitimacy question notwithstanding, the reports from the AU observation missions is getting increasingly better and has become reference material for electoral bodies.

The effectiveness of the work of the AGA Secretariat is still unknown partly because the Secretariat has not been able to do anything apart from organizing retreats, often in very inaccessible five-star hotels. If we use social media presence as a basis to judge the effectiveness of these retreats, then the AGA has been very effective in promoting itself. Some of its retreats are estimated to have reached millions of social media consumers. The 2014 High-Level Retreat in Dakar trended on Twitter during the two-day period, and the estimated number of people following it was around four million. The interesting question is how many of these were Africans; how many were from communities who actually need their governments to be responsible and accountable? It is likely that most of the people on Twitter were elites, highly connected, and socially engaged individuals who know most of the information that were sent through Twitter.

Efficiency: In terms of the cost-benefit analysis of AGA's work, the jury is still out. The AGA Secretariat is a recent addition to the DPA, and as of May 2015 the head of AGA did not have his own office. But as a general preposition, the cost of managing AU democracy promotion through AGA should not be prohibitive for either African states or donors. The AU in general is not an expensive institution, and the remuneration for its work-force is considerably less than comparable institutions such as the EU and OAS, to name a few. The AGA Secretariat has no full-time permanent staff that is entitled to benefits and all the costs associated with having a full-time employee. The Secretariat is dependent on donor funding, and the head of AGA is actually seconded to the DPA by the GIZ. To some extent it is a very cheap, and critics would say sweatshop-like, way of promoting good govern-ance on the African continent.

The mechanisms through which the AGA Secretariat is promoting good governance on the African continent may not, however, be the most efficient. Organizing retreats, workshops, and seminars in high-end hotels in capitals and major cities across the African continent is not the most efficient way of promoting political governance. At minimum, the AGA Secretariat may be preaching to the converted, and no effort is given to spreading AGA ideas in places such as schools, communities, clubs, and other locations where the majority of Africans tend to congregate.

The means through which the AGA Secretariat communicates may also not be the most effective way of promoting democracy on a continent that has a high rate of poverty and illiteracy. It is certainly trendy to transmit information through social media, but what is the point of doing so if the majority of the people you are trying to reach does not have access to the Internet, let alone has a social media account or is unable to read and under-stand the information? Other cheaper ways of promoting ideas on the African continent such as the integration of ideas into school curriculums and transla-tion of these ideas into local languages and other medium where a majority of Africans get their information from have all been neglected by the AGA Secretariat. Finally, the elitist approach to good-governance promotion has been tried before in the early 1990s and 2000s, yet every single study of democracy performance on the African continent shows that it has not been effective or efficient. They are easily captured and manipulated by the elite and used toward selfish ends.

NOTES

1. AQ: Missing note?

2. Donald Rothchild and E. Gyimah-Boadi, "Ghana's Decline and Development Strategies," in *Africa in Economic Crisis*, ed. John Ravenhill (New York: Columbia University Press, 1986).

3. Organization of African Unity, "Report of the Secretary-General to the Fifty-First Ordinary Session of Council of Ministers" (Addis Ababa: Organization of African Unity, 1990).

4. Edward R. McMahon, "The African Charter on Democracy, Elections, and Governance: A Positive Step on a Long Path," *Open Society Institute* (2007), http://www.afrimap.org/papers.php.

5. For comparative analysis, see Thomas Legler and Thomas Tieku, "What Difference Can a Path Make? Regional Regimes for Democracy Promotion and Defense in the Americas and Africa," *Democratization* 18, no. 3 (2010): 465–91.

6. Article 25 of the African Charter on Democracy, Elections, and Governance, http://www.achpr.org/files/instruments/charter-democracy/aumincom_instr_charter_democracy_2007_eng.pdf.

7. Dexter S. Boniface, "The OAS's Mixed Record," in *Promoting Democracy in the Americas*, edited by Thomas Legler, Sharon F. Lean, and Dexter S. Boniface, 40–62. Baltimore, MD: Johns Hopkins University Press, 2007.

8. Solomon Eborah, "The African Charter on Democracy, Election and Governance: A New Dawn for the Enthronement of Legitimate Governance in Africa?" *Open Society Institute* (2007). http://www.afrimap.org/papers.php; Sekai Saungweme, "A Critical Look at the Charter on Democracy, Elections, and Governance in Africa," *Open Society Institute* (2007). http://www.afrimap.org/papers.php.

9. Mmanaledi Mataboge, "AU's Dependence on Cash from the West Still Rankles," *Mail & Guardian*, June 12, 2015, http://mg.co.za/article/2015-06-11-aus-dependence-on-cash-from-the-west-still-rankles.

10. Allison Simon, "Think Again: In Defence of the African Union," September 9, 2014, http://www.issafrica.org/iss-today/think-again-in-defence-of-the-african-union.

11. African Union, The 23rd Ordinary Session of the African Union, in Malabo, June 30, 2014, http://summits.au.int/en/23rdsummit/events/23rd-ordinary-session-african-union-ends-malabo.

12. For the EU budget, see Council of the European Union, EU budget for 2015, http://www.consilium.europa.eu/en/policies/eu-annual-budget/eu-budget-2015/; and for the UN, see "Secretary-General Unveils $5.4 Billion 2014-2015 Budget to Fifth Committee, Net Reduction of Posts Draws Mixed Reviews from Delegates," United Nations, Meetings Coverage and Press Releases, October 28, 2013, http://www.un.org/press/en/2013/gaab4080.doc.htm.

13. Institute for Peace and Security Studies, "Five Priorities for Obama Ahead of AU Visit," http://www.ipss-addis.org/new-ipss/news-events/five_priorities_for_obama_ahead_of_au_visit/.

14. Eborah, "The African Charter on Democracy, Election and Governance."

15. McMahon, "The African Charter on Democracy, Elections, and Governance."

16. Chapter VIII (Article 23) of the African Charter on Democracy, Elections and Governance, http://www.ipu.org/idd-E/afr_charter.pdf.

17. Article 25 of Charter, African Commission on Human and Peoples' Rights, African Charter on Democracy, Elections and Governance, http://www.achpr.org/instruments/charter-democracy/.

18. For details see, Khabele Matlosa, "Assessing the African Charter on Democracy, Elections and Governance: Declaration vs. Policy Practice Policy Brief 53," *Centre for Policy Studies* (2008).

19. For more on this, see the section on norms.

20. Article 7 of Protocol Relating to the Establishment of the Peace and Security Council of the African Union, http://www.peaceau.org/uploads/psc-protocol-en.pdf.

21. Stef Vandeginste, "The African Union, Constitutionalism and Power-Sharing," *Journal of African Law* (2013): 4.

22. Matlosa, who is now the director of Political Affairs at AUC, was then the program director of the Electoral Institute of Sustainable Democracy.

23. For details, see the website of FAHAMU: Networks for Social Justice, http://www.fahamu.org/SOTU.

24. AU Assembly, *Decision on the Prevention of Unconstitutional Changes of Government and Strengthening the Capacity of the African Union to Manage Such Situations. Doc. No. Assembly/AU/Dec.269 (XIV) Rev.1, 6(i)(b),* February 2, 2010, http://www.africa-union.org/root/AR/index/Assembly Dec.268-288, Decl.1-3, Res E.pdf.

25. Eki Yemisi Omorogbe, "A Club of Incumbents? The African Union and Coups d'État," *Vanderbilt Journal of Transnational Law* 44, 123 (2012).

26. Omorogbe, "A Club of Incumbents? The African Union and Coups d'État."

27. 25(4 &6) of the Constitutive Act of the African Union.

28. Rothchild and Gyimah-Boadi, "Ghana's Decline and Development Strategies."

29. Lomé Declaration of July 2000 on the framework for an OAU response to unconstitutional changes of government (AHG/Decl.5 (XXXVI), http://www2.ohchr.org/english/law/compilation_democracy/lomedec.htm.

30. Lomé Declaration of July 2000 on the framework for an OAU response to unconstitutional changes of government (AHG/Decl.5 (XXXVI), http://www2.ohchr.org/english/law/compilation_democracy/lomedec.htm.

31. African Union, the OAU/AU Declaration on the Principles Governing Democratic Elections in Africa (AHG/Decl.1 (XXXVIII) and the African Union Guidelines for Election Observation and Monitoring Missions, both adopted in July 2002.

32. Martha Finnemore and Katherine Sikkink, "International Norm Dynamics and Political Change," *International Organization* 52, no. 4 (1998): 887–917.

33. The Mediation Team was established by the OAU and East African leaders through the Great Lakes Regional Initiative for Peace in Burundi. For details, see African Union in search of Peace in Burundi and Comoros, 2011. http://www.hdcentre.org/uploads/tx_news/The-AU-and-the-search-for-Peace-and-Reconciliation-in-Burundi-and-Comoros-FINAL.pdf.

34. Quoted in "Nigerias Intervention in Sierra Leone," Human Rights Watch, http://www.hrw.org/reports/1997/nigeria/Nigeria-09.htm; also see "OAU Summit Ends with Promise to get 'Tougher' on Coups," *South African Press Association*, Johannesburg, June 4, 1997.

35. Salim had invested so much energy in the Burundi peace process and in the process of creating the interim government to restore constitutional rule disrupted by the 1993 assassinations of the leaders of the first democratically elected government in Burundi and had led the campaign to impose sanctions on the Boyoya regime. Ibrahim Dagash, "OAU Gives 'Green Light' for Use of Force in Sierra Leone," South African Press Association, June 3, 1997.

36. Organization of African Union, *Introductory Note to the Report of the Secretary-General to the Thirty-Third Ordinary Session of OAU of Organization of African Unity* (Addis Ababa, 1997).

37. Organization of African Union, *Report of the Secretary-General to the Thirty-Fifth Ordinary Session of Organization of African Unity* (Addis Ababa, 1999); Lomé Declaration of July 2000 on the framework for an OAU response to unconstitutional changes of government (AHG/Decl.5 (XXXVI).

38. Organization of African Union, *Ushering the OAU into the Next Century: A Programme for Reform and Renewal* (Addis Ababa, 1998).

39. Organization of African Union, *Ushering the OAU into the Next Century.*

40. African Union, *The Constitutive Act,* Addis Ababa, 2001.

41. Lomé Declaration of July 2000 on the framework for an OAU response to unconstitutional changes of government (AHG/Decl.5 (XXXVI), http://www2.ohchr.org/english/law/compilation_democracy/lomedec.htm.

42. One of the minor language changes introduced was a move away from the idea that the states whose government came to power through unconstitutional means will be suspended from participating in the activities of just the policy organs. Article 30 of the Constitutive Act stipulates that they "shall not be allowed to participate in AU activities." The new language widened the punishment to include, for instance, eligibility to propose candidates for election into AU offices or asking AU to support the candidacy of any of its citizen for a position in other international organization.

43. George Mukundi Wachira, "Consolidating the African Governance Architecture," Policy Briefing 96, *South African Institute of International Affairs* (June 2014).

Chapter Six

Promotion of Peace and Security

INTRODUCTION

This chapter explores the AU's work in promoting peace and security on the African continent. It contends that the AU's peace and security ideas and institutions are among the most ambitious and novel continent-wide security governance mechanisms developed in the last two decades. They are grounded in a collectivist security system, the R2P framework, human security ideas, and lessons learned from UN postwar reconstruction activities. The AU peace and security work is anchored by the PSC. The assertiveness of the AU on African peace and security issues has put the Union in a position that it is increasingly sharing with the UN as the primary responsibility of maintaining peace and security in Africa. The power- and burden-sharing roles of the AU go beyond the UN Charter's paternalistic attitude to regional organizations. The absence of a legal cover in the UN Charter for the role the AU is playing is creating a number of frictions between the AU and the UN.

The AU has been able to attract significant resources and attention for its peace support operations, and it has used mediation to prevent the outbreak of full-blown wars and/or reduce tensions in various African states. Mainstream donors have appreciated the work of the AU and given the AU ringing endorsement by providing the majority of the financial resources that the AU has used to promote peace and security in Africa during the last decade.

The relative successes of the AU in the areas of peace and security have been achieved on a weak foundation. The AU relied more on ad hoc, temporal, and personality-driven measures. The long-term sustainability of the things that helped the AU the most to promote peace and security is in doubt. Although the AU has been very effective in firefighting issues such as reacting to major wars, it has been relatively ineffective when it comes to preventing conflict and building durable peace. Although the new AU peace and security agenda has attracted billions of resources into the AU system, the measures that are often funded are those that attract media attention, such as large-scale killings in places such as Darfur, Central African Republic, and Somalia. The endemic and sporadic yet damaging wars that do not attract a lot of mainstream media attention are often ignored. Finally, the AU work on peace and security has contributed to Africa's incessant dependence on donor agencies and countries.

The above arguments are advanced in five parts. The first part discusses the AU peace and security paradigm. It shows the extent to which the paradigm is novel, relevant to priority stakeholders, generates resources, is effective, and whether it the most efficient way to address African peace and security challenges. The second part takes a closer look at the AU peace and security rules and the extent to which the rules are novel, relevant, financially viable, and effective in managing Africa's insecurities. The third part explores the AU's peace and security policies within the novelty-efficiency continuum. The fourth part examines the level of AU's success in translating its peace and security ideas into norms and whether these norms are new, effective, and efficient in addressing African peace and security challenges. The last part shows the performance of the AU peace and security decision-making structures.

WORLDVIEW

The AU seems to have taken a three-pronged view to peace and security on the African continent. The first is what can be described as a collectivist security system that seems to be based on the way conflict is often resolved at the local level in many societies in Africa. Like most collectivist social systems, in which members of the in-group are collectively responsible for the maintenance of the internal peace and harmony of the group, the Pan-African peace and security architecture seeks to make every member of the AU responsible for the maintenance of peace and security on the African continent. Similar to collectivist entities that loathe any interference in their internal affairs by a member of an out-group, the AU security paradigm seeks to protect African people and their governments from foreign interventions. The collective defence that AU member states have mounted in support of the Sudanese president Omar al-Bashir and the AU's vocal opposition to the 2011 NATO's (North Atlantic Treaty Organization) military intervention in Libya are all part of the collectivist security mindset.

The second AU security paradigm is grounded in human security ideas.[1] The Constitutive Act of the AU affirmed the centrality of human security to the AU when it provided in Article 4(m, o) that every African has the right to live in peace and respect for democratic principles and rule of law. This opened the legal and political space for the AU to adopt in July 2002 the human security ideas articulated in the "Conference on Security, Stability, Development, and Co-operation in Africa" (the CSSDCA) as the cornerstone of its approach to security in Africa.[2] The CSSDCA was originally developed in the early 1990s by a group of African civil society organizations that called itself the Kampala Movement.[3] The document expanded the definition of security from traditional state security concerns to include the economic, political, and social security of the individual, the family, and the society. In a Memorandum of Understanding (MOU) adopted by the Assembly in July 2002 in Pretoria in South Africa, the AU accepted the expansion of the definition of security to embrace "all aspects of society."[4] Though the MOU version of the CSSDCA diluted the original formulation that demanded certain "standards of behaviour . . . from every government [in Africa] in the interest of common humanity," there is no doubt that the AU's peace and security ideas are consistent with the human security doctrine.[5] The definition of security as a multidimensional phenomenon surpassing military considerations informed the drafting of the African Defence Pact that was adopted in June 2005 in Abuja in Nigeria.[6] Human security language articulated in the MOU also shaped other key AU peace and security governance instruments, such as the PSC protocol and protocol to the OAU Convention on the Prevention and Combating of Terrorism (Terrorism Protocol), the Revised African Maritime Transport Charter (the African Maritime Charter), the African Union Convention on Cross-Border Cooperation (the African Cross-Border Convention), and even the African Governance Charter.

The third foundational idea of the AU peace and security reflects the spirit of the Responsibility to Protect (R2P) doctrine.[7] The R2P-like ideas are clearly articulated in the Ezulwini Consensus, in which AU member states endorsed R2P and submitted a common position on it to the 2005 World Summit Outcome.[8] The Ezulwini Consensus reiterated the three pillars of R2P, namely: the responsibility of states to protect their citizens; the responsibility of the international community to help states protect their citizens; and the responsibility of the international community to protect citizens of states that are unable or unwilling to protect their citizens.

While the AU peace and security paradigm is broadly consistent with the spirit of the R2P doctrine, the wording of the Ezulwini Consensus made the African approach to peace and security slightly different from the original R2P outlined in either the report of the International Commission on Intervention and State Sovereignty (ICISS) or the report of the 2005 World Summit Outcome. The African take on the R2P, for instance, sees regional organizations rather than the UN as the best-positioned organization to intervene for humanitarian purposes. There are other important caveats in the Ezulwini Consensus that are discussed in the next section.

Novelty: The three ideas can best be described as Africa's distinctive approach to peace and security. The collectivist security concept is certainly different from conventional security doctrines embedded in most international organizations. It is different from both collective security and the security community. The AU security system moves beyond the collective security system, which simply requires that an attack on one member in the group is an attack on all members, to impose an obligation on all AU member states to support an African government in dispute with a non-African entity. The PSC's response to the United Kingdom's arrest of Rwandan intelligence chief Lieutenant-General Karenzi Karake in June reflects this collectivist security mindset. A communiqué issued by the PSC after a hurriedly arranged extraordinary meeting of the PSC on June 26, 2015, called Karake's detention "not only an attack on a Rwandan national, but on Africa as a whole."[9] In effect, the PSC turned a dispute between the Rwanda national/ government and United Kingdom into a continental dispute and in the process threw the full weight of the AU behind Rwanda.[10]

The collectivist security paradigm transcends collectivist security in another respect. The former obligates AU member states to contribute to the maintenance of order at the domestic level. Thus, while collective security deals with interstate relations, collectivist security regulates both intrastate and interstate relations. If properly applied, collectivist security requires each member of the in-group, in this case each African government, to prevent, resolve, manage, and if possible remove any external and internal threat posed to any member of the group. The collective security system is also different from a security community, which makes it unthinkable for in-group members to use military force to settle any dispute between them. The AU system has not developed to a level at which the use of force is completely off the table in dealings between member states. Members in a collectivist social structure do not rule out the use of force as a conflict-resolution mechanism. Thus, although each AU member state is expected to ensure the maintenance of peace and security of citizens within the African international system, military conflict between AU member states is still possible.

The collectivist security mindset in large part explains why the AU said nothing when Ethiopia in 2006 and Kenya in 2011 invaded Somalia in pursuit of militants from the Somali Islamist group, al-Shabaab.[11] The AU did not only support these clear violations of Somalia's sovereignty through quiet diplomacy, its PSC actually endorsed it after the fact. The AU would have been up in arms if a non-African country had intervened in Somalia without the explicit authorization of either the UN Security Council or the AU and did exactly what Ethiopia and Kenya did in Somalia.

The AU may also be the first international organization to have legalized the human security doctrine, defined as the protection of people and communities, rather than of states, from violence and imminent danger. No international organization has embellished its binding agreements, key policy documents, treaties, memoranda of understanding, plans of action, mission and vision statements, communiqués, conventions, declarations, and decisions with human security ideas more than the AU. [12] The Constitute Act, the PSC, the Defense Pact, and the Post Conflict Reconstruction Policy, just to mention these four, are replete with human security ideas. Even the AU approach to political governance in Africa is human security–centered inasmuch as the Constitute Act commits member states of the AU to promoting "respect for the sanctity of human life." [13]

It is also significant that 3(g) enjoins member governments to promote democratic principles and institutions, popular participation, and good governance. This provision is important for the AU human security agenda because it is generally understood in the human security research community that democratic development is a critical aspect of human security. [14] Human securitization of AU appears to be at odds with post–September 11, 2001, institutional development, which often prioritized traditional military security issues. Traditional security seems to have regained its preeminent position in the post-9/11 international system. Most international institutions and structures that emerged post-9/11 provided privileged positions to counterterrorism and military security issues. Yet the AU, which was inaugurated a few months after the September 11, 2001, terrorist attacks on the United States of America, kept faith with its human security approach to continental cooperation in Africa.

Finally, the AUs understanding of R2P is slightly different from the convention thinking of R2P. The Ezulwini Consensus sought to shift to regional organizations the power to decide when, where, and how to intervene, contrary to the argument put forth by the original R2P report. The Ezulwini document argued that "the General Assembly and the Security Council are often far from the scenes of conflicts and may not be in a position to undertake effectively a proper appreciation of the nature and development of conflict situations." The collective wisdom of members of the AU is that regional organizations are the institutions best placed to make the appropriate assessment, and should be "empowered to take actions in this regard." The Ezulwini Consensus delinked R2P from regime change, noting that even though "it is important to reiterate the obligation of states to protect their citizens, this should not be used as a pretext to undermine the sovereignty, independence and territorial integrity of states."

Though the Ezulwini Consensus and the original R2P report converged on the idea that intervention by regional organizations "should be with the approval of the Security Council," an interesting and subtle qualification was inserted into the Ezulwini Consensus that effectively makes it possible for regional organizations to seek the Security Council's approval after interventions. The Ezulwini Consensus also indicated that the UN should "assume responsibility for financing such operations." The language used here in the document is meant to encourage the UN to take ownership for keeping peace imposed by regional organizations. This regional-led peacekeeping strategy was employed by ECOWAS in Liberia and Sierra Leone, and the AU copied it when it intervened in Burundi, Sudan, and Somalia.

Relevance: The three peace and security paradigms seem very relevant to African ruling elites, donors, civil society groups, and even nonelites. The importance African governments attach to them is reflected in the fact that they are willing to bind their states within a legal framework that obligates them to promote and defend these ideas. All three paradigmatic ideas are codified in the Constitutive Act of the AU, the Peace and Security Protocol, and the African Defense Pact. Each one of these legal instruments have clauses that seek to protect African states from intervention by non-African states while leaving room for African states to intervene collectively in each other's internal affairs with or without the consent of the target country. The intervention can take different forms, including: mediation, as in the case of Kenya in 2008; suspension from participation in activities of African international organizations, as in the case of Mauritania in 2008; rebuke and suspension of AU membership, as in the case of Côte d'Ivoire in 2011; economic sanctions, as in the Malian case in 2012; and, as a last resort, military intervention, as in the case of Comoros Island in 2007.

There is little doubt that the three worldviews have positioned African leaders in a better place to discuss pressing African security concerns. They have at least shifted the mindset of African leaders away from, in the words of a judge of the African human rights court, "non-intervention to non-indifference."[15] The shift from politics of regime survival to politics of caring for the security of vulnerable groups has allowed African leaders to discuss issues that have the greatest impact on African peace and security. African leaders are no longer second-guessing themselves as to whether they have the right to intervene in domestic affairs of each other for humanitarian purposes. Most of the African security challenges are discussed in a relatively frank manner in the PSC. They have sanctioned governments, including AU major funders whose actions have undermined one of the three paradigmatic ideas. For instance, Egypt was suspended in 2013 for a year for violating key human security principles, including human rights abuses and the overthrow of civilian governments by its army. This would have been unthinkable prior to the creation of the African peace and security architecture.

Donors have found the AU peace and security paradigm an appropriate framework to engage African political elites. For mainstream donors, the language of R2P, human security, and perhaps more important the slogan "African solutions to African problems" that became the rallying point for discussing the new AU peace and security paradigms is perhaps the best slogan that has ever emerged since African countries gained independence. It allows them to delegate the burden of maintaining peace on the African continent to African political elites. For mainstream donors such as the European Union and the United States of America, there is nothing more convenient for them to do than just provide resources in the form of money and military hardware for Africans to police themselves. It is an easy and a cheap way for them to support African peace and security within the context of the post–Cold War era where most of these donors feel that they do not have any strategic security interest in policing the African continent.

For the international community, represented by the UN, the AU paradigms opened up the space for the UN Security Council to engage in burden sharing and division of labor when it comes to African peace and security. It gave the Security Council the chance to pick and choose the conflict that it is willing to take on and parcel the rest to the AU. The AU language of R2P and human security provided the convenient cover for the Security Council to delegate to the AU peacemaking in places such as Burundi, where most of the permanent members of the Security Council have little interests and in some instances the Security Council cajoled the AU into conflict zones such as Somalia where the UN and major powers have tried and failed to make peace. This enables the Security Council to focus on countries such as Democratic Republic of Congo and Sudan, where some P5 members have strong economic and political interests.

The AU peace and security paradigms serve as enablers for both the UN and donors to micromanage African peace and security on the African continent from afar without actually doing the heavy lifting. In the context of peacekeeping fatigue, the openings created by AU paradigms have come at the perfect time. For donors and the UN, nothing is more convenient than for them to provide resources while the Africans provide the blood necessary to keep peace on the African continent. Donors and the UN have the language and the excuse to engage with Africa peace and security in a limited, cautious, and calculated way. This explains why the European Union, United States, and the UN have been making the necessary strides to ensure that the AU peace and security paradigms are translated into actionable and concrete policy instruments. Self-interest has been at the heart of all of the consultancy and technical services the UN and donors have been providing to the AU in the last thirteen years.

For civil society groups, the AU peace and security paradigms have given them a renewed sense of purpose and a platform to put pressure on African leaders to protect their own people. The creation of the AU security framework has energized mainstream NGOs and led to the creation of a plethora of new transnational African civil society groups and/or the establishment of new alliances within the NGO community. Alliances of NGOs such as the Africa Governance Monitoring and Advocacy Project (AfriMAP) were established a few months after the adoption of the PSC protocol in 2004 to provide a platform for African civil society to, among other things, influence the direction of AU peace and security. Together with OXFAM, they drafted a guide for civil groups to engage primarily with the AU on peace and security issues. For nonelite Africans and vulnerable groups in Africa, the AU paradigms are of tremendous significance to them given that it attempts to shift the focus of security away from the state and African elites toward the individual and the community.

Financial Viability: Of the three new paradigms, the R2P-like idea is the one that has generated excitement within the donor community. The European Union in particular finds this paradigm more convenient and appropriate with its engagement with the AU. Even if mainstream donors such as the EU are not serious about African security, they have shown through financial commitment that they are at least willing to financially support the AU to implement its R2P-like interventions. The European Union has given approximately $1.2 billion to the AU in the last ten years to promote R2P-inspired interventions in places such as Darfur and Somalia.[16] The United States of America and Germany provided smaller but significant resources to both the AU and troop-contributing states to AU's interventions in Burundi, Darfur, and Somalia.

The United States alone gives over $100 annually both in kind and money as well as pays for a full-time peace and security advisor at the AU Peace Support Operations division at a cost of more than $300,000.[17] Almost all the resources are directed toward AU interventions. The bulk of the resources have gone to troop-contributing countries. The United States estimates that since 2007, it has provided over $341 million in the form of equipment, logistics support, advice, and training to troop-contributing countries (TCCs) participating in the African Union Mission in Somalia (AMISOM).[18] While critics will point out, and rightly so, that the majority of the resources will go back into the U.S military-industrial complex, it is equally the case that the AU would not have been able to make inroads in Somalia's complex security landscape without U.S support.

The AU paradigms have also inspired some African states to make significant contributions to African security, usually in the form of troops, logics, and in-kind donations. The constant criticisms, sometimes richly deserved but often superficial accusations, of African governments ignore the fact that some of them have contributed in no small way to peace and security in the continent. It was largely African resources that created peace in a number of African states including Burundi in 2005, Comoros in 2007, and Mauritanian in 2009, among others. Some of these contributions have come at heavy cost to African states. For instance, the tiny state of Burundi, which is contributing over five thousand troops to AMISOM even in the midst of its own political problems, had fifty peace enforcement officers reportedly killed by al-Shabaab in June 2016 alone.[19]

Other African states have suffered similar casualties in places such as Darfur, yet the often-maligned African governments continue to offer the service of their security personnel to AU interventions. To put this in perspective, the number of Burundian troops in Somalia and the casualties they have suffered in Somalia are more than the combined troops' contribution and casualties sustained by G8 countries in multinational mission to anywhere in Africa since the AU emerged on the scene thirteen years ago. The meaning of the slogan "Africans give blood and others provide money" rings true when you look at the actual peace missions in Africa in the last decade.

Effectiveness: Although African states generally consider these three paradigms to be relevant, they are yet to integrate these ideas into policies and practices at the levels of state, community, and at the local level. The collectivist understanding of African security remains largely at the continental level, and more so when African countries engage with non-African entities. It does not reflect the way individual African countries resolve conflict within their state. Most African countries still continue to resolve conflict through traditional state-centric methods, and there is no effort on the part of the leadership of many states to create a critical mass of people to spread the collectivist security idea.

In African countries where the collectivist security mindset exists, it is only visible at the community level, and there is very little attempt by the political elite to mainstream these indigenous mechanisms into the state system. In many instances the states have not really paid attention to it and as a result have not had the capacity to shape and if necessary tweak it to be in line with national conflict-management and resolution mechanisms. The absence of a national policy framework to make the collectivist security system a national approach to peace and security has turned the collectivist security mindset into an "us versus them" mentality in intergroup relations in some African communities. While it is enhancing intragroup harmony, it also has the capacity to simultaneously increase intergroup tension if not managed.

Similarly, African leaders are willing to talk nicely about human security, praise it, and rhetorically dance around it, but their approach to peace and security at the state level still reflects traditional state-centric and military security. For most African governments, security primarily means security from fear rather than security from want. Like the other two paradigms, the R2P-like framework is still a continental thought. It is yet to be ingrained in the national psyche of most African societies. In many ways it is still a foreign concept to a number of African communities.

Efficiency: The AU security paradigms seem not to have cost a fortune to develop. The impact these ideas have had in mobilizing both African governments and the international community to try to manage and contain some of the worst insecurities on the African continent seems to suggest they have provided value for money. No price tag will be sufficient for the 360-degree turnaround in thinking of African leaders in the last thirteen years.

In comparative terms, the AU's R2P-like interventions have been relatively cheaper than other humanitarian interventions. For instance, it cost the AU less than U.S. $400 million a year between 2003 and 2005 to create peace in Burundi, but it cost the UN twice as much when it took over the mission in 2006. Other AU missions such as those in Darfur and Somalia, the Mandrup and Møller study show, are "much cheaper than comparable UN missions."[20] The former AU special representative to Burundi, the late Ambassador Bah, in his usual witty ways summed up why the UN mission cost more than the AU when he indicated "the AU blood is not as expensive as other bloods."[21] He then went on to explain that UN spends more money than AU in peace operations because, in his words, "where I will go without a car or bodyguard, my UN counterpart will go there with two armoured cars and many bodyguards." The huge differences in procedures and bureaucratic and administrative cultures between the AU and the UN will make the AU's peace missions far cheaper than that of the UN in the near future.

In addition, it takes the AU far less time to intervene compared to that of the UN. At minimum it takes the UN six months to deploy troops after the decision is made, but the AU has the capacity to deploy troops in less than three months. In Darfur and Somalia, the AU deployed troops in less than sixty days. Of the international security organizations, only NATO has demonstrated shorter deployment capacity than the AU, but NATO's intervention is more expensive and politically complex than even the UN's. Indeed, the only IO with comparative advantage to the AU may be ECOWAS, but as it is documented elsewhere, regional organizations are too close to conflict zones and are driven by the political interests of the big country in the region. Thus, compared to other IOs, the AU approach to peace and security seems more efficient.

RULES

Nature: A number of rules have been developed to ensure that the three security paradigms have the binding force of the law. Among them is Article 4(h), which gives the union the right to intervene along the lines of the R2P.[22] The grounds for intervention are to "prevent war crimes, genocide and crimes against humanity." Though Article 4(h) is yet to be invoked, it has provided the broader context and cognitive orientations for the AU to intervene in African countries to protect and save lives. Consistent with the human security paradigm, Article 4(0) of the Constitutive Act encourages respect for the sanctity of human life, and Article 4(m) promotes respect for democratic principles, the rule of law, and good governance. It is also significant that 3(g) enjoins member governments to promote democratic principles and institutions, popular participation, and good governance. This provision is important for the AU human security agenda. As indicated before, the widespread idea in the human security research community is that democratic development is a crucial cord in human security.[23] The collectivist security system is legalized in many aspects of the Constitutive Act of the AU, including 3(a, b, d), which encourages solidarity and greater unity among Africans and their governments, urges Africans and their governments take common positions on international subjects and defend issues that are of importance to the continent, in addition to calling on Africans and their governments to defend their independence. These clauses are understood in AU leadership circles as calling on African governments to defend each other against imperialist tendencies and attacks by foreign entities, especially criticisms by Western political, economic, and social elites. The collectivist security system is further enhanced by Article 4(f, i), which encourages peaceful coexistence and the right of African states to live in peace and security, and it also prohibits the use of force or threat to use force among AU members. These general legal provisions open the space for the AU leadership to adapt the PSC protocol, which enhanced the legalization of the three AU approaches to peace and security. In addition, all three security ideas are embedded in the AU Non-Aggression Pact, the human rights protocols, and others.

Novelty: Many of the rules that the AU has developed in the last thirteen years have broken a number of international legal grounds. Many of the rules go beyond the UN Charter's paternalistic attitude toward regional organizations. At least they have opened up the legal and political spaces for the AU to engage in power-sharing arrangements with the UN in ways that was not anticipated in the UN Charter. For instance, the Charter neither anticipated that a regional organization will be able to intervene in the internal affairs of UN members and only informed the UN after the fact, nor did it foresee situations in which regional organization independently deployed troops to UN member states to create the peace and then co-opted the UN to keep the peace. Co-optation of the UN by the AU into conflict zones occurred when the AU intervened in Burundi in 2003, Darfur in 2005, and Somalia in 2011.

Many of the peace and security rules the AU has developed make a number of regional organizations such as the OAS and the ASEAN look conservative, at least on paper. The Common African Defense Pact establishes a security paradigm that transcends collective security systems and alliance frameworks and most of the security and defense agreements that have been agreed upon by most international organizations. It imposes a higher form of obligation than what NATO expects of its members and certainly what is expected of members of both the OAS and the ASEAN.

Similarly, Article 4(h) of the Constitutive Act is unique in the IO system. The threshold condition provided by the AU for intervention, as Schoeman points out, "goes 'beyond' the provision made for intervention in the internal affairs of a country in the UN Charter."[24] The AU has actually set thresholds for military intervention lower than those outlined in any other international legal code.[25] The article was introduced with a view to protecting ordinary people in Africa from abusive governments. [26] The specification of war crimes, genocide, and crimes against humanity as grounds for intervention has created a clearer set of criteria by which the Union can decide to intervene in a state for human security purposes.[27]

Finally, the AU Protocol on Terrorism provides some of the clearest and most elaborate legal principles on acts of terrorism and the means to contain them. It is certainly an improvement over what the UN has done, which is very little. The world body cannot even get its members to agree on the definition of terrorism. All the Security Council resolutions on terrorism, including resolution 1566, do not contain any definition.

Relevance: The relevance of the various AU peace and security protocols, conventions, pacts, and treaties to African governments, the donor community, civil society groups, and the so-called ordinary Africans cannot be overstated. For AU member states, these rules have enhanced interstate security in a number of ways. Just to mention two of these: first, they have strengthened border security and enabled a number of African countries to settle border disputes peacefully. The low level of interstate conflicts on the African continent is in large part due to the tremendous work of the OAU on borders that has since been strengthened and solidified by the AU system. The AU accepted all the border rules that the OAU developed, including the controversial decision to affirm borders drawn during the colonial rule. The only exception to the colonial border rule is South Sudan, and the AU made it abundantly clear that the situation of South Sudan was one off thing and will not be repeated. The tragic state of South Sudan and the few border wars in Africa in general suggest perhaps that the OAU/AU has done the right thing by accepting colonial boundaries as a basis for statehood in Africa.

The PSC protocol that led to the creation of the AU PSC has enhanced African security in multiple ways. It has provided the space for African governments to discuss their security challenges and clarify misunderstanding. It has been an excellent forum for tension reduction, and the PSC also carries enormous deterrence effect.

For the donor community, the creation of a number of peace and security rules has allowed them to engage with African actors in ways that they would not have imagined prior to the emergence of the AU on the political scene. The European Union, for instance, established the African Peace Facility in response to the adoption of the PSC protocol. The PSC protocol paved the way for AU and NATO to develop a relationship that would have been richer had it not been for NATO's ill-advised, uninformed, poorly conceived, and naïve military campaign in Libya in 2011.

In the case of other IOs, the AU peace and security rules rekindled their engagement with Africa. The UN Security Council has taken advantage of the space to develop a unique and elaborate relationship with the PSC. The UN's relations with AU transcend any cooperation the world body has with other regional organizations. For instance, the Security Council and the PSC hold regular consultations, including annual meetings in Addis Ababa and New York.

Many civil society organizations seem to have found the AU's rules important in their own work. The International Community of the Red Cross, in particular, has taken advantage of the PSC's rules on civilian protection to develop a twenty-first-century protection regime for AU peace support missions. In the case of non-African elites, the rules have at least given them the hope that the AU will come to their aid in their hour of dire need. A number of civilians in places such as Burundi, Darfur, and Somalia have had their lives saved in large part because of the introduction of the Constitutive Act as well as the PSC Protocol. As Rodt's work showed, the AU peacekeeping in Burundi, for instance, "was able to discourage violence and contribute to the creation of a secure environment conducive to peace. The force managed the violent aspect of the conflict and prevented further diffusion, escalation and intensification of violence. . . . AU troops also helped facilitate the return of refugees and internally displaced people and delivery of humanitarian aid."[28]

Financial Viability: If there are any rules within the AU system that have proved to be financially viable, then they are the AU rules on peace and security. The rules on humanitarian intervention, in particular, have gained the most traction within the donor community. The EU $1.2 billion support for the AU in the last ten years is driven by the R2P-like rules that guide AU's missions. U.S. support would not have been forthcoming without the peace and security rules. Without these rules, the United States would certainly not pay out anywhere close to $358 million it gave to the AU to make and keep peace in Somalia in 2010.[29] The rules enabled the UN to provide in-kind and logistical support to the AU peacekeeping missions in places such as Somalia, Darfur, and Burundi. African countries themselves have also found it convenient to use the AU humanitarian legal language to attract resources toward their militaries. A number of them have reorganized their military and encouraged donor countries to provide training and logistical support in the hope that the skill sets that have been impacted will be made available to the AU.

The AU legal framework has also encouraged the creation of new security systems and alliance systems among African states that in itself has attracted resources. The creation of the West and East African brigades, which were made possible by the PSC protocol, have also attracted significant

funding for African states. The humanitarian language embedded in the brigade concept has to some extent allowed the AU Commission to push
African countries to put resources into the maintenance of peace and security
in their own backyard. The $50 million that African states pledged toward
the multinational intervention force in Mali and the in-kind support that they
have provided to the AU in the last ten years have all been made possible by
the Constitutive Act and PSC protocol. The AU would have been able to
mobilize more resources if the AU Commission had been more organized
and proactive in developing the institutional capacity to absorb large sums of
donor funding. In some instances, funding for the AU peace and security had
not been disbursed or has been redirected primarily because the AU Commission seems incapable or unwilling to absorb the funds. For instance, in 2014
the EU redirected to the UN 50 million euros it had originally earmarked for
the AU Commission for the promotion of peace and security on the African
continent. In short, the financial viability of the AU rules is plainly obvious.

Effectiveness: Many of the peace and security rules have been mainstreamed into peace missions authorized by the AU. They inform the work of
the organization, and indeed the rules are the primary reason why the AU is
known within the international community. The relative success of the AU
peace and security rules account for the prominence of the AU peace and
security department within the AU system. The rules have led to the creation
of many institutional mechanisms within the AU system. The Peace and
Security Department is larger than any division within the AU primarily
because the AU rules led to the creation of bodies such as the Panel of the
Wise, the African Union Conflict Management Division, the Early Warning
Systems, and the African Union Border Programs. The consensus within the
current AU Commission is that the Peace and Security Department is too big
and must be split. Many keen observers expect it to be one of the major
recommendations of the new organizational structure that the AU Commission will present to the next AU summit in January 2016.[30] Critics of the AU
Commission will argue and perhaps rightly so that the PSD is being punished
for being by far the most effective and functional unit within the AU system.
Even in the midst of its leadership struggles in the last two years and its worst
performing years, it is still seen as the king of kings department in the AU
system.

Efficiency: Any honest assessment of the efficiency of the AU peace and
security rules will conclude that it has been admirably cost effective. Although it is still very expensive to implement most of the rules, such as
Article 4(h), the AU has still done it in a relatively cheap way compared to
the implementation of similar rules by other international organizations.
Compared to other regional organizations, such as the EU and NATO, the
AU rules have not been too expensive to implement. As pointed out already,

the cost of operationalizing the rules on intervention is cheaper than what it will cost other IOs to implement the same rules.

Consultants who are continentals in orientations developed the rules, and it often charges relatively lower consultancy fees than the going market rate paid by IOs such as the EU and UN. The cost for developing these rules are relatively cheaper because the AU has gotten rid of some of the procedural barriers that one would encounter in a matured international organization such as the EU. The AU is also not following some of the international standards that have been established by international organizations regarding peacekeeping around the world. The AU also pays less than the amount of money that other IOs give to its peacekeepers. The logistics for implementing major AU rules such those on peacekeeping, which are provided to AU peacekeepers by either member states or donors, are often discounted or donated.

CAUSAL IDEAS

Nature: The AU peace and security ideas are captured in four major policy instruments. The first is the African Union Policy Framework for the Establishment of the African Standby Force and the Military Staff Committee (the Standby Force Policy), which was released in May 2003.[31] The second is the African Union Policy on Post-Conflict Reconstruction and Development (the Post-Conflict Reconstruction Policy) published in June 2006.[32] The third is the African Union Policy Framework on Security Sector Reforms (the Security Sector Reform Policy) released in April 2013.[33] The last and most recent is the Common African Position on UN Review of Peace Operations (the Peace Operation Policy) submitted to the UN in April 2015.[34] The Standby Force Policy instrument outlines the AU's position on military intervention in the internal affairs of member states as well as the division of labor that the AU would like to see established between the AU, African regional organizations, and the UN. It gives the PSC a central role in decision making on peacekeeping, peace operations, and peacebuilding on the African continent and suggests that AU institutions are best positioned to provide African ownership on peace and security issues. In addition to making the African regional organization the building blocks of the AU, the Standby Force Policy creates a Military Staff Committee made up of the most senior security officers on the African continent who will provide military advice to the AU on peace and security matters. The Post-Conflict Reconstruction Policy provides guidelines of best practices for peacebuilding on the African continent. The AU policy contends that peacebuilding processes of the past have not taken African ownership into consideration, and the document is designed to enhance African agency and leadership in the peacebuilding processes. The main purpose of the Security Sector Reform Policy is to articulate the best ways to create a culture of peace, respect for civilian leadership, and professionalism among the various security agencies in Africa. The Peace Operation Policy is actually not a policy instrument in the proper sense of the word but rather a wish list of things AU would like to see reflected in the report of the UN panel on peace support operations. It rehashes ideas contained in documents articulating common African positions on peace and security issues and emphasizes the imperative for African ownership and priority setting in the conflict prevention–peacebuilding continuum. It asks the UN to articulate its support to the AU. It argues for burden sharing and codecision making with the UN on peace and security issues, and calls on the UN to listen to the AU's voices on matters such as transitional justice, women and peace, mediation, peace support operations, and postconflict reconstruction. In other words, the policy advocates for a new deal with the UN that goes far beyond Chapter VIII of the UN Charter.

Novelty: The four policy instruments bring out a number of distinctive African perspectives on the prevention and reconstruction continuum. They provide a basic understanding of African views on conflict prevention, conflict management, conflict resolution, and peacebuilding. This section will analyze the postconflict reconstruction document, in particular, in further detail. The postwar policy is designed to discourage peace builders from trying to civilize citizens of postwar states by directing the peace builders' attention to local needs and encouraging them to respect local cultures. Leading figures at the AU Commission think current peacebuilding projects carry too many residues from the civilizing missions and projects of the eighteenth and nineteenth centuries.[35] They claim current peacebuilding projects are driven by a civilizing mission, because they try to: replicate representative government in the form of a presidential or parliamentary system of government (read democratization) that exists in donor states; replace traditional and customary rules with formal written laws similar to those in donor states (read promotion of the rule of law); and spread values and ideas held by external interveners and their donors (read promotion of good governance). The projects also attempt to stimulate local people's taste for merchandised goods produced in donor countries (read economic reforms). The AU leadership thinks that while these may be well intentioned, they are likely to have disastrous long-term impacts on postwar societies. The AU Commission attached to the postwar reconstruction policy a "flexible template" to help peace builders' move beyond civilizing goals to "pave the way for growth and regeneration in countries and regions emerging from conflict."[36]

The template is also designed to dissuade peace builders from prioritizing aspects of the reconstruction processes at the expense of others. A major complaint from civil society groups during AU–civil society consultations on postwar reconstruction was that many donors and practitioners tend to favor aspects of reconstruction that will generate publicity and media attention to the exclusion of other important, but less visible, areas. Often the ones that are neglected, such as psychological healing, retraining of former combatants, and the creation of sustainable jobs, are precisely those that are most needed by the people recovering from the war. The AU wants to end the discriminatory practices by producing a menu of items essential for peace builders to accomplish in war-ravaged African countries. Given the AU's complaints that current peacebuilding ideas are borrowed from outside of Africa, it is ironic that the template draws heavily from liberal capitalist democratic principles, such as the rule of law. Indeed, the democracy ideals they listed appear identical to the conventional liberal peacebuilding exercises the policy seeks to replace. Perhaps these ideas somehow lose their civilizing significance when they are articulated by African elites. The hypocrisy notwithstanding, the policy could minimize the potential for conflicts over the political objectives of postwar reconstruction in the African context.

The postwar reconstruction policy provided benchmarks for measuring successes and failures of peacebuilding. Given the attraction of human security discourses in AU circles, it was perhaps to be expected when the then-chairperson of the AU Commission claimed that every postwar peacebuilding process in Africa must strive to free the so-called ordinary Africans from "want and fear." [37] On the question of freeing people from want, the AU expects peacebuilding to create the conditions in which people affected by war can improve their living conditions; meet basic needs, such as for health, education, and food; and enhance their capacity to realize their potential. On freeing people from fear, the AU borrowed ideas from conventional disarmament, demobilization, and reintegration (DDR) programs. Thus, at the end of the postwar reconstruction, the AU expects peace builders to complete the demanding task of establishing conditions for social, political, economic, and physical transformations of affected areas, societies, and states.

The postwar reconstruction policy attempted to address the obvious question of how African these ideas are as the document reads like a poorly attributed paper or, even, a plagiarized review of peacebuilding literature. The template and the broader policy documents claimed the state-building ideas are not African ideas per se, but that they can be adapted and embedded in certain principles to suit local African conditions. The AU has consequently developed six principles; namely, African leadership, national and local ownership, inclusiveness, equity and nondiscrimination, and cooperation and cohesion, as well as capacity building for sustainability to guide peacebuilding exercises. Though many of these principles lack specifics, the AU leadership hopes the principles of national and local ownership will empower local actors to domesticate peacebuilding projects and to exercise oversight in the reconstruction processes. The AU Commission thinks local Africans will use the ideas to set the terms of peacebuilding engagements with external actors.

African Union members recognize that peacebuilding can easily be used to reconstruct the identities of people in societies emerging from war. The principles of African leadership are meant to help Africans determine the content of peacebuilding projects. Rather than turning war-torn societies into photocopies of outside cultures, AU members hope national bureaucrats and local authorities will use the template to design, assess, implement, monitor, and evaluate peacebuilding projects in such a way that they reinforce core local identities and values. The AU is acutely aware that it is not enough to make Africans take leadership positions. It is equally vital that ordinary Africans get involved in order to ensure local acceptance of peacebuilding projects. The principles of inclusiveness, equity, and nondiscrimination, with their emphasis on equitable distribution of power, wealth, and organic links between peace builders and the local population, are designed to ensure that ordinary people are involved in reconstruction exercises.

Coordination and cooperation are problems of legendary severity in the current aid system, and peacebuilding projects that depend heavily on donor support carry this baggage as well. The principles of cooperation and coherence are meant to promote synergy among different peacebuilding activities, encourage genuine partnership among actors involved in reconstruction, and promote donor cooperation and coordination. As a Pan-African organization, the AU would ideally like Africans based in Africa to manage every aspect of peacebuilding projects, but it knows that the expertise is unavailable. It developed the principles of capacity building for sustainability to encourage peace builders and donors to prioritize capacity building of locals so that the local people will make the necessary efforts to consolidate and sustain peacebuilding projects.

African Union members are acutely aware that intermediaries can sometimes be spoilers in peacebuilding processes.[38] Intermediaries such as peacebuilding consultants, nongovernmental organizations, and donors are not necessarily altruistic, however morally superior the outlook they project. Intermediaries are quick to tell those who will listen that their main goal is to help war-torn states resolve the root causes of conflicts; but in practice, as the volume edited by Dayton and Kriesberg showed, few have pursued this objective in any meaningful way.[39] It is not uncommon to find intermediaries putting their interests above those of the people they are supposed to be helping. The AU's aim is to minimize the incentive for self-seeking donors to turn the peacebuilding exercises into a lucrative industry. The benchmarks and principles are meant to discourage intermediaries from treating their work as mere jobs or careers.

Though AU peacebuilding ideas are general and imprecise, and at times contradictory and incoherent, their drafters made an excellent move by establishing linkages between the postwar reconstruction ideas and extant AU policies. The security elements were thus embedded in human security ideas outlined in the African Non-Aggression and Common Defence and Security Pact. The political governance element draws extensively from the AU Declaration on Political, Economic, and Corporate Governance of 2002, which contains the textbook conception of political governance. The drafters of the postwar reconstruction policy thus attempt to prevent illegal seizure of power in countries emerging from war by drawing on the 1999 OAU Declaration against unconstitutional change of governments in Africa. The clear definition of unconstitutional change of government in the declaration—as the replacement of a democratically elected government through a military coup d'état, or mercenary intervention, or armed rebellion, or by the refusal by an incumbent government to relinquish power to the winning party after free, fair, and regular elections—together with the mechanical way in which the anticoup principles in the Declaration have been applied, has provided an effective mechanism with which to close a loophole in the current peacebuilding system. The current system has no means, except the court of public opinion, to prevent unconstitutional changes of governments during a statebuilding period.

The postwar reconstruction policy seeks to prevent war-torn states from sliding into electoral dictatorship. It is easy for postwar societies to practise electoral politics—or to, at least, hold an election with international support. Consolidation of postwar democracies has, however, become one of the most difficult activities in peacebuilding exercises. Governments that emerge from postwar electoral processes often try to use legal means to undermine democratic institutions. The recent history of Africa is replete with examples, and studies also show that authoritarian tendencies have crept into the administrations of a number of ostensibly democratic postwar states.[40] Ethiopia, Sierra Leone, Uganda, and Rwanda, for example, have all become casualties of democratic backsliding. To deal with the problem, the postwar reconstruction commits the AU to defending and protecting African democracies by linking peacebuilding exercises to the African Charter on Democracy, Elections, and Governance (the African Democratic Charter), which entered into force on February 15, 2012.[41]

The AU seeks to introduce a third-party oversight into peacebuilding processes in order to deal with the current system, which has no institutional mechanisms for either international or African peace builders to render accounts of their performance on key aspects of their work. African Union members want to make the AU Commission the overarching institution to which peace builders and postwar societies can submit reports that show how they are performing in key areas, such as democratization. That development would be a major corrective to the current system, which is based on the belief that international pressure will be enough to nurture critical projects, such as democracy, once elections are organized and elected leaders take office in war-ravaged states. Without a third-party obligation, it has become too easy for elected leaders to use legal and constitutional means to erode democratic gains, as the cases of Burundi and Rwanda show. The AU instrument introduces third-party oversight by empowering the AU Commission to monitor progress made by postwar states in areas such as good governance, respect for the rule of law, consolidation of peace agreements, disarmament and the reintegration of former combatants, and the return of refugees and internally displaced persons.

Finally, the postwar reconstruction policy tries to offer institutional mechanisms for parties in postwar societies to resolve electoral disputes. Electoral disputes are major challenges in countries emerging from war, and the current postwar reconstruction system has few institutionalized mechanisms to resolve disagreements over electoral results. The policy links reconstruction to other rules, regulations, and norms the AU has developed to minimize postelection disputes. These include requiring member states to inform the AU Commission of any scheduled elections and to invite the AU Electoral Assistant Unit to send an electoral observer mission and to give detailed rules for elections in member states. The AU Commission has the power to conduct election monitoring without the express consent of member states. The AU Commission's ability to monitor elections has thus been enhanced, as clever governments often use the "by invitation only" prerogative to negotiate the terms of the observation mission. This prerogative has been used by incumbent governments in places such as Latin America to issue an invitation so close to an election that it gives the observers little time to prepare.[42] Other governments have used the "by invitation" principle to negotiate for a sympathetic mission, to limit access to electoral institutions, and to shape the election observation mission to their liking. African governments would seek to mainstream and globalize these ideas if a new Agenda for Peace were to be discussed and adopted in 2012.

Relevance: The policy frameworks are relevant to African governments inasmuch as they provide a consensual view of African states on key peace and security issues. The policy framework on the UN Review of Peace Operations enabled African states to provide a common African position to the UN panel. It created some semblance of unity and coherence and a common frame of reference for the UN panel. It also gave African states the language and talking points to engage with the UN system on peace and security issues.

Similarly, the international community and donor agencies see policy instruments as relevant. The policy document for the ASF gave the UN a clear understanding of how to work with the AU in preventing and responding to conflicts on the African continent. The UN seems to have found it relevant enough to encourage senior UN staffers to decide to engage with the AU in the operationalization of the ASF. Indeed, the UN has been paying close attention to every step that the AU has been taking in the implementation of the framework. In many instances, the UN has seconded some of its experts to the AU or helped the AU translate the document into implementable instruments. In other words, the ASF policy framework has been the guiding principle of UN and donor engagement with the AU.

Equally significant has been the policy framework to civil society groups and non-African elites. Both the postconflict reconstruction framework as well as the security sector reform policy are designed to help local African actors to take ownership of security sector reforms and postconflict reconstruction in their areas. They have both given the language, the templates, and the benchmark for civil society groups and local actors to measure the performance of peacebuilding and postconflict reconstruction activities. The big question is, how many are aware of the existence and content of these policies?

Financial Viability: Of the four policy instruments, the ASF's document seems to have captured the imagination of the mainstream donor community. It has galvanized the UN to develop some form of coherent relationship with the AU in the area of peace operations. The UN has provided a number of in-kind contributions and expert services toward the operationalization of the ASF. Mainstream donors such as the GIZ and the United States have been able to provide unprecedented funding, including building a multipurpose complex specifically for the DPS. This partnership was made possible in large part because of the policy frameworks that exist for donors to engage with the AU on peace and security issues.

Although African countries themselves have not in the past provided enough funding for the implementation of these policies, the attraction of donor communities to AU peace and security have shamed them to the extent that they have now committed themselves to providing the bulk of funding for AU peace-and-security-related activities in the future. The budget that was approved for the AU in 2016 almost doubled the African government's contributions to AU peace and security activities.

Another way of looking at how much the AU has attracted funding is to compare the funding that African states provided to the OAU and the AU. In comparative terms, African countries' contributions to peace-related activities have increased over 500 percent since 2000 (from under $30 million in 2000 to over $200 million in 2015). The change of orientations of African governments may have something to do with the plethora of peace and security instruments that the DPS has developed over the last decade.

Effectiveness: Most of the policy instruments have been adapted in bits and pieces by AU member states, and none of them have been mainstreamed into national policy instruments or legislations of any of the member states of the AU. The postconflict reconstruction idea, the policy framework on UN reforms, and the security sector reforms are all aspirational policy instruments as far as most African states are concerned. Many of them do not have a national policy instrument that reflects the wonderful ideas that the AU has articulated. The national policy instruments do not reflect these ideas primarily because consultants and AU bureaucrats wrote the AU's policies, and few African countries had a role to play in the development of these policies. The closest African governments got to the development of these polices was through the consultative processes, but these consultative processes are very much controlled by AU bureaucrats.

Take, for instance, the development of the postconflict reconstruction policy. The consultative processes included: a Brainstorming Retreat for members of the PSC and the PRC, held on September 4 and 5, 2005, in Durban, South Africa; a Technical Experts Meeting of AU members, held on February 7 and 8, 2006, in Addis Ababa, Ethiopia; an AU and Civil Society Dialogue, held from April 5 to 7, 2006, in Abuja, Nigeria; a Validation Workshop for the AU Commission, held on May 31, 2006, in Addis Ababa; and, finally, a Governmental Experts Meeting held on June 8 and 9, 2006, in Addis Ababa. In September 2006, the AU Commission discussed with civil society groups the best ways to promote the postwar policy. The AU leadership believes these processes used to develop the postwar policy gave a broad spectrum of Africans the chance not only to shape peacebuilding ideas in Africa but also to stop the dumping of foreign ideas on Africans. In truth, the draft policy instruments developed by consultants did not really change that much after going through these consultative processes. The processes were more of an information session than a consultative process.

The AU itself has not been able to implement these policies in any coherent basis. Of the four policy instruments, the one that the AU has been able to operationalize to a limited extent is the policy framework on the establishment of the ASF. It has led to the establishment of the West, East, and Southern African brigades. Even so, the North and Central African regions are not close to establishing their brigades. The inability of the AU to operationalize the ASF in full has led to South Africa proposing the creation of the Rapid Reaction Force as an interim measure. This has been a hotly debated issue in the last two years, and at the last AU summit held in Johannesburg it became clear that the political will to create a rapid reaction force is not there. The AU has gone back to the drawing board and is now exploring ways to operationalize the ASF.

The other documents are perhaps too new and will take some time for us to know if African countries are willing to integrate them into national policy instruments and implement them. Perhaps they will join other policy instruments and remain on the shelves gathering dust.

Efficiency: A major reason for developing these policy instruments stem from the painful experience that the UN approach to African peacekeeping is too top-down, cumbersome, and does not provide value for money. Subregional organizations such as ECOWAS can provide relatively efficient peace operations, but as ECOWAS's intervention in Liberia and Sierra Leone showed, these African regional institutions are easily manipulated and monopolized by regional hegemons. Interventions by African regional communities impose too much cost on regional hegemons to the extent that few of them are willing to get involved in such peace-and-security-related activities on a sustainable basis. The AU framework brings with it some form of African legitimacy while at the same time it offers some distance between national interests of countries in their region and what needs to be done to maintain peace in a particular country.

The development of these policy frameworks did not cost the AU resources beyond what most international organizations offer. In actual fact, the development of these policies are relatively cheap in part because the AU is able to draw on the expertise of a select group of Pan-African intellectuals who are often able and willing to provide their services either very cheaply or for free. The AU postconflict reconstruction program was written in large part by a number of Pan-Africanists who took nothing more than a small per diem and seating allowances. In some instances, per unit costs of consultancy services provided to the AU are cheaper than in other parts of the world. In short, these policy frameworks can be described as relatively cost effective, although translating them into national legislation may end up costing individual African countries perhaps as much as what they would have spent in developing and implementing similar policies at the national level.

NORMS

Nature: The AU peace and security activity has led to the emergence of a number of norms to guide the behavior of African states in the area of peace and security. The first norm is the so-called norm of nonindifference, which is the idea that the AU will no longer ignore domestic issues that impact on the peace and security of the African continent. It has become the practice for the AU to discuss and interfere in peace and security matters that are within the jurisdiction of individual African countries. This is a fundamental shift from the OAU days when domestic affairs of African states were seen as out of bounds for international organizations. The OAU could not discuss issues that bordered on domestic affairs of African states. Any discussion of such matters were considered interference in the internal affairs of member states and shut down.

In contrast to the OAU system, every peace and security concern can be discussed in PSC. Indeed, the expectation is that the AU will discuss any threat to African peace and security. In the words of the former chairperson of the AU Commission, Alpha Oumar Konaré, the AU has shifted "from the old norm of 'non-interference' in armed conflicts to a new posture of 'nonin-difference' to member states' internal affairs."[43]

The second and the most underrated norm that the AU has introduced into the African international system is a norm that prevents individual member states from acquiring and developing nuclear weapons. The norm is so strong to the extent that South Africa and Libya had to give up their nuclear weapon programs as part of the process of rejoining the African international system in the 1990s. Though Western policymakers took credit for Libya's decision to suddenly abandon its nuclear weapons program, those who follow closely the late Gaddafi's politics knew he gave it up as part of the transformation from an Arab troublemaker to a Pan-African statesman. He knew it was a taboo for an African state to have a nuclear weapons program or even harbor an ambition to have one, and would have found it difficult to establish legiti-macy for his Pan-African leadership if he had not abandoned the nuclear weapons program. It is not a sheer coincidence that Africa is the only conti-nent that has no nuclear weapons state. The OAU took a firm no-nuclear-weapons stance, and the AU continued the pace set by the OAU. The norm is firmly imbedded in key AU legal instruments, including the African common defense policy.

The norm that has enhanced peace and security in Africa is the Pan-African solidarity norm, which is a widespread belief among African ruling elites that the proper and ethically acceptable behavior of Africa's political elites is to demonstrate a feeling of oneness and support toward other Africans, at least in public. This feeling of "we-ness," or public show of support, among African leaders goes "beyond the merely rhetorical level" to impose "on African rulers a sense that, at any rate, they *ought* to act in harmony."[44] The solidarity norm not only discourages African leaders from disagreeing with each other in public, it also puts "pressure on the rulers of individual African states not to step out of line over issues where a broad continental consensus had been established."[45] The norm was developed "at the first [Session] of OAU Council of Ministers [held in] Lagos" in 1963.[46]

The fourth norm that the AU has been promoting is the norm around territorial integrity of African states. Here the AU accepted the OAU's norm of respecting borders that were drawn during the colonial era. This norm is so strong that only South Sudan has defied the norm, with the AU grudgingly agreeing to it and indicating that the Sudanese case is an exceptional one and will not be repeated elsewhere. This territorial integrity norm that the AU has been promoting has contributed to the historically low rate of interstate con-flict on the African continent. It may paradoxically have contributed to the rate of internal wars on the African continent, but the broader significance in terms of reducing interstate war on the African continent should not be underestimated.

Finally, the AU has also introduced and promoted the anticoup norm as part of a broader approach to conflict prevention on the African continent. The respect and importance that African states attached to the norm is not in doubt. The justification that is often provided by breakers of the anticoup norm is a strong indication of the level of institutionalization of the norm.

Novelty: All five norms are distinctively African in nature. There is no region in the world where a regional organization has the freedom to discuss every peace-and-security-related matter or has the freedom to discuss issues that are purely internal matters of states. Asia, Latin America, and the Middle East still hold on to the traditional interpretations of noninterference. The Arab League, the ASEAN, and the OAS were all built and stand on very strong noninterference norms. Even the EU does not have a very strong voice when it comes to the maintenance of the peace and security within the area of its jurisdiction.

There is also no other continent beside Africa that has made the acquisition of nuclear weapons an inappropriate act that is subject to social sanctions. Asia, the Americas, Europe, and the Middle East are all not nuclear-free zones. Africa is not only a nuclear-weapons-free zone; it appears most African countries do not aspire to acquire nuclear weapons. This is not out of the blue but a conscious effort among the African elite to dissuade themselves against the will to acquire nuclear weapons. It is a taboo subject within the institutional framework of the AU to discuss or even raise the issue of an African country acquiring nuclear weapons. There is also no continent in the world where there is a very strong anticoup attitude. Almost all coups that have occurred since the emergence of the AU have been punishable by sanctions and their membership to the AU suspended. They have only been able to rejoin the AU after an election has been held and a constitutional system of government established. The AU anticoup norm is so strong that it became the only international organization to have taken a firm stand against one of its own big funders, Egypt, even when most Western states such as the United States refused to call it a coup.

Relevance: All five norms have proven their relevance to African governments, the donor community, and to non-African elites. The Pan-African solidarity norm, for example, allows African countries to develop a common position and maintain some semblance of unity and cohesion. This has been very important in part because Africa exhibits enormous diversity in terms of governance, social structures, beliefs, attitudes, languages, and more. Without an operating broader norm such as the Pan-African solidarity norm, it would have been very difficult for African political elites to do anything together. It has also enabled the ruling elite to protect themselves from the global power configuration that is unequal and in which they find themselves to be very invisible within. African leaders such as Omar al-Bashir and Uhuru Kenyatta have found it convenient to seek the shelter of the Pan-

African solidarity norm when they have had conflict with a non-African entity. The downside of it is that the norm has also prevented non-African elites from getting the justice they deserve and for holding their leaders accountable.

The nonindifference norm has allowed the African Union to intervene in a number of places where ordinary citizens were at risk of being massacred or where there is a possibility of genocide, crimes against humanity, and war crimes. The nonindifference norm enabled the AU to deploy troops in Burundi in 2003, Darfur in 2005, and Somalia in 2011. While these interventions have not been universally positive, there is little doubt that they have contributed to saving the lives of thousands if not millions of ordinary Africans. As Gettleman showed in the case of Somalia, "The African Union has done a better job of pacifying Mogadishu, Somalia's capital and a hornet's nest of Islamist militants, clan warlords, factional armies and countless glassy-eyed freelance gunmen, than any other outside force, including 25,000 American troops in the 1990s."[47] The norm against nuclear acquisition has largely contributed to the relative security that Africans have from nuclear annihilation. At least most Africans do not live under the constant fear that a neighboring state may use nuclear weapons, unlike in other parts of the world. The donor community does not have a nuclear Africa to worry about.

The anticoup norm has also contributed to some extent to the lives of ordinary Africans as it has greatly reduced the rate of coups and the acceptance of military governments on the African continent. The abuses that military governments perpetrated against civilians are generally seen as a thing of the past. This can only be a good news story for ordinary Africans. The donor and international community have also found some of the AU norms very useful. The UN and Western governments have found the anticoup norm to be a good framework with which to engage with other African countries. Although the UN still does not have anticoup norm, the AU position on coups has given the UN a clear and easy way to close its doors to coup makers from the African continent. It must be pointed out that not all the norms have been very relevant to the donor community. Many donors despise the Pan-African solidarity norm because it shields African leaders from some of the accountable measures that have been promoted in the international system.

Financial Viability: The five norms have not been used explicitly to solicit funds or as a basis for donors to give money to the AU or African states. The AU has not used these norms as a tool for mobilizing funds. Implicitly, however, some donors have provided resources to the AU in part because of its stance on coups and nuclear weapons. In other words, the norms may not have attracted money to the AU explicitly, but they have provided a foundation for the good image that the AU enjoys. The norm themselves have not encouraged African countries to provide resources but have implicitly galvanized them to be more engaged in Pan-African affairs. The commitment of the Kenyan and Sudanese governments to the AU and their willingness to pay their countries' annual contributions is due in part to the benefit that they enjoy from norms such as the Pan-African solidarity norm. Although it is difficult to assess the financial viability of AU peace and security norms, it is safe to say that the AU peace and security system has attracted more resources than any other unit in part because of the peace and security norms the AU has developed over the last decade.

Effectiveness: All five norms have operated very effectively and in some cases too effectively. The Pan-African solidarity norm, for example, has permeated too deep into the fabric of African political elites to the extent that is it actually undermining open and engaging conversation. It has prevented African governments from disagreeing and criticizing each other or even encouraging each other to do better. Critics of the AU can point out that the effective operation of the Pan-African solidarity norm is partly to blame for the poor human rights situation on the continent and the widespread culture of impunity.

The norm on nuclear weapons has also been very effective, as there has been no major attempt by any African state to put nuclear weapons on the agenda of the AU. It may have crossed the minds of the African political elite, but they know it is a taboo subject and no one will gain traction with the idea of making an Africa state a nuclear zone. The effectiveness of the anticoup norm is widely documented, and there is no need to repeat them.[48]

Efficiency: The cost-benefit analysis of producing each one of these norms should be deemed as efficient. The benefit of having a nuclear-free Africa, few military governments, and the benefits associated with the AU norms on borders cannot be overestimated. No money can buy them. The price tag for the limited amount of interstate conflict on the African continent should be high in monetary terms. Although the benefits of the Pan-African solidarity norm has not been universally positive, overall it has been a very important normative framework for a continent that is so diverse and super weak in the global power configuration. While non-Africans and those that look at Africa at the superficial level are quick to point fingers at the negative impact of the Pan-African solidarity norm, perceptive observers of African politics do recognize that overall it has been a positive norm for the continent. It was relatively cheap to produce, and its benefits are enormous.

DECISION-MAKING STRUCTURES

African Union peace and security ideas are promoted by an organizational structure headed by the PSC.[49] The PSC, established to make swift, timely, and efficient decisions relating to all peace and security issues in Africa, is comprised of ten members who are elected for a two-year term, and five members who are elected to serve for three years. There is no permanent or veto-wielding member. Membership is merit based, though every effort is made to ensure regional balance in the allocation of seats. So far, the two-year term and three-term seats have been distributed equally among the five subregions of Africa. The AU Commission acts as the administrative unit of AU peace and security architecture, while a Military Staff Committee comprised of Senior Military Officers from various African military establishments offers the necessary technical advice to the civilian managing the AU peace and security system. The PSC agenda is set by a chairperson, a position rotated among PSC members on a monthly basis. Decisions of the PSC are binding, and do not require approval by heads of state to take effect. The binding nature of PSC decisions, together with the seriousness of its deliberations, has given the PSC the highest profile in the AU system.[50]

The other members of the AU peace and security organizational structure are the Panel of the Wise, the Early Warning System (EWS), the Peace Fund (PF), and the African Standby Force (the ASF). The Panel of the Wise is composed of five highly respected African personalities who have made outstanding contributions to the cause of peace and security in Africa. They are selected by the chairperson of the Commission on the basis of competence and regional representation to serve for a renewable three-year term. The Continental Early Warning System consists of an observation and monitoring center known as "the Situation Room" located at the AU headquarters in Addis Ababa. The Situation Room is supposed to be linked to similar structures at the subregional levels. The feed from the regional systems, together with independent data collected by the Situation Room at the AU headquarters, is supposed to help the PSC get accurate and timely information about potential trouble spots on the African continent. The Peace Fund is made up of roughly 6 percent of AU annual assessed contributions, voluntary contributions from African states, and donations from external partners. As of the time of writing, over 90 percent of contributions to the peace fund came from external actors, primarily the European Union and the United States. The African Standby Force has multidisciplinary contingents of civilian and military brigades assembled at each of the five subregions of Africa. When fully operational, the ASF will be able to deploy within thirty days, and stay in combat theatre for up to ninety days. As of the end of July 2015, West Africa, East Africa, and Southern Africa had established the nucleus and policy basis for a regional brigade. So far two major field military exercises called AMANI AFRICA (meaning peace in Africa in the Kiswahili language) I and II, aimed at testing the readiness of the ASF, has been held in North Africa and Southern Africa.

Novelty: All AU peace and security institutions bring something distinctive to the regional and global security landscape. At the global level, creators of the PSC integrated the positive side of the Security Council into the PSC system, and they made a conscious effort to avoid defects of the UN system. The PSC addressed the delicate balance between big states' desire for preferential treatment in representation and the principle of equality of states in more creative ways than was provided for in the UN Charter. The creators of the PSC did not appease powerful states by trading permanent and veto-wielding seats for their commitment. Rather, the drafters of the PSC protocol invented renewable three-year term seats that five egomaniac states can fight for while other renewable two-year term seats were established for the other states to compete for.[51] The creators of the PSC learned the right lessons from the inequitable geographical representation on the UN Security Council. They provided for equitable representation for all five subregions of Africa. Each subregion was allocated three seats.

At the regional level, the drafters of the PSC protocol recognized the importance of drawing on domestic conflict-resolution mechanisms and the special role elders play in dispute settlement within the community. The Panel of the Wise, made up of five elderly and supposedly wise Africans who will provide second sober thoughts and can be used to diffuse tension, was added to the security apparatus. The Council is a distinctively African concept and does not exist in a formal sense in any IO. The Panel members have so far been highly respected retired heads of states, senior public policy officials, diplomats, and politicians. The drafters of the AU peace and security system recognized that gender is an important element in thinking about peace and security. A conscious effort was made to ensure gender balance in the appointment of members of the Panel of the Wise.

The creators of the AU peace and security system did not want to fall into the problem that the UN has encountered in enforcing its decisions. Building on the often discussed but discarded idea of a standby army for the UN, an African Standby Force made up of a multinational, multiethnic, and multi-purpose rapid deployment force was added to the peace and security institutions. If operationalized in full, the AU will be the only major IO in the world with a standby army. The standby force also brought its own innovations. It co-opted African regional communities by locating the five brigades of the Standby Force within African regional communities, thereby making them building blocks of the Force. The African regional communities are mandated to create one brigade for each one of the five regions of Africa.

Drawing lessons from the UN's lack of an intelligence unit, the AU peace and security system proposed a military staff committee that will not only enhance the AU's intelligence-gathering capacities but would serve as a technical unit for the African Standby Force. Equally interesting is the Early Warning System that is supposed to gather information and analyze and forecast potential trouble spots for rapid and swift action of the PSC. Almost all of these institutional mechanisms are absent in comparable international

organizations, including the OAS and the ASEAN. They offer something
new in the design of regional security systems.

Relevance: All five security institutions, perhaps with the exception of the
African Standby Force, have demonstrated their relevance to African governments, donor agencies, civil society groups, and non-African elites. For
African governments, the PSC is the most important security institution outside of the UN Security Council. In some cases, African leaders actually hold
the PSC in a higher regard than the UN Security Council. They see the PSC
as more legitimate and fair in institutional design than the UN Security
Council. Almost all African countries are willing to put their cases across to
the PSC. It is the first IO African leaders go to whenever they face any major
peace and security challenge. It was the PSC that the Rwandan government
contacted and complained about when its intelligence officer was detained in
the United Kingdom in June 2015. The PSC decisions have so far been
treated with enormous respect by many African countries. Almost all African
leaders and state representatives that have been summoned before the PSC
have appeared before the Council, and there is a tremendous diplomatic
effort on the part of African governments to influence the agenda and decisions of the PSC. In addition, the PSC provides a forum for African political
elites to localize global and transnational security norms to reflect local
African situations and identities. Thus, the PSC has become an important
institution for the localization of transnational norms. [52]

The Panel of the Wise is equally highly regarded by many African states,
although its usefulness has been limited to trouble spots and countries where
AU mediation is particularly needed. Donors and foreign entities have found
the PSC to be a good forum for gathering information about African states
and where they stand on pertinent global issues. Like the UN, it is a good
source for gathering human intelligence. The PSC has contributed to the
growth and high concentration of diplomats from rich countries in Addis
Ababa. In general, mainstream donors seem to find the PSC as a useful
interlocutor and an institution they can work with to enhance not only
African security but also the peace and security of their own countries.

Civil society groups seem to have found the PSC to be a very relevant
institution to engage with. There is intense lobby within the civil society
community for the attention of PSC members and to gain access to PSC
meetings, documents, and events. The status of a PSC observer is a prized
asset in the NGO community as they see the PSC as an important source of
information for their advocacy works. Because the PSC "mediates between
the AU's approach to conflict management and the expectations of outisiders, some of the ambassadors representing PSC members are often given
preferential treatment and even treated like a mini-celebrity in some circles in
Addis Ababa.[53] The early warning system has also become a very important
source of information for African leaders, civil society groups, and foreign

diplomatic establishment in Addis Ababa, although the open source of information that analysts of the Early Warning System depend on have often
undermined the credibility of the information that is often provided.

Financial Viability: Of the five institutions, the ASF and the Panel of the
Wise seem to have inspired the most donor support. The concept of the
African standby army staffed by Africans has captured the imagination of the
donor community. For one thing, rich countries, that do not like the idea of
sending their people to keep peace in Africa but do not want to be seen as
standing idle while innocent people are killed, like the division of labor that
the ASF will inevitably bring. It allows governments of rich countries to
avoid the delicate politics of foreign intervention. The bulk of the 1.2 billion
euros that the EU has provided to the AU in the last ten years has gone to
activities related to the ASF or the work that the Force is supposed to. The
generous donor support for the African peace support operations is driven in
large part by the ASF idea. The GIZ, which has given over $500 million to
the AU, is financing a multi-million-dollar building for the African Union in
part because of the expectation of increase in the volume of work and activities that a well-functioning ASF will generate. The United States has provided millions to the AU, including a recent announcement of $110 million
per year in the next five years toward the operationalization of the rapid
deployment aspect of the ASF.

The expectation of donors such as the United States seems to be that the
ASF will not only absolve the work of the AU Peace Support Operation
Division but also will take the burden of keeping peace in Africa off the
shoulders of the security forces of rich societies. The Panel of the Wise has
also generated excitement within the donor community. Funding for the bulk
of its programs has been provided by external partners, particularly the middle powers such as Sweden, Norway, Denmark, and Canada. The Early
Warning System has also received credible sources of funding from donors.
Indeed, the Peace and Security budget of the AU is the largest program item
in the AU budget, and over 80 percent of this funding of DPS programs
comes from external partners of the AU. It should be pointed out that African
governments have also contributed to making the Peace and Security institutions the cash cow of the AU. They have shown the capacity to set aside the
largest amount of the annual contributions to the DPS. During the June 2015
Summit in South Africa, the AU pledged to fund 100 percent of the operational budget of the DPS and 75 percent of the program budget. To put this
into context, the budget that was approved for 2016 has a $150 million
operating budget and $267 million designated for programs. Over 90 percent
of the $267 million is funded by donors, and almost 60 percent is earmarked
for Peace and Security initiatives. In terms of the allocation of the operational
budget, the PSD receives three times as much as other departments. For
instance, in 2015, the DPS received 17.2 percent of the AU's operational

budget while only 3.24 percent went to the DPA. The money provided by African states seems to suggest they value PSD more than comparable departments in the AU system.

Effectiveness: Overall, the AU peace and security institutions have demonstrated a decent level of effectiveness compared with other IOs. Gettleman's research pointed out that any honest assessments of the AU's mission in Somali, for instance, will conclude that "the African Union has done a better job of pacifying Mogadishu, Somalia's capital and a hornet's nest of Islamist militants, clan warlords, factional armies and countless glassy-eyed freelance gunmen, than any other outside force, including 25,000 American troops in the 1990s."[54] Of the five institutions, the PSC has proved to be the most effective in both institutional design and in terms of the work that it has done for the continent over the last decade.

Most analysts give the AU peace and security institutions credit for making an impact in the peace and security landscape of the continent. It serves as a good deliberative space for African governments, allows civil society groups to transmit their ideas to the AU system, and it has become a very important diplomatic and political space for tackling major African security challenges. Like many international political institutions, it has its challenges. For instance, it is still an elitist body, and many ordinary Africans have very little access to the organization. Even the civil society groups that have gained access are the cream of the NGO world or the leaders of the groups. Its discussions do not often pay enough attention to the daily struggles of the common African. The Panel of the Wise has equally demonstrated its effectiveness in many ways. It has been very effective and influential in mediating disputes on the African continent. Most of its best work has often been done behind closed doors. It served as a mediation body during the Egyptian political crisis in 2013, and has often assisted in calming tension down in disputes that did not make it to headlines of major newspapers. It would have played a far greater role if the AU had given it the necessary funding and administrative support.

In one sense, the ASF's effectiveness cannot be measured since it is yet to be operationalized, but in another sense it is in part because of the ASF that the AU is still engaged in peace support operations in places such as Somalia, Darfur, and Burundi. The effectiveness or lack thereof of AU peace support operations is a good barometer of how the ASF will work. The ASF would likely inherit some of the institutional coordination problems that the AU peace support operation currently has. At the moment, the relationship between the DPA and the headquarters of missions does not enhance effective communication and reporting. The AU does not even have in-house expertise and capacity to deploy peacekeepers on its own. It depends on the generosity of external partners for basic things such as airlifting, intelligence gathering, troop training, and logistic provisions, among other things. The AU Peace

Support Operation is not only heavily dependent on donor funding and support, but the AU itself does not have the capacity to deploy troops on the ground for more than a year. It often sends peace missions on the assumption that the UN and external partners will come to its aid. The question then becomes, what happens if they do not? This is a question that the AU would have to seriously consider as it moves to operationalize the ASF.

Efficiency: The AU institutional structures have a mixed record in terms of efficiency. The PSC has shown a relatively good level of efficiency over sister institutions within the international system. It is certainly more efficient than the UNSC. It makes quicker, better, and often more frequent decisions compared to that of the UNSC. Although it is a political organization, it is often not held into ransom by a few big countries similar to the way that the UNSC has become a tool for P5 members. It is also not a very expensive institution to run in the grand scheme of things. Its monthly meetings and support structures are not administratively burdensome compared to sister organizations.

The Panel of the Wise, if properly managed, can equally be a very efficient institution and a cheaper way of resolving conflict than peace support operations, peacekeeping, or peacebuilding missions. However, the age, mobility, and durability of members of the Panel often limit their ability to deliver the services that they are supposed to provide in a timely manner. The Panel still does not have proper administrative support and relies mainly on ad hoc and informal relationships in order to do its work.

The ASF is the most expensive and in some ways the most inefficient way to solve conflict. Whether is it peacekeeping, peacebuilding, or peace support operations, it costs more to deploy and manage troops than any other means of resolving conflict. That said, the AU system of intervention is still cheaper than comparable peace missions. The AU administrative staff and consultants are not paid as much as those who work for IOs, such as UN, EU, OAS, or ASEAN. The AU also does not have the human capacity itself, and as a result it depends on only a few individuals who are often overworked, underpaid, and in some sense underappreciated. As indicated earlier, over 90 percent of the professionals working on AU peace and security issues are on a limited-term appointment, meaning they have no benefits or long-term job security. Overall, the AU peace and security institutions operate on a shoestring budget.

NOTES

1. For a detailed discussion of the human security ideas in the AU, see Thomas Kwasi Tieku, "Pan-Africanization of Human Security," in *Handbook of Human Security*, ed. Taylor Owen and Mary Martin. London: Routledge, 2012.

2. See MOU for the CSSDCA: http://pages.au.int/sites/default/files/Solemn_Declaration_on_CADSP_0.pdf.

3. O. Obasanjo and F. G. N. Mosha, "Africa Rise to the Challenge," Conference Report on the Kampala Forum, Abeokuta/New York: Africa Leadership Forum, 1992; Thomas Kwasi Tieku, "Explaining the Clash and Accommodation of Interests of Major Actors in the Creation of the African Union," *African Affairs* 103, no. 411 (2004): 249–67.

4. African Union, *Memorandum of Understanding on Security, Stability, Development and Cooperation* (Durban, 2002); Thomas Kwasi Tieku, "A Pan-African View of a 'New' Agenda for Peace," *International Journal* (2012).

5. Kwasi Tieku, "A Pan-African View of a 'New' Agenda for Peace."

6. A. Omar Touray, "The Common African Defence and Security Policy," *African Affairs* 104, no. 417 (2005): 635–56.

7. Jide Martyns Okeke, "African Union and the Challenges of Implementing 'Responsibility to Protect' in Africa," Paper presented at the XIIIth *CODESRIA* General Assembly, 2011, http://general.assembly.codesria.org/IMG/pdf/Jide_Martyns_Okeke.pdf.

8. African Union, *The Ezulwini Consensus: The Common African Position on the Proposed Reform of the United Nations*, New York: United Nations, 2005c, http://www.cfr.org/world/common-african-position-proposed-reform-united-nations-ezulwini-consensus/p25444; African Union, *Report on the Elaboration of a Framework Document on Post Conflict Reconstruction and Development (PCRD)*, Banjul, The Gambia: 2006.

9. African Union, Communiqué of the 519th PSC meeting on Universal Jurisdiction, 26 June 2015. See more at: http://www.peaceau.org/en/article/communique-of-the-519th-psc-meeting-on-universal-jurisdiction-26-june-2015 -sthash.365l6KtJ.64Yh7pGv.dpuf.

10. "PSC Stands with Rwanda on Universal Jurisdiction," Peace and Security Council Report, https://www.issafrica.org/pscreport/addis-insights/psc-stands-with-rwanda-on-universal-jurisdiction.

11. Xan Rice, "Ethiopia Ends Somalia Occupation," *The Guardian*, January 26, 2009, http://www.theguardian.com/world/2009/jan/26/ethiopia-ends-somalia-occupation; Alex Perry, "Kenya Invades Somalia. Does It Get Any Dumber?" *TIME*, October 19, 2011, http://world.time.com/2011/10/19/kenya-invades-somalia-does-it-get-any-dumber/.

12. For detailed examination of this, see Thomas Tieku, "Pan-Africanization of Human Security."

13. The Organization of African Unity, *The Constitutive Act*, Lomé, Article 4(0), Togo: July 11, 2000.

14. A. Hammerstad, *African Commitments to Democracy in Theory and Practice: A Review of Eight NEPAD Countries*, South African Institute of International Affairs, Monograph, 2005, https://www.issafrica.org/pubs/Other/ahsi/HammerstadMono/Contents.html.

15. Ben Kioko, "The Right of Intervention under the African Union's Constitutive Act," *International Review of the Red Cross* 85, no. 852 (2003): 819; See also Paul D. Williams, "From Non-Intervention to Non-Indifference the Origins and Development of the African Union's Security Culture" (Oxford University Press, March 12, 2007).

16. "African Peace and Facility Evaluation—Part 2: Reviewing the Overall Implementation of the APF as an Instrument for African Efforts to Manage Conflicts on the Continent," European Union Final Report, October 2013.

17. U.S. Department of State, "U.S. Assistance to the African Union–Fact Sheet," http://photos.state.gov/libraries/usau/231771/PDFs/us_assistance_to_the_au_fact_sheet.pdf.

18. U.S. Department of State, "The United States and the African Union," Washington, DC, April 19, 2011, http://www.state.gov/r/pa/prs/ps/2011/04/161212.htm.

19. Reuters News Agency, "Somali Militants Attack African Union Base," http://www.reuters.com/article/2015/06/26/us-somalia-militants-idUSKBN0P60BX20150626.

20. Thomas Mandrup and Bjørn Møller, "African Union: A Common Security Structure in the Making?" in *International Organisations: Their Role in Conflict Management*, ed. Peter Dahl Thruelsen. Royal Danish Defence College, 2014.

21. Interview by author, Bujumbura, Burundi, October 10, 2008.

22. Organization of African Unity, *The Constitutive Act*, Lomé, Togo: July 11, 2000.

23. Hammerstad, *African Commitments to Democracy in Theory and Practice*.

24. Maxi Schoeman, "The African Union after the Durban 2002 Summit," *Centre of African Studies, University of Copenhagen* (February 2003).

25. Thomas G. Weiss, "The Sunset of Humanitarian Intervention? The Responsibility to Protect in a Unipolar Era," *Security Dialogue* 35, no. 2 (2004): 135–53.

26. Mark Malan, "New Tools in the Box? Towards a Standby Force for the African Union," *Johannesburg: Institute of Security Studies* (2002); Jakkie Cilliers and Kathryn Sturman, "The Right Intervention: Enforcement Challenges for the African Union," *African Security Review* 11, no. 3 (2002), https://www.issafrica.org/pubs/ASR/11No3/Cilliers.html. The article has been amended to include intervention to "restore peace and stability" and in response to "a serious threat to legitimate order."

27. Kristiana Powell and Thomas K. Tieku, "The African Union and The Responsibility to Protect: Towards a Protection Regime for Africa?" *International Insight* 20, no. 1 and 2 (2005): 215–35.

28. Annemarie Peen Rodt, "The African Union Mission in Burundi," *Civil Wars* 14, no. 3 (September 2012): 379.

29. U.S. Department of State, "The United States and the African Union," Office of the Spokesman, Washington, DC, April 19, 2011, http://www.state.gov/r/pa/prs/ps/2011/04/161212.htm.

30. "Transforming the AU a Momentous Task," ISS Peace and Security Council Report, July 13, 2015, https://www.issafrica.org/pscreport/addis-insights/transforming-the-au-a-momentous-task.

31. The African Union Policy Framework for the Establishment of the African Standby Force and the Military Staff Committee, adopted by the Third Meeting of African Chiefs of Defense, May 15–16, 2003, http://www.peaceau.org/uploads/asf-policy-framework-en.pdf.

32. African Union Policy on Post-Conflict Reconstruction and Development (PCRD), adopted in Banjul, Gambia, July 2006, http://www.peaceau.org/uploads/pcrd-policy-framwowork-eng.pdf.

33. The African Union Policy Framework on Security Sector Reform, African Union Commission, Addis Ababa, Ethiopia, http://www.peaceau.org/uploads/policy-framwork-en.pdf.

34. African Union, Common African Position on the UN Review of Peace Operations, Peace and Security Council 502nd Meeting Addis Ababa, Ethiopia, 29 April 2015, PSC/PR/2(DII), http://www.peaceau.org/uploads/psc.502.peace.operations.29-04-2015-1-.pdf.

35. Interview by author, Addis Ababa, February 24, 2012.

36. African Union, Policy on Post-Conflict Reconstruction and Development (PCRD), vi, Banjul, Gambia, July 2006, http://www.peaceau.org/uploads/pcrd-policy-framwowork-eng.pdf.

37. Jean Ping, "Opening Remarks by the AUC Chairperson H. E. Dr. Jean Ping on the occasion of the First Annual US-African Union High Level Meeting," Washington DC, April 21, 2010, http://www.africa-union.org/root/au/index/index.htm.

38. Desirée Nilsson and Mimmi Söderberg Kovacs, "Revisiting an Elusive Concept: A Review of the Debate on Spoilers in Peace Processes," *International Studies Review* 13, no. 4 (2011): 606–26; John Stephen Stedman, "Spoiler Problems in Peace Processes," *International Security* 22 (1997): 5–53.

39. Bruce W. Dayton and Louis Kriesberg, *Conflict Transformation and Peace Building: Moving from Violence to Sustainable Peace* (New York: Routledge, 2009).

40. Michael Bratton, Robert Mattes, and E. Gyimah-Boadi, eds., *Public Opinion, Democracy, and Market Reform in Africa* (Cambridge: Cambridge University Press Brooks, 2005).

41. On the African Charter on Democracy, Elections, and Governance, see Solomon T. Eborah, "The African Charter on Democracy, Election and Governance: A New Dawn for the Enthronement of Legitimate Governance in Africa?" *Open Society Institute* (2007), http://www.afrimap.org/papers.php.

42. Thomas Legler and Thomas Tieku, "What Difference Can a Path Make? Regional Regimes for Democracy Promotion and Defense in the Americas and Africa," *Democratization* 18, no. 3 (2010): 465–91.

43. Paul D. Williams, "The African Union's Conflict Management Capabilities," *Council on Foreign Relations* (October 2011): 1.

44. This understanding of solidarity norm comes from Christopher Clapham's discussion of politics of solidarity and Ali Mazrui's analysis of the concept of "we are all Africans." Christo-

pher Clapham, *Africa and the International System: The Politics of State Survival* (Cambridge: Cambridge University Press, 1996); Ali Mazrui, "On the Concept of 'We Are All Africans,'" *The American Political Science Revie w* LVII: 1 (March, 1963): 88–97; and Ali Mazrui, *Towards a Pax Africana: A Study of Ideology and Ambition* (Chicago: University of Chicago Press, 1967).

45. Clapham, *Africa and the International System*, 106–7.

46. Scott Thompson and I. William Zartman, "The Development of Norms in the African System," in *The Organization of African Unity after Ten Years: Comparative Perspectives*, ed. Yassin El-Ayouty (New York: Praeger, 1975): 10–11.

47. Jeffrey Gettleman, "African Union Force Makes Strides Inside Somalia," *New York Times*, November 24, 2011, http://www.nytimes.com/2011/11/25/world/africa/africa-forces-surprise-many-with-success-in-subduing-somalia.html?_r=0.

48. See Issaka K. Souare, "The African Union as a Norm Entrepreneur on Military Coups d'état in Africa (1952–2012): An Empirical Assessment," *Journal of Modern African Studies* 52, no. 1 (March 2014): 69–94, doi: 10.1017/S0022278X13000785.

49. For detailed examination of the PSC, see Paul D. Williams, "The Peace and Security Council of the African Union: Evaluating an Embryonic International Institution," *Journal of Modern African Studies* 47, no. 4 (2009): 603–26.

50. Williams, "The Peace and Security Council of the African Union," 603–26.

51. So far only Nigeria has taken advantage of the arrangement to behave like a permanent member of the PSC by bouncing between a two-term seat and three-term seats and finding a way to remain on the PSC since 2014.

52. Amitav Acharya, "How Ideas Spread: Whose Norms Matter? Norm Localization and Institutional Change in Asian Regionalism," *International Organization* 58, no. 2 (2004).

53. Paul D. Williams, "The African Union's Conflict Management Capabilities," *Council on Foreign Relations* (October 2011).

54. Gettleman, "African Union Force Makes Strides Inside Somalia."

Chapter Seven

Promotion of Human Rights

INTRODUCTION

This chapter examines the performance of the AU in the area of human rights promotion and defence. It contends that the AU has developed path-breaking human rights rules, instruments, and institutional mechanisms, but priority stakeholders have not internalized the rules, and the AU human rights bodies are not working effectively and efficiently. A majority of the rules have neither been integrated into national legalization of member states nor implemented at the levels of the state, community, and the individual. With the possible exception of a few elites in Africa and some human rights activists and organizations that have used these instruments to fight state officials, AU human rights instruments have had minimal impact at the state and community levels. Though it is early to draw the conclusion that they have failed, the early signs are not encouraging.

The chapter is organized into five sections. Section one examines the paradigm that shapes the AU's approach to human rights promotion and defense. It shows that the AU merges African human rights values with mainstream human rights ideas in ways that enable the coexistence of both collective and individual rights. Section two explores the extent to which the AU rules are novel, relevant to stakeholders, generate resources for the AU, and how effective and efficient the rules are in addressing Africa's human rights concerns. It shows that the rules are very innovative and elaborate, but they have not been used in any effective and efficient way. Section three evaluates AU policies on human rights in terms of novelty, relevance, financial viability, effectiveness, and efficiency in addressing African human rights problems. It reveals that the AU does not have any coherent policy framework to guide its human rights agenda. Similarly, section four shows that the AU's human rights ideas have not moved from rules into norms. The final section takes a critical look at the performance of AU human rights institutions. Perhaps unsurprisingly, it shows that the AU human rights bodies are underresourced, overburdened, weak, and poorly managed.

WORLDVIEW

The AU has continued the OAU's effort to create a new human rights paradigm that places collective rights on an equal footing with individual rights. [1] The OAU conception of human rights, reflected in the African Charter on Human and Peoples' Rights (the Banjul Charter), tries to merge an African community-based understanding of rights and a mainstream individualist approach to rights. [2] It tries to strike a delicate balance between the African conceptions of the individual in relational and interdependent terms and a mainstream human rights conception of the person as an independent, atomistic, and self-interested agent. As Okere's gender-insensitive but philosophically well-grounded argument alluded to, "The African conception of man ([*sic*] i.e., person) is not that of an isolated and abstract individual, but an integral member of a group animated by a spirit of solidarity. [3] Okere goes on to contrast the African notion with that of a mainstream conception of human rights, which he described as principles whose essential purpose is to be invoked by the individual against the group with which she or he is in conflict. [4]

It is widely acknowledged in the literature that the African Charter on Human and Peoples' Rights pioneered the idea of collective rights with its insistence on the notion of peoples' rights. [5] The OAU's introduction of a people-centered approach to human rights was controversial, yet there is no doubt that it represents an innovation in the discourse and practice of human rights in the international system. The AU has embraced this and created more legal and institutional structures to advance a collectivist approach to human rights promotion and practices on the African continent.

The Banjul Charter and the other AU human rights instruments challenge the priority that mainstream human rights groups and Western governments place on first- and second-generation rights over third- and fourth-generation human rights. The Banjul Charter elevates the status of rights of social solidarity, such as the right to peace, security, health, and environment, as well as rights to economic, social, and cultural development, and places these rights on equal terms with first- and second-generation rights. [6] The AU inherited and fully embraced the OAU insistence that collective rights such as self-determination, economic rights such as the right to development, and social rights such as nondiscrimination must be given an equal pride of place in the discourse and promotion of human rights. The human rights instruments that the AU has developed to complement the Banjul Charter, such as the African Youth Charter, the protocol on the rights of women in Africa, and the protocol on the African Court of Justice and human rights, all advanced the idea that third- and fourth-generation rights should be at the heart of human rights promotion in Africa, similar to the way political and civil rights have been at the center of mainstream discourse and the practice of human rights.

Novelty: A major paradigmatic shift that the AU has introduced into the African human rights landscape is broadening the scope of international crime that can be prosecuted by African regional courts. The protocol to the AU Convention on the Prevention and Combating of Terrorism[7] and the Protocol on Amendments to the Protocol of the Statutes of the African Court of Justice and Human Rights (the ACJHR)[8] broadened the scope of crimes that can be prosecuted by the ACJHR to acts such as election rigging, unconstitutional change of governments, human trafficking, drug trafficking, terrorism, piracy, slave practices and slavery, corruption, and money laundering.[9]

The novelty that came from the expansion of the jurisdiction of the Court largely explains why discerning observers of African politics thought that the outraged newspaper headlines, NGO protests, and the harsh criticisms that followed the adoption of the changes during the summit of African leaders in Malabo in June 2014 were based on a simplistic understanding and reading of the amendment to the ACJHR protocol. As Allison insightfully noted, "African leaders did vote to protect themselves in the African Court protocol, but they also broke new legal ground in adopting a holistic approach to the prosecution of serious crimes."[10] Many of these acts covered in the amendment to the ACJHR protocol have not been criminalized in international conventions, and most international courts do not have jurisdiction over them.[11] The scope of the ACJHR certainly goes far beyond the provision covered by the Rome Statute.

Another distinctive aspect of the AU approach to human rights promotion lies in the fact that it is promoting human rights from many angles. There is the African Commission of Human and Peoples' Rights to promote and protect human rights through naming, shaming, and other soft measures; there is ACJHR to prosecute human rights offenders; there is the AUC to provide bureaucratic and administrative support for the promotion of human rights; there is the Peace and Security Council and the Assembly to provide political support; and there are a plethora of courts in regional economic communities and at the state level whose works interface with and enhance the capability of the AU human rights system. Take, for instance, the ACJHR. It is in theory unique in the international system. It has the Assembly and the PSC to turn to for political cover, the AUC for administrative assistance, and other sister institutions it can draw technical and human resources from. In the words of Agwu, the ACJHR "prides itself as unique in the sense that unlike the International Criminal Court (ICC) and the ad hoc international criminal tribunals . . . [that operate] in instances where they were the only institution in their respective environments dealing with the issues they were established to deal with, the African Court will be operating in an 'ecosystem' where there are other organs and institutions that would share some of the division of labour."[12]

Equally unique to the AU's approach to human rights has been the breadth and depth of issues that the AU considers to be part of the human rights regime. The AU has developed a series of international legal principles and binding legal instruments that deal with the rights of the child, women, youth, environment, and transnational crime, among others. The obligation that these legal instruments impose on state parties goes far beyond what even the world body of the UN has been able to impose on its member states. For instance, even the African Charter on the Rights and Welfare of the Child, which has been criticized for providing inadequate measures to pro-hibit acts such as child labor, imposes higher obligations on state parties than most international legal instruments. As Evans pointed out, "The measures required of States Parties is more extensive than those of the UN Conven-tion."[13]

The AU has also pioneered a paradigmatic shift in women's rights. The Women's Protocol is generally considered to contain many "global firsts" on women's rights.[14] It provided for the first time in an international human rights treaty a woman's right to abortion, the right to self-protection, and to be protected against sexually transmitted infections, including HIV/AIDS as well as the first to provide that every African woman has the right to be informed on their health status, including their HIV and AIDS status. The Women's Protocol is also the first international treaty to impose obligations on state parties to eliminate female genital mutilation (FGM).

The progressive nature of the Women's Protocol reflects a fundamental shift in both the perception and treatment of women at the continental level in the last decade. Pan-Africanism and continental integration was seen as a man's job until the late 2000s, when women's groups made a breakthrough in adding women's rights to the agenda of continental institutional-building processes. The claim that Pan-Africanism and continental integration was generally considered a man's business can be supported in multiple ways. The OAU Charter was not only gendered but also boldly proclaimed that only men founded the Pan-African organization. The Charter repeatedly makes references to "founding fathers," even though the Pan-African Wom-en's Organization (the POWA), which was formed before the creation of the OAU, had campaigned vigorously for independent African states to unite. In 1962, a delegation of the POWA paid a courtesy call on the then Tanzanian leader Julius Nyerere, urging him to bring together African leaders who had formed the Casablanca and Monrovia group and also to encourage him to champion the cause of women in postcolonial Africa. [15]

In spite of the POWA's advocacy and the tremendous role played in the liberation struggle, the OAU leadership never placed women's rights on the agenda of deliberation of African leaders during OAU summits, nor even acknowledged in a genuine way the role that POWA played in either the liberation struggle or the merger of the Monrovia and Casablanca groups that paved the way for the formation of the OAU. In the words of the former commissioner of social affairs of the AUC, Bience Gawanas, OAU officials elected to ignore women's rights despite the fact that women brought issues on gender inequalities to the African agenda through their participation in liberation struggles and drew its "attention to the position of women in society." [16] In other words, the neglect of women's issues by the OAU for almost three decades was not because of the absence of the mobilization of women and advocacy by women's groups.

The lack of attention on women's rights reflected a deeper worldview that saw Pan-Africanism and continental integration as man's work. As a result of this paradigm, African leaders did not deem it necessary to consider, let alone select, a women to serve as Secretary-General or Under-Secretary of the OAU. The professional staffs of the OAU were overwhelmingly male. Less than 20 percent of women who managed to get a job at the OAU were put in pink ghettos—they were placed at the bottom of the organization and usually in the nonprofessional class. The perception was that the women were only good at doing menial jobs such as secretarial work and cleaning.

It even appeared that OAU leadership did not recognize that women had rights. The OAU declarations, binding decisions, and treaties were conspicuously silent on women's issues. Even the most progressive legal instruments such as the African Charter on Human and Peoples' Rights had little to say about women's rights. In the flamboyant language of an African scholar, the Charter placed women's rights in "a legal coma." [17] The conspicuous omission of women's rights in a Charter purported to be addressing human rights of all Africans was corrected only after the AU had emerged in 2001. The adoption of a protocol on women's rights formed part of the paradigmatic change that occurred in the early 2000s with the emergence of the AU. Unlike the OAU days, every legal instrument adopted by the AU makes provisions for women's rights.

Relevance: The relevance of the AU's approach to human rights to priority stakeholders cannot be overstated. The approach that the AU has taken is significant, particularly to groups such as women, children, and youth, who often do not have privileged access to state institutions. The approach has also empowered human rights groups and civil society organizations to push for greater accountability from those who are in positions of authority. The importance that priority stakeholders attached to AU's approach to human rights is reflected in the outraged headlines and campaigns that greeted the expansion of the jurisdiction of the ACJHR. Over "140 organizations with a presence in 40 African countries issued a mass group declaration in August 2014 calling for African states to reject" an amendment to the ACJHR proto-col. Global human rights groups, including Human Rights Watch and Am-nesty International, endorsed it. Another equally important sign that priority stakeholders take the AU's approach to human rights seriously is the fact that African states agreed to make 2015 the year of the woman, and by extension, women's rights. The theme of the Twenty-Fifth Summit of the AU was on human and women's rights, which dominated the discussion of the summit.

Financial Viability: Only the gender-equality paradigmatic has attracted meaningful funding from both the donor community and African states. It seems the AUC has little problem raising money to support women's rights activities. Donors have also showed keen interest in supporting the women's rights work of the AU. On average, almost U.S. $1 million has been raised annually by the Women's Directorate since it became operational.

This is in spite of the fact that the AUC has not developed any major systematic or strategic fund-raising mechanisms to attract donor funding. The absence of a conscious donor fund-raising approach is in part a function of limited human and technical resources at the gender directorate and in part driven by a deeper belief in the key section of the AUC that they do not want to be seen with a cup in hand roaming foreign capitals begging for money. One senior member of the AUC retorted back when asked about the absence of a coherent strategy to attract donor funding, "We do not want to be like some African leaders who have effectively become globetrotting beggars."[18] In any case, why should they turn themselves into fund-raising bureaucrats if donors are already flooding in looking for viable women's rights projects to fund?

There is a strong view among African regional managers of women's issues that good things sell themselves, and women's rights promotion is a good thing that needs no marketing to the donor community. As one of them phrased it, promoting women's rights "is not a favour to women. . . . And, it is not only a right, but it is the right and smart thing to do."[19] There is no doubt in the minds of the people working in the gender directorate that their work will attract donor support even if they do not make any concerted effort to court the attention of the donor community. The broader message to high-light here is that women's rights work of the AUC is financially viable and would have attracted far more resources if the AUC had consciously and systematically designed and implemented an effective donor fund-raising strategy.

The shift in thinking about women's rights has attracted financial assis-tance from even African governments, who are often willing to make all sorts of decisions but are unwilling to pay for them. African leaders agreed in 2009 to set aside 1 percent of the AU regular budget for women-related activities. The Women Fund, which became operational in 2011, distributes money in the amounts of U.S. $15,000 to grassroots African women's organizations. In addition, a number of AUC departments have earmarked resources for women-related activities. Some of the richest departments, such as the Peace and Security Department, that have not earmarked resources to women-related activities, transferred resources on a regular basis to the budget of the Women Directorate. At the Twenty-Fifth Summit held in South Africa in mid-June 2015, the AU Foundation organized a series of fund-raising activities, including a gala dinner and a golf day, that "raised several million dollars' worth of pledges over the course of the summit."[20] Many of the pledges were directed toward work related to women's empowerment, the theme of the summit.

The mainstream donor community has greeted with both suspicion and utter contempt the other two human rights paradigms. The expansion of the jurisdiction of the ACJHR has killed any appetite that mainstream donors may have for the Court, and they are likely to vote with their money. And few mainstream human rights organizations are willing to support or provide resources for the AU to promote collective and people's rights. Most donor agencies do not feel that collective rights are the most important rights to be promoted across the African continent. For most donors, human rights are about civil and political rights, and they are not willing to support any fundamental paradigmatic shift.

Effectiveness: The new approach is yet to be integrated into national legislation across the African continent on a systematic basis. There are pockets of countries whose constitutions emphasize collective rights. Others have also developed national legislations designed to capture some of the gender-neutral and gender-equity ideas that the AU is promoting. Overall, however, the effectiveness of the AU worldview on human rights remains in doubt in spite of the political support and lobbying that the Kenyan government has mounted to mobilize the necessary signatures for the adoption of the malleable protocol on extending the jurisdiction of the Court. As of the time of writing, fifteen countries have not yet signed the protocol, meaning that within the AU system the new approach has not attracted universal endorsement even from governments.

Efficiency: The efficiency of the worldview is difficult to assess in part because not many countries have actually adopted it, and we still do not know whether it is the most cost-effective way to promote human rights across the continent. The cost of changing national legislation to reflect these ideas and the cost of socializing a significant number of domestic constituents to believe in the importance of collective rights, gender equality, and new legal principles is still not known. But if the African Court becomes operational and is able to prosecute criminals across the African continent, then we may perhaps say that the new worldview is a more effective way of doing it, but that jury is still out.

RULES

The African Union has introduced many rules designed to promote human rights across the African continent. The preeminent of them is Article 5(h, m) and (o) of the Constitutive Act, which commits member states of the AU to respect human rights and the sanctity of human life. This provision is supported by detailed and more precise rules in the form of charters, conventions, and protocols. The rule that imposes the highest human rights obligations on state parties can be found in the Banjul Charter, the PSC protocol, the African Governance Charter, the ACJHR protocol and its amendments, the AU protocol for the Protection of Internally Displaced Persons in Africa, the African Charter on the Rights and Welfare of the Child, and the protocol on the African Charter of Human and Peoples' Rights on the Rights of Women in Africa.[21]

Novelty: Many of these rules are groundbreaking in the international legal system. For instance, the rules provided in the protocol on women's rights incorporate both the UN's legal principles on women and advances these rules in so many ways. Its definition of "violence against women" transcends the definition contained in UN Declaration on the Elimination of Violence against Women. Unlike the UN Declaration, it expanded the definition of violence against women to include acts causing economic hardship in addition to adding acts committed both in peacetime and during war. It also has elaborate rules against practices that constitute violence against women. Another innovation that the protocol on women's rights introduced into the international legal community is that for "a legal ban on female genital mutilation."[22] The women's protocol provided sanctions against those regimes that commit violence against women.

Relevance: There is no doubt that a set of human rights rules for a continent that has experienced more than a fair share of human rights abuses will be considered extremely relevant by all key stakeholders. These rules are particularly germane to the work of human rights groups and nonstate actors. Many international NGOs have used the rules in the Banjul Charter to seek redress for human right abuses of Africans whose rights have been infringed upon by their governments. For instance, in a landmark ruling in 1999, Amnesty International, the Lawyers' Committee for Human Rights, and the Association of Members of the Episcopal Conference of East Africa dragged the government of Sudan to the African Commission on Human Rights for disregarding the antidiscrimination rule in Article 2 of the Charter and also for not respecting the protection of religious freedom in Article 8 in the Banjul Charter.[23]

The complainants had alleged that since 1990, the government of Sudan had been violating human rights of the southern Sudanese, including extrajudicial executions; arbitrary arrests and detentions; the arrest, detention, and torture of opposition group members; and the suppression of Sudanese Christians.[24] In a Communication, the African Human Rights Commission ruled against the Sudanese government, stating that it "cannot countenance the application of law in such a way as to cause discrimination and distress to others."[25] It asked the government of Sudan and Sudanese courts not to apply Shari'a law to non-Muslims, arguing that "it would be fundamentally unjust that religious laws should be applied against non-adherents of that religion."

Similarly, domestic advocacy groups have used some of the human rights rules to defend the rights of groups and individuals whose rights would not otherwise be respected by their states. For instance, a number of advocacy groups, including the Malawi African Association, shamed the Mauritania government for human rights abuses, including slavery of a section of its population. They took the Mauritanian government to the African Human Rights Commission for violating sections of the Banjul Charter. In a Communication, the African Human Rights Commission ruled against the Mauritanian government and recommended to the government to establish independent inquiry to identify and punish perpetrators of the human rights violations, ensure payment of compensations to victims and relatives, ensure the eradication of the root causes of discrimination and degrading practices, and to ensure the complete abolition of slavery in Mauritania.

The significance of these rules to the work of advocacy groups is reflected in the outcry and campaign that the NGO community mounted against the Malabo protocol. The anger of human rights groups at the Malabo protocol did not in any way disguise the importance they attached to the creation of a regional human rights regime for Africa. At least some member states of AU see these rules as important even if they are doing so for selfish reasons. The Kenyan government's decision to put its governmental machinery behind the implementation of the Malabo protocol is due to the fact that it felt that those rules would provide protection for at least some Kenyans, including government officials.

Equally relevant to priority stakeholders has been the interpretation of these rules. The African Human Rights Commission has interpreted the Banjul Charter in such a progressive way that many of the rules in the Charter do not only reflect the best international human rights practices but also has advanced human rights laws in many significant ways. For instance and as Hansungule indicated, the African Human Rights Commission has interpreted rules on the right to life and dignity in the Banjul Charter in such a way that it is almost similar to the antidiscrimination clauses.[26] The interpretation covers many acts unanticipated in the original text. Governments are deemed to have violated the article if their citizens go into hiding for fear of their life, and if states representatives deny food and medical attention to prisoners. Governments can also be held responsible for any forced disappearance in their areas of jurisdiction. The Commission has used this interpretation to rule against Nigeria and Rwanda, just to mention these two, for violating the right to life and dignity because of the way they treated some prisoners.

Financial Viability: Donor support for the rules has been very uneven. Most donors are willing to provide resources to the African Commission on Human and Peoples' Rights to promote the rules that deal with civil and political rights. Others are also willing to provide resources to the AU to promote gender equality within the Commission and across the African continent. But there is an acute shortage of donors who are willing to provide resources to the AU to promote the integration of the entire human rights rules into national legislation. In other words, donors have been very selective and cautious with respect to the sort of human rights rules that they are willing to support.

Mainstream donors that have shown interest in providing funding for the human rights rules that challenge the authority of the state and hold African governments accountable seem to attract relative support from the donor community. Similarly, the leading human rights groups have demonstrated a considerable desire to spend a considerable amount of resources to ensure that state authorities respect the political and civil rights sections of the Banjul Charter. In many instances, they have taken state authorities to the African Human Rights Commission. Hansungule's assessment of interactions between the NGO and the African Human Rights Commission concluded that complaints tend to increase against a state party depending on the political situation in the country. For example, during the era of military rule in Nigeria, it monopolized the communications to the African Human Rights Commission; more recently it was Zimbabwe that took the lead. Although there has not been a complaint by a legal person like a corporate entity, this is not totally unlikely.[27]

But donors and mainstream human rights groups seem to have little appetitive for providing resources for the rules that promote collective rights and second- and third-generation rights. Conversely, African governments are willing to provide financial support to strengthen the human rights system that enhances regime survival and protects the political class. For instance, the budget for the African Human Rights Commission have often been designed in such a way that it does not empower it to promote rules that undermine state control and authority.

Little money is often given to the African Human Rights Commission to visits countries to promote the Banjul rules to ordinary citizens, to conduct research, and to embark on special activities that promote and protect human rights. A report of the African Human Rights Commission laid this bare when it indicated in 2007 that its work continues to be severely compromised by the fact that the Commission has little money for "research, training, capacity building, special mechanisms, activities, projects, seminars and conferences."[28]

The resources African governments are prepared to spend to promote and protect rules relating to solidarity rights or second- and third-generation rights are not impressive. For instance, the AU came under heavy criticisms for not raising enough funds to protect the people of the Horn of Africa during its recent famine experience, which posed a great threat to the economic, health, livelihood, and cultural rights of the population. It was reported that only three African countries: Algeria ($10 million), Angola ($45 million), and Egypt ($5 million) provided significant money to the AU to help the people in the Horn. Nigeria gave only $2 million, and the South African government donated around $1.3 million though other sources of funding, which made the South African pledge respectable.[29] Overall, the AU Human Rights rules have at best demonstrated an uneven financial viability, and at worst their ability to generate resources is questionable.

Effectiveness of Rules: Most of these rules have not been operationalized at the state level. Few countries have directly integrated them into national legislations. The best known is Nigeria, which made the African Human Rights Charter Chapter 10 the federal law of Nigeria. Some African countries, especially those that developed national constitutions and human rights legislations after the AU was born in 2001, drew inspiration and ideas from the AU human rights system. Others such as South Africa, Ghana, Cape Verde, and Mauritius, just to mention these four states, have human right rules consistent with and in many instances advanced the AU human rights rule, but most of these rules were introduced in spite of AU rather than because of the AU human rights system. Perhaps not surprising, the rules that have been operationalized to some extent are those contained in the African Human Rights Charter. The rest have remained at the headquarters of the AU gathering dust.

The ones that have been operationalized, such as those monitored by the African Human Rights Commission, are not working to their fullest potential. Most honest assessments of the performance of the rules in the African Human Rights Charter have all come to the conclusion that they have had mixed impact. On one hand, they have provided an opportunity for landmark rulings, the shaming of misbehaving governments in Africa, and they have given advocacy groups tools to promote and defend human rights. On the other hand, most of the rules came with little enforcement mechanisms and remedies. Take, for instance, the African Human Rights Commission's landmark decision in the case of *Social and Economic Rights Action Centre and the Centre for Economic and Social Rights v. Nigeria*, a seminar ruling on social, economic, and cultural rights.[30] The two NGOs had complained to the African Human Rights Commission that the Nigeria government through its majority shareholding in the Nigeria petroleum consortium (Shell is the major shareholder in the consortium) had violated the right to life, the right to health, the right to a healthy environment, the right to property, the right to housing and food, and the protection of the family. They argued that the petroleum consortium released toxic waste in the environment; polluted local waters and air; destroyed soil, crops, and animals; caused avoidable oil spills; and in put in danger the food sources of inhabitants of people living near oil-producing areas. The NGOs claimed that the environmental impacts of the oil production are causing skin infections, gastrointestinal and respiratory diseases, increased risk of cancers, and neurological and reproductive problems. In a landmark decision in 2000, the African Human Rights Commission sided with the NGOs for the most part, arguing that the right to health and the right to a satisfactory environment were violated, although it pointed out that the Nigerian government had the right to produce oil. The African Human Rights Commission could not provide any remedies to the affected people, and indeed it was unable to ensure that the Nigeria government gave the people the satisfactory environment it had eloquently articulated. Thus, although the rules in the Banjul Charter and indeed the African human rights system have made significant inroads in the protection of the rights of a number of Africans, they have not protected the rights of most Africans in the most effective way.

Efficiency: The cost-benefit analysis of the existence of these rules is reasonable given how important they are to the well-being of Africans. The cost of producing these legal instruments is actually relatively low. This is why the OAU and its successor, the AU, the most resource-challenged international organization in the world, were able to produce them. It did not cost the AU more than U.S. $10 million to produce the human rights rules in the Banjul Charter, the Youth Charter, the Women's Rights Protocol, and other important AU human rights instruments. The total cost of producing them is well within the budget for creating a decent national legislation in many societies. To put this in perspective, the Institute for Socio-Economic Research and Information (IRIS) estimated that the Canadian omnibus Bill C-10, which provided for mandatory prison sentences for drug-related crimes and child sex offenders, will cost around $2.3 billion.[31] The AU is able to produce these elaborate rules within a tight-fisted budget because it does not have to engage in a broad national consultations and studies before developing these rules.

African consultants prepared most of these documents at a relatively low fee. Many of the consultants do not charge more than $200 a day to prepare these documents compared with the standard consultancy fee paid by governments to domestic lawyers, which is usually more than $500 a day. For instance, most Canadian lawyers charge around $500 a day to prepare legal-related materials for governments. And unlike the deliberative and consultative processes associated with law making in domestic settings, the AU only convenes an expert meeting composed of lawyers of member states to discuss drafts of these rules. These experts meetings do not often last more than four days, and the cost of lodging, feeding, and per diem paid to these government lawyers are relatively low compared with standard charges by lawyers in domestic settings.

The integration of these laws into national legislation will not impose any cost beyond the standard way that most international rules are ratified and incorporated into domestic laws. It will, however, be expensive to provide the necessary conditions for the full enjoyment of many of the rules. For instance, the full implementation of the socioeconomic and cultural rights is beyond the means of most African governments. The prohibitive cost has nothing to do with the fact that they were produced at the AU level. These rights are just expensive to enjoy. In some instances, the technology for ensuring that all can enjoy the rights is unavailable or prohibitively expensive. Take the decision by the African Human Rights group in respect of the right to life and healthy living in the oil-rich Niger Delta. The know-how to ensure that the right of the Nigeria government to produce oil and the inhabitants' right to live in a good and a healthy environment seems to be unavailable or prohibitively expensive. In addition, much of the cost, especially the indirect costs associated with the implementation of the AU human rights rules, are simply unknown. There are no meaningful and systematic cost assessment of the rules that have been implemented, and because most of the rules have not been implemented, it is difficult to assess the true cost of spreading these rules across the African continent.

CAUSAL IDEAS

In terms of causal ideas, the AU has yet to articulate a solid and broader policy framework for its approach to human rights. There is no one or single document that outlines the AU's broader approach to human rights and the strategies to enforce them. Most of the human rights ideas are scattered in a variety of different documents and lack coherence. The only document that comes closest to a policy framework is the AU's Human Rights Strategy for Africa developed by the DPA. This document, however, is not only very short but also reads like a poorly written manifesto for donors. The entire document is around twelve pages and contains a very poorly articulated view of the human rights mechanisms, processes, and institutional structures to promote human rights. This is not surprising given the deficit of human resources at the AU Commission for promoting human rights. The unit given the responsibility of overseeing the AU's human rights promotion is staffed by one full-time AU employee and a couple of other part-time employees. Many of these individuals do not have extensive experience in legal practices or human rights advocacy. They have diplomatic and administrative experiences. There is little wonder why they have not been able to articulate the broader strategic policy goals of the AU human rights protocol.

The absence of a very well-drafted human rights strategy may also be the result of not only limited human resources but also may reflect a general disinterest on the part of AU leadership and African states to make human rights a cornerstone of the work of the AU. After all, the AU is a political organization, and those who work for the AU have often decided to pick their battles, and it appears that human rights is not one of them. Because of the limited human and institutional resources at the disposal of the AU Commission to promote human rights, the Human Rights Strategy for Africa has not been marketed or advertised to a number of AU member states. Although extensive research will be needed to determine how many African states are aware of the document, it is not an exaggeration to say that a number of key African policymakers who are aware of the existence of such a document will be a minority. None of the policymakers, including senior diplomats who have served at the headquarters of the AU who were interviewed in the course of doing this particular book, were aware of the content of the Human Rights Strategy. Even within the AU Commission itself, only a few people outside of the Political Affairs Department knew the existence of this particular document. Many civil society groups are unlikely to be aware of it, or even if they are aware will not be aware of what to do with this sort of document due to the fact that it does not contain any meaningful advocacy information. Certainly ordinary Africans do not even have access to the language that the strategy is written in. The point here is that stakeholders do not know even the little document that exists that the AU may want to call a policy framework of promoting human rights on the African continent, and as a result it is difficult to know whether they care or are aware of this document. The fact that they do not know the existence of the document questions the relevance of the document to priority stakeholders.

Financial Viability: The AU's Human Rights Strategy has certainly not received a ringing endorsement from donors considering that most of the donors have not put money forward for the document or have generally not provided any meaningful money to the AU. Part of the reason why the unit promoting the AU's human rights protocol is extremely weak has been the absence of donor support. African states have generally also not provided resources to promote human rights, let alone provided resources as a result of a specific policy framework that the AU has developed.

Effectiveness: It is obvious that the AU has no effective mechanism to promote human rights on a domestic level. There is no policy framework for domestic groups or for states to integrate into their legislation, and neither is there a policy framework for civil society groups to use to advance the protection of human rights. The cost effectiveness is unknown because the policy does not exist, nor does the AU have the capacity to produce it in the first place.

NORMS

The AU's approach to human rights has not moved from rules and worldview into a normative standard, although few works have emerged suggesting that the AU has developed certain norms for promoting human rights on the African continent. Only two of these rules seem to have made progress in terms of their institutionalization. These are the AU's rules on antidiscrimination and collective rights. It is generally considered a distinct part of the African human rights system that nondiscrimination and self-determination are essential parts of human rights protection across the African continent. Discrimination on the basis of color, race, and ethnicity are generally seen within the African system as an abuse of human rights. The idea of the protection of communities and their rights to existence is widely held among the political class, yet in practice there have been consistent reports of widespread discrimination of Africans, particularly on the basis of class, religion, and ethnicity. In other words, although there is a general acceptance that discrimination is a violation of human rights, it has not moved beyond awareness to become a normal part of the everyday life of most Africans. Although the idea of discrimination on the basis of color is to some extent alien to most parts of Africa, racial discrimination between black Africans and their Arab counterparts is very common.

The second human rights rule that seems to be on its way to becoming a norm is the acceptance, particularly within the political class, of third- and fourth-generation rights. These rights are seen as important as first- and second-generation rights. The political class now accepts that Africans have both economic, social, and cultural rights, as indicated in Articles 15 to 18 of the African Charter of Human and Peoples' Rights. While the notion of economic, social, and cultural rights is widely accepted, the practice of this idea has yet to emerge. It is very common for the political class to deny economic, social, and cultural rights to individuals and groups if it serves their interests. Almost two-thirds of African countries have laws that discriminate against the lesbian, gay, bisexual, and transgender (LGBT) community. In other words, although the importance of group rights is recognized, the politic class has no internalized them. Even when these rights are respected, the political class does so as a matter of right or because of political expediency rather than as a matter of appropriateness. The political class in Africa takes a very instrumental approach to economic, social, and cultural rights. State elites provide economic, social, and cultural rights to individuals in groups only when it serves their political interests. For example, groups that often support the ruling political class are often given enormous economic, social, and cultural rights, while those who oppose or are unwilling to do the bidding of the elites are denied these rights.

Even advocacy groups have not made effective use of the consciousness that has emerged on economic, social, and cultural rights. Most of the cases that they have often campaigned or sought redress from the African Human Rights Commission have often centered on civil and political rights. While they may genuinely believe that social and economic rights are as important as civil and political rights, they are still stuck in the idea that the key to human rights is the protection of civil and political rights. Individuals across the African continent do not often seek redress from state institutions, international bodies, and even the African Human Rights Commission on the basis of social and economic rights. This suggests that while a number of individual Africans think they have social, economic, and cultural rights, they have not internalized it to the extent that they would defend and seek redress whenever those rights are infringed upon or not respected by the state. The broader point here is that awareness about these rights seems to be unaccompanied by the necessary internalization and institutionalization that would move them from rules to norms. They are yet to be normalized in the everyday life of African political elites, African civil society groups, and certainly the so-called ordinary Africans.

Financial Viability: Similar to the way stakeholders have treated the human rights "norms" across the African continent, donors have often recognized the importance of protecting economic, social, and cultural rights, but most of their funding is directed toward the protection of civil and political rights. Few donors have internalized the importance of economic, social, and cultural rights to the extent that they are willing to provide sufficient resources for the enjoyment of Africans. Most donors provide the excuse that the challenges facing the protection of civil and political rights are so enormous that they feel compelled to spend almost all of their money on the protection and defense of those rights. They are yet to broaden their scope into areas such as economic, social, and cultural rights. To be fair, donors have to some extent been smart to avoid economic, social, and cultural rights in part because the resources required to ensure the full enjoyment of these rights are beyond the capacity of most donor agencies. Most donors do not have the resources to ensure full enjoyment of the right to development, let alone have the money to promote social and cultural rights.

African state parties who are supposed to advance these rights have been reticent in advocating for resources on the basis of social, economic, and cultural rights. Most of them know that the enjoyment or demand for the enjoyment of these rights would impose enormous burdens on them. For strategic reasons, they have decided not to promote them even if they genuinely believe that Africans have a right to economic, social, and cultural rights. Most states have not operationalized these rights and integrated them into national legislation. Where there are references to these rights in national legislations, they are often confined to the aspirational parts of these documents. Even when they exist in binding legislation they are often ignored or neglected in the implementation of those documents. Most African states do not even have a decent welfare system, let alone mechanisms to provide for the enjoyment of economic, social, and cultural rights. The costs of operationalizing these ideas are somewhat prohibitive for some African states, while others think promoting them may not be the most efficient way of using state resources. The AU itself has often stayed away from even defining what some of these rights mean in practice. For example, the concept of peoples' rights has not been defined or provided in vague language in almost all AU documents. It is widely known that a definition will create a political and economic problem for both the AU and state parties. Most of the state parties would not have signed on to human rights rules if the concept of peoples' rights had been defined the way it is conceptualized by most scholars.[32]

Effectiveness: Most of the AU human rights ideas have not become norms across the African continent. In many instances, states have developed rules and institutional mechanisms to undermine the spirit, if not the letters, of these human rights. Take, for example, the AU human rights on nondiscrimination, which is widely held at a continental level, but a number of legislations have been passed at the state level that actually reinforce discriminatory practices. Countries such as Uganda have come out with national legislation on homosexuality that is discriminatory in nature. Others have introduced antiterror legislation in response to the September 11, 2001, attacks on the United States (henceforth 9/11), which have ended up undermining human rights promotion in these countries. The post 9/11 security architecture is generally considered to have curtailed some of the human rights advances that were made in the late 1990s and early 2000s.[33] The edited collection by Wafulu Okumu and Anneli Botha clearly demonstrate that many African countries put in place counterterrorism legislations, institutions, and security apparatuses that have negative implications for the promotion of rights across the African continent. With prodding by the United States, a number of East, West, and North African countries have introduced legislation similar to the PATRIOT Act that undermines many of the political and civil rights principles embedded in the AU human rights system. Many of the African countries would not have introduced these anti–human rights legislations if they internalized AU human rights principles. Put differently, African states would not have introduced unfriendly human rights laws after 9/11 if the elaborate AU human rights rules were everyday practices or norms.

Efficiency: Since the AU, human rights rules cannot be described as norms, yet it is difficult to assess the cost of institutionalizing it or turning it into norms. That said, it is unlikely that its financial impact may be different from the cost of institutionalizing international norms. It may, however, be more expensive to turn them into norms, particularly at the local level given that they did not develop organically. Many ordinary citizens will find it relatively difficult to relate to these human rights ideas in part because of the top-down processes that were used to develop them. As indicated already, many of these rules were written by consultants and lack the socialization and awareness that often accompany the development of ideas that involves broad masses or deliberative processes. In some instances, the human rights rules contradict local practices, and some African and local people are unaware that their practices are against AU human rights principles. A classic example is the AU's position on marriage. The African human rights regime affirms the importance of monogamy, but this is contrary to marriage practices in a number of African communities. For the AU human rights principles of marriage to be institutionalized as a norm, it first has to displace the traditional normative standards of polygamy in these communities. This will not happen unless enormous resources are put into creating awareness and dissuading people from engaging in these practices. This will be an expensive exercise. Some of the costs would have been avoidable had the rules emerged organically from these communities.

DECISION-MAKING STRUCTURES

Nature: The AU human rights agenda is supposed to be managed by four institutions, the African Human Rights Commission, the African Committee of Experts on the Rights and Welfare of the Child (the Committee on the Rights of the Child), the AU Commission, and the ACJHR (replaces the African Court on Human and Peoples' Rights[34] and the nonexisting African Court of Justice and the Human Rights Court).

The Banjul Charter created the African Human Rights Commission in 1986 to protect and promote human and peoples' rights. It has eleven members who are elected by the AU Assembly for a renewable term of six years.[35] The African Charter on the Rights and Welfare of the Child created the Committee on the Rights of the Child in 1999 to promote and protect the rights and welfare of African children as enshrined in the Charter.[36] Human Rights promotion and protection are supposed to be mainstreamed in the work of all the departments and units of the AU, but the DPA and Directorate of Women, Gender and Development (the DWGD) have been explicitly mandated to protect and promote human rights across the African continent. The DWGD manages all the women and children's rights while the DPA is supposed to handle the other rights. The ACJHR, whose protocol was adopted in 2008 and signed by thirty African states, will come into force thirty days after the deposit of an instrument of ratification by fifteen African states.[37] When operational, the Court will have sixteen judges who are will be empowered to make binding decisions and issue advisory opinions on a wide range of human rights issues provided in the African human rights system.

Novelty: Of the four, the Africa Human Rights Commission and the ACJHR are the most innovative in institutional design. The ACJHR may well be the only one in the international system that has a "two-pronged objective to provide for justice and human rights under one roof."[38] It will act as the supreme court of the African human rights system with powers to make binding decisions on a wide range of human rights issues. This is a remarkable improvement over the African Human Rights Commission, which only has the power to make recommendations and nonbinding decisions.

The decision of the Court will be final, meaning that no domestic African court can overturn its rulings. A major distinctive addition to the African international human rights system is that the Court is empowered to make pronouncements on all acts, decisions, regulations, and directives of the organs of the AU. It can even rule on bilateral agreements that AU member states may conclude in the future, provided the parties agree to give jurisdiction over these bilateral issues to the Court. Thus, the ambit of the Court can potentially include every bilateral and multilateral human rights–related agreement that states parties have adopted. This is a major innovation in the international legal system, where most courts have jurisdiction over issues that are specifically mandated in treaties that created them.

Another innovation introduced by the ACJHR is the wide range of organizations, groups, and individuals that are eligible to file a case with the Court. In addition to state parties, individuals, African human rights groups, and the African Committee of Experts on the Rights of the Child can access the ACJHR. The protocol of the ACJHR enhanced further accessibility to the Court by providing free legal aid for individuals whose cases are in the interest of the public.[39] This is a major improvement over the existing legal system, though the public interest requirement together with the elitist procedures for accessing the court may prevent illiterate and poor Africans from filling cases with the Court.

Another uniqueness the Court introduced is the access that it grants to complainants to find any suitable individual(s) and/or group(s) to represent them.[40] In practice, this means that complainants have the opportunity to employ seasoned lawyers and/or human rights groups to file and defend their case. The opening up of the legal space to third-party representation is extremely important. The relative success of the African Human Rights Commission is very much due to the cases filed and defended by human rights groups. Most of the landmark decisions and complaints lodged with the African Human Rights Commission were NGO driven. Without this third-party defence system, it would be difficult for many Africans to access the Court given the low level of formal education across the continent and the formal processes required to file a case with the ACJHR. It should, however, be pointed out that some aspects of the institutional design of the African Court of Justice and the African Human Rights Commission are not necessarily new in the international legal system. Their creators borrowed extensively from international human rights regimes such as the UN Commission on Human Rights and the Inter-American Commission on Human Rights.

Relevance: All of the four institutions managing the African human rights system are generally considered as important, but not in equal terms. The African Commission of Human and Peoples' Rights is broadly seen to be an extremely important institution in the promotion of human rights across the continent. The numerous cases that have been referred to it by individuals, NGOs, and state parties affirm the importance of the Commission. Many of the decisions and communications by the Commission have been historic. Numerous rulings have been against governments and are generally considered by human rights groups to have advanced human rights on the African continent. For instance, the Minority Rights Groups International praised the 2013 decision by the Commission to prevent the eviction of the Ogiek community from their ancestral homes in Kenya's Maomau Forest.[41] Another institute that is highly rated by the African states and human rights community is the ACJHR. Its creation, the International Federation for Human Rights indicated, "is an essential step towards the establishment of a coherent and effective system of human rights protection on the African continent."[42] The outcry that greeted the expansion of the jurisdiction of the Court is a strong indication that a number of civil society groups and even the donor community see the Court as an important institution. Interestingly, not many priority stakeholders think about the AU Commission and the Committee on the Rights of the Child as key human rights institutions or know about them, though both have important human rights mandates. A critical mass of priority stakeholders is unaware that the Secretariat of ACJHR reports to the Department of Political Affairs of the AU Commission.

Financial Viability: Donor support for human rights promotion has reflected the importance they attach to each of the four principal human rights institutions. Of the four institutions, the African Human Rights Commission has received the most funding from mainstream donors, such as the GIZ, the

European Union, and more recently, the Americans have joined the donor list. The donor community has traditionally provided the entire program budget of the African Human Rights, while African member states often pay for the operating budget of the human rights body. For instance, of the U.S. $ 6,395,466 budget approved for the African Human Rights Commission for the 2014 fiscal year, U.S. $ 4,821,043 came from the assessed contribution of AU members, while U.S. $ 1,569,423 was provided by donors.[43]

The African Human Rights Court is increasingly gaining traction in the donor community. In 2014 fiscal year, out of the U.S. $8,969,947 total budget approved for the Court, donors pledged U.S. $2,362,315 while the AU member states offered U.S. $6,607,632 from their assessed contributions.[44] Some donors have provided resources to the African Human Rights Commission, though not at the level expected by the Commission and most keen observers of African human rights system.[45] Donors have largely stayed away from supporting the unit of the DPA in charge of human rights, the African Committee of Experts on the Rights of the Child and the ACJHR.

The financial commitment by African governments to the four human rights bodies have not gone beyond the operational budget and pledges. All four institutions face acute financial problems, but the financial challenges of the African Committee of Experts on the Rights of the Child and the human rights unit of the DPA are the most critical. The financial viability problem of the African Committee of Experts on the Rights of the Child has more to do with its invisibility in the donor community. The challenge could be overcome by serious outreach and credible performance. The DPA problem in attracting donor support, as documented in a previous section, is more systemic and will take good and savvy leadership to overturn it.

It is unlikely that there will be a queue of mainstream donors for the ACJHR, at least in the short term. In actual fact, there is a major campaign, especially in Western diplomatic circles, to kill the Court even before its birth in part because it affirmed customary international law practices that grant immunity from prosecution to public officials.[46] As Human Rights Watch shrewdly put it, "Some activists, diplomats, and academics have queried the appropriateness of having regional courts with this authority and this is likely to be a debated issue for some time to come."[47] Some of the key public officials and bureaucrats in mainstream donor states feel strongly that the broadening of the scope of the Court would effectively render the ICC moribund, and this might discourage the usual donors of the AU such as the EU from funding the Court.

The public argument against the ACJHR relies on two closely related logics. First, that the creation of the African Court demonstrates African leaders' lack of genuine commitment to fighting impunity and ensuring justice for victims of international crimes.[48] The second is that crimes committed in Africa should be tried by a reputable international judicial system. In their view, the ACJHR will at best duplicate the work of the ICC and at worst will just provide cover for African political elites to evade justice. The subtext and the real problem mainstream donor governments have against the ACJHR is that it will compete with ICC, and because thirty-four African countries have already accepted its jurisdiction, there is a genuine fear that it will render the ICC moribund. Such a turn of events will effectively undercut the ability that major donor states want to have over human rights discourse and promotion. Critics will even say that many donor states are complaining about the ACJHR only because it seeks to undermine donor governments' desire to use humanitarian language and the legal system to advance their political interests.

The insecurities of ICC supporters is perhaps warranted given that the drafting of the amendment to the ACJHR protocol occurred at the time that the AU had asked its member states not to cooperate with the ICC and given that the amended protocol did not explicitly acknowledge ICC's jurisdiction over some of the crimes included in the amended protocol. The only entities mentioned as complementary courts were domestic African courts and legal bodies of regional economic communities. Critics of the ACJHR think that the lack of acknowledgment of the ICC's position is a deliberate attempt to weaken and kill it by other means. They may have a case, because without Africa the ICC would have found it difficult to justify its existence and the over a billion dollars it has spent since it was established. The ICC's relevance since its creation has been built on the backs of African citizens. Some middle countries, such as Canada, Sweden, Norway, and Switzerland, who are big supporters of the ICC, fear an effective AU court of justice will put the nail in the coffin of the ICC. Interestingly, the vehement opposition to the ACJHR has emboldened some African countries to commit funding to the AU's approach to human rights. The Kenyan government, for example, has pledged $1 million toward the establishment of the ACJHR and is mobilizing African countries to support its creation.[49]

Effectiveness: Of the four institutions, the African Human Rights Commission is the only one that has demonstrated some level of effectiveness in promoting and defending human rights across the African continent. It has received numerous cases and made landmark rulings. It has at least given an opportunity to Africans to seek redress for human rights abuses. Its creation has allowed individuals, NGOs, and state parties to send communications alleging violations of human rights by state parties.

Yet any honest assessment of its effectiveness (and the Commission is the first to admit) will come to the painful conclusion that it has had decidedly mixed results. Its overall performance could have been way better. One critic argues that the underperformance of the Commission is at least partly the fault of the Commissioners. He writes that "[m]ost Commissioners are there to promote their personal interests: very few are there to promote rights."[50]

This may well be the case, but there are structural problems relating to the design of the Commission that makes it difficult for even the most well-intentioned commissioners to be effective. The Commission framework is not the most suitable institutional structure to promote and defend human rights across the African continent. The Commission was given little tools besides issuing communications and recommendations; shaming; organizing seminars, symposia, and conferences; the dissemination of information; and putting pressure on human rights bodies at the state level to promote and protect human rights. These toothless tools are not what are needed to promote human rights in a challenging human rights environment.

Another structural barrier to the work of the African Human Rights Commission is that it can act on communication its receives only when it is deemed that the individuals, group, or state party filing the complaint has exhausted all available legal remedies at the state level. In other words, it is a court of last resort. Savvy state parties can and often put impediments in the way of individuals and groups who want to access the African Human Rights Commission. The problem of the Commission is compounded by the fact that is not widely known, particularly to vulnerable groups who are likely to have their rights' violated. The working methods and means of communications are not accessible to those who do not have formal education, which is a majority of Africans. Only the elites or those who are well connected to mainstream NGOs (often the elites) can often seek redress. The Commission has thus become the commission of the elites. The cases it has dealt with since the creation of the African Human Rights Commission are mostly complaints that the African social and economic elite has against the political class. It has often been out of reach of most ordinary Africans who need it the most.

The African Human Rights Commission takes too long to investigate and issue communications. It can take up to eight years upon receipt of a communication for the human rights body to review, investigate, and issue decisions. Some of the decisions are often made after the fact or after complaints have suffered deadly consequences. For instance, the late human rights activist Ken Saro-wiwa was killed by the Nigerian military regime before the Commission issued its final communication. Critics of the African Human Rights Commission accuse it of "trying to focus on settlements at the expense of efficiency."[51] The critics of the Commission cite poor prioritization of communication and vague proceedings as major contributors to the ineffectiveness of the African Human Rights Commission.

Efficiency: The efficiency of the four institutions is very questionable. As already pointed out, the procedure for judging cases is slow and not the most efficient way to promote human rights. There have been numerous incidents in which complainants have endured human rights abuses while their cases continued to be examined. It is also not clear if the processes for arriving at a decision are the best available for promoting human rights across the African continent. The Human Rights Commission does not provide remedy or have the power to force parties to provide remedies. Thus, although the Commission's budget is very small, estimated to be around nine million per year, critics would say, what is the point of spending that amount of money to investigate cases and arrive at decisions that may well be ignored? There are few instances in which governments have responded to the ruling of the Commission by providing remedies to victims, but for the most part state parties ignore the Commission's decisions and recommendations. Perhaps the naming and the shaming that comes as a result of the filing of complaints may put pressure on a number of African governments to put their houses in order, but we still do not know if this actually happens. In short, the jury of the Commission's efficiency is still out.

As for the other three institutions, they have not done enough for us to know for sure if they are cost effective. The AU Commission has done very little on promoting human rights. The Experts on the Rights of the Child has done little besides organizing a few workshops and other promotional events. The African Court of Justice and Human Rights is yet to be operationalized. Perhaps it is too early to assess the performance of these three institutions in terms of efficiency. Yet the past records of older regional human rights bodies do not provide any convincing evidence that they are the most cost-effective way to promote human rights across the African continent.

NOTES

1. See the Constitutive Act of the African Union, African Charter on Human and Peoples' Rights, January 25, 2005; Protocol on African Court of Justice and Human Rights, Protocol on the Rights of Women in Africa, the African Youth Charter, the African Charter on Democracy, Elections and Governance, http://www.achpr.org/instruments/achpr/.

2. Pamphlet No. 6 Minority Rights under the African Charter on Human and Peoples' Rights, http://www.ohchr.org/Documents/Publications/GuideMinorities6en.pdf.

3. B. Obinna Okere, "The Protection of Human Rights in Africa and the African Charter on Human and Peoples' Rights: A Comparative Analysis with the European and American Systems," *Human Rights Quarterly* 6, no. 2 (May 1984): 148.

4. Obinna Okere, "The Protection of Human Rights in Africa and the African Charter on Human and Peoples' Rights," 148.

5. Francesca Klug, *A Magna Carta for All Humanity: Homing in on Human Rights* (New York: Routledge, 2015), 58.

6. Klug, *A Magna Carta for All Humanity*, 58.

7. African Union, The Protocol of the OAU Convention on the Prevention and Combating of Terrorism, July 2004, http://www.au.int/en/sites/default/files/PROTOCOL_OAU_CONVENTION_ON_THE_PREVENTION_COMBATING_TERRORISM.pdf.

8. Protocol on Amendments to the Protocol of the Statutes of the Statutes of the African Court of Justice and Human Rights.

9. The Court also has jurisdiction over the traditional crimes, such as war crimes and crimes against humanity, that are covered in international legal instruments.

10. Allison Simon, "Think Again: In Defence of the African Union," *Institute for Security Studies*, September 9, 2014, http://www.issafrica.org/iss-today/think-again-in-defence-of-the-african-union.

11. Chacha Bhoke Murungu, "Towards a Criminal Chamber in the African Court of Justice and Human Rights," *Journal of International Criminal Justice* 9 (2011); 1085–86.

12. Fred Aja Agwu, "The African Court of Justice and Human Rights: The Future of International Criminal Justice in Africa," *Africa Review* 6, no. 1 (2014).

13. Malcolm D. Evans and Rachel Murray, ed., *The African Charter on Human and Peoples' Rights: The System in Practice, 1986–2000* (Cambridge: Cambridge University Press, 2002).

14. Sheila Keetharuth, "Major African Legal Instruments and Human Rights," in *Human Rights in Africa: Legal Perspectives on Their Protection and Promotion*, ed. A. Bosl & J. Diescho (Namibia: Macmillan Education Namibia, 2009).

15. Interview with Litha Musyimi-Ogana, director of AU Gender, Women and Development Directorate, June 28, 2014.

16. Bience Gawanas, "The African Union: Concepts and Implementation Mechanisms Relating to Human Rights," in *Human Rights in Africa: Legal Perspectives on Their Protection and Promotion*, ed. Anton Bösl and Joseph Diescho (Windhoek: Macmillan Education Namibia, 2009), 152–53.

17. Quoted in Gawanas, "The African Union," 135.

18. Musyimi-Ogana interview.

19. Diop Ngone, quoted in "African Union Gender Equality Ministers Adopt Common Position on the Post-2015 Development Agenda," UN Women, 2014, http://www.unwomen.org/en/news/stories/2014/2/african-union-post-2015-position#sthash.wzQY6fFg.dpuf.

20. Louis Napo Gnagbe, the director of the AU Foundation, quoted in African Peace and Security Report, "Beyond Bashir: What Else Happened at the AU Summit?" *Institute of Peace and Security Studies*, http://www.issafrica.org/pscreport/addis-insights/beyond-bashir-what-else-happened-at-the-au-summit.

21. For a discussion of these human rights rules, see Joseph M. Isanga, "The Constitutive Act of the African Union, African Courts and the Protection of Human Rights: New Dispensation?" *Santa Clara Journal of International Law* 11, no. 2 (2013); also see Manisuli Ssenyonjo, *The African Regional Human Rights System: 30 Years after the African Charter on Human and People's Rights* (New York: Martinus Nijhoff Publishers, 2011).

22. Christine Ocran, "The Protocol to the African Charter on Human and Peoples' Rights of Women in Africa," *African Journal of International and Comparative Law* 15, no. 1 (2007): 148–49.

23. *Amnesty International and Others v. Sudan*, African Commission on Human and Peoples' Rights, Comm. No. 48/90, 50/91, 52/91, 89/93 (1999), University of Minnesota, Human Rights Library, http://www1.umn.edu/humanrts/africa/comcases/48-90_50-91_52-91_89-93.html.

24. *Amnesty International and Others v. Sudan*.

25. *Amnesty International and Others v. Sudan*.

26. Michelo Hansungule, "The African Charter on Human and Peoples' Rights," in *The African Union: Legal and Institutional Framework: A Manual on the Pan-African Organization*, Abdulqawi A. Yusuf and Fatsah Ouguergouz, 435 (Martinus Nijhoff Publishers, 2012).

27. Michelo Hansungule, "African Courts and the African Commission on Human and Peoples' Rights," (Konrad-Adenauer-Stiftung), http://www.kas.de/upload/auslandshomepages/namibia/Human_Rights_in_Africa/8_Hansungule.pdf.

28. Report of the African Commission on Human and Peoples' Rights, Executive Council, Eleventh Ordinary Session, June 25, 2007, Accra, Ghana, EXCL/364 (X).

29. Mark Tran, "African Union Summit Struggles to Raise Funds to Combat Horn of Africa Crisis," *The Guardian*, August 25, 2011, http://www.theguardian.com/global-development/2011/aug/25/african-union-summit-funds-somalia.

30. For detailed account of the case, see Sheila Keetharuth, "Major African Legal Instruments and Human Rights," in *Human Rights in Africa: Legal Perspectives on their Protection and Promotion*, ed. A. Bosl and J. Diescho (Namibia: Macmillan Education Namibia, 2009).

31. Marianne White, "Controversial Crime Bill to cost Canadians $19 Billion: Study," *Postmedia News*, December 8, 2011, http://www.vancouversun.com/Controversial+crime+bill+cost+Canadians+billion+study/5832700/story.html.

32. Hansungule, "The African Charter on Human and Peoples' Rights."

33. Wafula Okumu and Anneli Botha, *Understanding Terrorism in Africa: In Search for an African Voice* (Pretoria: Institute for Security Studies, 2007); Mutegi Njau, "An Incentive to Clamp Down: With U.S. Prodding, 3 East African Nations Get Tough on Terrorist Suspects—Even When Evidence Is Lacking," International Consortium of Investigative Journalists.

34. The African Human Rights Court was established by the protocol to the Banjul Charter in 2004 to judge and ensure compliance of AU member states with the Banjul Charter. The Human Rights Court is composed of eleven judges, who are elected by the Executive Council for renewable a term of six years.

35. See the African Commission on Human and Peoples' Rights, http://www.achpr.org/.

36. See the African Committee of Experts on the Rights and Welfare of the Child (ACERWC), http://acerwc.org/mandate-of-the-committee/.

37. As of the July 2015, only five states have ratified and deposited their instruments of ratification, but most keen observers of African politics expect the Court to be in operation within a year or two years.

38. Hansungule, "The African Charter on Human and Peoples' Rights," 237.

39. ACJHR Article 52(2).

40. ACJHR Article 36.

41. Minority Rights Group International.

42. International Federation for Human Rights, "The African Court on Human and Peoples' Rights towards the African Court of Justice and Human Rights," *International Federation for Human Rights* (April 2010): 19.

43. 37th Activity Report of the African Commission on Human and Peoples' Rights, http://www.achpr.org/.

44. Activity Report of the African Court for the Year 2013, Executive Council Twenty-Fourth Ordinary Session, 21–28 January 2014. Addis Ababa, Ethiopia, http://www.au.int.

45. Joseph M. Isanga, "The Constitutive Act of the African Union, African Courts and the Protection of Human Rights: New Dispensation?" *Santa Clara Journal of International Law* 11, no. 2 (2013).

46. International Justice Resources Centre, "African Union Approves Immunity for Government Officials in Amendment to African Court of Justice and Human Rights' Statute," July 2, 2014, http://www.ijrcenter.org/2014/07/02/african-union-approves-immunity-for-heads-of-state-in-amendment-to-african-court-of-justice-and-human-rights-statute/.

47. Human Rights Watch, "Statement Regarding Immunity for Sitting Officials Before the Expanded African Court of Justice and Human Rights," November 13, 2014, http://www.hrw.org/news/2014/11/13/statement-regarding-immunity-sitting-officials-expanded-african-court-justice-and-hu.

48. Mireille Affa'a-Mindzie, "Leaders Agree on Immunity for Themselves During Expansion of African Court," *The Global Observatory*, July 23, 2014, http://theglobalobservatory.org/2014/07/leaders-agree-immunity-expansion-african-court/.

49. John Ngirachu, "Uhuru Kenyatta: Let's Have an African-Funded Court," *Daily Nation*, January 31, 2015, http://www.nation.co.ke/news/politics/Uhuru-Kenyatta-African-Court-of-Justice-and-Human-Rights/-/1064/2609206/-/15qapjj/-/index.html.

50. Michelo Hansungule, "The African Charter on Human and Peoples' Rights," in *The African Union: Legal and Institutional Framework: A Manual on the Pan-African Organization*, Abdulqawi A. Yusuf and Fatsah Ouguergouz, 250 (Martinus Nijhoff Publishers, 2012).

51. International Federation for Human Rights, "The African Court on Human and Peoples' Rights towards the African Court of Justice and Human Rights," April 2010, 26–27.

Chapter Eight

Conclusion

Summary and Theoretical Implications

This book sought to conceptualize the nature of International Organizations (IOs) and to provide the framework for assessing the performance of IOs. It used the AU as empirical turf to illustrate these two primary ideas. The book showed that IOs such as the African Union (AU) are three-dimensional organizations composed of intergovernmental bodies, supranational agencies, and transnational networks and organizations. The three bodies exist in a symbiotic relationship, and each dimension plays a central role in setting the agenda and directing the daily work of the organization. The best way to understand and study IOs is therefore to approach them as three organizations put into one.

The membership and role of intergovernmental bodies are not in doubt. They are spelled out in binding legal instruments. In the AU context, the intergovernmental bodies are clearly outlined in the Constitutive Act as the Assembly, the Council, and the Permanent Representatives' Committee (PRC), among others. At the ideational level, there are three blocs within the intergovernmental AU: statists, regionalists, and continentalists. The statists are more interested in defending the colonial borders that were bequeathed to Africans. Some of the proponents of the statist school are native-statists, and they loathe attempts to cede any aspect of sovereignty to supranational authority, however insignificant. They do not like to see the AU pushing African states to adopt common standards, values, and beliefs that have been agreed upon at the continental or regional levels. Left to the native-statists alone, there will be no room for AU bureaucrats in the management of African states. There are also transnational-statists who want to defend the colonial boundaries but are relatively open to cooperating with other African states based on national interests and preferences of individual African governments. For the transnational statists, the AU should be nothing more than a forum to develop a common position for African states on global issues.

The regionalists, by contrast, are more interested in creating regional identity, and they see the African regional economic communities as building blocks for constructing such an identity. They loathe the idea of a continental union and want IOs, such as the AU, to serve as a forum for the five regions of Africa to coordinate their international activities. Like the statists, they want to limit the role of the AU and its bureaucrats, also known as Africrats, in African states affairs. The dominance of the statists and regionalists in the intergovernmental part of the AU in large part accounts for the slow process in the operationalization of key AU supranational ideas, such as the African Standby Force (ASF), and the poor performance of the AU at the national level.

The continentalists are interested in building a stronger and united Africa. They consider the European colonial boundaries that gave birth to the African state system as problematic and, even, illegitimate. Those who subscribe to this view claim that the boundaries impeded organic development of political organizations and institutions. As a result, they call for the re-building of political organizations in Africa. For proponents of this thesis, a continental union government—in the form of a federation, a confederation, or similar union—that brings all African people together will be the most appropriate replacement for the European state system. Like every broader ideational group, there are also differences within the group. There are the continental federalists who like to replace the colonial states with a federal system of government. For them, colonial boundaries are artificial creations that should give way to one federal government for Africa. There are also confederal continentalists who favor a more malleable form of continental governance. They are interested in the dissolution of the state system into either a confederal or a hybrid form of federation and confederation and see the AU as the start of the process to dissolve this system.

The three major paradigmatic orientations (worldviews) drive both the conduct of, and the discourse on, cooperation in Africa. Supporters of the three paradigmatic groups engaged in a heated debate in the late 1950s and early 1960s about a master frame idea for the African continent. A decisive victory for the statists led to the creation of the Organization of African Unity (OAU). The statist ideological influence made the OAU focus on legitimization and promotion of statehood in Africa. The influence of neoliberal ideas and the International financial institutions in the 1980s led to a shift in focus on the OAU as a tool for building the African state. Domestic African and transnational private businesses became the main center of attention. The change in focus generated so much indifference toward the work of the OAU that in the 1980s the continental organization became virtually moribund. The OAU, however, reasserted itself as a mover of African politics in the first half of the 1990s. Africrats led by the former OAU Secretary-General Salim Ahmed Salim are largely responsible for putting the focus back on continental initiatives with the adoption of the African Economic Community (AEC) at the Twenty-Seventh Ordinary Session of the OAU held in Abuja, Nigeria, in 1991. Salim also broadened the scope of the OAU to include conflict prevention, management, and resolution. The reformist agenda of Salim together with structural factors, such as the end of the Cold War, created conditions for the second grand debate in the late 1990s. The AU is a product of this particular debate.

Unlike intergovernmental bodies, the identity of IOs as supranational organizations is debatable. There are scholars who are willing to accept that at least some IOs have supranationality. Many scholars will agree that some European Union (EU) institutions, such as the Parliament and Court, have supranational identity. This book argued that the AU should be added to the list of supranational institutions. The African Union Commission (AUC) possesses all the attributes of a supranational body. The AUC's supranationality comes from the relative independence that its staff enjoys, and the functional roles and activities that the Commission staff and supporting actors, such as consultants, perform on a day-to-day basis. The day-to-day work of the AUC staff includes treaty drafting, rule making, rule enforcement, agenda setting, proposal initiation, research, and dissemination and monitoring of states' compliance. The AUC supranational roles are compartmentalized into eight departments and three units.

The most controversial member of IOs are the outisiders. They can be categorized into at least three different groups. The first are individuals who are formally affiliated with organizations outside of the AU system but seek to influence, direct, and in some cases shape the direction of the Union. These individuals tend to engage with the AU either as consultants, technical experts, members of a commission, or as independent researchers and academics. In some instances they engage with the AU within the institutional framework of think tanks. These groups and individuals feed the AU with ideas, advice, and policy instruments, among other things. Most of the AU's ideas including the African Peace and Security Architecture (APSA), the African Governance Charter, and African Court of Justice originated from these groups. The second type of outisiders is the donors of the AU. These groups tend to use indirect means to shape and influence the direction of the AU. They have carved out a space for themselves, and in particular they are in charge of directing, influencing, and in some cases encouraging the development of AU programs.

The third group of outisiders are the international organizations that have tremendous interest in the work of the AU. The first group of international organizations are the ones based on the African continent, usually referred to as the African Economic Communities. These organizations often serve as testing grounds for AU ideas and have also become a source of ideas for the AU. The APSA draws ideas and lessons from the work of the Economic Community of West African States (ECOWAS). The other type of IO that engages with the AU is the international organizations outside of the African continent. The most prominent of these organizations are the United Nations and the European Union. These two organizations provide lessons learned and resources to the AU.

The fourth and last type of outsiders is the civil society groups. The transnational and local African civil society groups are prominent players within the AU system. The transnational civil society groups that have been central in the AU system are those interested in promoting peace, security, good governance, and human rights, particularly gender rights. These transnational groups often provide knowledge, information, and technical expertise to the AU. A good amount of information that the AUC and intergovernmental AU tend to use is drawn from knowledge and research produced by the International Crisis Group. These transnational organizations also provide feedback to the AU system. Many of them help to sharpen AU ideas and work by making them more relevant to non-African elites. The second civil society group that has played a fundamental role to the AU project is the local indigenous African civil society groups. These local nongovernmental organizations (NGOs) engage in the AU through the institutional framework of the United Nations Economic and Social Council (ECOSOC). These local NGOs, a majority of which are dealing with human rights issues, have become the transmission belt of AU ideas. They transmit these ideas to local communities and non-African elite. They are not just recipients of ideas of the AU, but they modify these ideas to suit the local context. In other words, they serve as the interlocutor between transnational ideas, norms and practices, and local practices and norms. They also provide feedback to the AU and are primarily responsible for ensuring a reality check on most of the AU ideas. Together with the transnational civil society groups, they have become the critics of the AU.

The question that may come to the mind of the curious reader after reading the nature of the AU is, Where did this IO with such a complex membership come from? Chapter 3 tells that story, arguing that a combination of factors including criticisms by outsiders made Africrats and African leaders acutely aware that its predecessor, the OAU, was incapable of helping African states to address challenges that Africans will face in the twenty-first century. In the early 1990s, Africrats began to search for alternative institutional frameworks that would assist African governments to organize and govern African societies better. Africrats consciously defined the interests that drove the creation of the AU. Salim Ahmed Salim, a well-connected former Tanzanian foreign minister with considerable persuasive skills, and a few senior professional staff members at the OAU Secretariat used ideas and policy documents deliberately to construct interests for the majority of African governments. Salim and the OAU staff members persuaded African governments, first, to renegotiate rules and norms of interstate politics in Africa; and, second, to create new institutional mechanisms to embed those rules and norms. Africrats in collaboration with Pan-African outisiders put forth a number of proposals, including a single charter that would bring together the plethora of institutions that African states had established since the formation of the OAU in 1963. Since African leaders and the inter-governmental institutional framework that they inhabit are divided along the statist, regionalist, and continental fault lines, their governments had to bring together states lawyers and other representatives from the fifty-three members of the OAU to negotiate the content of the AU between 1999 and 2000.

Chapter 4 documented the negotiation processes, showing that Africrats helped state representatives select the specific content of the AU. The chapter suggested that Africrats used their entrepreneurial skills, the OAU's institutional mechanisms, and arguments to persuade representatives of states to select ambitious principles, rules, institutional structures, and decision-making procedures. Africrats did not persuade all state representatives, but they did convince sufficient numbers of them to generate a broad agreement on the appropriate institutional mechanisms for Africa. As soon as the broad consensus emerged on the appropriateness of the AU institutional mechanism, Pan-African solidarity then set in to compel the unconvinced governments to sign on. The AU that Africrats helped to construct and African leaders in Lomé adopted in 2000 differed remarkably from what state representatives wanted. It did not reflect the statists' project, or preferences of regionalists, or meet the expectations of the institutional order that continental federalists had imagined. Rather, it reflected an ambitious and in many cases innovative institutional structure. The institutional mechanisms of the AU undermine the international norm of the territorial integrity of states, and it set limits on core sovereign prerogatives of African states. It is ironic that African states would establish and commit to an organization that undercuts the international norm that has protected the existence of postcolonial states. The significance of the AU becomes more profound when it is placed within the broader structural global power context. Many of the states that formed the AU are weak, and have much to lose should the international norm of territorial integrity of states wither. The question then becomes, Did African governments really mean to implement the ambitious AU agenda, or did they just agree to it for presentational and symbolic purposes?

The next three chapters are therefore devoted to an assessment of the AU since it was created in 2001. To ensure that the assessment is done in a systematic way, an analytical framework was developed. The framework has indicators on both vertical and horizontal axes. The vertical axis showed the extent to which the AU helped member states acquire worldview, binding rules, norms, policies, and decision-making bodies. The horizontal axis provided indicators to measure the extent to which the worldview, rules, norms, policies, and decision-making structures are novel, relevant, effective, financially viable, and efficient in addressing African challenges. The framework was then used to assess AU performance in the areas of good political governance, peace, and security as well as human rights promotion. The issues were selected because almost every political scientist who pays even superficial attention to the African continent will notice that the three issues are at the heart of Africa's political problems, and they offer the best possible opportunity for the continent to take its rightly discursive and material place in the world.

Chapter 5 examined the AU's performance in promoting good political governance. It demonstrated that the AU's good political governance ideas and institutions have introduced a paradigmatic shift in terms of regional and global thinking about democracy promotion and defense. At the regional level, the AU has introduced new benchmarks and an African consensual understanding of what good political governance is. These ideas have been legalized in multiple ways, including treaties, protocols, charters, and declarations. The most elaborate and up to date of these legal instruments is the African Governance Charter, which imposes an obligation on state parties that goes way beyond obligations that a number of IOs have imposed on member states. The rules are certainly more precise and intrusive than comparable charters that exist within the international system. Some of these rules have developed to the extent that they have been normalized and routinized in the practice of African leaders. The chapter demonstrated that the rule on unconstitutional change of government has been transformed into an anticoup norm. The AU good governance political ideas are embedded within an institutional framework managed by the African Union's Department of Political Affairs. Under the so-called African Governance Architecture, the AU political governance ideas are being diffused within the AU itself and in African countries. The diffusion of the ideas has proceeded relatively well within the AU itself, but they have not been transmitted or diffused to individual African states, other African institutions, or local African communities. To put it in another way, the AU has been able to develop new, innovative, game-changing ideas, but these ideas have not traveled beyond the confines of the AU itself.

Chapter 6 picks up the story of the performance of the AU in peace and security, including counterterrorism activities. The chapter showed that the AU has developed the state-of-the-art security worldviews, norms, rules, policy instruments, and decision-making structures. A majority of them make other IOs look conservative, and some of the ideas are novel to the international security landscape. The AU performance in the area of security is comparably better than its performance on other issues. The chapter demonstrates that the AU has been able to deploy peace support operations that were cheaper and more effective than peacekeeping of even the United Nations. The AU has also been able to help African states develop a number of security norms that have a strong regulatory impact on member states. The AU work is, however, grounded on a very weak foundation. Most of its activities are ad hoc in nature, based on short-term thinking, and in many instances they are not done in a systematic or coherent way. A majority of the individuals who were instrumental in making AU peace and security relatively effective were on short-term contracts, and there seems to be no sustainable plan in place for the AU to continue some of the good work that it has done so far. In other words, the AU has introduced novel peace and security ideas and institutions that are already making positive inroads in different parts of Africa, but the gains made are built on an unsustainable foundation.

Chapter 7 explores the AU's performance in the area of human rights promotion. The AU has developed innovative and at times game-changing human rights worldviews, norms, rules, instruments, and decision-making structures. But unlike in the areas of peace and security, the implementation of the sound human rights tools has been decidedly poor. In particular, the AU has been unable to diffuse and implement most of the rules at the state, community, and individual levels. It does not even have a good policy framework to anchor the human rights worldviews, norms, rules, instruments, and decision-making structures. Most of the institutions that have been created to promote human rights are weak, and many do not have any teeth. The African Commission on Human and Peoples' Rights, for example, does not have the power to enforce its decisions. Similarly, the African Human Rights Court also does not have power to enforce its decisions. In fact, the Libyan authorities ignored its first major ruling, and the Court is toothless in forcing the Libyan government to respect its decisions. The scope of the African Court of Justice, which came with useful enforcement mechanisms, has been broadened to the extent that the major perpetrators of human rights abuses across the African continent may end up escaping prosecution or may not be brought to justice. This has been a major source of complaints and criticisms of the AU by human rights groups. Overall, therefore, the performance of the AU on the three important issues—governance, peace and security, and human rights—has been very average at best. The AU has performed creditably well on peace and security issues, but it has largely been very inefficient and ineffective in promoting human rights and good governance.

A number of theoretical insights were advanced in the book. For the sake of brevity, three of these will be highlighted. The first theoretical insight is that the long-standing debate between intergovernmental and supranational is actually mute in the sense that every IO has both an intergovernmental and supranational dimension. The key question for scholars of IOs to explore is not whether IOs are intergovernmental or supranational or whether IOs are driven by intergovernmentalism or supranationalism. Both actors are key players in the IO system. What is important for those interested in IOs scholarship to explore is, under what circumstance would one dimension of an IO be more effective in advancing the goals of the organization, or what makes one actor more effective on a particular issue at a particular time in history?

Conceptualizing IOs in intergovernmentalism verses supranationalism actually undermines our understanding of IOs because it obscures the critically important role played by outisiders in the IO process. The debate between intergovernmental and supranational oversimplifies very dynamic and complex interactions between intergovernmental, supranational, and outsiders. As chapter 2 showed, outisiders provide ideas to both intergovernmental and supranational bodies through consultancy services, advocacy, reports, studies, and policy instruments, and use moral suasion and incredible access to decision makers to set parameters of choices available to intergovernmentals and supranationals.

Even the relationship between intergovernmentals and supranationals is not as straightforward and unidimensional as the intergovernmentals verses the supranationals binary suggests. On one hand, both chapters 3 and 4 showed that Africa's international bureaucrats do not perform mere functional roles for states, nor are they mere servants of politicians, as the liberal intergovernmentalists maintain; instead, they are active political players. They persuaded governments to commit their states within institutional mechanisms that many of them would have otherwise rejected. The institutional deficiencies and human resource deficits combined with the transient nature of staffing of government agencies such embassies allowed Africrats to perform the function normally reserved for intergovernmental bodies. Africrats made rules, regulations, and decisions that they sometimes enforce on governments, and they used their position to establish long-term goals and strategic plans for the AU. On the other hand, Africa's international bureaucrats need approval (even if they were mere rubber stamps) from intergovernmental bodies, such as the Assembly, for most of the things they do, while operating within the financial parameters policed by intergovernmental organizations such as the PRC.

Second, the discussion of the role of Africrats in both the creation and the performance of the AU highlights interesting theoretical insights. It draws attention to the fact that the prevailing view in the study of African politics and international relations, that regional African politics in general, and the creation of an IO in Africa in particular, is driven by powerful African political leaders is overstated. It seems transnational bureaucrats play more of a vital role in the institutional formation in Africa than has been acknowledged in the literature. In addition, the book suggests that the successes of

Africrats depended heavily on argumentation, rather than bargaining. This was particularly evident during the AU negotiation processes documented in chapter 4. The analyses of the AU negotiations suggested that delegations rarely used strategic or manipulative instruments and tactics. Little bargaining speech acts, such as threats, material inducements, and side payments, among others, were instead deployed. These observations seem to contradict the dominant rationalistic analysis of international relations, which suggests that material resources, bargaining, and strategic speech acts are drivers of major interstate negotiations. As chapter 4 showed, the selection of elements of the AU was rule guided and reflected more of a social setting than anything else.

FUTURE RESEARCH DIRECTION

The arguments of the book raise exciting questions and intriguing ideas for future research. The performance indicators can be adopted and used to do a compelling comparative study between the AU and other comparable IOs such as the Organization of American States (OAS), the League of Arab States (or Arab League), the Association of Southeast Asian Nations (ASEAN), and even the EU. Issue-area comparison might place IR scholars in a good position to gauge whether or not the case of the AU represents a significant movement toward a rule-governed world, given the recent interest in legalization. It will also give IR scholars a good basis to judge the state of global governance. The AU's integration orientation also offers scholars interested in regional integration a good opportunity to embark upon a more rigorous comparative work and to develop sophisticated analytical tools for a better understanding of the integration process. The AU's limitations on core sovereign prerogatives of states and the seeming similarities between the AU and the EU lend themselves to comparative analysis that might yield groundbreaking results.

The book also shows that IR scholars are missing important knowledge by neglecting the independent political role that international bureaucrats operating in regions other than continental Europe play. These international bureaucrats are neither tools in the working bags of politicians nor passive recipients of ideas and instructions. They do more than is acknowledged by IR conceptual and analytical tools. It is, perhaps, time for IR scholars to think about regional organizations outside of Europe as political arenas, perhaps in a fashion similar to the one in which their colleagues in public administration and public policy treat bureaucracy at the state level. This book has provided grounds for IR scholars to inquire into the role that international bureaucrats working with regional institutions in the developing world play in the construction of international politics and social reality.

Closely related, the book provides ample evidence to illustrate the fact that political scientists and African studies scholars are losing significant knowledge by ignoring the role of outsiders in IOs and in regional politics. A comparative study of the role of outsiders in other IOs and regional organizations, such as the EU, the North American Free Trade Agreement (NAFTA), Asia-Pacific Economic Cooperation (APEC), the Common Market of the South (Mercosur), and the ASEAN will improve our understanding of IO politics a great deal.

Similarly, the analysis indicates that political scientists and African studies scholars are missing a great deal of insights by neglecting the impact of norms rooted in regional social structures. Though the universalistic approach that many constructivists have adopted to study norms has improved the understanding of world politics, it has, paradoxically, impaired scholars' view of the effects that norms embedded in regional and subnational entities have on international affairs. This book has shown that the understanding of world politics would be improved if scholars would devote attention to the study of norms embedded in entities other than the international system.

The book prompts scholars to pay attention to the impact of arguing and bargaining in international politics. The ubiquitous nature of both modes of communication in international politics notwithstanding, we know little about their relative significance in a wide range of issue areas. For instance, does international negotiation lead to a more successful outcome under conditions of arguing than of bargaining, or vice versa? In what kind of conflict would it be more useful to employ arguing as opposed to bargaining, or vice versa? Which of the two modes of communication provides a more suitable environment for nonstate actors to play an independent political role? These questions require answers from scholars interested in IOs.

Finally, the observation in the book that the AU Commission, ably supported by outsiders, basically provided the intellectual power that has fueled the work of the AU, since its creation prompts us to reconsider the romantic and idealized way in which we think about state capacity. Because most IR theories have Western-developed states in mind, they conceptualize the state as a well-organized entity with the capacity to supervise IO institutions and transnational bureaucrats. Most IR scholarship assumes that government officials have the competence to set priorities and give policy directions. There is little room in the theories for states that do not have the capacity to develop long-term strategic priorities at the regional level, and that have to rely on transnational bureaucrats and think tanks to do so. A careful study of state capacity that is not grounded in any romantic assumptions about state capacity will go a long way to help us understand politics and society a little better.

Bibliography

Abass, Ademola. "The Proposed International Criminal Jurisdiction for the African Court: Some Problematical Aspects." *Netherlands International Law Review* (2013): 27–50. doi:10.1017/S0165070X12001027.

Abdullah, Ibrahim. "Bush Path to Destruction: The Origin and Character of the Revolutionary United Front." *Africa Development* 3, no. 4 (1997): 45–76.

Abraham, Arthur. "Dancing with the Chameleon: Sierra Leone and the Elusive Quest for Peace." *Journal of Contemporary African Studies* 19, no. 2 (2001): 205–28.

Acevedo D., and C. Grossman. "The OAS and the Protection of Democracy." In *Beyond Sovereignty: Collectively Defending Democracy in the Americas*, edited by Tom J. Farer, 132–49. Baltimore: Johns Hopkins University Press, 1996.

Acharya, Amitav. "Dialogue and Discovery: In Search of International Relations Theories Beyond the West." *Millennium* 39, no. 3 (2011): 619–37.

———. "How Ideas Spread: Whose Norms Matter? Norm Localization and Institutional Change in Asian Regionalism." *International Organization* 58, no. 2 (2004): 239–75.

Addo, Prosper. "Transnational Threats to Peace in Africa," *Social Science Research Council Forum: Kujenga-Amani (2013)*. http://forums.ssrc.org/kujenga-amani/2013/09/26/transnational-threats-to-peace-in-africa/.

Addona, A. F. The Organization of African Unity. Cleveland and New York: World Publishing Company, 1969.

Adedeji, Adebayo. "History and Prospects for Regional Integration in Africa." Presented at the third meeting of the ECA's African Development Forum, Addis Ababa, March 5, 2002.

Adisa, Jimmi, Senior Coordinator and Head of CSSDCA. Interview. February 20, 2004.

Affa'a-Mindzie, Mireille. "Leaders Agree on Immunity for Themselves During Expansion of African Court." *The Global Observatory*, July 23, 2014. http://theglobalobservatory.org/2014/07/leaders-agree-immunity-expansion-african-court/.

African Heads of Government (OAU). *Lomé Declaration* (AHG/Decl.5 (XXXVI). Lome, Togo: July 10–12, 2000. http://www.peaceau.org/uploads/ahg-decl-2-xxxvi-e.pdf.

African Union. *African Charter on Democracy, Elections, and Governance*. Adopted by the Eighth Ordinary Session of the Assembly. Addis Ababa, Ethiopia: January 30, 2007. http://www.achpr.org/files/instruments/charter-democracy/aumincom_instr_charter_democracy_2007_eng.pdf.

———. *African Charter on Human and Peoples' Rights*. Adopted by the eighteenth Assembly of Heads of State and Government. Nairobi, Kenya: June 1981. http://www.achpr.org/instruments/achpr/.

———. African Union, *Agenda 2063*. http://agenda2063.au.int/en/about.

————. *African Union Convention for the Protection and Assistance of Internally Displaced Persons in Africa* (Kampala Convention). Kampala, Uganda, October 23, 2009. http://au.int/en/sites/default/files/AFRICAN_UNION_CONVENTION_FOR_THE_PROTECTION_AND_ASSISTANCE_OF_INTERNALLY_DISPLACED_PERSONS_IN_AFRICA_(KAMPALA_CONVENTION).pdf.

————. "The African Union (AU) Establishes a Team to Investigate Allegations of Sexual Exploitation and Abuse (SEA) by the AU Mission in Somalia (AMISOM)." http://www.peaceau.org/en/article/the-african-union-au-establishes-a-team-to-investigate-allegations-of-sexual-exploitation-and-abuse-sea-by-the-au-mission-in-somalia-amisom#sthash.3q4PGFRq.dpuf.

————. The African Union Non-Aggression and Common Defence Pact, Adopted by the Fourth Ordinary Session of the Assembly. Abuja, Nigeria, January 31, 2005. http://au.int/en/sites/default/files/AFRICAN_UNION_NON_AGGRESSION_AND_COMMON_DEFENCE_PACT.pdf.

————. "The African Union Releases the Key Findings and Recommendations of the Report of Investigations on Sexual Exploitation and Abuse in Somalia." *African Union Peace & Security*, April 21, 2015. http://peaceau.org/en/article/the-african-union-releases-the-key-findings-and-recommendations-of-the-report-of-investigations-on-sexual-exploitation-and-abuse-in-somalia.

————. *African Youth Charter, adopted by the Seventh Ordinary Session of the Assembly.* Banjul, Gambia, July 2, 2009. http://www.au.int/en/sites/default/files/AFRICAN_YOUTH_CHARTER.pdf.

————. *Algiers Declaration, AHG Decl. 1 (XXXV)*, OAU 35th Assembly of Heads of State and Government (Algiers: July 12–14, 1999).

————. *The Common African Defence and Security Policy.* Addis Ababa: African Union Commission, 2007.

————. Common African Position on the UN Review of Peace Operations. Peace and Security Council 502nd Meeting. Addis Ababa, Ethiopia, April 29, 2015, PSC/PR/2(DII). http://www.peaceau.org/uploads/psc.502.peace.operations.29-04-2015-1-.pdf.

————. Communiqué of the 519th PSC meeting on Universal Jurisdiction, June 26, 2015. http://www.peaceau.org/en/article/communique-of-the-519th-psc-meeting-on-universal-jurisdiction-26-june-2015 -sthash.365l6KtJ.64Yh7pGv.dpuf.

————. *The Constitutive Act.* Addis Ababa, 2001.

————. *The Constitutive Act.* Lomé, Togo, July 11, 2000.

————. *Decision on the Prevention of Unconstitutional Changes of Government and Strengthening the Capacity of the African Union to Manage Such Situations.* Doc. No. Assembly/AU/Dec.269 (XIV) Rev.1, 6(i)(b), February 2, 2010. http://www.africa-union.org/root/AR/index/Assembly Dec.268-288, Decl.1-3, Res E.pdf.

————. *Declaration of the Heads of State and Government of the African Union on the Fourth Ordinary Session of African Union.* Addis Ababa, Ethiopia: African Union, 2005.

————. *Explanatory Note on the Draft Constitutive Act of the African Union.* Addis Ababa, Ethiopia: General Secretariat, June 2000.

————. *The Ezulwini Consensus: The Common African Position on the Proposed Reform of the United Nations.* New York: United Nations, 2005c. http://www.africa-union.org/News_Events/Calendar_of_%20Events/7th%20extra%20ordinary%20session%20ECL/Ext%20EXCL2%20VII%20Report.doc.

————. *Political, Economic, and Corporate Governance.* 2002.

————. *The Protocol of the OAU Convention on the Prevention and Combating of Terrorism.* Addis Ababa: July 8, 2004. http://www.au.int/en/sites/default/files/PROTOCOL_OAU_CONVENTION_ON_THE_PREVENTION_COMBATING_TERRORISM.pdf.

————. *The Protocol on Amendments to the Protocol of the Statutes of the African Court of Justice and Human Rights.* Adopted by the Eleventh Ordinary Session of the Assembly. Sharm El-Sheikh, Egypt, July 1, 2008. http://www.au.int/en/sites/default/files/PROTOCOL_STATUTE_AFRICAN_COURT_JUSTICE_AND_HUMAN_RIGHTS.pdf.

———. *Protocol on the African Charter on Human and Peoples' Rights on the Rights of Women in Africa*, Adopted by the 2nd Ordinary Session of the Assembly of the Union. Maputo July 11, 2003.

———. *Protocol on the Amendments to the Constitutive Act of the African Union*. Addis Ababa, Ethiopia: African Union, 2003.

———. *The Protocol Relating to the Establishment of the Peace and Security Council of the African Union*, adopted by the First Ordinary Session of the Assembly of the African Union. Durban, South Africa: July 9, 2002. http://www.peaceau.org/uploads/psc-protocol-en.pdf.

———. *Report of the African Commission on Human and Peoples' Rights, Executive Council, Eleventh Ordinary Session.* Accra, Ghana, June 25, 2007.

———. *Report of the 3rd Ordinary Session of the Executive Council on the Proposed Structure, Human Resources Requirements and Condition of Service for the Staff of the Commission of the African Union and Their Financial Implications* (Doc. EX/CL/39 (III). July 4–8, 2003. Maputo, Mozambique. http://webmail.africa-union.org/REFERENCE/EX CL 34 (III) _E.PDF.

———. *Report on the Elaboration of a Framework Document on Post Conflict Reconstruction and Development (PCRD)*. Banjul, Gambia: 2006.

———. *Sirte Declaration EAHG/Draft/Decl. (IV) Rev. 1, Fourth Extraordinary Session of the Assembly of Heads of State and Government* (Sirte, Libya, September 8–9, 1999). http://www.au2002.gov.za/docs/key_oau/sirte.pdf.

———. "South Sudan Commission of Inquiry Established and Members Appointed." Addis Ababa, Ethiopia: African Union Commission, March 7, 2014. http://www.peaceau.org/en/article/south-sudan-commission-of-inquiry-established-and-members-appointed#sthash.WdBv4VEd.dpuf.

———. *The Statute of the Commission of the African Union.* Durban, South Africa: Assembly of the African Union. July 9–10, 2002. http://www.au2002.gov.za/docs/summit_council/statutes.pdf.

———. *Strategic Plan of the Commission of the African Union Volume 3: 2004–2007 Plan of Action*, May 2004. https://repositories.lib.utexas.edu/bitstream/handle/2152/4763/3851.pdf?sequence=1.

———. *The 23rd Ordinary Session of the African Union, in Malabo*. Malabo, June 30, 2014. http://summits.au.int/en/23rdsummit/events/23rd-ordinary-session-african-union-ends-malabo.

———. *Union Government for Africa, AHG/Resolution.10 (I)*. Assembly of Heads of State and Government, First Ordinary Session (Cairo, UAR: July 17–21, 1964).

———. "Vision and Mission of the African Union Commission." Addis Ababa, Ethiopia: African Union 2005b. http://www.africa union.org/root/au/AboutAu/vision_mission.htm.

———. *Yaoundé Declaration (Africa: Preparing for the 21st Century)*, AHD/Dec.3 (XXXII) 32nd OAU Summit (Yaoundé: July 1996).

Agwu, Fred Aja. "The African Court of Justice and Human Rights: The Future of International Criminal Justice in Africa." *Africa Review* 6, no. 1 (2014): 30–43.

Ahmed Salim, Salim. "Introductory Note to the Report of the Secretary-General." *Organization of African Unity* (Harare, 1997): 10.

———. "Introductory Note to the Report of the Secretary-General to the Fifty-Ninth Ordinary Session of Council of Ministers." *Organization of African Unity* (Addis Ababa, 1994), 7.

———. "Report of the Secretary-General to the Fifty-Fifth Ordinary Session of Council of Ministers." *Organization of African Unity* (Addis Ababa, 1992): 4–5.

———. "Report of the Secretary-General to the Fifty-First Ordinary Session of Council of Ministers." *Organization of African Unity* (Addis Ababa, 1990): 8–10.

———. "Report of the Secretary-General to the Fifty-Second Ordinary Session of Council of Ministers." *Organization of African Unity* (Addis Ababa, 1990).

———. "The Report of the Secretary-General to the Special Session of the Council of Ministers on Economic and Social Issues in African Development." *Organization of African Unity* (Addis Ababa, 1995): 130–35.

————. "Ushering the OAU into the Next Century: A Programme for Reform and Renewal in the Introductory Note to the Report of the Secretary-General to the Thirty-Third Ordinary Session." *Organization of African Unity* (Addis Ababa, 1997).

Ake, Claude. *Democracy and Development in Africa*. Washington: The Brookings Institution, 1996.

Algathafi, Muammar. "Unity Will Make Us Strong." 2001.

All Africa. "Commission of the AU Rejects Damning Report on Zimbabwe." http://allafrica.com/stories/200407061180.html.

Alter, Karen J. "The Multiple Roles of International Courts and Tribunals: Enforcement, Dispute Settlement." *Constitutional and Administrative Review, Buffet Centre Working Paper* 12, no. 2 (2012).

Amoo, Sam. "Role of the OAU: Past, Present and Future." In *Making War and Waging Peace: Foreign Intervention in Africa*, edited by David R. Smock. Washington DC: United States Institute of Peace, 1993.

Armstrong, K., and S. Bulmer. *The Governance of the Single European Market*. Manchester: Manchester University Press, 1998.

Asamoah, Obed. Interview. Accra, July 2, 2005.

Ayebare, Adonia. "Regional Perspectives on Sovereignty and Intervention." Discussion Paper of ICISS Round Table Consultation, Maputo: March 10, 2001. Available online at: http://web.gc.cuny.edu/icissresearch/maputu.htm.

Babiker, Mohamed Abdel Salam. "The International Criminal Court and the Darfur Crimes: The Dilemma of Peace and Supra-National Criminal Justice." *International Journal of African Renaissance Studies* 5, no. 1 (2010): 82-100. doi: 10.1080/18186874.2010.500033.

Barker, Debi, and Jerry Mander. "The WTO and Invisible Government." *Peace Review* 12, no. 2 (2000): 251–55.

Barnett, William C. "The Geography of Africa." In *African History before 1885, Volume One*, ed. Toyin Falolom, 43. Durham: Carolina Academic Press, 2000.

Barrett, Michael, and Martha Finnemore. "Political Approaches." In *The Oxford Handbook on the United Nations*, edited by Thomas G. Weiss and Sam Daws, 42. Oxford: Oxford University Press, 2007.

————. "The Politics, Power and Pathologies of International Organizations." *International Organizations* 53, no. 4 (1999): 711.

————. *Rules for the World: International Organizations in Global Politics*. Ithaca: Cornell University Press, 2004.

BBC News. "World: Africa, Gaddafi calls for United States of Africa." *BBC News*, August 20, 1999. http://news.bbc.co.uk/2/hi/africa/425929.stm.

Berman, Eric. "African Regional Organizations' Peace Operations: Developments and Challenges." *African Security Review* 11, no. 4 (2002): 33–44.

Biersteker, Thomas J. "Globalization and the Modes of Operation of Major Institutional Actors." *Oxford Development Studies* 26 (February 1998): 15–31.

Bohlen, Rachel. "Questioning Authority: A Case for the International Criminal Court's Prosecution of the Current Sudanese President, Omar Al-Bashir." *George Washington International Law Review* 42, no. 3 (2010): 687–712. https://www.lib.uwo.ca/cgi bin/ezpauthn.cgi/docview/1026586048?accountid=15115.

Bomberg, E., and J. Peterson. "Prevention from Above? Preventive Policies and the European Community." In *Health Prevention and British Politics*, edited by M. Mills, 139–59. Aldershot: Avesbury Press, 1993.

Boniface, D. S. "The OAS's Mixed Record." In *Promoting Democracy in the Americas*, edited by Thomas Legler, Sharon F. Lean, and Dexter S. Boniface. Baltimore, MD: Johns Hopkins University Press, 2007.

Bratton, Michael, Robert Mattes, and E. Gyimah-Boadi, eds. Public Opinion, Democracy, and Market Reform in Africa. Cambridge: Cambridge University Press Brooks, 2005.

Bratton, Michael, and Nick van de Walle, eds. *Democratic Experiments in Africa*. New York: Cambridge University Press, 1997.

Brehm, John, and Scott Gates. *Working, Shirking, and Sabotage: Bureaucratic Response to a Democratic Public*. Ann Arbor, MI: University of Michigan Press, 1997.

Breitmeier, H., O. R. Young, and M. Zürn. *Analyzing International Environmental Regimes: From Case Study to Database*. Cambridge, MA: MIT Press, 2006.

Brighton, Claire. "Avoiding Unwillingness: Addressing the Political Pitfalls Inherent in the Complementarity Regime of the International Criminal Court." *International Criminal Law Review* 12 (2012): 629–64. doi: 10.1163/15718123-01204002.

Brooks, Stephen G., and William C. Wohlforth. "Power, Globalization, and the End of the Cold War: Reevaluating a Landmark Case for Ideas." *International Security* 23, no. 3 (2000–2001): 5–53.

Cambridge History of Africa, Volumes II. Edited by J. D. Fage. Cambridge: Cambridge University Press, 1979.

———. *Volumes IV*. Edited by Richard Gray. Cambridge: Cambridge University Press, 1970.

Cameron, M. A. "Special Issue on the Inter-American Democratic Charter." *Canadian Foreign Policy* 10, no. 3 (Spring 2003).

Caporaso, James. "The European Union and Forms of State: Westphalian, Regulatory or Post-Modern?" *Journal of Common Market Studies* 34, no. 1 (March 1996): 29–52.

Chisti, Sumitra. "Democratic Decision Making in the World Trade Organization: An Assessment." *International Studies* 37, no. 2 (2000): 90.

Cilliers, Jakkie, and Kathryn Sturman. "The Right Intervention: Enforcement Challenges for the African Union." *African Security Review* 11, no. 3 (2002). www.iss.co.za/PUBS/ASR/11NO3.

Clapham, Christopher. *Africa and the International System: The Politics of State Survival*. Cambridge: Cambridge University Press, 1996.

Claude, Inis L., Jr. "Peace and Security: Prospective Roles for the Two United Nations." *Global Governance* 2, no. 3 (1996): 289–98.

———. *Swords into Plowshares: The Problems and Prospects of International Organization*. New York: Random House, 1956.

Comprehensive African Agriculture Development Program (CAADP). http://caadp.net/.

Cooper, A. F. "The Making of the Inter-American Democratic Charter: A Case of Complex Multilateralism." *International Studies Perspectives* 5, no. 1 (February 2004): 92–113.

Cooper, A. F., and T. Legler. *Intervention without Intervening: The OAS Defense and Promotion of Democracy in the Americas*. New York: Palgrave MacMillan, 2006.

———. "The OAS in Peru. A Model for the Future?" *Journal of Democracy* 12, no. 4 (2001): 123–36.

Council of the European Union. EU budget for 2015. http://www.consilium.europa.eu/en/policies/eu-annual-budget/eu-budget-2015/.

Curtis, Devon. "The Contested Politics of Peacebuilding in Africa." In *Peacebuilding, Power, and Politics in Africa*, edited by Devon Curtis and Gwinyayi A. Dzinesa, 1–28. Athens, OH: Ohio University Press, 2012.

Dagash, Ibrahim. "OAU Gives 'Green Light' for Use of Force in Sierra Leone." *South African Press Association*, June 3, 1997.

Dahl, Robert A. "Can International Organizations Be Democratic?" In *Democracy's Edges*, edited by I. Shapiro and C. Hacker-Cordon, 19–36. Cambridge: Cambridge University Press, 1999.

Daily Graphic, May 2, 1959.

Danso, Kwaku. "The African Economic Community: Problems and Prospects." *Africa Today* 42, no. 4 (1995): 31–55.

Dayton, W. Bruce, and Louis Kriesberg. *Conflict Transformation and Peace Building: Moving from Violence to Sustainable Peace*. New York: Routledge, 2009.

Deng, David K. "The Silencing of the AU Commission of Inquiry on South Sudan." *Sudan Tribune*, May 13, 2015. http://www.sudantribune.com/spip.php?article53903.

De Waal, Alex. "What is New in the New Partnership for Africa's Development?" *International Affairs* 78, no. 3 (2002): 468.

Dirar, Abdelrahim, former director of EDECO. Interview. July 27, 2005.

Dobbins, F. James. "America's Role in Nation-Building: From Germany to Iraq." *Survival* 45, no. 4 (2003): 87–110.

————. "The UN's Role in Nation-Building: From the Belgian Congo to Iraq." *Survival* 46, no. 4 (2004): 81–102.

Dreher, Axel, Jan-Egbert Sturm, and James Raymond Vreeland. "Politics and IMF Conditionality." *Journal of Conflict Resolution* 59, no. 1 (2015): 120–48.

Du Plessis, Max. "Implications of the Decision to Give the African Court Jurisdiction over Mass Atrocity Crimes." *Institute for Security Studies* no. 235 (June 2012). http://www.issafrica.org/uploads/Paper235-AfricaCourt.pdf.

Easterly, William. *The Tyranny of Experts: Economists, Dictators, and the Forgotten Rights of the Poor*. New York: Basic Books, 2013.

Easton, David. *A Framework for Political Analysis*. Englewood Cliffs, NJ: Prentice-Hall, 1965.

————. *Systems Analysis of Political Life*. New York: Wiley, 1965.

Eberechi, Ifeonu. "Armed Conflicts in Africa and Western Complicity: A Disincentive for African Union's Cooperation with the ICC." *African Journal of Legal Studies* 4 (2009): 53-76.

————. "'Rounding Up the Usual Suspects': Exclusion, Selectivity, and Impunity in the Enforcement of International Criminal Justice and the African Union's Emerging Resistance." *African Journal of Legal Studies* 4 (2011): 51–84. doi: 10.1163/170873811X567970.

Eborah, Solomon T. "The African Charter on Democracy, Elections, and Governance: A New Dawn for the Enthronement of Legitimate Governance in Africa?" *Open Society Institute* (2007). http://www.afrimap.org/papers.php.

el-Ayouty, Yassin, ed. *The Organization of African Unity after Ten Years: Comparative Perspectives* (New York: Praeger, 1975), 3–46.

European Union. African Peace and Facility Evaluation—Part 2: Reviewing the Overall Implementation of the APF as an Instrument for African Efforts to Manage Conflicts on the Continent." European Union Final Report, October 2013.

Evans, Graham. "South Africa's Foreign Policy after Mandela: Mbeki and His Concept of an African Renaissance." *The Round Table* 352, no. 1 (1999).

Evans, Malcolm D., and Rachel Murray. *The African Charter on Human and Peoples' Rights, The System in Practice, 1986–2000*. Cambridge: Cambridge University Press, 2002.

Fado, Gilles Oscar. Interview. Addis Ababa, July 26, 2005.

Fagbayibo, Babatunde. "The (Ir)relevance of the Office of the Chair of the African Union Commission: Analysing the Prospects for Change." *Journal of African Law* 51, no. 1 (2012): 21.

FAHAMU: Networks for Social Justice. http://www.fahamu.org/SOTU.

Finnemore, Martha. *National Interests in International Society*. Ithaca: Cornell University Press, 1996.

Finnemore, Martha, and Kathry Sikkink. "International Norm Dynamics and Political Change." *International Organization* 52, no. 4 (1998).

Forji, Amin George. "Should Africa Quit the International Criminal Court?" *Nordic Africa Institute*, October 29, 2014. http://naiforum.org/2013/10/should-africa-quit-the-international-criminal-court/.

Gaddafi, Muammar. "Unity Will Make Us Strong." http://www.algathafi.org/index-en.htm.

Garrett, Geoffrey. "International Cooperation and Institutional Choice: The European Community's Internal Market." *International Organization* 46, no. 2 (1992): 533–60.

Gawanas, Bience. "The African Union: Concepts and Implementation Mechanisms Relating to Human Rights." In *Human Rights in Africa: Legal Perspectives on Their Protection and Promotion*, edited by Anton Bösl and Joseph Diescho, 152–53. Windhoek: Macmillan Education Namibia, 2009.

George, S. "Supranational Actors and Domestic Politics: Integration Theory Reconsidered in the Light of the Single European Act and Maastricht." Sheffield University Press: 1993.

Gettleman, Jeffrey. "African Union Force Makes Strides Inside Somalia." *New York Times*, November 24, 2011. http://www.nytimes.com/2011/11/25/world/africa/africa-forces-surprise-many-with-success-in-subduing-somalia.html?_r=0.

Gnagbe, Louis Napo, the director of the AU Foundation, quoted in African Peace and Security Report. In "Beyond Bashir: What Else Happened at the AU Summit?" *Institute of Peace and*

Security Studies. http://www.issafrica.org/pscreport/addis-insights/beyond-bashir-what-else-happened-at-the-au-summit.

Gordenker, Leon, and Christer Jonsson. "Knowledge." In *The Oxford Handbook on the United Nations* , ed. Thomas Weiss and Sam Daws, 82–94. Oxford: Oxford University Press, 2007.

Greenawalt, Alexander K.A. "Introductory Note to Documents Regarding the Failure by Malawi & Chad to Comply with ICC Requests." *International Legal Materials* 51, no. 2 (2012): 393–417. http://www.jstor.org/stable/10.5305/intelegamate.51.2.0393.

Gueli, Richard. " South Africa: A Future Research Agenda for Post-Conflict Reconstruction." *African Security Review* 17, no. 1 (2001): 83–98.

Gutner, Tamar, and Alexander Thompson. "The Politics of IO Performance: A Framework." *Review International Organization* 5, no. 3 (2010): 227–48.

Gyimah-Boadi, E. Democratic Reform in Africa: The Quality of Progress . Boulder, CO: Lynne Rienner, 2004.

Hammerstad, A. *African Commitments to Democracy in Theory and Practice: A Review of Eight NEPAD Countries*. South African Institute of International Affairs, Monograph, 2005. http://www.africanreview.org/forum/docs/feb04partmeet/saiia1.pdf.

Hansen, Thomas Obel. "The Policy Requirement in Crimes against Humanity: Lessons from and for the Case of Kenya." *George Washington International Law Review* 43 (2011): 1–41.

Hansungule, Michelo. "The African Charter on Human and Peoples' Rights." In *The African Union: Legal and Institutional Framework: A Manual on the Pan-African Organization*, Abdulqawi A. Yusuf and Fatsah Ouguergouz, 435. New York: Martinus Nijhoff Publishers, 2012.

———. "African Courts and the African Commission on Human and Peoples' Rights." Konrad-Adenauer-Stiftung. http://www.kas.de/upload/auslandshomepages/namibia/Human_Rights_in_Africa/8_Hansungule.pdf.

Hawkins, Darren. "Protecting Democracy in Europe and the Americas." *International Organization* 62 (Summer 2009): 373–403.

Hazlewood, Arthur. "The End of the East African Community: What Are the Lessons for Regional Integration Schemes?" *Journal of Common Market Studies* 18, no. 1 (1979): 41.

Heads of Independent African State. "The Declaration of the Ghana-Guinea Union." Ghana and Guinea Summit, May 1, 1959.

———. "Resolution on Cooperation." Conference of Independent African States, Accra, Ghana. December 13, 1958.

———. "Resolution on Frontiers, Boundaries and Federations." All-African Peoples Conference, Accra, Ghana: December 13, 1958.

Huliaras, Asteris. "Qadhafi's Comeback: Libya and Sub-Saharan Africa in the 1990s." *African Affairs* 100, no. 298 (2001).

Human Rights Watch. "Nigeria's Intervention in Sierra Leone." *Human Rights Watch*, May 20, 2014. http://www.hrw.org/reports/1997/nigeria/Nigeria-09.htm.

———. "The Power These Men Have Over Us: Sexual Exploitation and Abuse by African Union Forces in Somalia." *Human Rights Watch*, September 8, 2014.

———. "Rwanda: Allow Human Rights Watch to Work." *Human Rights Watch* (2010). http://www.hrw.org/en/news/2010/04/23/rwanda-allow-human-rights-watch-work.

———. "South Sudan: AU Putting Justice on Hold." *Human Rights Watch*, February 16, 2015. http://www.hrw.org/news/2015/02/03/south-sudan-au-putting-justice-hold.

———. "Statement Regarding Immunity for Sitting Officials Before the Expanded African Court of Justice and Human Rights." November 13, 2014. http://www.hrw.org/news/2014/11/13/statement-regarding-immunity-sitting-officials-expanded-african-court-justice-and-hu.

Huntington, S. P. *The Third Wave: Democratization in the Late Twentieth Century.* Oklahoma: University of Oklahoma Press, 1991.

Hurd, Ian. *International Organizations: Politics, Law and Practice*. Cambridge: Cambridge University Press, 2011.

Ibok, Sam. "The OAU Mechanism for Conflict Prevention, Management and Resolution and Conflict Situation in Africa." Original Document: Addis Ababa, 1999.

International Crisis Group. "Burundi: Democracy and Peace at Risk." *Africa Report* 120, no. 30 (November 2006).

International Federation for Human Rights. "The African Court on Human and Peoples' Rights towards the African Court of Justice and Human Rights." *International Federation for Human Rights* (April 2010): 26–27.

International Justice Resources Centre. "African Union Approves Immunity for Government Officials in Amendment to African Court of Justice and Human Rights' Statute," July 2, 2014. http://www.ijrcenter.org/2014/07/02/african-union-approves-immunity-for-heads-of-state-in-amendment-to-african-court-of-justice-and-human-rights-statute/.

Isanga, Joseph M. "The Constitutive Act of the African Union, African Courts and the Protection of Human Rights: New Dispensation?" *Santa Clara Journal of International Law* 11, no. 2 (2013).

Iyanda, Layi-Kayode. Head of Mission at the Nigerian Mission in Addis Ababa. Interview. September 27, 2005.

Jackson, Richard. "The Dangers of Regionalising International Conflict Management: The African Experience." *Political Science* 52, no. 1 (2000): 41–60.

Jackson, Robert H., and Carl G. Rosberg. "Sovereignty and Underdevelopment: Juridical Statehood in the African crisis." *Journal of Modern African Studies* 24, no. 1 (1986): 1–31.

———. "Why Africa's Weak States Persist." *World Politics* 35, no. 1 (1982): 1–24.

Jalloh, Charles C., Dapo Akande, and Max du Plessis. "Assessing the African Union Concerns about Article 16 of the Rome Statute of the International Criminal Court." *African Journal of Legal Studies* 4 (2011): 5–50. doi: 10.1163/170873811IX563947.

Johnson, Carol A. "Conferences of Independent African States." *International Organization* 16, no. 2 (1962): 426–29.

Johnstone, Ian. "Law-Making by International Organizations: Perspectives from International Law/International Relations Theory." In *Interdisciplinary Perspectives on International Law and International Relations: The State of the Art*, edited by Jeff Dunoff and Mark Pollack. Oxford: Cambridge University Press, 2012.

Jonah, James. "The OAU: Peace Keeping and Conflict Resolution." In *The Organization of African Unity After Thirty Years*, edited by Yassin El-Ayouty. Westport: Praeger, 1994.

Jorgensen, Knud Erik, Sebastian Oberthu, and Jamal Shahin. "Introduction: Assessing the EU's Performance in International Institutions—Conceptual Framework and Core Findings European Integration." *Journal of European Integration* 33, no. 6 (November 2011): 599–620.

Kane, Ibrahima, and Nobuntu Mbelle. *Towards a People-Driven African Union: Current Obstacles & New Opportunities*. AfriMAP, AFRODAD: Oxfam: Harare, 2007.

Keck, Margaret E., and Kathryn Sikkink. *Activists Beyond Borders: Advocacy Networks in International Politics*. Ithaca: Cornell University Press, 1998.

Keetharuth, Sheila. "Major African Legal Instruments and Human Rights." In *Human Rights in Africa: Legal Perspectives on Their Protection and Promotion*, ed. A. Bosl and J. Diescho. Namibia: Macmillan Education Namibia, 2009.

Keohane, Robert O. *After Hegemony: Cooperation and Discord in the World Political Economy*. Princeton: Princeton University Press, 1984.

Keohane, Robert O., and Stanley Hoffmann (eds). *The New European Community: Decision Making and Institutional Change*. Boulder: Westview Press, 1991.

Keohane, Robert O., Stephen Macedo, and Andrew Moravcsik. "Democracy-Enhancing Multilateralism." *International Organization* 63, no. 1 (2009): 1–31.

Keohane, Robert O., and Joseph S. Nye, Jr. "Globalization: What's New? What's Not? (And So What?)." *Foreign Policy* 118 (Spring 2000): 104–19.

———. *Power and Interdependence: World Politics in Transition*. Boston: Little, Brown, 1977, 3–19.

———. "Transnational Relations and World Politics: A Conclusion." *International Organization* 25, no. 3 (1971): 721–48.

Keppler, Elise. "Managing Setbacks for the International Criminal Court in Africa." *Journal of African Law* 56, no. 1 (2012): 1–14. doi: 10.1017/S0021855311000209.

Kimundi, Elizabeth. "Post-Election Crisis in Kenya and the Implications for the International Criminal Court's Development as a Legitimate Institution." *Eyes on the ICC* 7, no. 1 (2010–2011). https://www.lib.uwo.ca/cgi-bin/ezpauthn.cgi/docview/1026586048?accountid=15115.

Kioko, Ben. "The Right of Intervention under the African Union's Constitutive Act." *International Review of the Red Cross* 85, no. 852 (2003): 807–26.

Kleine, Mareike. *Informal Governance in the European Union: How Governments Make International Organizations Work*. Ithaca, NY: Cornell University Press, 2013a.

———. "Trading Control: National Fiefdoms within International Organizations." *International Theory* 5, no. 3 (November 2013): 321–46. http://journals.cambridge.org/action/displayFulltext?type=1&fid=9073727&jid=INT&volumeId=5&issueId=03&aid=9073724&bodyId=&membershipNumber=&societyETOCSession=.

Klug, Francesca. *A Magna Carta for All Humanity: Homing in on Human Rights*. New York: Routledge, 2015.

Knight, Andy. *Adapting the United Nations to a Post-Modern Era: Lessons Learned*, 2nd edition. Houndmills: Palgrave/Macmillan Press/St. Martin's Press, 2005.

———. "The Future of the United Nations Security Council: Questions of Legitimacy and Representation in Multilateral Governance." In *Enhancing Global Governance*, ed. Andrew Cooper, 19–37 (Tokyo: United Nations University Press, 2002).

Kodjo, Edem. "Report of the Administrative Secretary General covering the period September 1970 to February 1971." (Addis Ababa: Organization of African Unity, 1971), 351.

———. "Report of the Secretary General covering the period June 1980 to February 1981." (Addis Ababa: Organization of African Unity, 1981), 2.

Koenig-Archibugi, Mathias. "Explaining Government Preferences for Institutional Change in EU Foreign and Security Policy." *International Organization* 54, no. 1 (2004).

Koremenos, Barbara. "When, What, and Why Do States Choose to Delegate?" *Law and Contemporary Problems* 71 (Winter 2008): 151–192. http://scholarship.law.duke.edu/lcp/vol71/iss1/7.

Korman, Sharon. *The Right of Conquest: The Acquisition of Territory by Force in International Law and Practice*. Oxford: Clarendon, 1996.

Kotzian, Peter, Michele Knodt, and Sigita Urdze. "Instruments of the EU's External Democracy Promotion." *Journal of Common Market Studies* 49, no. 5 (2011): 996.

Krasner, S., ed. *International Regimes*. Cambridge, MA, Cornell University Press, 1983.

Kwame, Nkrumah. *Africa Must Unite*. New York: International Publishers, 1963, 218–20.

Landsberg, Chris. "Promoting Democracy." *Journal of Democracy* 11, no. 3 (2000): 107–21. http://muse.jhu.edu/journals/journal_of_democracy/v011/11.3landsberg.html.

Lavergne, Real. *Regional Integration and Cooperation in West Africa: A Multidimensional Perspective*. Ottawa: International Development Research Centre, 1997.

Legler, Thomas, and Thomas Tieku. "What Difference Can a Path Make? Regional Regimes for Democracy Promotion and Defense in the Americas and Africa." *Democratization* 18, no. 3 (2010): 465–91.

Legum, Colin. *Pan Africanism : A Short Political Guide*. London: Pall Mall Press, 1962.

Levitt, B. S. "A Desultory Defense of Democracy: OAS Resolution 1080 and the Inter-American Democratic Charter." *Latin American Politics & Society* 48, no. 3 (Fall 2006): 93–123.

Luck, Edward. *UN Security Council: Practice and Promise*. New York: Routledge, 2006.

Lusthaus, C., M. H. Adrien, G. Anderson, F. Carden, and G. Montalvan. *Organizational Assessment: A Framework for Improving Performance*. Ottawa: IDRC, 2005.

MacLeod, Scott. "A New Dawn for Africa?" *Time*, March 2, 2001. http://www.time.com/time/world/article/0,8599,101184,00.html.

Magliveras, Konstantinos D., and Gino J. Naldi. "The International Criminal Court's Involvement with Africa: Evaluation of Fractious Relationship." *Nordic Journal of International Law* 82 (2013): 417–46. doi: 10.1163/15718107-08203004.

Majone, G. "Ideas, Interests and Policy Change." *EUI Working Papers* SPS 92/21. Florence: European University Institute, 1992.

Malan, Mark. "New Tools in the Box? Towards a Standby Force for the African Union." *Johannesburg: Institute of Security Studies* (2002).

Maloka. Eddy. *A United States of Africa*. Pretoria: African Institute of South Africa, 2001.

Maluwa, Tiyanjana. "Reimagining African Unity: Preliminary Reflections on the Constitutive Act of the African Union." *African Yearbook of International Law* 9 (2001).

Mandela, Nelson. Address to the Summit Meeting of the OAU Heads of State and Government, Ouagadougou, June 8, 1998. http://www.anc.org.za/ancdocs/history/mandela/1998/sp980608.html.

———. "South Africa's Future Foreign Policy." *Foreign Affairs* 72, no. 5 (November/December 1993). http://www.foreignaffairs.org/19931201faessay5221/nelson-mandela/south-africa-s-future-foreign-policy.html.

———. Speech to Assembly of OAU Heads of State and Government at the 30th Ordinary Session of Organization of African Unity, 1994. http://www.anc.org.za/ancdocs/history/mandela/1998/sp980608.html.

———. "Statement of the President of the Republic of South Africa at the OAU Heads of State and Government Summit," Tunisia, June 1994.

Mandrup, Thomas, and Bjørn Møller. "African Union: A Common Security Structure in the Making?" In *International Organisations: Their Role in Conflict Management*, ed. Peter Dahl Thruelsen. Royal Danish Defence College, 2014.

Marble, Andrew D. "The 'Taiwan Threat' Hypothesis: Ideas, Values, and Foreign Policy Preferences in the United States." *Issues & Studies* 38 (March 2002): 170.

Maru, Mehari Taddele. "The Future of the ICC and Africa: The Good, the Bad, and the Ugly." *Aljazeera*, October 11, 2013. http://www.aljazeera.com/indepth/opinion/2013/10/future-icc-africa-good-bad-ugly-20131011143130881924.html.

Mataboge, Mmanaledi. "AU's Dependence on Cash from the West Still Rankles." *Mail & Guardian*, June 12, 2015. http://mg.co.za/article/2015-06-11-aus-dependence-on-cash-from-the-west-still-rankles.

Matlosa, Khabele. "Assessing the African Charter on Democracy, Elections and Governance: Declaration vs. Policy Practice Policy Brief 53." *Centre for Policy Studies* (2008).

Mazrui, Ali. "On the Concept of 'We Are All Africans.'" *American Political Science Revie w* LVII: 1 (March 1963): 88–97.

———. *Towards a Pax Africana: A Study of Ideology and Ambition*. Chicago: University of Chicago Press, 1967.

Mazzeo, Domeico. *African Regional Organizations*. London: Cambridge University Press, 1984.

Mbeki, Thabo. "The African Renaissance Statement." Pretoria, August 13, 1998. http://www.anc.org.za/ancdocs/history/mbeki/1998/tm0813.htm.

———. Speech delivered at the launch of the African Renaissance Institute, Pretoria, October 11, 1999. http://www.polity.org.za/html/govdocs/speeches/1999/.

McCoy, J. L. "International Response to Democratic Crisis in the Americas, 1990–2005." *Democratization* 13, no. 5 (December 2006).

McGowan, P. "African Military Coups d'Etat, 1956–2001: Frequency, Trends and Distribution." *Journal of Modern African Studies* 41, no. 3 (2003): 339–70.

———. "Coups and Conflict in West Africa, 1955–2004." *Armed Forces & Society* 32, no. 2 (2006): 234–53.

McMahon, Edward R. "The African Charter on Democracy, Elections, and Governance: A Positive Step on a Long Path." *Open Society Institute* (2007). http://www.afrimap.org/papers.php.

Mearsheimer, John J. "The False Promise of International Institutions." *International Security* 19, no. 3 (Winter 1994–1995).

Melber, Henning. "South Africa and NEPAD: Quo Vadis?" http://www.sarpn.org.za/documents/d0000682/index.php.

Miles, E. L., A. Underdal, S. Andresen, J. Wettestad, J. B. Skjærseth, and E. M. Carlin. *Environmental Regime Effectiveness: Confronting Theory with Evidence.* Cambridge, MA: MIT Press, 2002.

Mills, Kurt. "'Bashir Is Dividing Us': Africa and the International Criminal." *Human Rights Quarterly* 34, no. 2 (2012): 404–47. doi: 10.1353/hrq.2012.0030.

Mkwezalamba, Maxwell. Statement on the Occasion of the Opening of the Meeting of Governmental Experts on Alternative Sources of Financing the African Union, African Union, Addis Ababa, 2006. http://www.africa-union.org/root/UA/Conferences/Mai/EA/29mai/WELCOME%20STATEMENT%20%20Alternative%20source%20of%20funding.pdf.

Moore, Will H., and James R. Scaritt. "IMF Conditionality and Polity Characteristics in Black Africa: An Exploratory Analysis." *Africa Today* 37, no. 4 (1990).

Moravcsik, Andrew. "Preferences and Power in the European Community: A Liberal Intergovernmentalist Approach." *Journal of Common Market Studies* 31 (1993).

———. "Taking Preferences Seriously: Liberalism and International Relations Theory." *International Organization* 51, no. 4 (Autumn 1997): 512–53.

Muller, Marie. "South Africa's Economic Diplomacy: Constructing a Better World for All." *Diplomacy & Statecraft* 13, no. 1 (2002).

Murray, Rachel, and Steven Wheatley. "Groups and the African Charter on Human and Peoples' Rights." *Human Rights Quarterly* 25, no. 1 (2003): 213–36. http://www.jstor.org/stable/20069658.

Murungu, Chacha Bhoke. "Towards a Criminal Chamber in the African Court of Justice and Human Rights." *Journal of International Criminal Justice* 9 (2011): 1085–86.

Musengeyi, Itai. "AU Rejects Damning Report on Zimbabwe." *The Herald*, July 6, 2004. http://allafrica.com/stories/200407061180.html.

Mutua, Makau. "The African Human Rights Court: A Two-Legged Stool?" *Human Rights Quarterly* 21 (1999): 342–63.

Muyangwa, Monde, and Margaret A. Vogt. "An Assessment of the OAU Mechanism for Conflict Prevention, Management and Resolution, 1993–2000." *International Peace Academy*, New York, November 2002.

Ndulo, Muna. "Harmonisation of Trade Laws in the African Economic Community." *International and Comparative Law Quarterly* 42 (1993): 101–18.

Ngirachu, John. "Uhuru Kenyatta: Let's Have an African-Funded Court." *Daily Nation*, January 31, 2015. http://www.nation.co.ke/news/politics/Uhuru-Kenyatta-African-Court-of-Justice-and-Human-Rights/-/1064/2609206/-/15qapjj/-/index.html.

Nilsson, Desirée, and Mimmi Söderberg Kovacs. "Revisiting an Elusive Concept: A Review of the Debate on Spoilers in Peace Processes." International Studies Review 13, no. 4 (2011): 606–26.

Njau, Mutegi. "An Incentive to Clamp Down: With U.S. Prodding, 3 East African Nations Get Tough on Terrorist Suspects—Even When Evidence Is Lacking." *International Consortium of Investigative Journalists* (2003).

Nkrumah, Kwame. *African Must Unite.* New York: Panaf, 1963.

Nuruzzaman, Mohammed. "Revisiting 'Responsibility to Protect' after Libya and Syria," *E-International Relations*, March 8, 2014.

Nye, Joseph S. *Pan-Africanism and East African Integration.* Cambridge, MA: Harvard University Press, 1965.

Nyerere, Julius. "A United States of Africa." *Journal of Modern African Studies* 1, no. 1 (1963): 6.

Obasanjo, O., and F. G. N. Mosha. "Africa Rise to the Challenge." Conference Report on the Kampala Forum, Abeokuta/New York: Africa Leadership Forum, 1992.

Obote-Odora, Alex. "An AU Absurdity: African Leaders Promote Impunity for Themselves." *The Nordic Africa Institute*, October 18, 2013. http://naiforum.org/2013/10/an-au-absurdity/.

Ocran, Christine. "The Protocol to the African Charter on Human and Peoples' Rights of Women in Africa." *African Journal of International and Comparative Law* 15, 1 (2007): 148–49.

Oestreich, Joel E. *International Organizations as Independent Actors: A Framework for Analysis.* New York: Routledge, 2012.

Oette, Lutz. "Peace and Justice, or Neither?: The Repercussions of the al-Bashir Case for International Criminal Justice in Africa and Beyond." *Journal of International Criminal Justice* 8 (2010): 345–64. doi: 10.1093/jicj/mqq018.

Okeke, Jide Martyns. "African Union and the Challenges of Implementing 'Responsibility to Protect' in Africa." Paper presented at the XIIIth CODESRIA General Assembly, 2011. http://general.assembly.codesria.org/IMG/pdf/Jide_Martyns_Okeke.pdf.

Okere, B. Obinna, "The Protection of Human Rights in Africa and the African Charter on Human and Peoples' Rights: A Comparative Analysis with the European and American Systems." *Human Rights Quarterly* 6, no. 2 (May 1984).

Okumu, Wafula, and Anneli Botha. *Understanding Terrorism in Africa: In Search for an African Voice.* Pretoria: Institute for Security Studies, 2007.

Olivier, Gerrit, and Deon Geldenhuys. "South Africa's Foreign Policy: From Idealism to Pragmatism." *Business & the Contemporary World* 9, no. 2 (1997).

Olonisakin, Funmi. "African 'Homemade' Peacekeeping Initiatives." *Armed Forces and Society* 23, no. 3 (1997): 340. http://afs.sagepub.com/content/23/3/349.full.pdf+html.

Omorogbe, Eki Yemisi. "A Club of Incumbents? The African Union and Coups d'État." *Vanderbilt Journal of Transnational Law* 44, no. 123 (2012).

O'Neill, Kate, Jorg Balsiger, and Stacy D. VanDeveer. "Actors, Norms and Impact." *Annual Political Science Review* (June 2004): 250. doi: 10.1146/annurev.polisci.7.090803.161821.

Onu, Peter. "Report of the Secretary General covering the period June 1983 to February 1984." Addis Ababa: Organization of African Unity, 1984.

Organization for Economic Cooperation and Development. *Regional Integration in Africa, Report of the Forum of the OECD Development Centre and the African Development Bank devoted to Regional Integration in Africa.* Paris, France: 2002.

Organization of African Unity. Assembly of Heads of State and Government. Ouagadougou Declaration. *Organization of African Unity.* Addis Ababa, 1998.

———. *The Draft Constitutive Act of the African Union.* Tripoli, Libya: 2000.

———. *Draft of the Establishment of the Union of African States.* Sirte, Libya: 1999.

———. *Introductory Note to the Report of the Secretary-General to the Thirty-Third Ordinary Session of OAU of Organization of African Unity . Organization of African Unity.* Addis Ababa, Ethiopia, 1997.

———. *Lagos Plan of Action for the Economic Development of Africa 1980–2000.* Addis Ababa, Ethiopia: 1981.

———. *OAU: Twenty-Fifth Summit Meeting. Keesing's Record of World Events,* 1989.

———. *Organization of African Unity Consultants on the Sirte Declaration, The Draft Treaty Establishing the African Union.* Addis Ababa, Ethiopia: 2000.

———. "The Political and Socio-Economic Situation in Africa and the Fundamental Changes Taking Place in the World." Addis Ababa, Ethiopia: Organization of African Unity, 1990.

———. *Report of the Council of Ministers and of the Assembly of Heads of State and Government.* Cairo, Egypt: 1964.

———. *Report of the Meeting of Legal Experts and Parliamentarians on the Establishment of the African Union and the Pan-African Parliament.* Addis Ababa: 2000.

———. *Report of the Ministerial Conference on the Establishment of the African Union and the Pan-African Parliament.* Tripoli, Libya: 2000.

———. *Report of the Second Meeting of Legal Experts and Parliamentarians on the Establishment of the African Union and the Pan-African Parliament.* Addis Ababa: 2000.

———. *Report of the Secretary-General to the Fifty-First Ordinary Session of Council of Ministers. Organization of African Unity.* Addis Ababa, Ethiopia, 1990.

———. *Report of the Secretary-General to the Fifty-Second Ordinary Session of Council of Ministers. Organization of African Unity.* Addis Ababa, Ethiopia: 1990.

———. *Report of the Secretary-General to the Thirty-Fifth Ordinary Session of Organization of African Unity. Organization of African Unity.* Addis Ababa, 1999.

———. *Resolutions Adopted by the First Conference of Independent African Heads of State and Government Held in Addis Ababa, Ethiopia,* May 22 to 25, 1963.

———. The Sanniquellie Summit. Declaration of Principle, July 19, 1959.

———. *Ushering the OAU into the Next Century: A Programme for Reform and Renewal.* Organization of African Unity. Addis Ababa, 1998.

Ostry, S., and T. K. Tieku, *Trade Advocacy Groups and Multilateral Trade Policy-Making of African States* (Toronto: Munk Centre for International Studies, 2007).

Oumarou, Ide. "Report of the Secretary General covering the period June 1988 to February 1989." (Addis Ababa: Organization of African Unity, 1989), 4.

Padelford, Norman J. "The Organization of African Unity." *International Organization* 18, no. 3 (1964): 526.

Paris, Roland, and Timothy D. Sisk, eds. *The Dilemmas of Statebuilding: Confronting the Contradictions of Post-War Peace Operations.* New York: Routledge, 2009.

Parish, R., M. Peceny, and J. Delacour. "Venezuela and the Collective Defense of Democracy Regime in the Americas." *Democratization* 14, no. 2 (April 2007): 207–31.

Park, Susan. "Norm Diffusion within International Organizations: A Case Study of the World Bank." *Journal of International Relations and Development* 8, no. 2 (2005): 113. doi:10.1057/palgrave.jird.1800051.

———. "Theorizing Norm Diffusion within International Organizations." *International Politics* 43, no. 3 (2006): 342–43. doi:10.1057/palgrave.ip.8800149.

Pedersen, Thomas. "Cooperative Hegemony: Power, Ideas and Institutions in Regional Integration." *Review of International Studies* 28 (2002): 677–96.

Perfect, David. "The Gambia under Yahya Jammeh: An Assessment." *The Round Table* 99, no. 406 (2010): 53–63. doi: 10.1080/00358530903513681.

Perry, Alex. "Kenya Invades Somalia. Does It Get Any Dumber?" *TIME*, October 19, 2011. http://world.time.com/2011/10/19/kenya-invades-somalia-does-it-get-any-dumber/.

Peterson, J., and Bomberg, E. "Prevention from Above? Preventive Policies and the European Community." In *Health Prevention and British Politics*, ed. M. Mills, 137–76. Aldershot: Avesbury Press, 1993.

Pierson, Paul. *Dismantling the Welfare State? Reagan, Thatcher and the Politics of Retrenchment.* Cambridge: Cambridge University Press, 1994.

———. "Increasing Returns, Path Dependency, and the Study of Politics." *American Political Science Review* 94, no. 2 (2000): 251–67.

———. *The New Politics of the Welfare State.* Oxford: Oxford University Press, 2001.

———. "The Path to European Integration: A Historical Institutional Analysis." *Comparative Political Studies* 29, no. 1 (1996).

———. *Politics in Time: History, Institutions, and Social Analysis.* Princeton, NJ: Princeton University Press, 2004.

Ping, Jean. "Opening Remarks by the AUC Chairperson H. E. Dr. Jean Ping on the occasion of the First Annual US-African Union High Level Meeting." Washington DC, April 21, 2010. http://www.africa-union.org/root/au/index/index.htm.

Powell, Kristiana, and Thomas K. Tieku. "The African Union and The Responsibility to Protect: Towards a Protection Regime for Africa?" *International Insight* 20, no. 1 and 2 (2005): 215–35.

Puchala, Donald. "Institutionalism, Intergovernmentalism and European Integration: A Review Article." *Journal of Common Market Studies* 37, no. 2 (June 1999).

Rabkin, A. Jeremy. *Law without Nations? Why Constitutional Government Requires Sovereign States.* Princeton, NJ: Princeton University Press, 2005.

———. *Why Sovereignty Matters.* Washington, DC: American Enterprise Institute Press, 1998.

Rapkin, David P., and Jonathan R. Strand, "Representation in International Organizations: The IMF," August 29, 2010.

Raustiala, Kal. "States, NGOs, and International Environmental Institutions." *International Studies Quarterly* 41, no. 7 (1997): 720.

Renaissance Institute." Pretoria, 1999. http://www.polity.org.za/html/govdocs/speeches/1999/.

Rice, E. Susan. "Remarks by Ambassador Susan E. Rice, U.S. Permanent Representative to the United Nations, At a Security Council Open Debate on UN-AU Cooperation." *U.S. Permanent Representative to the United Nations, New York, 2012.* http://usun.state.gov/briefing/statements/180554.htm.

Rice, Xan. "Ethiopia Ends Somalia Occupation." *The Guardian*, January 26, 2009. http://www. theguardian.com/world/2009/jan/26/ethiopia-ends-somalia-occupation.

Rittberger, Volker, and Peter Mayer. *Regime Theory and International Relations*. Oxford: Oxford University Press, 1993, 27.

Rittberger, Volker, Bernhard Zangl, and Andreas Kruck. *International Organization*. UK: Palgrave Macmillan, 2012.

Rodt, Annemarie Peen. "The African Union Mission in Burundi." *Civil Wars* 14, no. 3 (September 2012): 379.

Ronen, Yehudit. "Libya's Diplomatic Success in Africa: The Reemergence of Qadhafi on the International Stage." *Diplomacy & Statecraft* 13 (2002): 68.

Rothchild, Donald, and E. Gyimah-Boadi. "Ghana's Decline and Development Strategies." In *Africa in Economic Crisis*, ed. John Ravenhill. New York: Columbia University Press, 1986.

Rubenfeld, Jed. "Unilateralism and Constitutionalism." *New York University Law Review* 79, no. 6 (2004): 1971–2028.

Saine, Abdoulaye. "Military and Human Rights in The Gambia: 1994–1999." *Journal of Third World Studies* 19, no. 2 (2002): 167–87.

———. "Presidential and National Assembly Elections, Gambia 2006 and 2007." *Electoral Studies* 27 (2008): 151–90. doi: 10.1016/j.electstud.2007.07.002.

Saki, Otto. "Celebrating Minor Victories? Zimbabwe at the African Commission on Human and Peoples' Rights." November 13, 2007. http://www.pambazuka.org/en/category/comment/44417.

Salim Ahmed Salim. "Introductory Note to the Report of the Secretary General." Addis Ababa: *Organization of African Unity*, 1997.

———. "Introductory Note to the Report of the Secretary-General to the Fifty-Ninth Ordinary Session of Council of Ministers." Addis Ababa: *Organization of African Unity*, 1994.

———. "Introductory Note to the Report of the Secretary-General to the Sixty-Fourth Ordinary Session of Council of Ministers." Addis Ababa: *Organization of African Unity*, 1996.

———. "Opening Address to the Meeting of Legal Experts and Parliamentarians on the Establishment of the African Union." Addis Ababa, April 17, 2000.

———. "Report of the Secretary-General to the Fifty-First Ordinary Session of Council of Ministers." Addis Ababa: *Organization of African Unity*, 1990.

———. "Report of the Secretary-General to the Fifty-Second Ordinary Session of Council of Ministers." Addis Ababa: *Organization of African Unity*, 1990.

Sandholtz, Wayne, and Alec Stone Sweet. *European Integration and Supranational Governance*. Oxford, UK: Oxford University Press, 1998.

Sandholtz, Wayne, and John Zysman. "1992: Recasting the European Bargain." *World Politics* 42, no. 1 (1989): 95–128.

Sandholtz, Wayne, John Zysman, Michael Borrus et al. *The Highest Stakes: The Economic Foundations of the Next Security System*. New York: Oxford University Press, 1992.

———. "Membership Matters: Limits of the Functional Approach to European Institutions." *Journal of Common Market Studies* 34, no. 3 (1996): 404–29.

Saungweme, S. "A Critical Look at the Charter on Democracy, Elections, and Governance in Africa." *Open Society Institute* (2007). http://www.afrimap.org/english/images/paper/ACDEG_Saungweme.pdf.

Saxena, Suresh Chadra. "The African Union: Africa's Giant Step toward Continental Unity." In *Africa at the Crossroads : Between Regionalism and Globalization*. Westport: Praeger, 2004.

Schoeman, Maxi. "The African Union after the Durban 2002 Summit." *Centre of African Studies, University of Copenhagen*, February 2003. http://www.teol.ku.dk/cas/nyhomepage/mapper/Occasional%20Papers/Schoeman_internetversion.doc.

Schraeder, Peter J. "South Africa's Foreign Policy from International Pariah to Leader of the African Renaissance." *The Round Table* 359, no. 1 (2001).

Senarclens, Pierre de. "Governance and the Crisis in the International Mechanisms of Regulation." *International Social Science Journal* 50, no. 155 (March 1998).

Seymour, Vernon. "Human Rights and Foreign Policy: A Window of Opportunity?" *Indicator* 13, no. 4 (1996).

Simon, Allison. "Think Again: In Defence of the African Union." *Institute for Security Studies*, September 9, 2014. http://www.issafrica.org/iss-today/think-again-in-defence-of-the-african-union.

Snyder, F. "Institutional Development in the European Union: Some Implications of the Third Pillar." In *The Third Pillar of the European Union: Cooperation in the Fields of Justice and Home Affairs*, ed. J. Monar and R. Morgan, 85. Brussels: European Interuniversity Press, 1994.

Souare, Issaka K. "The African Union as a Norm Entrepreneur on Military Coups d'état in Africa (1952–2012): An empirical Assessment." *Journal of Modern African Studies* 52, no. 1 (March 2014): 69–94, doi: 10.1017/S0022278X13000785.

South African Press Association. "OAU Summit Ends with Promise to Get 'Tougher' on Coups." *South African Press Association*, Johannesburg, June 4, 1997.

Sriram, Chandra Lekha, and Stephen Brown. "Kenya in the Shadow of the ICC: Complementarity, Gravity and Impact." *International Criminal Law Review* 12 (2012): 219–44. doi: 10.1163/157181212X633361.

Ssenyonjo, Manisuli. *The African Regional Human Rights System: 30 Years after the African Charter on Human and People's Rights*. New York: Martinus Nijhoff Publishers, 2011.

———. "The Rise of the African Union Opposition to the International Criminal Court's Investigations and Prosecutions of African Leaders." *International Criminal Law Review* 13 (2013): 385–428. doi: 10.1163/15718123-01302002.

Stedman, John Stephen. "Spoiler Problems in Peace Processes." *International Security* 22 (1997): 5–53.

Stone Sweet, A., and James Caporaso. "From Free Trade to Supranational Polity: The European Court and Integration." In *European Integration and Supranational Governance*, edited by W. Sandholtz and A. Stone Sweet (Oxford: Oxford University Press, 1998).

Sudan Tribune. "AU Inquiry Wants Kiir Excluded from Transitional Leadership." February 16, 2015. http://www.sudantribune.com/spip.php?article54201.

Suttner, Raymond. "South African Foreign Policy and the Promotion of Human Rights." *South African Yearbook of International Affairs* (1997).

Tavares, Rodrigo. *Regional Security: The Capacity of International Organizations.* London and New York: Routledge, 2010.

Taylor, Ian. "The Democratization of South African Foreign Policy: Critical Reflections on an Untouchable Subject." In *Democratizing Foreign Policy? Lessons from South Africa*, eds. Philip Nel and Janis van der Westhuizen. Lexington: Lanham, 2004.

Taylor, Ian, and Philip Nel. "New Africa, Globalization and the Confines of Elite Reformism: Getting the Rhetoric Right, Getting the Strategy Wrong." *Third World Quarterly* 23, no. 1 (2002).

Telli, Dailo. "Introduction to the Report of the Administrative Secretary-General covering the period February 1969 to August 1969." Addis Ababa: Organization of African Unity, 1969, 22.

Thakur, Ramesh, and Thomas G. Weiss. "United Nations 'Policy': An Argument with Three Illustrations." *International Studies Perspectives* 10, no. 1 (2009): 18–35.

Thompson, Scott W. *Ghana's Foreign Policy 1957–1966: Diplomacy, Ideology, and the New State*. Princeton: Princeton University Press, 1969.

Thompson, Scott, and I. William Zartman. "The Development of Norms in the African System." In *The Organization of African Unity after Ten Years: Comparative Perspectives*, edited by Yassin el-Ayouty. New York: Praeger, 1975.

Tieku, Thomas Kwasi. "Explaining the Clash and Accommodation of Interests of Major Actors in the Creation of the African Union." *African Affairs* 103 (2004): 249–67.

———. "The Formation of African Union: Analysis of the Role of Ideas and Supranational Entrepreneurs in Interstate Cooperation." Ann Arbor: ProQuest, 2006.

———. " Multilateralization of Democracy Promotion and Defense in Africa." *Africa Today* 56, no. 2 (2009): 74–91.

———. "Pan-Africanization of Human Security," in *Handbook of Human Security*, ed. Taylor Owen and Mary Martin. London: Routledge, 2012.

———. "A Pan-African View of a 'New' Agenda for Peace," *International Journal* (2012).

Tieku, Thomas Kwasi, and Sylvia Ostry. *Trade Advocacy Groups and Multilateral Trade Policy-Making of African States*. Toronto: Munk Centre for International Studies, 2007.

Tieku, Thomas Kwasi, and Kristiana Powell. "The African Union and the Responsibility to Protect: Towards a Protection Regime for Africa?" *International Insights* 20, no. 1 and 2 (2005).

Touray, A. Omar. "The African Union: The First Ten Years 2002–2012." (Forthcoming)

———. "The Common African Defence and Security Policy." *African Affairs* 104, no. 417 (2005) : 635–56.

Tran, Mark. "African Union Summit Struggles to Raise Funds to Combat Horn of Africa Crisis." *The Guardian*, August 25, 2011. http://www.theguardian.com/global-development/2011/aug/25/african-union-summit-funds-somalia.

Tsilimbiaza, Soanirinela, director of Trade and Industry, African Union). Interview. July 22, 2005.

Udombana, Nsongurua J. "So Far, So Fair: The Local Remedies Rule in the Jurisprudence of the African Commission on Human and Peoples' Rights." *American Journal of International Law* 97, no. 1 (2003): 1–37. http://www.jstor.org/stable/3087102.

Umozurike, U.O. "The African Charter on Human and Peoples' Rights." *American Journal of International Law* 77, no. 4 (1983): 902–12.

UNESCO. *The Pearson Report, A New Strategy for Global Development. UNESCO Courier*, February 1970. http://unesdoc.unesco.org/images/0005/000567/056743eo.pdf.

UNESCO General History of Africa. Volumes V. edited by B. A. Ogot. California: James Currey, 1999.

———. Volumes VIII. edited by Ali A. Mazrui and C. Wondji. California: Heinemann, 1993.

United Nations Organization. "African Union Gender Equality Ministers Adopt Common Position on the Post-2015 Development Agenda." February 12, 2014. http://www.unwomen.org/en/news/stories/2014/2/african-union-post-2015-position#sthash.wzQY6fFg.dpuf.

———. "An Agenda for Peace: Preventive Diplomacy, Peacemaking, and Peace-Keeping." Report of the Secretary-General Pursuant to the statement adopted by the Summit Meeting of the Security Council on January 31, 1992.

———. "Cooperation between the United Nations and Regional and Other Organizations." A/67/280-S/2012/614. New York: United Nations, 2012. http://www.operationspaix.net/DATA/DOCUMENT/7490~v~Cooperation_entre_lOrganisation_des_Nations_Unies_et_les_organisations_regionales_ou_autres__S_2012_614_.pdf.

———. Disarmament, Demobilization, and Reintegration Resource Centre (2009). http://unddr.org/.

———. "In Larger Freedom: Towards Development, Security, and Human Rights for All." http://www.un.org/en/events/pastevents/pdfs/larger_freedom_exec_summary.pdf.

———. Lomé Declaration of July 2000 on the framework for an OAU Response to Unconstitutional Changes of Government (AHG/Decl.5 (XXXVI). Office of the United Nations High Commission for Human Rights, July 2000. http://www2.ohchr.org/english/law/compilation_democracy/lomedec.htm.

———. Pamphlet No. 6 Minority Rights Under the African Charter on Human and Peoples' Rights. http://www.ohchr.org/Documents/Publications/GuideMinorities6en.pdf

———. "Secretary-General Unveils $5.4 Billion 2014–2015 Budget to Fifth Committee, Net Reduction of Posts Draws Mixed Reviews from Delegates." United Nations, Meetings Coverage and Press Releases, October 28, 2013. http://www.un.org/press/en/2013/gaab4080.doc.htm.

University of Minnesota. *Amnesty International and Others v. Sudan*, African Commission on Human and Peoples' Rights, Comm. No. 48/90, 50/91, 52/91, 89/93 (1999). University of Minnesota, Human Rights Library. http://www1.umn.edu/humanrts/africa/comcases/48-90_50-91_52-91_89-93.html.

U.S. Department of State. "The United States and the African Union." Washington, DC, April 19, 2011. http://www.state.gov/r/pa/prs/ps/2011/04/161212.htm.

———. "U.S. Assistance to the African Union—Fact Sheet." http://photos.state.gov/libraries/usau/231771/PDFs/us_assistance_to_the_au_fact_sheet.pdf.

Vale, Peter, and Sipho Maseko. "South Africa and the African Renaissance." *International Affairs* 74, no. 2 (1998).

Vandeginste, Stef. "The African Union, Constitutionalism and Power-Sharing." *Journal of African Law* (2013): 1–28.

Viljoen, Frans, and Lirette Louw. "State Compliance with the Recommendations of the African Commission on Human and Peoples' Rights, 1994–2004." *American Journal of International Law* 101, no. 1 (2007): 1–34. http://www.jstor.org/stable/4149821.

———. "The Status of the Findings of the African Commission: From Moral Persuasion to Legal Obligation." *Journal of African Law* 48, no. 1 (2004): 1–22. 2014. doi: 10.1017/S0021855304481017.

Vogt, Margaret. "The African Union and Subregional Security Mechanisms in Africa." In *Africa: Problems and Prospects* (2002). http://www.codesria.org/Links/Home/Abstracts GA 12-20/Security_Vogt.htm.

Wachira, George Mukundi. "Consolidating the African Governance Architecture." Policy Briefing 96, *South African Institute of International Affairs* (June 2014).

Wallerstein, Immanuel. *Africa: The Politics of Independence and Unity*. New York: Random House, 1967.

Waltz, Kenneth N. *Theory of International Politics*. Reading: Addison Wesley, 1979.

Weiss, Thomas G. *Humanitarian Intervention: Ideas in Action*. Cambridge, UK and Malden, MA: Polity Press, 2007.

———. "The Sunset of Humanitarian Intervention? The Responsibility to Protect in a Unipolar Era." *Security Dialogue* 35, no. 2 (2004): 135–53.

Weiss, Thomas G., Tatiana Carayannis, and Richard Jolly. "The 'Third' United Nations." *Global Governance* 15 (2009): 123.

Weiss, Thomas G., and Ramesh Thakur. "Global Governance and the UN: An Unfinished Journey." *Ethics & International Affairs* 25, no. 4 (Winter 2011).

Weldehaimanot, Simon M. "Arresting Al-Bashir: The African Union's Opposition and the Legalities." *African Journal of International and Comparative Law* 19, no. 2 (2011): 208–35. https://www.lib.uwo.ca/cgi-bin/ezpauthn.cgi/docview/1026586048?accountid=15115.

White, Marianne. "Controversial Crime Bill to Cost Canadians $19 Billion: Study." *Postmedia News*, December 8, 2011. http://www.vancouversun.com/Controversial+crime+bill+cost+Canadians+billion+study/5832700/story.html.

Williams, Paul D. "The African Union's Conflict Management Capabilities." *Council on Foreign Relations* (October 2011): 1.

———. "The Peace and Security Council of the African Union: Evaluating an Embryonic International Institution." *Journal of Modern African Studies* 47, no. 4 (2009): 603–26.

Wodzicki, M. "The Inter-American Democratic Charter and the African Charter on Democracy, Elections, and Governance: A Comparison." Background document prepared for the conference on "Democracy Bridge: Multilateral Regional Efforts for the Promotion and Defense of Democracy in Africa and the Americas." Organization of American States, Washington, DC, July 11–12, 2007.

World Bank. World Development Report 2003 : Sustainable Development in a Dynamic World—Transforming Institutions, Growth, and Quality of Life . https://openknowledge.worldbank.org/handle/10986/5985.

World Trade Organization. "Azevedo Highlights Role of Academics in Policymaking of Developing Countries," *WTO News*, February 11, 2014.

Woronoff, Jon. *Organizing African Unity*. Metuchen, NJ: Scarecrow Press, 1970.

Young, Oran R. *Governance in World Affairs*. Ithaca, NY: Cornell University Press, 1999.

Zacher, Mark. "The Territorial Integrity Norm: International Boundaries and the Use of Force." *International Organization* 55, no. 2 (2001): 217.

Zanotti, Laura. *Governing Disorder: UN Peace Operations, International Security, and Democratization in the Post–Cold War Era*. University Park: Penn State University Press, 2011).

Zartman, I. William. "Africa as a Subordinate State System in International Relations." *International Organization* 21, no. 3 (Summer 1967): 545–64.

Zartman, I. William, and F. Deng. *A Strategic Vision for Africa: T he Kampala Movement.* Washington, DC: The Brookings Institution Press, 2002.

Lightning Source UK Ltd.
Milton Keynes UK
UKHW040712130219
337169UK00001B/138/P

9 781786 610317